2010
COACH OF THE YEAR CLINICS
FOOTBALL MANUAL

Edited by Earl Browning

www.coacheschoice.com

ISBN: 978-1-60679-104-2
ISSN: 1534-925X

Telecoach, Inc. Transcription: Emmerson Browning, Kent Browning, Tom Cheaney, and Dan Haley

Diagrams: Steve Haag

Book layout and cover design: Bean Creek Studio

Cover photos: Kent Gidley, The University of Alabama, Director of Athletic Photography

Special thanks to the Nike clinic managers for having the lectures taped.

Coaches Choice
P.O. Box 1828
Monterey, CA 93942
www.coacheschoice.com

Contents

Contents

BUILDING A PROGRAM THROUGH CHARACTER

University of Idaho

It is great to be here today. I will talk loud so you do not fall asleep. We did not invent anything, but we did make some progress in turning our program around at the University of Idaho. I have some strong beliefs about how you should go about turning around a program. I want to share those ideas with you today.

I played college ball at Weber State under Mike Price. I played there and then started coaching at Weber State. I was the defensive line coach at Weber State, and I coached there for four years.

I moved to Northern Arizona University as defensive line coach in 1995. I moved up to defensive coordinator after one year. In 1999, Coach Mike Price called with an opportunity for me to coach at Washington State University. I coached the Cougars' defensive line for four seasons before being elevated to defensive coordinator in 2003. That step on the ladder included three 10-victory seasons, three top-10 finishes.

The reason I am going through all of the problems I had getting started as a head coach is because I believe you can learn from the things I went through to get to this point today. When I went to Washington State, people asked me why I would leave a job as a coordinator to be a defensive line coach at Washington State. I had a hard time explaining why I thought we were going to win at Washington State. As I said, we had one hell of a run. We had three consecutive 10-win seasons, three consecutive top-10 finishes, a PAC-10 championship, and a trip to the Rose Bowl. The point I am trying to make is this: I think you can make anything happen if you work at it.

After we played in the Holiday Bowl, the University of Idaho called to see if I was interested in the head coaching position. They had fired their coach, and they were not in a conference at that time. They did not have an athletic director, and they were still looking to name a president to the university. I told them I was not interested in the job. I did not think that was the time to be thinking about going to a new job. I declined the job offer. The coach they did hire left in two years. The next coach was there for only about 10 minutes and he left. I got that same phone call again in a few years. By that time, Idaho had made it into the WAC, and the facilities had come a long way. Things were a lot better this time.

I told them I knew how to recruit in this area, and I liked the area. Therefore, I decided I wanted to be a head coach. I jumped in with both feet. I had spent 20 years as an assistant coach, and finally I was going to get the opportunity to run my own program. What we are doing at Idaho is very similar to what we did at Washington State when I was there. People tell me it must be hard to recruit in Idaho. The things a lot of people look at as disadvantages, I look at as advantages. A lot of the time, it is how you look at things.

I accepted the job in December of 2007. When I got into the job as head coach, holy moly! There were things there I had not seen in 20 years of college football.

The first experience was my first press conference. It was a big day. It is what coaches dream of doing. It was my chance to be a head coach. This is true, especially when it is your first head coaching job.

After the press conference, Coach Price called me and said he watched the press conference. He said, "I thought you were awesome." He went on to say that he bet it was a lot of fun. I told him it was fun. He replied, "You make sure you remember this day, because it is the last day you are going to have fun." He assured me I was going to get a lot of headaches from being the head coach. I assure you, he was joking.

After the press conference was over, it was as if I had been given the keys to a new Cadillac, but the Cadillac was not there. I got this job, but I did not have a team. They were home on Christmas break. I had a situation where I had to hire the staff, and I had to get myself introduced to the football team.

I knew I had to win the football team over. When I accepted the job at Idaho, I was the fourth head coach in a five-year period. That is a lot of changes. They had four head coaches in five years. What did that mean? They had changes with the assistant coaches as well, and that is whom the kids were looking to. The kids they were coaching, so many of them come from broken homes and have very little family life. It was as if their dad had run away from them when they were growing up, and now he had run off on them again. We knew we would have to be able to build trust in those players. This was my thinking about our future football team. I knew exactly how I wanted to go about building trust with this new team. I had the plan laid out. I knew we had to build trust in the coaching staff again.

I got all of the stats on the players and a picture of each player on the team. I had a phone list of every kid on the team. As I called them on the phone, I looked at their picture as I introduced myself as their new head football coach. I told them I could not wait to meet them in January and get them going in our program. I went through the entire team. It took me about two days to get that done. I talked with players until 10:00 at night. It is rude to call after 10:00 p.m., so at 10:01 p.m., I started calling coaches. I stayed on the phone until 2:00 a.m. on some of those calls to the staff. We had to get the staff put together, and we had to get the staff organized. Our staff got things going with recruiting, and then we had the team come back from the winter break.

The school took me on a tour of the facilities. I went to visit the dome. We were walking down the tunnel. It is quite a dome. I can assure you, weather is not a problem for us. Regardless of the weather outside, we tell our recruits the sun always shines at our place.

As we walked down the tunnel, I saw the sign on the door to the team meeting room. The AD told me I did not have to go in the room. I told him I wanted to see the team room. I walked into that room and it had a cement floor. There was a rental car in the back of that room used for storage, and it had a fence around the car. The band had their crap in one corner, and the trainer had some of his supplies in the other corner. I assured the AD that the room was one area to improve.

I decided our first team meeting would not be in that concrete room in the tunnel. It was more like a cave than a meeting room. We had our first meeting in a very nice room on campus. I got a nice room, and I told the players we were going to do things first class and that was why we were meeting in a first-class room.

The way you build trust is to tell people you will do something and then you back it up. This was my first message: "Gentlemen, there are going to be consequences for certain actions, regardless of who that someone may be." We set three major goals for our program.

- Everyone that plays football for us is going to graduate.
- We will win the WAC championship and the bowl game that goes with it. We could go to one of several different bowls.
- We want to make sure we are turning out first-class young men.

That last goal is very critical in this day and time. We want to graduate young men who conduct themselves in a way that our community, our school, our athletic department, our fans, and our alumni can be proud of. We want to make sure the mothers and fathers are just as proud to get them after they leave us as they were when they first came to school to be with us. This is very important to us—that is character. Character is who you are when no one else is looking. That is how you find things that matter.

We are a lot closer to getting those goals met now that we have our program started. From last year's seniors, we only have one player who has not graduated. The group this year, we only have one senior who will not be eligible to graduate this session. We have two players who are getting triple majors. We had two others who graduated the summer before last with triple majors. Things have come a long way from when we started in December of 2007.

Last year, with three games to play in our season, we were still competing for the WAC championship. We did not win the championship, so we still have lots to accomplish. However, we did win the bowl game we played in. We do feel we have turned the program around by stressing the character issue.

When I took the job, I made it clear that I did not want to be a high school principal. I did not want to be the sheriff. I wanted to be the head football coach. To do what we need to do, there is one rule you are going to follow: Do the right thing! It is as simple as that. What does that mean? Is it hard to figure out what the right thing is? I think it is very simple. If you have to think about it before you do it, don't do it. It is very simple.

If your name is going to run across the bottom line of ESPN or be on the front page of USA Today, will mom and dad be proud of you or not? Will your grandparents be proud of you? On the other hand, will it be something that will disgrace them, you, and your school? Remember the principle: Do the right thing.

Drugs are illegal. Don't have an experience with them. You must be 21 to legally drink alcohol. If you are 21, you must be smart about drinking, and you better have a driver available when you are out drinking.

We only have two things we can own in this world today. You can buy cars and homes and things such as that. However, the only two things you can own are your name and your word. If your name and word indicate you are a liar and a thief, then you do not own too much, do you? We are not going to put up with stealing. I am going to be honest with the players, and I expect the players to be honest with me. If we can do this, we can have a great future.

I let the players know we are all starting over with a clean slate. The players were there before me, and I come in new. None of us have a history together. We are all starting clean. As far as I know, all of the players are angels. I tell them to keep being angels. Some of you may have been on the wrong side of life, but none of you have been on the wrong side with me. I let them know everyone gets a fresh start on that first day we meet.

For some of these kids, it is a matter of restoring faith in the players. Some of them will ask, "Why should we believe you because the last head coach told us the same thing? Why are you any different?" I let them know we are going to be here for them and that we will back them up.

We modeled our program after parents and the family. The question is why we would choose the family to build a foundation for our program. I think this comes with the character issue. Let me explain what I mean. I have a younger brother. We fought like cats and dogs when we were growing up. I am sure most of you were the same. Families can have their own individual spats within the family. However, when it comes down to outsiders and fighting time, the family backs each other. The family has each other's back.

We have 107 players on the team. They all want to be treated the same way. We know that is not going to happen. There are going to be different situations, and you have to be able to work through those situations. When it comes time to go get someone else, we are united. That is the reason we selected the family as a model.

We got the kids in the classrooms and in the weight room for the second semester. The coaches were busy recruiting. We got to the first weekend of the new semester, and everyone had a new beginning.

I will not bore you with all the things that happened in those first few weeks. I had never been around anything in college football where so much nonsense was going on.

We got through to the next to the last day of spring practice. The next day we were having our spring game. We knew we would have 5,000 to 6,000 people show up to watch the spring game. The game was in the dome. We got a new field installed in our dome that first year. It was the same type of field turf installed at the new Cowboys Stadium in Dallas.

Before practice, on the day before our spring game, the athletic director came to see me just before practice. He told me the "big tackle" missed practice the last two days. I told him I was aware of this because we decided if they did not have the grades to be eligible, we would not allow them to practice. Instead, we sent them to a study hall with tutors available. In this case, we were talking about a good-looking, 6'7", 320-pound offensive tackle. He passed the look test in every respect. The AD said, "I know about the study hall. He has not been in the study hall for the last two days."

Now, I started thinking. I went along with the AD and asked him where the big tackle was. He told me he was in jail for selling dope. That ended his career at Idaho.

After practice that day, I held a meeting with the team. I told them I was very upset that they had not said anything to the coaches about what was going on. I told them they needed to take control of their team and clean their acts up. I let them know they had known about incidents of the players stealing in the locker room but did nothing to let the coaches know about the situation.

After the spring game, I let them all know that if anyone wanted to get his release from the team, I would gladly grant him his wish. I wanted them to get in or out. We needed to clean up the program, and we wanted to get rid of the bad apples. The next Monday, the coaches hit the road to catch up on recruiting.

I was on the road that Monday, and I received a phone call. It was one of the players. He told me he wanted a release. I assured him that I would sign the release with no problem. A little later that day, I received a second call from a player that wanted a release, which I granted.

We made it to the last week of the regular semester, and we were looking for any players that may have a problem with grades to become eligible for the fall semester. I was in my office, and I received a call from one of the police officers. He asked me if I knew about the bookstore situation. I assured him I did not know about the situation. He filled me in on what had happened.

Four of our players had gone to the bookstore. When they went in the bookstore, they had two lines. One line was for people selling their old books back to the bookstore. The other line was for people buying books. The players went in the bookstore, took books from the shelves, and got in the line to sell the books. After they sold the books, the security people reviewed the films the bookstore had and identified the four players. They had four cameras in the bookstore for security purposes. The security identified the four players. They were charged with stealing the books and selling them back to the bookstore. They wanted me to talk with them before the police moved on the case.

I called the players in to get their side of the story. I did not want to get involved with a story where it became a "he said, I said." I asked the position coach for each player to come in when I talked with each player. It was amazing the story they tried to tell me about what had happened. I assured them it was all on tape and there was no question about their intentions. It took over 40 minutes for the first player to finally admit he stole the books and sold them back to the bookstore. The second player was a lot easier to convince. In the end, we did get rid of all four of those players before summer practice.

A few days after the semester ended, we had a couple of players come in to visit with us. They wanted to thank the coaching staff for getting rid of some of the guys that were not willing to buy into the program as we had asked them to do earlier. After that, we knew we had established some sort of a foundation that we could start to build from. The players knew we were going to demand that they do things the right way.

At the end of that semester, I had a one-on-one conversation with each of the players. In addition, the position coach talked with each of his players one-on-one. A lot of the things that were going on started to come out. By that time, it became evident to me one group of bad guys were in one group, and the other guys were scattered in one big group. The team was split in several groups, and we were a long way from being a team. No one wanted to be around those who did not want to follow our structured program. That was the reason no one had taken over and tried to fix the problems on the team.

Now, we had an opportunity to begin to build a team. We got into football, and we did the right things. When you do the right things in a program, it spills over into the game of football. When I talk about character, I am talking about it as the way you behave. It is what we are expected to teach young men how to live. Character is football as well. Character, to us, is important to the game of football. It means working hard, playing hard, and playing physical. Football is a physical game, and it should be played that way.

We have to teach players how to win. That is what we need to work on. We only redshirted two offensive linemen last year. Everyone else got a chance to play this past fall. You have to give kids the opportunity to play the game. The more freshmen we can get to play, the better they will be the next year. Then, the next year, we play true freshmen and true sophomores. We feel this is the way to build a program. This will be our third year coming up next fall.

We still have a lot rebuilding to do. We have some of the problems weeded out. That is one of the good things about the NCAA. I love the NCAA.

They have this thing they call the APR which is the Academic Progress Rate. Put together, it is a great idea. I will tell you one story about this concept. We were under the academic standards as it was. I had to send 18 players packing. Fourteen of those players were on scholarship. Do you think those players made an effort to finish the semester and try to raise their grades? No, they were gone.

The way the rule works is this: If a player stays in your program, you get a point for him. If he stays eligible, you get another point for him. If he is not eligible the next semester, you lose a point. If any player goes zero for two, he becomes ineligible and they take the scholarship away from him. You do not lose the kid, but he loses his scholarship. It is a long-drawn-out process. I think you can see where I am going with this.

At one time, the most scholarships they could take away was eight. Later, they rounded anything over 8.5 to 9 scholarships to be lost. With the class I started out with, we lost 9 of them from the get-go. I had lost 14 before and then the additional 9 players and it hurt. You can only sign 25 players per year. The rule makes it difficult to build a team. We are in the low 68 to 70 players on scholarships. We have a long way to go to get to the 85 players allowed on a team. This is a great rule in theory, but it is not protecting the kids.

I can tell you this: Our community was happy when I got the "garbage" off our team. Everyone around was happy those guys were gone.

What would happen if I recruited your grandson? If your grandson has a locker next to one of those "bad" dudes we got rid of, would you be glad we built our program on character? A lot of coaches would not have done what we did. Some coaches would have kept some of those marginal players. They do this to avoid the numbers issue. They may not want to deal with those parents. If we have players that are stealing from the players and players that are selling dope, then you do not want me to recruit your grandson. Don't tell me parents and grandparents do not want coaches to build character.

Now, we are ready to go on the field and play football. We are not very good. That was the part I could do something about. I knew football.

We had some players in our program that were not very good players and they were not very strong. We had one fifth-year senior who was 6'3" and weighed 280 pounds, and he could not bench press 400 pounds. It was not because we did not have a good strength coach. No one on our team looked as if they had ever been in a weight room when we took over that first year. The class we recruited this year is much better. We have size and strength coming in with this next class.

In my first game as a head coach, we went to play the number-one team in the country in USC at the Coliseum. We played them in front of 90,000 people on national TV. We were starting a freshman quarterback. The last time he had played in a football game, it was in North Platte, Nebraska in front of 90 beagle hound dogs. I was worried he would walk up under the guard and call the cadence. The kid stayed very composed. Our kids competed. They played hard. They played hard in every game that year. That told our staff we were working in the right direction. We only won one football game that first year. That was against a 1-AA team, Cal Poly.

A lot of teams will stop playing hard when they see they are not going to have a winning season and are not going to a bowl game. Our kids played hard all year. The fact that we were playing against the second and third teams of our opponents may have helped some, but our kids played hard. It still made for a long year for us.

We got into the second season, and we won two games that year. We played hard, but we did not play good enough to win any more games. As the head coach, you stand in front of the team after another loss, and you tell them what they need to do to get better and what we have to do to win the next game. You do that from game to game. It is like Groundhog Day—it comes again, and again, and again. Don't think I do not hate to lose. I do. There is nothing worse than losing. We had a plan, and we knew it would take time for the plan to work the

way we expected it to work. We could see we were getting better each game.

We know the fans want to see the score, and they want to see us win. As a staff, we had to figure out what we needed to do to win. We started talking about the individual things we needed to do to have a chance to win. We needed to create more turnovers. We needed to complete more passes, and we needed to gain more yards rushing. We had to figure out what we needed to do to win.

At the same time, we listed the things we were getting better at. We told the players, this is what is good, and it is going to get better. We asked them to continue to work hard, and we would get the job done. We told them to keep playing their tails off, and this is how we are going to get it done. I kept telling my coaches to stick with the plan because it would work. I had to talk myself into staying with the plan as well as the assistants and the players.

I was concerned the players might start thinking, Coach is saying all of these things and telling us he has a plan, but we are not winning. We had been there two seasons, and we did not have much to show in the win column. We won two games that second year. One of the wins was in the conference. We won three games in two years. I will have to live with that beside my name forever. However, we are going to make things better.

After that second year and during the holidays, I watched every bowl game. During those bowl games, I would text individual players to see if they were watching the same game I was watching. I would tell them something like this: "This is the bowl game we are going to be playing in next year." I started planting the idea in their heads. I sent some of the leaders more than one text message.

We came back to school in January, and it was time to go to work. Every team does mat drills to some extent. Teams do it every winter, and the players hate those drills with a passion. The truth of the matter is that the drills got old and it was not fun for anyone. We worked them hard and made them go until they got sick to their stomachs. We made them go six times in the mornings.

We started thinking, the players move better in the afternoon. We do not play games at 6:30 a.m. We made a change in our program. This had a lot to do with the way we approached the game of football.

Instead of having eight stations in the mat room, we only used four stations. We selected a leader for each of the basic positions on the team. We had eight leaders. Each of the eight leaders had their own team. They drafted the other players to make up the teams. We divided the players according to their skills. We drafted those players first. Then, we went to the next level of skills. We continued to draft the players until everyone was on a team. Our players know the other players better than we know them. We may think we know them, but the players know them a lot better.

We set up a schedule where each of the teams would compete against each other. We referred to the competition as the BCS Challenge. We kept standings in the competition. We made the program just like the bowl games. If a team goes undefeated in the WAC, you are going to play in a BCS bowl game most of the time. With the four stations instead of eight, we would play the first half. We had different drills for each day. Each group ran the same drills. We ran the drills as relays. The player who completed the drill first scored a point for his team.

We still coached football fundamentals in the drills. We made the drills competitive for each group and allowed them to compete just like a game. I never heard one coach yell at a kid to finish his run. We had kids who were dying to get across the lines. They were trying to score points for their teams. By competing, they were getting each other to work hard. We were getting everything we wanted, and the players were learning how to compete. We knew we had to teach our kids how to win. That is the character of the game. That is the nature of teams. We challenged each player to compete for the team.

On Thursday mornings, we have breakfast with our players. We talk about their schoolwork. We want to make sure they are doing things the right way. I was sitting next to a couple of players, and I overheard what they were saying. "We play team four tomorrow, and if we beat them, and, then, if we can win on Tuesday, we will be in first place." I was shocked that these players were excited about running mat drills. We knew we had something going here.

To make a long story short, at the end of the indoor workouts, we had one undefeated team, one team with one loss, and those teams were made up of our quarterbacks and tailbacks. They played each other in the BCS Challenge. The tailbacks were undefeated, and they won the competition. We gave everyone who was bowl eligible a T-shirt. Every member of a team that won their bowl game got to eat steak dinners one special night. All of the others who did not win a bowl game ate hotdogs and beans that night. We did not want to punish anyone, but we did want to reward winners. We wanted to create competition.

Once football practice started in the spring, we carried those competitive drills into practice. One drill we did was to knock a player off the board. We liked the drill and we used it in practice. It is a very competitive drill.

We started doing drills involving each position on the team. We worked with receivers against defensive backs. We worked individual drills at each position on the team. We lined up the offensive man against the defensive man, and we go 1-on-1 with each individual against a defender. We have seven stations, and we work each station 1-on-1. The players who win their individual drills do not have to run at the end of practice. We always run at the end of practice. The entire team can see those drills, and they are cheering for the offense or the defense.

We even did this in the middle of our spring game last year. We know that third down is a very important down in football. We get to third down, and we go live on the drill right where the ball is on the field. We take the ball and move it to seven different down and distances on the third-down play. We start with third and 10, third and 7, third and 5, third and 4, third and 3, third and 2, and third and 1. This is a live drill. We get the first down or we don't. We stop them or we do not stop them. We can run our first offensive team against the second defense and the second offense against the first defense. The team that wins most of the seven plays wins. We are just finding ways to reward the players for competing and for winning.

We run other drills to stimulate competition. We place the ball on our own two-yard line. We give the offense the down and distance. Either we get out of the danger zone or we do not get out of the danger zone. We compete and we have a reward for winning the drill.

Competition has helped our football team. We needed to teach our players how to win. The team that won our BCS Challenge came to my house for dinner one evening during our two-a-days. It was a good way to reward those players who won the competition. It gave them a nice change of pace, and that was what we needed to do.

We knew we would be better going into the 2009 season. We were bigger, stronger, and faster. The question was this: Would we be mentally able to compete in our league? We knew we needed to have success early. That was critical for our team. That was a must for our team.

I needed to help the team set their goals. We all set goals. That is how we get our players to work hard. I can have a long list of goals. We have to make realistic goals. One of the goals we had was to go to a bowl game. In every meeting we had, we had our staff talk about our goal of going to a bowl game. I wanted them to write that goal on the chalkboard. When I meet with our team I want to have my bowl game ring on. We did achieve the goal of going to a bowl game this year. A lot of people thought I was nuts to set a goal to go to a bowl game when we had only won three games in two years. I needed to let the players know that was a realistic goal for us. You cannot accomplish anything if you do not say you are going to do it. You have to commit to doing it.

We had our first meeting in the fall. We started with a kickoff dinner. When the players went up to the buffet line to get their food, we did not have any plates. We only had bowls. Players asked where the plates were. I told them we did not have plates. We were going to a bowl, and we wanted everyone to eat out of the bowls provided. We wanted them to know what our theme was for the year.

We were going to an away game, and we were leaving the day before the game. We had to take a bus ride about 30 minutes to the airport. I got a call after about 15 minutes into the bus ride and I found out the plane was going to be late picking us up. It was too late to go back to the school and practice a pre-game again. I did not want to have the players sit in the small airport waiting for the plane. So what did we do? We had the bus hang a left and we pulled into a bowling alley. We went inside and we had the team bowl until we got the word the plane was waiting for us. We wanted them to know we wanted to go to a bowl game in 2009.

We had a six-game win streak. We had things happen that had never happened before in the history of the school. However, we had to learn how to win. We had to learn how to deal with success.

I want to close off here. Sometimes you need to have success early to have a chance to go to a bowl game. You need to have success winning after you have lost a game after a winning streak. We accomplished those goals. If you do not have the success early and win after you have lost in a season, you run the risk of players thinking, here we go again.

Our players gained confidence because they learned how to compete and they learned how to win. We got things turned around. We did it by building character and by doing things the right way. We paid attention to detail and to the character of the game. We won our bowl game, and we did it in style.

I hope I did not bounce around too much and that you can take something from this talk. Thanks for your attention. Good luck to everyone.

PRESSURING THE SPREAD OFFENSE

Murray State University

I want to thank Nike and Clinic Director Terry Rogers for this opportunity to speak here today. In addition, I want to thank my head coach, Chris Hatcher, for giving me the time to be here today. I have used a 4-3 defensive scheme all of my coaching career. The spread offense as it is today has become the dominant offense. A couple of years ago, I did a lot of homework and started branching out to running a three-man front. I have used both fronts the last couple of years.

I feel very comfortable in the three-man front against the spread offense. This is not saying we will not use the four-man front against the spread. We used the three-man front most of the time at Georgia Southern University. After coaching against the spread offense over the years, I feel more comfortable with a linebacker or a defensive back dropping into space than a 3-technique end dropping back into the open space.

I want to go over a few points to cover my philosophy, and then I will go over a few things we do in attacking the spread offense. I feel you must attack the spread offense. I do not think you can sit back and play your base defense against the spread offense play after play. I think that is part of what you have to do, but my feeling is that you have to give multiple looks for the offensive coordinator and the players on the field as well.

The first thing you must do is to have a solid base defense. We must have a solid base defense. We rush four down linemen and run twist moves with them. When we talk about rushing four men, and I am in a three-man front, I am always going to bring a linebacker on the blitz. I do not think we looked at one snap where we only rushed three down linemen. We do not just rush three men against the spread offense. Therefore, when I talk

about our base defense, I am talking about rushing four defenders in either our 4-3 set or our 3-4 look.

If we are in the 4-3 set, we rush the four down linemen (Diagram #1). We are a two-high-safety defense. That could be cover 4 or cover 2. The defense you feel comfortable with is what you should use. That is what I do with our defense. I feel the two-high-safety look is versatile in that you can run everything that you can run out of the one-high-safety look.

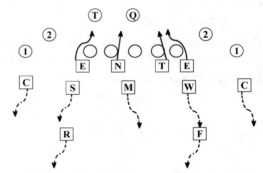

Diagram #1. 4-3 Base Defense Rush 4

Out of the 3-4 look, we can still rush four defenders and play with two high safeties (Diagram #2). We rush the three down linemen plus the Sam linebacker. We are rushing four defenders and playing a two-high-safeties look. In this defense, we have the ability to bring any defender we want to make the fourth rush man.

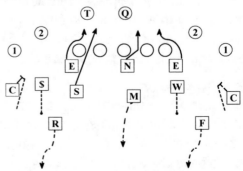

Diagram #2. 3-4 Base Defense Rush 4

I think it is important to give the offense multiple looks. We do this with different defensive moves, and we disguise the defense. We do this for the offensive coordinator, for the quarterback, and for the offensive line on their pass protection.

Out of the multiple looks, you must be able to move the defense. It is a lot easier for the offensive linemen to block a defender if that defender lines up head-up on the blocker. It makes it more difficult for the blocker if you can move on defense, especially if you have better athletes on defense.

I believe in disguising the secondary coverages. In addition, I believe it is important to disguise where you are coming from on your side of the ball.

Here is an example of what we do to disguise the coverages. We show cover 2, but we play man-free coverage (Diagram #3). This is a big deal with us because we run a two-high-safety look. When I talk about a cover-2 look, or a cover-4 look, most of the time our safeties are going to be 12 to 14 yards deep, depending on what we have called. We like to give the same look on each of the calls.

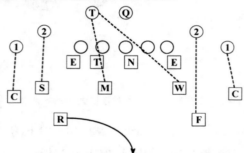

Diagram #3. Show Cover 2, Play Man-Free

All of our zone coverages are numbers or words, and all of our man coverages include a color in the call. I may not be the smartest coach in the world, but I believe I can teach a player this defense. If we call coverage with a color in the coverage, he will know we are in man coverage. If we call a number, then he has to decide which cover we are calling.

We show cover 2 or cover 4, and out of those two looks, we can play man-coverage. We can show our cover-3 look, and use a spin and end up in cover 2 (Diagram #4). We are blitzing the Will backer. We have the safety rolled down to show a

3-5 look, but we are rolling the free safety to the outside and bringing the opposite corner back on the opposite side to be a post player. We are rolling to cover 2 from a one-high look.

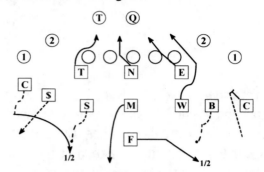

Diagram #4. Show Cover 3, Spin Cover 2

We may start in a two-high-safety look, and stem the man down to make the quarterback think we are going to bring pressure. The quarterback may think we are in man coverage when the corner starts backing out.

When you are in a one-deep safety look, you can do just so many things. If the corners are up in the box, and the quarterback sees only one deep back, he will most likely think the defense is going to be in man-free coverage.

The next point of concentration for our defense is that we believe we must attack protection and lesser players. The first thing I am going to look at when I break down the film and look at the pass protection, I want to know how good is the running back at pass blocking. The offensive linemen work on blocking all day. They do not run out for passes, or run the ball in drills. Their job is to protect the quarterback and to block. They are going to get a lot more reps over the course of practice and over the course of the week in doing their job. The offensive player that does not get the reps is the running back. He has to be involved in the pass protection. We want to know if the running back can pass block. If he is not a good protector, we are going after him on the pass rush. We want to get our linebacker or defensive end 1-on-1 with that running back. We want to force him to block one of those two defenders. In my thinking, we should win that battle.

If the offense has a running back who can pass block better than average, we are going to look at the five offensive linemen. We look at them and try to determine which one of them is the least able blocker of the five linemen. Chances are, not all five of them are going to be good pass protectors. There is going to be a weak link somewhere. Things we look at with the five offensive linemen are speed and footwork. We want to know if they can step well on pass protection. We want to know if they have heavy feet, and are slow moving their feet. We are looking at how well they use their hands. Different things go into what we are looking at with the offensive linemen as far as we are trying to determine which one of them to attack.

We are talking about attacking the protection. We see a lot of slide protection (Diagram #5). I am sure you see a lot of slide protection. I would think every offense in the country runs some version of slide protection. We look to see how we can attack slide protection.

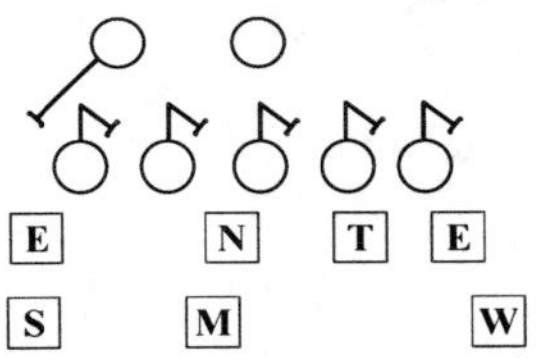

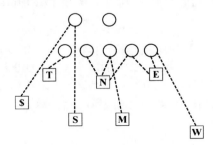

Diagram #5. Slide Protection

The way we set our defense up the blitz can come from different position but it will attack a certain spot every time. Our defense has the ability to use certain tags. We can bring the pressure from any direction. If we are going to attack the back who is pass blocking, and the offense is in a shotgun look, our blitz is going to come from the side in which the back is blocking. If the quarterback is under center, we designate the area we are going to attack. If the defense blocks the back away from the slide protection, we can call a minus blitz, and it allows us to bring the blitz away from the backside. We can attack the back, or we can attack away from the back.

Slide protection:
• Slide to back/away from back = check or minus
• Slide to field/away from field = field or boundary

• Slide to formation/away from formation = strong or weak
• Slide to tight end/away from tight end = T or open

We use tags to designate where we are going to attack the pass protection. By using different tags, we do not have to run the stunts from the field every time, or the strongside every time. We can bring a blitz from eight different scenarios or looks, with only one blitz. We do that by using a tag in front of the blitz.

First, we are going to attack the running back on his ability to pass block. Then we are going to find the weakest link on the line as a pass protector, and we attack him. I tell our linebackers they set the tone early in the game. If they rush the pass and end up on the running back, we want to knock his feet back. We want that linebacker to run over the blocking back. We do not care about the rush, the sack, or anything else except to run over that blocker. We want to let that back know it is going to be a long afternoon for him. We want to set the tone for him on pass protection. We want to set him up for a bad experience.

Next, we talk about man protection (Diagram #6). We want to cover these questions about their pass protection:
• Big-on-big?
• Where does the center block?
• Where does the back block?
• Do they throw hot routes?
• Overload side?
• Attack weak link?

Diagram #6. Man Protection

We want to know where the center blocks. If we are in a four-man front, we want to know if the center always steps toward the nose man. If we are in the three-man front, it is obvious he has to block the noseman. We also want to know where the back blocks. In a man-protection scheme, most of the time, the back blocks away from the center. These points are factors that determine the blitzes we are going to use for that game.

We want to know if the offense is big on throwing the hot routes. If they are throwing the hot routes, this is where the disguise comes into play. You want the quarterback to read one defense, but we end up in another defense by disguising the defense. We use other techniques against teams that throw the hot routes.

We like to overload one side of the defense to rush the quarterback. We want to show the offense our overload, and get someone to come free from the other side of the defense. In addition, we like to attack the weak link of the offensive line.

Another point we consider is the injury report before the game. Even during the game, if a player gets hurt and has to be replaced, we are going to go after his sub. We want to test his water. It is obvious he is not as good a player as one of the other five linemen, or he would be starting.

I believe in multiple coverages with the blitz. At one time, we had several different blitzes with only two coverages. We cut down on the number of blitzes and added a couple of additional coverages and it makes it a lot tougher for the quarterback to read the coverage. That gives us a fraction of a second to get to the quarterback when he holds the ball that short additional amount of time.

We feel it is important to believe in your pressure. You must get good at it. In addition, you must make the quarterback hold the ball. It may only be three generic blitzes, but if you believe in them, you have to sell the players on those three blitzes.

You have to get good at the blitzes you do run. If you cut them down to a working number where you are efficient with them, you can run them all year long. We want three or four blitzes that we can hang our hat on as a base defense. To get good at the blitzes, you have to rep them.

We want to make the quarterback hold the football. The triggerman is the key in the spread offense. If we can confuse him for one step, we feel we have a chance. We want to make him hold the football.

Let me get into some X and O things. First is the NCAA blitz. Here is one of the basic blitzes we use (Diagram #7). I would say that 95 percent of the teams in college football use this blitz. They run this blitz for a reason. The offense is going to see this stunt every week. They still have to protect against this scheme.

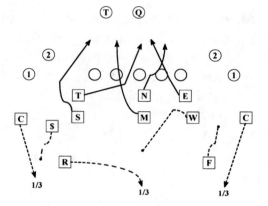

Diagram #7. Three-Deep Coverage: 2x2 Stack Strong Sword Outlaw—Heat

The line and the quarterback can see the three down linemen, but the quarterback is concerned with what is going on in the secondary. When we get to a third-down situation, I like to go to a three-man front because I feel the linebacker or safety is a better pass defender than the defensive end who is dropping into pass coverage. We tag the word "sword" on the call to check for the quarterback draw play. This is our three-under, three-deep coverage for us.

Next, we look at the 3x1 three-deep coverage. We do not want our Will backer coming across the middle to cover the third receiver. We cannot ask that Will backer to play the hot route against the #3 receiver to the opposite side of the formation. We run a sword blitz with three under. We are in three-deep coverage (Diagram #8). We have a racer lined up behind our Sam linebacker. He is our DOT player. It is a "drop on three," which is the third receiver inside. He is checking for the hot route.

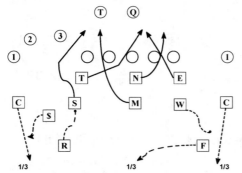

Diagram #8. Sword Blitz With Three Under: Three-Deep Coverage

This is a trips check for the safety looking for the hot route. If we get a hot route in the area where the Sam linebacker is blitzing, the racer picks up the third receiver on the hot route. If the three-receiver catches the hot route, he better end up with a headache from the hit on him by our racer.

Here is another example. We are still in our three-deep concept. Now, we run stack strong shank heat (Diagram #9). Strong for us means we are coming from the passing strength. We can bring the blitz from the field or from the boundary. We are bringing a double-edge pressure from the passing strength or from the field.

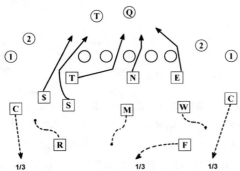

Diagram #9. Stack Strong Shank Heat

Going back to our sword concept we talked about previously, we are giving the defense the same look. We have run three under and three deep. We want to test the quarterback by running a different look. We are in the two-deep concept against a 2x2 look. We run stack strong sword: 2 choke (Diagram #10). We are playing cover 2 with

the corners. They are our trail players. We are still going to funnel the receivers inside, but we are going to play underneath the curl with the corners. We are trying to rob the corner on the call.

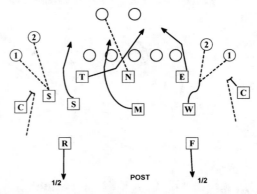

Diagram #10. Stack Strong Sword: 2 Choke—2x2

On the 3x1 look on the 2 choke, we still funnel the outside receiver to the inside and play the corner underneath. The Mike backer takes the #3 receiver inside (Diagram #11). We will assign the noseman the back in the spread set. We are not going to ask the noseguard to cover a swing route. If the back is releasing outside, we expect the end to hit him in the mouth as he comes outside. We still have a corner who will leverage the swing back in the flat to a degree.

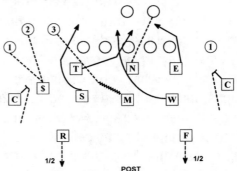

Diagram #11. Stack Strong Sword: 2 Choke—3x1

If the back peels off as soon as the ball is snapped, we peel off and run to the back immediately. We take on the back in what we call "peel alert" to take away the hot route to counter our blitz. We are still running pressure, and we have the flare back covered. We want to take the quarterback's hot read away from him.

Another variation of our cover 2 is our stack strong shank X spin (Diagram #12). We are rotating the corner on the backside to the deep zone. We play the corner on the callside, the same as we played before. He funnels the widest receiver inside, and drops into coverage to the outside flat.

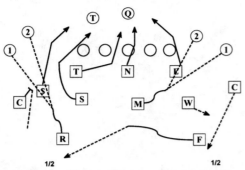

Diagram #12. Stack Strong Shank X Spin

Now, I want to go back to the man-free concepts. This is our 2x2 look. We are going back to sword. We are moving around and we are disguising our defense. We may bring the corners and backers up to show blitz, but then drop back into our coverage before the ball is snapped. We are showing two deep safeties, but the offense does not know if we are going to play cover 2. They do not know if we are going to play Cover-4 or if we are going to blitz or not.

I feel you must play man-free coverage to some degree. You may have three players who are good playing man coverage, and you may have one man who is weak playing man coverage. You have to roll the dice and play what you think is the best in your situations. You do not have to hang your hat on one coverage or man coverage. However, you have to play man coverage at some point in time. If you are playing a team that is in the spread offense, and they have a third down and four yards to go, and they throw the five-yard out route and move the chains, you know you must play man to stop them. You do not have to get up tight and press all of the time. I am not saying that. You must be able to sit tight and play the receivers in those situations to force the offense from picking the defense apart.

We can run our stack strong sword outlaw blue and play our man concept against the 2x2 (Diagram #13). We would have our possible peel alert to contain the blitzer if the back is not check releasing.

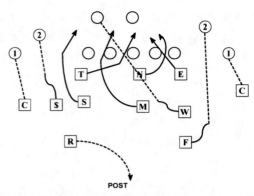

Diagram #13. Stack Strong Sword Outlaw Blue Versus 2x2 Alignment

Again, our man coverage is all colors. If a player is not blitzing and we are playing blue coverage, they know the linebackers are running the blitz. The defensive backs know none of the deep backs are going to be involved in a blitz when we call a blue call. Our team knows the B in blue is for "backers," and they are blitzing. We never tie a defensive back to a blitz with blue coverage. The deep backs play man coverage (Diagram #14).

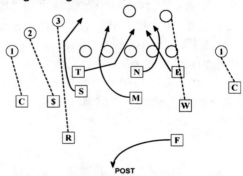

Diagram #14. Stack Strong Sword Outlaw Blue— Backs in Man Coverage

Whoever is playing man-to-man on the back always blitz-engages the back. The backer on the back must go with the back if he swings outside. If he flares outside, the backer takes him immediately. We are going to take away that play at that moment. If the back steps up to block and then releases, we send the backer immediately. The back does not know if the backer has him man-to-man, or if he is blitzing. If the backer is coming, the back has to stay in to block.

It all goes back to what I said before. There is a lesser player out there somewhere. We are going after that player, and we should win most of those battles.

We ran shank with the cover-2 concept. Now, we are going to run shank with the man concept. We are going to run stack strong shank brown. The brown coverage alerts our defensive backs that there is a possibility one of the defensive backs may be blitzing. It also alerts the linebackers that one of them may have to cover man-to-man, depending on the blitz called. Ideally, I like our Will backer on a second man inside in the slot. This is a mixer for us (Diagram #15). We are taking the sword blitz and the shank blitz, and we are running the same coverages with both of them. A different player may have a different assignment, but we are changing things up. We are trying to confuse the quarterback by giving him multiple looks.

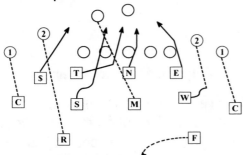

Diagram #15. Stack Strong Shank Brown

The offense had six players to block, so we are going to bring six on defense. We are going to run a zero no-help concept. Our no-help blitzes are designated by Indian names. We may only have two or three, but we will carry at least one into a game. Our guys know if Seminole or Apache is called, we tighten down and bring the house. We do tie our black coverage with this package. Black alerts our players that there is no help for them. They are playing man-to-man (Diagram #16). They must know the ball is coming out quick because we are getting after the quarterback. We have one more rusher than the offense has to block us.

On a zero blitz, we have an assigned scout who is our peel-alert man. If we call "scout," it kills the blitz, and that scout becomes the peel-alert man. If that back peels off for a pass, we have our assigned defender peel off with him. If he steps up to block,

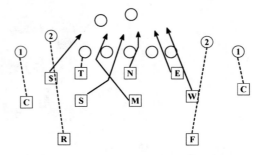

Diagram #16. Stack Seminole Black

we come after him. We have the tackle as the scout, playing the slow screen pass. We have one more man than the offensive blockers have, so we assign the tackle the slow read.

Let me sum up the philosophy and the things I have covered. I have given you two samples of coverages that we use and the blitzes we use with the coverages. The thing that has helped us the most against the spread offense is changing up our coverages. It has helped us tremendously. We only have so much time to practice. The question comes down to this: do you want to run several blitzes, or do you want to run a few blitzes and get good running those few blitzes with different coverages?

The offense is going to run their best plays every week. I feel the defense must do the same. Run what you believe in. Rep it, and rep it consistently. It is the same for the blitz plays.

We take the best five running plays and the top five passing plays, and that first day we run nothing but our base defense against them. We want our kids to see the offense as many times as we possibly can see the offense from day one. On the second day, we do the same, except we are ready to start looking at our blitz plays with a certain coverage. On the third day, we do the same thing, but we add a second coverage to the defense. The players must see those plays against what they are doing. We are going to run our stunts against their top five plays in practice over and over.

I appreciate your attention. If you have any questions about our defense, let me hear from you. Thank you.

THE PISTOL OFFENSE

University of Nevada

I want to give you a quick background on how we came up with the *pistol offense* and what it is all about. All offenses have strengths and weaknesses, and this offense is no different. I do not want anyone in this room to think we do not throw the football. I coach the quarterbacks at the University of Nevada, and I love to throw the football. From 1993 to 1996, we led the country, one way or another, in throwing the football. We really enjoy throwing the football. We are a one-back offense most of the time.

When the shotgun offense came out, I enjoyed watching those teams move the football. The thing I did not like was the idea of a running back getting the ball running east and west. This was true on an inside zone or outside zone play. Teams have taken this offense and they have done a good job with the counter play and the trap plays off those zone plays.

We have always been a north and south running game offense. We led the country in rushing this year, and the year before that we were third in the country in running the ball. We can run the football. We do this because of our play-action passing game. This coming year, our emphasis is going to be on the dropback part of the passing game.

There are no gimmicks in our offense. The beauty of the pistol offense is this: To win a championship, and to compete every year at the championship level, you must be able to run the football. This is true in our conference. Somewhere along the way, you will have to run the football.

We went to the pistol offense in 2005. I brought the staff together and I told them this is what I want to look at during spring practice. I want to move the quarterback four and one half yards off

the ball in the shotgun set. We want our deep back to line up seven to seven and one half yards from the center or the ball (Diagram #1). I wanted to know if we could move the quarterback off the line and still be able to run our offense. In most situations, teams had the quarterback five yards off the ball in the shotgun.

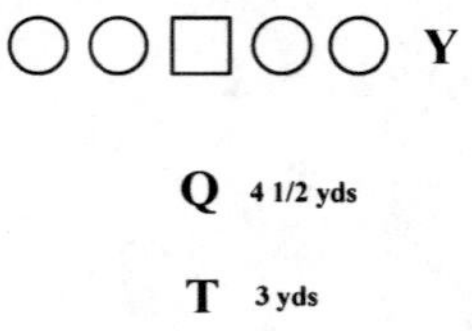

Diagram #1. Pistol Alignment

When I presented this to my staff, they looked at me as if I had really lost my marbles. We agreed in January to look at the concept. I had no film to study because there was nothing you could compare it to. I came back to the staff and told them we had to do something different. I did not like what we were doing, so I decided we were going to run the offense.

We had 15 days in the spring to practice. I decided if we were in a fourth-and-one situation, we were going to stay in the pistol offense. Our practices are very physical. I started calling the offense the pistol. The quarterback was the trigger, and the deep back was the hammer of the pistol. We went out to practice for the first four days. The quarterback was four yards deep behind the center. The deep back was three yards deeper than the quarterback.

The things we did not realize are things I will share with you today. This is why we liked the system. The running back gets the ball deeper. We took the kids out on the field and ran all of the tests on the depth of the back. We lined the quarterback up four and one half yards deep. Occasionally, we will go under center. We lined up the tailback three yards behind the quarterback. It was difficult to see the running back directly behind the quarterback three yards away.

At five yards away, the linebackers could see the running back better. By having him seven yards deep, we can get the ball to him deeper than we would if the quarterback was under center. If we are under center with the quarterback and we run an isolation play, we get the ball to the deep back at five yards. In this formation, we get it to him six yards deep (Diagram #2). This gave the back more time to make his cut. This increased his vision for his cut.

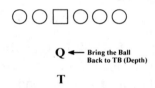

Diagram #2. Depth of the Tailback

The first thing we teach is the zone play. If you came to our practice today, you would see the same play we ran from the get-go. It has not changed. We believe in this offense and it starts with the zone. In this formation, it hides the running back. I am not saying the linebackers cannot see the backs, but the backs come from behind the quarterback from three yards away, and it is difficult for them to pick the back up on his cut.

We found out the formation helped hide the running back, and this made it hard on the linebackers to key the back. In addition, the defense cannot set their front based on the offset back. We can use all formations in the game. With the one-back set, we are able to do some things against the defense. We can run to either side of the formation. We can use one tight end, two tight ends, a wingback, and we can use motion. We enjoyed this a great deal. We can be a power team, an option team, a split-zone team, an I-back team.

At the time we designed the pistol, we were not sure what we could do with the offense. We

wanted to take the offense we had been running, which was the power offense, and the I formation offense, and adapt it to the pistol offense. That is how the pistol offense evolved.

The second year, we went to the read offense as well. You will see what we are trying to do with our offense. The first thing we teach is the zone play. It is the inside zone play. We teach it differently than most teams. We teach it different in terms of our steps for the offensive line. Our steps are always into the line of scrimmage. We go six inches out and two inches up. We are all stepping up and into the line of the zone. Most teams that were teaching the zone play at that time were not too concerned about getting into the line. We bring the foot forward. We teach hip progression with everyone on our football team to start with. Our front line has been very good over the last few years.

After we teach the inside zone play, everything evolves from this concept. We want the line split two feet across the board. We want the quarterback to get the ball back as deep as he can to the back so he can cut off our 2 technique or 3 technique. We really stress that the quarterback gets the ball back deep to the back. Our backs are north/south players. This year, our deep backs were 4.6 kids, and they were very physical. They were north/south runners.

People have gone to a lot of man coverage to take our quarterback away from our two-man read. The thing I am stressing now is the depth at which the tailback gets the football on the zone play. We work on this play from the time we start stretching until we go to our punt formation in our fourth period. The reason for that is because the handoff on the play is going to simulate so many plays that we run later.

The tailback reads the block of our guard. His aiming point is the inside hip of our guard (Diagram #3). It is the back cheek of that inside guard. It is downhill from there.

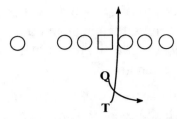

Diagram #3. The Inside Zone Play

The split for our linemen is two feet across the board. We may split our tight end out a little wider. We can run the play to the quickside or the strongside based on our game plan. Again, all of our linemen are stepping forward on that first step. We tell our kids to block the defensive front first. We will work our way up to the next level, but we want to block the front first.

We are a multiple-formation team. We can run wing, unbalanced, spread, and a lot of other formations. We do a lot of different formations. They all have a common denominator this way.

From the zone play comes what we call the slice play (Diagram #4). It is the same exact zone play, with this exception: It will have a receiver, who may be a wingback or an extra tight end, come across the formation in motion and slice the defensive end on the split end side. The motion man comes down the heels of our offensive line and his rule is to slice block the first man outside our offensive tackle. It is a full zone offense off the zone play. We have all of the reads and other aspects we work against depending on the scouting report. The tailback cuts back toward the center on the slice play.

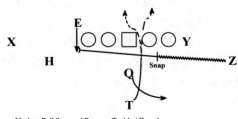

Motion: Ball Snapped Between Tackle / Guard

Diagram #4. Zone Slice Play

We can run the play with a wide receiver in motion, with a wingback in motion, or we can run it from a two-back set. When we start spring practice, these are the first two plays we work on.

We run the play with all of our receivers. A combination of people can run this play and not change the basic concept.

It is the exact same play for our linemen. Our left tackle knows he does not have to worry about any defender on his outside shoulder. He can pull on up into the second level.

In the pistol, the ball is always snapped when the motion man is on the inside hip of the near tackle. We do have some plays with motion where we do not snap the ball until the motion man is across the formation to change the strength of the formation. The motion for the misdirection on the pistol is to have the ball snapped when that motion man gets on the inside hip of the near tackle. The snap comes when he is between the tackle and guard.

Before we ran the pistol offense, we ran the slice with the quarterback under center. However, we wanted to create something that would make it difficult for those linebackers to see when we run the motion. We do have a play where we hand the ball to the motion man and he runs the ball outside. I am not going to cover that play in this session.

We want to be able to run the zone and the slice plays against any defense. We averaged 5.7 yards per carry last year. In practice, we will not move off this play until they can run it correctly. When we run the zone (slice) play, we can run the ball off the hip of the offensive guard. If we ran 30 plays, five of them would be off the hip of the guard, and the others would be on the cut over the center. It is a change-up for us to run the play off the center and the guard.

The key to the play is that the tailback cannot be more than three yards behind the quarterback. He has to be able to read what is going on up front. He has to see what is taking place up front. We get double-team blocks across the front of our offensive line. He has to see those double-teams and make his cut off the blocks.

Our offense starts with the zone play. We run it on the goal line as well as in the middle of the field. I tell our offensive coaches that no one can penetrate our offensive line from tackle to tackle. Someone may get in the tight end and tackle gap, but no one is to get in a gap from tackle to tackle. We keep our splits at two feet. Our GA places the ball ready for play, stands behind our line, and calls out, "Two-foot splits." He will write down the names of any player who is not taking his proper splits. You must be disciplined on this play.

The thing we did this past year was to bring the wide receiver in motion on the slice play and have him block on the defensive end. The defensive end did not see the motion man as a threat. We did it with live receivers. We do not expect that motion man to blow the defensive end up. We expect to get a piece of him on the inside shoulder to keep him from coming down inside on the play. If he does come down inside, we are going to run the two-man game against him.

When the end comes down inside, we run the two-man game. We call the play *zone bluff* (Diagram #5). We added this phase to our offense two years ago. It can be a two-man game or a three-man game. Here, we see the two-man game. You can run the play from all formations. We can run the play to either side. If we run the play to the weakside, we are reading the end and blocking down with the tackle.

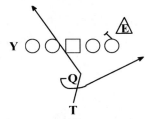

Diagram #5. Zone Bluff

In practice, we call our running game the thunder period. We have a 20-minute *thunder period*. In that 20-minute period, we tell the offensive line coach he has seven minutes to work on the zone bluff play. That is our 24 and 25 bluff plays. The beauty of this is the fact that it is the same blocking on the backside as our 32 and 33 zone plays, and the only thing that is different is the block by our quickside tackle. Once we get the zone play installed with our bluff scheme, he can practice both plays during that seven-minute time period. It is the same blocking technique except for

the quickside tackle. If the end is coming down, the tackle is going to screen the linebacker on his side.

The difference on the play is for the quarterback. The quarterback takes an open step on the bluff. The running back runs the same path but his aiming point is the right cheek of the center. That is our 32 play. On the zone play, the aiming point is the inside cheek of the guard.

The steps for the quarterback on the zone play are to open, hand the ball to the back on the second step, and then complete his bootleg action. On the bluff, he opens and rides the tailback hip to hip. We do not want the ball out in space. We want it on the hip of the quarterback. We say hip to hip so everyone knows how we are going to run the play. He reads the defensive end and runs toward the line of scrimmage on this particular play.

We run the play to both sides. It is the same exact blocking. The onside tackle checks to make sure no one is coming down inside, and then he blocks the first man to show at the next level.

Our tight end does an arc release on the play. If the defense overloads to the tight end side, we run an audible away from the strength of the defense. Our offensive line is not huge but we are quick.

The quarterback reads the end man on the line of scrimmage. The defense will play a lot of games against us. We have a lot of techniques to use with our fronts. The tackle blocks down inside, and we read the end man on the line of scrimmage. We did not invent this play, but we did invent the pistol. If the tackle is coming down hard, we are going to come with the two-man bluff game.

The thing I love about this offense is that it does not matter what the defense plays, and seldom do we see a base front—the blocking is the same up front. Against the three-man front, you are blocking man on everything except the option.

Some teams call our slice and bluff plays the midline offense. We did not want to call it the midline because we did not want the kids to think we were going to run in the crack of the center. We tell the tailback to run over the hip of the center. That is what we want.

In the five years that we have run this offense, we have led the league in rushing three of those years. We have had two 2000-yard rushers two of those three years. We had one 3000-yard rusher one year. We have only had one year without a 1000-yard rusher.

The motion man is not going to run into the line tiptoeing. He is a wide receiver—just like the wide receivers you have. He is going to go into the line and block the first man outside our tackle. He wants a piece of the defensive tackle. If the tackle is coming down tough, we are going to run the two-man bluff game. That is the beauty of the thing because we can run the play with the same exact motion.

We can motion the wingback and bring him across the formation. His assignment is alley. We block down and read the defensive end. The wingback blocks the first man in the alley. The H-back has the safety, and the split end has the corner. We come back and run the slice play, and the assignments stay the same for the receivers.

The bluff game is our two-man game. The quarterback is reading the end man on the line of scrimmage. Our tackle has the B gap. Everyone else blocks the same as they do on the slice play.

When we tell our receivers to block the alley, we do not tell them a particular defender to block. We do not tell them to block the linebacker or to block the safety. We want them to block the cover. That is what we call an *alley*.

Our backup quarterback is a 4.75 runner. The way he runs is as if he were a 4.6 runner. If you see him run, you will think he is a lot faster. Just because he is a 4.75 runner, we will not change the offense. We may not call his number as much as we normally would call for the quarterback.

Again, the thing we like is this: We can tell the line coach to work on the zone and bluff plays. He is on the same play, with the exception of the tackle. He can work on this day after day. He is working on our base zone play repeatedly, except for one man.

When the quarterback opens to the playside, he is running the slice game. When he opens away from the playside, he is running the bluff game. Some defenses will try to key how the quarterback opens on each play. The next thing they see is the motion with the plays and it causes confusion; at least it has worked out that way for us.

Our two-man game is with the tailback and quarterback. The tailback runs the ball on the slice and bluff, and the quarterback runs the ball on the two-man game(Diagram #6). We do include some options in the offense, depending on the defenses we are seeing. We can run these plays to both sides of our offense.

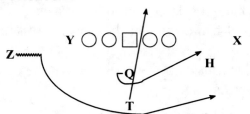

Diagram #6. Two-Man Game

Next, we run the triple option. It is the same as we run with motion on slice and bluff. Now the Z-back starts in motion and comes back behind the tailback and becomes the pitchman (Diagram #7). The blocking to the runside is the same as our zone blocking. There is no penetration allowed from the strong guard back to the backside tackle. You may slip a defender through on the end, but we are going to get rid of the ball before the defender can make a play.

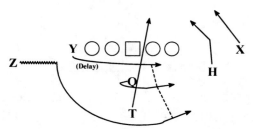

Diagram #7. Triple-Option Pitch

It is the same read for the quarterback. We can run the triple option from all kinds of different sets. When we bring the Z-back in motion behind the tailback, we call that *buck motion* (Diagram #8). We can bring the wingback or H-back inside and have him block out. This means he is blocking the read man. We expect the quarterback to read the end and to make a decision to keep or pitch the football. We can bring him back in motion and still run the base slice and bluff plays.

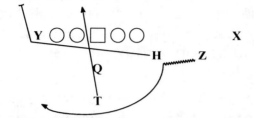

Diagram #8. Slice—Fake Option

In 1986, we named our offensive line the *Union*. They have Union membership cards, Union hats, and it is a big deal for us. They have their own private meeting room called the *Union Room*. When players come back to visit us after they have moved on, they will ask us how the Union is doing that year. The team takes pride in the Union. It is one of the best things I have done as a football coach. The kids that come back to visit make it a big deal. It is all based on an award system. We take care of the Union.

We can run the offense from several different formations including the unbalanced line. Everything stays the same for the guys up front. We run the slice play a lot. When defenses see our Z-back start in motion, most of the time they are thinking slice play (Diagram #9). That is when we can get the ball to the alley. The reading is the same, which is the man outside our end on the playside.

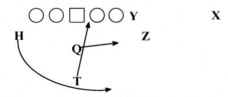

Diagram #9. H-Back Motion, Slice

We do not want to be known as an option team. We want to be known as a team that runs the option. We are not an option team. We include the play-action passing game to complete our offense. This slice and buff have helped us with our play-action passing game. We did not put the pistol offense in our system to run the option repeatedly. Now, it is a big part of our offense without question.

The way we like to dress it up is from the different types of formations and blocking schemes that we like.

What I like about the pistol offense is the fact that we can hide our tailbacks. We want our backs to carry the football. We think the alignment gives us an edge and holds the linebackers long enough to give the back a chance to see what is going on up front.

I want to talk about the play-action pass. This is where we can take advantage of the pistol offense. We run the bluff pass off the downhill motion. It gives us a little more of a variety. The quarterback has great depth position after the fake. The move by the running back is tough on the linebackers. The pistol creates advantages over the shotgun formation. In the pistol when we open up, two things happen. First is the attack of the running back, which we call the attack phase of the play-action pass. That is the run off the zone play.

The quarterback opens and seeds the ball. He puts his left hand in the belly of the tailback and reads the end. He wants to get a depth of eight yards. We want to attack the corner. Very seldom do we run the naked play. Most of the time we run a slice action toward our quickside end and our backside tackle.

I want to show you the attack mode pass. We took this play from our I-formation plays as our number-one way to run the play-action pass. We attached it to our pistol attack. We can run it two ways. We can put the Z-back in motion and bring him back behind the tailback on a circle route, or we can release him on a post route (Diagram #10).

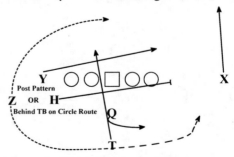

Diagram #10. Play-Action Pass

We are going to block the area outside our tackle on the backside. We do not want the quarterback to be run down before he can get his feet under him. The line is blocking zone. The quarterback is throwing the ball on the run.

In our practice session, we take a seven-minute period every day and work on throwing the ball on the run. We take a three-minute period every day and run the scramble drill. So, we are spending 10 minutes a day with our quarterback throwing on the run every day. This is the most dominate play-action pass that we run. We have been more consistent with this pass.

Every year, we come up with something to add to the offense. You can do so many things with this offense. You can motion either way. You can motion one back and swing another back. Again, you can do so many different things. We do run the fly sweep. In addition, we do run the option pass sometimes. We are not a big fly sweep team, but occasionally we see the defensive end is not worried about our outside, and we will run the fly sweep.

The thing we are trying to influence is the second level of the defense. We are going to block the fronts. You may be more physical than us, but we are going to at least get in front of the defensive line before they can get to the ball. The thing we have to do is to take care of the second level with our action in the motions and with our play-action game.

I see my time is up. I appreciate the opportunity to visit with you. Thank you very much.

THE 4-3 DEFENSE AND STUNTS

University of Cincinnati

I want to get into the football aspect of this lecture because I know that is what you want to hear. I do not know how much confusion we are causing the offenses, but I do know this: we are going to try to give the offense a lot of different looks, but we do not want to confuse ourselves. I talk about a lot of different looks when I am talking in terms of our fronts.

How many of you play field fronts? I am sure a large percentage of the people in this room play a field front. We are not reinventing the wheel; we can dictate to the offense by setting our front to the field, or we can set it to the boundary.

We also play some under by calling the front to the tight end. We call the under toward the tight end our Eagle call. We have a strip call we can make to the field, and one we can make to the boundary, and now we have a call we can call to the tight end. Next, we have an over front. We set our front to different people. I will get into that later.

Next, we start talking about our coverages. We do not do a lot of different things, but we are doing enough to keep the offense guessing. We call it keeping the offense honest. We are going to play two-deep, and we are going to play some form of three-deep coverage. We are going to play some man coverage, and we are going to play some combo coverages. It can be a zone defense to one side and man defense on the other side of the coverage. Those are the four basic principles we talk about in our coverages.

I want to talk about specific aspects of the defense. I think we need to discuss how to adapt to the conference teams we are playing. I came from the MAC. I compare the MAC to the PAC-10

Conference. These teams throw the ball all around the ball field. Many of the offensive coordinators in the MAC are also the head coaches.

Why is that important? There are no consequences for them. We are talking about them using all four downs. When you are the head coach and the offensive coordinator, you can do what you want on offense. You are going to see all of the offense. Half of the MAC is set up that way. If they are not calling the plays, they are offense-oriented and they once coached on that side of the ball. You have to realize this and adapt to the style of offense you will be facing. They are going to throw the ball a great deal of the time. Adapt to your conference. You need to know if your conference is a power conference or a pass conference.

When you start putting your defense together, you must decide what type of offense you are going to be facing most of the time in your league. In the Big East Conference, we must be prepared to stop the power running game.

The next thing you must talk about in establishing your defense is how to adapt to your personnel. The first question we must answer is what positions we must stress the most. We need to list our strengths and weaknesses. We need to look at the players to see what positions we have an extra supply, and what areas we need to find additional players. These are factors to talk about when you are putting your defense together.

We use the same basic numbering system to communicate with our players as most of you use. If we are talking about an alignment on the outside shoulder of the offensive tight end, we call it a 9 technique. Head-up with the end is the 6 technique.

Inside shoulder of the end is our 7 technique. On the outside shoulder of the tackle is the 5 technique. Head-up with the tackle is the 4 technique. Inside shoulder of the end is the 4i technique. On the outside shoulder of the offensive guard is the 3 technique. Head-up with the guard is the 2 technique, and inside the guard is the 2i technique. The shoulder of the center is the 1 technique, and head-up with the center is the 0 technique. We build from this alignment.

We give our defense names to indicate the player we are dealing with. In our field defense, we call the 9 technique our Leo (Diagram #1). The tackle is in the 3 technique, the nose is in a 1 technique, and the defender in the 5 technique is our end. Some teams call that end the buff end. This is for teaching purposes.

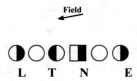

Diagram #1. Field Alignment Players

As we progress, you will see we are a role-playing team. We are going to role-play. Some people question us on the alignment of the defender over the tight end. We actually play a different technique than most teams. We can line him up in a 9 technique and jam him down into a 6 technique. However, he lines up outside the tight end.

We play with a boundary corner and with a field corner. We play with a strong safety and free safety. We play with Mike, Will, and Sam linebackers. All of these players have unique skill sets that we use in unique ways, and we want those players to get used to playing certain techniques.

My first coaching job was at Farris State. I coached there for two years. I can remember going to so many different clinics. I wanted to learn as much football as I could. I always said if I got the chance to lecture at a clinic, I would give the coaches who are willing to listen to me the things I was looking for when I was a young coach. I always

try to keep my lectures very informal. Feel free to ask questions if you have anything you would like to know about what I am covering.

I coached at the University of Maryland earlier in my career. I coached linebackers there for three years. In my last year at Maryland, I coached our secondary. In that last year, our defensive coordinator retired. His name was Gary Blackney. He had been the head coach at Bowling Green University before he came to Maryland. In addition, he was the defensive coordinator at Ohio State University for a number of years. He was a great mentor to me. He taught me 90 percent of the defense I know. The first thing he talked about was having a plan. He talked about the plan before he talked about stopping the run or defending the pass. He always talked about a teaching progression. The first thing we want to talk about is how we are going to defend our bubble. In our defense, our bubble is always our B gap. The first thing we must do is to defend that area.

We feel it is important to have carryover in the principles and rules you apply to your defense. We do this to so we do not have to teach a great deal to the kids. We try to teach with a hands-on approach, and we try to make it as simple as we can.

The first stunt I want to cover is very simple. It is how we defend the B gap. We take the end in the 5 technique and bring him on an inside lateral step, and then up into the B gap. That is our field blood stunt (Diagram #2). He takes what we call an L step inside, keeping his shoulders square, and he is trying to get across the line and up the field. That is our first run stunt on the defense.

Diagram #2. Field Blood

To continue the run stunts, we take the L end, tackle, noseman, and slant to the inside gaps. We call that our field blaze stunt (Diagram #3). Again, this is coming off field principles. When we say "field," it is where the end lines up. This is a right call for us as it is set in the diagram. Our noseman, our end, and our Mike backer go to that side. We are saying the big field is to our right side facing the defense. The T. L, and W go away from the call on field. We are still trying to defend the B gap. We are taking the bubble away.

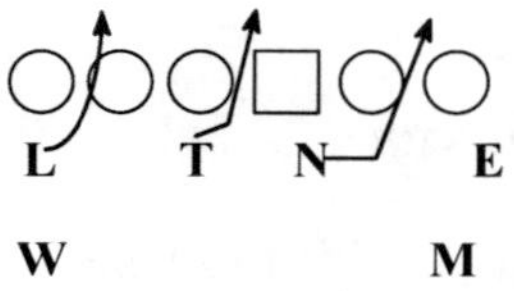

Diagram #3. Field Blaze

To the offense, this defense looks exactly the same each time. We are showing the same front, but we are defending the B gap in a different way.

The characteristics of our players are very important. The role the players fill is important. Our end is a bigger man than most of our other front line. He should be a strong and stout-type player; the noseguard is a strong, stout player, but not as big as the tackle. Our tackle, or 3 technique is our Stud. He is the best pass rusher between the nose and end. He is the defender we like to play over the guard. The Leo is more athletic than the other front line defenders. We ask him to do more than we do the other linemen.

The next stunt is our field heat stunt (Diagram #4). We are sending the tackle through the A gap, and the Leo end is going into the B gap.

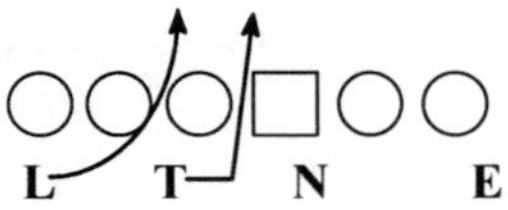

Diagram #4. Field Heat Stunt

Our next stunt is our field Tex (Diagram #5). It is a stunt with the tackle and Leo. The tackle goes first, and the Leo comes off his tail into the B gap.

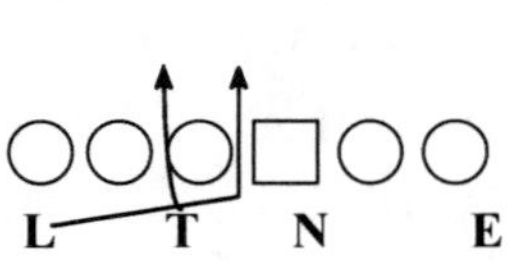

Diagram #5. Field Tex

The next front we put in our system is called Falcon (Diagram #6). Right now, we are just defending the field. This is a stunt with our noseman and our end. As I said earlier, our end is bigger, stronger, and better as a pass rusher. I have the ability to defend the field first. Next, we want to defend the tight end. You may have a great tight end, but we do not know where he is going to line up. The offense has a good tight end, and they are running the ball to the tight end. I want to put my best run defensive end to his side. We call it Falcon. This is how we do it.

Diagram #6. Falcon

The Will makes a Rip or Lil call to the tight end. As the offense gets to the line of scrimmage, we find out where the tight end is and make a Rip call. This means our end is going to the tight-end side. If we call Lil, our end is going opposite the tight end.

For simplicity sake, our Mike and Will are still lining up with field principles. Our Mike and Will and the entire secondary are lining up in field principles. If the offense has a great blocking tight end, we do not want him beating up our 240 Leo, so we want to get our big man matched up on the tight end. This is where we get to our Falcon call.

To the offense, our defense looks very similar. All we are doing is changing players on the tight end. This gives us a better match-up with the tight end.

Next, we want to run our stunt with the Falcon. We call Falcon blood (Diagram #7). We do not want to add a new stunt. We are still running the blood stunt. The first time we ran the blood, it was a stunt for the end from the field. We are going from the field stunt to a stunt by technique. Now, we are running a 1- and 5-technique stunt. The Leo is running the stunt. He is taking the B gap. It is the same stunt as we ran before on blood, but now it is with a different person. We did not have to come up with a whole new term. We have only changed from words to techniques on the stunt.

Diagram #7. Falcon Blood

From there, we add our Falcon blaze stunt (Diagram #8). We are taking away the B gap. We have our best defender to the tight end. We can eliminate the gaps. That is the blaze stunt. We are trying to make the offense blink.

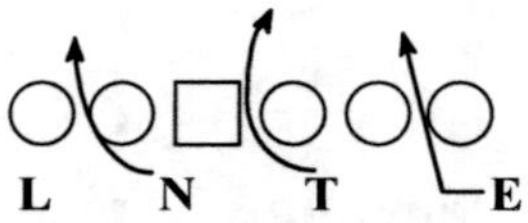

Diagram #8. Falcon Blaze

I did not show you our X stunt to the field. We can run the X stunt and our Tex stunts out of both the field and the Falcon. The Falcon X stunt is more of a pass-rush stunt (Diagram #9). It is a second-level stunt for us.

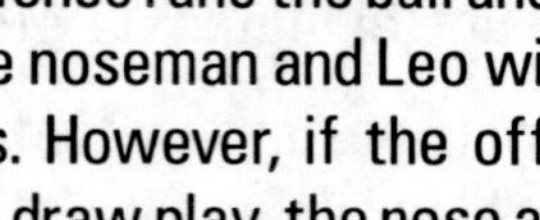

Diagram #9. Falcon X

The X stunts for us are what we call secondary stunts. If the offense runs the ball and we have an X stunt called, the noseman and Leo will stay in their respective gaps. However, if the offensive tackle shows pass or a draw play, the nose and Leo run the X stunt.

When we ran the blood stunt earlier; that was a first-level stunt. That means he is running to the gap, come hell or high water. It is an all-out blitz. We want to have the ability to do both types of covering the B gap.

We run the Falcon heat call, which is similar to the field Tex stunt (Diagram #10). Here, the end is

coming down into the B gap. We are doing the same stunt as the Tex, but now we are running the end into the gap. This is a 3- and 6-technique call. The Tex stunt is a 1- and 5-technique call.

Diagram #10. Falcon Heat

Our next front is what we call tuff (Diagram #11). It is played with two 3-technique players. We use this on the passing downs. We more than likely will not be in this front unless it is a passing situation. Some teams use the front against the run, but we do not like it against the run. The nose and tackle are in 3 techniques. The end and Leo are in 5 techniques.

Diagram #11. Tuff Front

If we do not make a specific call such as field or boundary, or under, or Falcon, our players know we are going to play field principles. If we do not make a specific call, they know we are playing field principles. For the nose and end, it is their field alignment. This is a different look for the quarterback. We can still run what we want to run out of this alignment. If we make the call "tuff return," it means we are going to stunt back to our base defense.

Our base defense versus a one-back set is field. If I call "return," the defense knows we are returning to our base defense. That noseman will take the A gap. It is very simple.

The next thing we do is to run the tuff blaze (Diagram #12). Some players may ask how we are going to run the blaze if the defense is already lined up in the right play. That is fine; now, we do not have to move them. We are running the same call but from a different alignment.

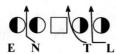

Diagram #12. Tuff Blaze

We have looked at the heat stunt before. We have a whole series off heat. Again, we are running the same stunt but from a different front when we run the tuff heat stunt (Diagram #13). We can get a ton of reps running heat, but we put them in different alignments.

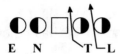

Diagram #13. Tuff Heat

I did not talk about our tuff slant stunt (Diagram #14). We are able to run the slant stunt from any front. If I can run slant out of tuff, I can do the same thing out of field. We have not used this stunt much in the last two years because of the tight-end run game. We prefer to bring the entire front against the tight-end run game, but we did use it a few times. All we have to do to run this stunt is to bring the tackle and noseman over. If we had the noseman lined up in the A gap he would be slanting to the B gap in case we ran the slant stunt out of the field alignment. Because we are in a tuff alignment already, the noseman will stay where he is. He is already in position to slant into the B gap. Next, we'd bring the tackle on the other side down to the A gap on the other side. That is our tuff slant.

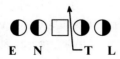

Diagram #14. Tuff Slant

When I look at the call sheet, I have a bunch of plays or stunts I can utilize. However, the front players know they simply change their alignment from running the same stunts. It is muscle memory, and it allows our front people to play fast.

The under defense is next. A lot of coaches use the term Eagle to describe the under defense. That

is what we call it. We just call it Eagle defense (Diagram #15). Now we are setting the call to the tight end. We have just looked at setting the defense to the field. We set it to the field, left and right. When we were in Falcon, we had two calls. We called right or left, or a Roger or Lucky to the field, and we had a Rip or Liz call to the tight end. Now that we are in the under defense, we are setting the defense to the tight end. Our tuff was a field-oriented call as well.

Diagram #15. Under Defenses to the Tight-End Side

We are moving the end down into a 5 techniques on the tight-end side. That is why he must be a bigger player than the Leo end. He lines up in a 5 technique.

We can run the tuff under return defense (Diagram #16). We did not run a lot of this defense, but we could by moving the nose and tackle in the gaps. The nose covers the A gap, and the tackle has the B gap.

Diagram #16. Tuff Under Return

We have already talked about our blood stunt (Diagram #17). We line the end up in the 5 technique and slant him down into the B gap. We run the under blood stunt with the end coming into the B gap from the 5 technique.

Diagram #17. Under Blood

If we want to run the Tex and X stunts from the under front, we can. It is very simple.

The under heat is with the Leo and the tackle on the backside, or split-end side (Diagram #18). We bring the tackle down to the A gap, and the Leo down inside to the B gap.

Diagram #18. Under Heat

Next, we look at our boundary defense. Again, it is a different look for the offense. You may ask how this is different. You may even say it looks like a field defense to you. Now the boundary is on the right, and the field is to the left (Diagram #19). We are setting our 3 and 6 techniques to the fieldside of our defense. Before, we set our 1 and 5 techniques to the field. This is our boundary defense.

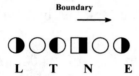

Diagram #19. Boundary Defense

Our linebackers are always stepping one gap opposite of the linemen on their calls. We are trying to help everyone on our defense play fast. We are only asking the individuals to learn a few techniques but from different areas of the line. A blood is a blood is a blood. They learn the terms and know what to do on each of the calls. Once they learn the six or seven moves they have, it is up to the coaching staff to be creative and to change the look to execute the same defense.

Boundary is an eight-man front for us. The Sam is on air outside the end to the boundary. The Mike is in a 30 alignment, and the Will is in a 30 alignment. We drop our strong safety down to the field. It is a different look for the offense. However, for us, we have been doing the same thing.

If we call boundary even return, we are lining up in 2 techniques inside (Diagram #20). The nose and tackle are over the guards in 2 techniques. We are moving back to the field defense. When we call return, it is the same as all return calls. We line up in 2 techniques and cover the gaps away from the call.

Diagram #20. Boundary Even Return

We have covered four different fronts. However, we execute the same stunts or moves. The opposite of even return is our boundary even slant (Diagram #21). We slant the tackle and nose toward the boundary. We have the Leo playing the 6 technique.

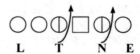

Diagram #21. Boundary Even Slant

When I was a young coach, I wanted to see as many fronts as possible. I wanted to run every front. It was the same way when it came to coverages. As I visited with other coaches, went to clinics, and learned more about coverages, I wanted to run everything. However, as a coordinator, it is a different story. Now, my job is on the line, and I think twice about adding a front or coverage to our package. I have simplified our defense a great deal. We do want we need to do to stop the run. Our red zone defense has always been very sound.

We were ranked 17th in the country in stopping the run last year. Here is the key to our red zone defense: we did not change what we were doing on defense. Whatever I like against 11 personnel in the big field was the same defense we ran in the red zone.

What is the red zone to our defense? That is from the plus 20-yard line to the 3-yard line for us. What we did against 12 personnel, we did in the red zone. We did not change very much. We did not change a lot until they got down to the eight-yard line. Then we played our 4 red. I will talk about that later.

Our philosophy was simple. We were not going to try to reinvent the wheel when the defense got down in the red zone on us. We made our coverages very simple and cut down on the different coverages we did play before. That philosophy paid dividends when we got down to the red zone. We stayed with what we were playing and became better at what we were doing. The key was the fact we played our base red defense more in the red zone.

With that being said, I will give you one defense we played that was unique for us. It is our 4 red defense (Diagram #22). I will show it against 11 personnel. I use a PowerPoint® with my players and staff. My staff does not want me to get on the chalkboard to draw up defenses, so you will have to stay with me on these diagrams. I am a PowerPoint guy, not because I think it is cool, but because the players can't read my writing.

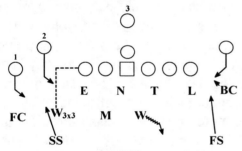

Diagram #22. Field 4 Red Triangle

I will not talk about the front stunts from here on, because we did that earlier in the lecture. We are playing 2x2 red coverage. We tell the nickel player we want him in a hip alignment. He is four yards wide of the tight end, and three or four yards deep off the line of scrimmage. He is in a hip alignment. We tell our 5-technique end he can run. If he reads a zone play, he comes hard across the line. He takes the first thing that shows, particularly the dive play. We have our Mike backer in a nesting position. He is covered up inside.

This left the nickel in an unblockable position. We tell the strong safety he has #2 up or out. If #2 would release vertical or outside, the strong safety took him. The field corner had #1 up or out. The nickel has #3 outside. We number the receivers

from the outside to the inside. The linebackers still take their drops.

The boundary corner has the #1 receiver to his side on the up or out. The free safety has #2 up or out. The Will and Mike backer are dropping off on #1.

2x2 Red Coverage

Strong safety: #2 up or out

Field corner: #1 up or out

Nickel: #3 out

Boundary corner: #1 up or out

Field safety: #2 up or out

Will and Mike backers: Drop off #3

This is the way we teach it. We always start with the number-one route that we see in our 2x2 alignment. We must talk about how we are going to stop the double-slant route, and the slant-flat route. We build from those principles.

When the offense runs double slants, it means the #2 receiver is tough. Our strong safety will tie on him. The #1 receiver is up the field, and the field corner will buy him. If the #3 receiver stays in the backfield to block, the nickel will push right through the window. If the offense throws the ball to the #1 receiver, the nickel should be in that window. The Mike backer should start to expand as the quarterback makes his move.

To the boundary, the free safety has #2 up or out. If the #2 man is not there, the free safety is diving. The boundary corner is squeezing the play down inside, playing #1 up or out. This is it in a nutshell versus 2x2.

If you want to put the red coverage in layman's terms, all it means is this: the #1 and #2 receivers, the corners, the strong safety, the free safety, and the boundary corner have their men on the up or out routes. They are dropping. When we talk about alignment, the corner is always heavy inside. We play the both safeties head-up to outside. Most of the time, well, I would say 90 percent of the time, the offense throws the slant to the man outside.

They do not throw the slant to the man inside very much. That is why we line up heavy inside. Some teams will play cover 2 and try to pattern-match the coverage. I prefer to play it our way.

I tell the corners if they get beat on a slant route down in the red zone, it is a sin. Where is the softness in the coverage? The speed out to the #2 receiver is the soft spot. On everything else, we should be in good shape. It is a run defense. We are taking the nickel, and we are getting him tight in the box. We have an eight-man box plus the free safety to play the offense. It is a great run defense against the one-back set.

Against the 3x1 set, we can be in our field or Falcon defense (Diagram #23). This is our triangle call we play in the big field. There are a lot of ways to play against the triangle look. We are not going to get exotic when we see the 3x1 look. The first thing I am going to do is to take away your easiest throw or your best receiver. Where is the easy throw on a 3x1 look? It is the backside. You have two different ways to play the boundary corner. You can cone him, you can play first out, first in, or however you want to play it. In our triangle, we are going to take the easiest throw away.

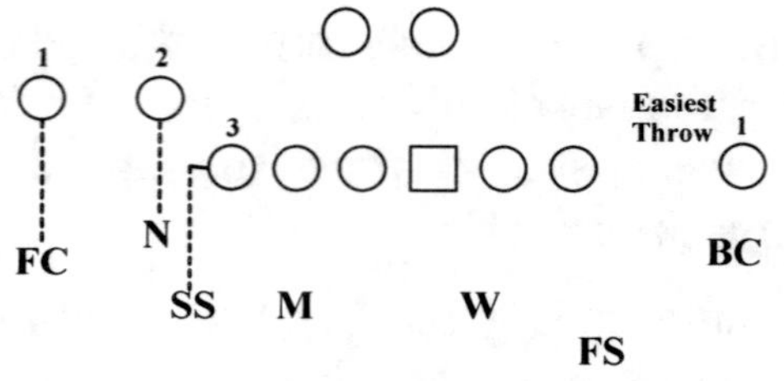

Diagram #23. Red Zone vs. 3x1

We can play it like cover-2 principles, or we can play it more like man double principles. We are always going to double on the backside.

Then, we are going to decide where we want our one-on-one match-up to be. If we are double-covering on the backside, we are shorting someone on the frontside. I know it is going to be 1-on-1, but I want to decide where it is going to be. I can take a linebacker and put him on the tight end 1-on-1. Then, all of a sudden, the tight end is better than my Mike

backer is. I do not want that coverage. From a day-one principle, I want to put my 1-on-1 to the longest throw, which is to the outside on the strongside. Where is that? It is the widest receiver. I am going to play straight man outside. Next, we search the field. We take the nickel, play him in the alley, and have him play #2. I am going to play the strong safety on the inside eye of #2.

The nickel is pattern reading the #3 receiver in the backfield. Mike is walling off #3. The strong safety knows he has #3 if he is up and over. If #3 goes outside, the nickel has him. If the #3 blocks, the nickel buys #2. It is like a combo-read zone coverage we play between #2 and #3.

If the #1 and #2 receivers outside are tight or close together, we are going to make a zone call. This means we are going to pattern-match them.

If you ask me my philosophy, I like to dictate match-ups. You can only play coverages so many different ways. I want to dictate what we are going to play. I do not want the offense dictating to me what we are going to play. This is why "empty" is such a big deal, because the offense is trying to dictate match-ups. I am not going to allow you to dictate match-ups. I am telling the offense on the 3x1 if they want to throw the 1-on-1 route, they have to throw the ball wide to the outside receiver. I know they are not going to throw the fade route into that three-man side. Generally, they want to throw the fade to the boundary corner.

To give you a change-up on the 3x1 look, we can run what we call stress coverage. We check the coverage to what we like to play on the 3x1. We roll the boundary corner up on the split end. We roll the free safety back to cover the outside third deep. The strong safety covers the deep middle third, and the field corner drops back to cover the outside deep third. It is our three-deep coverage (Diagram #24). The nickel is playing 2-to-1 dropper on the receivers. The Mike backer is going to be a 3-to-2 dropper on the inside receiver and the tight end. The Will backer has the curl area. Now, we are playing our three-deep zone coverage.

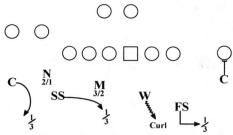

Diagram #24. Three Deep vs. 3x1

If the tight end attaches to the formation, the strong safety is playing with his outside foot and puts it on his inside foot. If the tight end is detached, the strong safety puts his outside foot on the outside foot of the detached end. This may be different for some teams, but again, our battle cry has always been this: We want to stop the run, we want to pressure the quarterback, and we always want to win third downs. That is our blueprint for winning.

When we talk about the end detaching, that is a red light for us to look for the run game. It alerts us to the bubble. It is a bubble alert for us. Our battle cry is to stop the run, so we have to stop the bubble.

We line our nickel up at five yards deep. Some teams will line him up on the #2 man's nose. We do not do that. We want to get some air under his drop.

We can play buzz, which is another form of three-deep. We take a nickel, and instead of playing 2-to-1, he is going to be a flat dropper right away. Instead of sending the strong safety to the middle third, we drop him to the hash mark. He is going to pattern-read the #2 man. Our Mike backer is just going to be a middle dropper. Now the free safety is coming to the middle to play a third. Our Will linebacker is going to be our hook/flat player. That is another way to get to three-deep.

If we play star, we are playing quarter coverage. The nickel is a quarter flat player. That means if the #2 receiver goes out right now, the nickel matches him. The corner is playing quarters off the #2 receiver. Mike is a three-hook player, and he is

dropping off on the #3 receiver. Will is still the curl/flat player to the weakside. That is star coverage for us.

Those are change-ups for us. We can play straight quarters across the board if we want. We can play two forms of three-deep: one is buzz, and one is stress. We have three different ways to match up, depending on what the offense is doing.

Let me talk about our empty coverage (Diagram #25). Here is our rule on empty: any time we see an empty set and we are in any of our cover 2, cover 6, or any of our zone coverages, we go to our base check rule. We can check into our two-deep coverage, three-roll coverage, or we can check into our triangle coverage. If we are in man coverage and we see an empty set, we are going to play man. Period! If we are in a fire zone and they give us an empty, we are playing the fire zone. Our true zone coverage always checks to what we have set up as our check for that week or game. For everything else, we play what we have called.

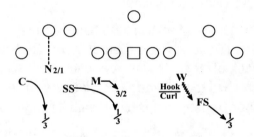

Diagram #25. Empty Cover 3

If we see a 4x1 set, the only thing that changes for us is the Will. He border-punches his drop, and he goes the other way. He had the fourth man or the first man to cross on his pattern.

I know I spent a lot of time talking about our defensive fronts. You are all welcome to see us. With me, you get what you see. I am just like you in that I am always trying to learn football. Our door is always open if you want to come to visit. I appreciate you coming to hear this lecture, and I appreciate your time.

Jay Bateman

FUNDAMENTALS OF COACHING LINEBACKERS

Elon University

When I first came to Elon University in 2005, it did not take long to realize we had a lot of work to do. In my first year, we finished 90th in the country in run defense and 90th in pass defense. We finished over 87th in total defense. Last year, we were second in the country in total defense, third in scoring defense, and second in defense on third downs, and we were 15th against the rush, and sixth against the pass. You can see we have gotten a lot better in four years.

I am going to talk about linebacker play. In the last four years at Elon, we have had three All-Conference linebackers, and three were second team All-Conference players.

The game of football has changed a great deal in the last 15 years. Back then, if we talked about a one-back offense, it was very unusual. It was a big deal. We had to practice all week to try to get ready for that offense. Things have really changed now.

Let me give you an idea of what type of plays we saw last year. We saw 39 bubble screen plays last year. They just raised up and threw it outside. We saw seven isolations plays.

The linebacker position has changed more than any other position over the last few years. You have to be able to run and cover to play linebacker today.

Let me talk about what I look for in selecting a linebacker. This is what we look for in our linebacker. Our Will and Sam linebackers were tailbacks in high school. Two of our linebackers were quarterbacks in high school. The only true linebacker for us is our Mike. The traits I look for in linebackers are as follows:

- Runner and hitter
- Speed: Must be able to run and chase
- Ability to play in space
- Great punch: Ability to create violent collisions
- Football IQ: Ability to diagnose a play
- Consistently play with great pad level.

We want players who can run and can strike a lick. When you are evaluating linebackers, you need to look for kids who can run. When they get to the ballcarrier, they must be able to create an impact. I do not think they can be 185 pounds in our league. In our 4-3 defense, we are going to try to keep those guys out of contact if we can. We want them to be able to dominate the point of attack. If that is the fullback, tailback, or if he is just making a tackle, we want them to be able to generated speed and power in a small area.

The equation for force is mass times velocity. I ask the players I am recruiting this question: Would you prefer I throw a bowling ball at you, or would you prefer I throw a baseball at you as hard as I can possibly throw it? If I throw a bowling ball at you, you can get out of the way. If I throw a baseball at you, it is going to hurt you a lot more. We are looking for the baseball kind of players.

The next thing we look for is a player with length. We do not get the tallest players in the world, but length is important.

The ability to diagnose a football play is important. I am not going to be able to recruit many linebackers from high school. I love to go watch the players when they are in a gym class. I like to see them playing a pick-up basketball game, 5-on-5. There are no rules. Someone is calling plays. You watch some of the players who are watching the ball movement, and he picks off a pass, and goes down and scores a basket.

How did he know where to go to intercept the pass? It was not as if he spent a lot of time with a coach watching film. He uses body language, and he reads the eyes of the passer. I think these qualities are important for a linebacker. If I can see that in a kid, it helps evaluate him for football.

The first thing I talk to linebackers about is what we call their stance takeoff. I do not think you should hammer a linebacker stance home. We view films from some high schools, and every linebacker is in the same stance. Linebackers have to go in all different directions. The one position on the field that can go all over the field is the linebacker. Think about it. Most backs are going back right away, or they are coming downhill. The offensive line knows where they are going. The receivers know where they are going. Linebackers on the snap of the ball may have to go left, right, forward, or backward.

They must be comfortable in their stance. When I first started coaching linebackers, I told them not to put their hands on their knees, and you must be in this type of stance. I do not worry about that anymore. I try to get them in a comfortable stance. I think this is important. Half of the teams we play now are coming to the line of scrimmage in the shotgun offense, looking over the defense.

We get in our stance, and we want the feet a little more than shoulder-width apart. I have changed on this aspect of the stance. I used to get them in a wide stance like the NFL linebackers. The NFL linebackers are worried about the pass. It is different for us. We went back and changed the stance so our linebackers are more comfortable in their stance. We do not want them spread out as much now.

A lot of coaches ask us why we play the 4-3 defense. For us, the defensive ends can be smaller players. Our defensive tackles are going to be big guys, and our ends are going to be smaller. The two ends who played for us last year, one was 6'0" and 250 pounds, and the other one was 6'6" and 235 pounds. They are small for ends in college, and that helps us. That is one reason we play the 4-3.

- Flexibility of personnel: Can play with smaller people
- Ability to adjust to all the different formations we see in today's game
- Puts more speed on the field
- Blitz alignments
- Disguise: Ability to pre-snap always look the same

We all have the same problems. It does not matter where we coach. We all are trying to find big players. If you are playing the 3-4 defense, at some point those 5-technique players must be B-gap defenders. Any time you ask a player to defend the B gap at the line of scrimmage, you need some players who are sturdy and big enough to defend the gaps.

When I played football, we saw the pro-I formation, and we saw the Twins formation. Anything else, we say, was a radical change for us. Now we see the pro set only about 50 snaps per year. Most of the time, those plays are play-action plays.

With the 4-3 defense, we can play with smaller players, which means we can put a lot more speed on the field. Our Sam and Will could play tailback for us if they had to.

In some of the other defenses, it is hard to disguise the coverages. In the 4-3, we like to line up the same as much as we can.

What Is Important to a Linebacker?
- Stance takeoff
- Key read
- Tackling
- Movement skills
- Block protection
- Pass coverage

When I am setting up an individual drill or setting up practice during the season, I am going to go in that order in working with the linebackers. We work on our stance first. Then, we work on our key reads.

Next, we work on our tackling, and then movement skills, block protection, and then pass coverage.

We hear coaches tell their players to get into a good football position. What they are really saying is for the players to get into a linebacker's stance. We are going to have three bends. We are going to have bends in the ankles, knees, and in the hips.

We want the linebacker stance to be with the feet slightly wider than the shoulders, with the knees bent. I do not care if they put their hands on their knees. I used to say no way can they put their hands on the knees. The coach I played for would have shot me if I had my hands on my knees.

We said the linebacker has to go in every direction. Comfort is important. I do not want their pad level to change when they are in their stance. I harp on this a great deal of the time.

One thing I get on the linebackers about is wasted movement. "Do not move just to be moving." The first thing I do from my stance is to rise up or ride down to create the center of gravity where I need to move. That is what I do first.

We feel it is important to develop movement skills. We do not want wasted movement, as I said before:

- If the ballcarrier is in the tackle box, the linebacker's shoulders are square and my feet are underneath me!
- Once the ballcarrier leaves the tackle box, the linebacker presses the ballcarrier's inside hip as fast as possible.
- Shuffles with quick feet, toes straight ahead, no heel click, and consistent pad level. Presses the line of scrimmage.
- Crossover run: Hips mirror the ballcarrier, shoulders parallel to the line of scrimmage. Snaps the hips back into place when he throttles.

Next, I talk to them about takeoff. We do not teach them to take a back step. If you are a 4.8 linebacker and you take a back step, you become a 4.9 linebacker and you have not moved yet. Does that make sense? We cannot waste movement. I want them to get into a comfortable stance from which they can go forward.

We talk about a read step and a gather step. The read step is going to be in the direction of the flow.

We read backs. Why do we read backs? We do not see the wing-T offense. We do not have to worry about that type of offense. We do see a lot of double slots in our conference. Most of the time, we're going to get a true read against the double slot.

The backs are a true read for us most of the time. That is the number-one reason why we read backs. It is difficult for the linebackers to read the guard. We start our read on the near back.

Why Read Backs?

- Our linebackers align in a lot of different spots. It is hard to start your read on guards.
- We get less misdirection, much truer reads than high school (no wing-T).
- So much of what we do we base off flow, easier to work back to a surface key.

We key the "flow" of the back. There are four types of flow:

- Dive: Straight ahead
- Tight: Inside the tackle box, off the midline
- Wide: Stretch, speed option, toss sweep
- Split: Two-back set. Backs go in opposite direction.

We get five trashcans set up and run a simple drill to teach the flow of the backs. We line a running back behind the cans, and I tell the back to run through between one of three of the cans. The linebackers get in a stance, and they must react with their feet to the direction the running back goes.

The first step is very important. Here are the points we talk about with the first stance:

- Great stance
- Good football position
- Must be able to go in every direction
- Comfort is important

- Pad level should never change
- Great takeoff
- No wasted movement; don't move just to move.
- Downhill
- Read step, gather step

The hard thing to teach the fast linebackers is to take the first step forward. They want to go east or west. They are not used to the play coming straight at them. We were second in the country in total defense, and the worst play for us to defend was the isolation play. If the offense runs a sweep, our linebackers are going to contain the play. We have changed the steps for our linebackers on flow downhill. If they get a flow downhill, we want them to flow that way.

One of the most important aspects of coaching linebackers is on the second step. No coaches teach them to take a crossover step. We tell our linebackers that the first step is a read step. If we froze the film on a play after that first step, the linebacker should be back in their stance with that second step.

Our linebackers are like robots. It is: one, two, one, two. I get them lined up in groups of three. I film the session. I take a step, and they take a step. I want them in their stance, and I want them to move their feet with me. We do that a ton of times. I think this is an important part of playing linebacker. If you can teach them those two steps, and if you can teach them a few footwork drills, then they have a chance to play linebacker.

Once we get our initial key (the flow of the back), we then work to our surface key. If flow goes in one direction, we start our read. We talk to our kids about the stack. When we talk about the stack, it is a double-team. If you are in a 4-3 defense, the two inside linebackers must read the double-team or pull.

There is a double-team block or a pull on each of those plays. If flow goes one way, we tell the linebacker to throw his eyes to the stack. We use that term. He throws his eyes to the stack where the double-team is going to happen. It could be on the shade of the 3 technique or at the 5 technique.

The stack is going to tell us what is going on. If a blocker is coming off the double-team to try to block the linebacker, he has confirmed his key. Now, he needs to go play football. If he gets a high-hat pull, and it can be the guard or tackle, from the stack, the linebacker is wrong on his key, and the ball is going the other way.

The first thing we do is diagnose flow. If it is a one-back set, it is easy; it is that one back. If it is two backs, we make a decision from week to week. If the offense does not run the counter play, we are going to read the tailback. That man is going to get the ball. If the fullback is offset, or moves to a wing, he is going to take you to the ball.

Next, we talk about their movement skills. It means, as a linebacker, moving his body in a way to protect himself. We have laminated on the wall our rules for movement skills. This is what we tell them.

Movement Skills

- If the ballcarrier is in the tackle box, the linebacker's shoulders are square, and my feet are underneath me.
- Once the ballcarrier leaves the tackle box, the linebacker presses the ballcarrier's inside hip as fast as possible.
- Shuffle: Quick feet, toes straight ahead, no heel click, consistent pad level. Presses the line of scrimmage. Never shuffles more than two times. We want consistent pad level.
- Crossover run: Hips mirror the ballcarrier, shoulders parallel to the line of scrimmage. Snaps his hips back into place when he throttles.

The first thing we do is what we call positional warm-up. We do it for five minutes every day. We get on the bags, and we shuffle through them. We do our stance and starts out of the bags.

We talk to our guys about run sets. We talk about three guys on a string. We are talking about the Sam, Mike. and Will linebackers with a string between them. If I am the Mike, I have a string on my hip going to Sam, and a string going from my hip to Will. If at any time that string is pulled, Mike gets pulled. If the Sam linebacker is out in space, he tells the Mike that he is out ("I am out! I am out!"). He pulls the string. Mike slides with him, and Will slides with Mike.

- Three linebackers are on a string. Any movement by one affects the other two. If the Will has to leave the box the Mike and Sam will slide in that direction.
- Easy gap control: Attack your gap on flow to you; replace each other on flow away.
- Spill all blocks; run everything down.
- Very easy to align; Linebackers just slide to any spread formation.

The same is true is we are in the box and we get a run at one of the linebackers. One linebacker punctures, and the other two replace.

One thing about playing the 4-3 defense it is easy to control the gaps. When you play a 50 defense, there are a lot of different things that can happen. We do not have a man on our team that does not know how to be a two-gap player. In the 50 defense, you are changing shades all of the time. In the 4-3 defense, it is easy. I tell our linebackers this: if there is a big butt in front of you, that man has the gap. If there is not a big butt there, odds are that is the linebacker's gap.

If I am the Mike, and the ball goes into the gap toward Sam, I have to replace Sam's gap. If the ball goes to Will, I go to replace Will's gap. If I am Will and the ball comes toward me, I attach the ball. If the ball goes away, I replace Mike's gap. We spill everything. It goes back to our speed guys, and the fact we have players who can run.

Dive flow occurs when the back we are keying attacks the line of scrimmage right down the middle of the center (Diagram #1). Common plays include trap and midline option.

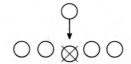

Diagram #1. Dive Flow

Tight flow occurs when the back we are keying attacks the line of scrimmage at a 45-degree angle

(Diagram #2). Common plays include power, isolation, counter, and inside zone.

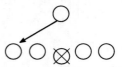

Diagram #2. Tight Flow

Confirm Your Key

- Once the linebacker has identified his flow, he throws his eyes to the offensive line in the direction of the flow.
- Any pull in the opposite direction of the flow cancels his key. Follow the puller!
- If there is no pull, then the key is confirmed; identify the blocking scheme, and fit into the play as needed.

Here is our base defense. You can see the gaps the linebackers key (Diagram #3).

- Will in B gap
- Mike in A gap
- Sam in D gap

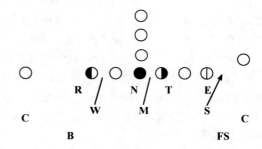

Diagram #3. Base Defense

Let me talk about an example of tight flow (Diagram #4). Notice there is no pull with an open window.

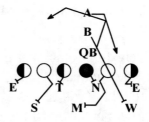

Diagram #4. Tight Flow: No Pull, Open Window

This is an example of tight flow with the guard and tackle pulling (Diagram #5). The guard/tackle Pull cancels the key, and the linebacker redirects.

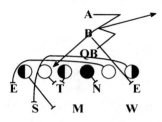

Diagram #5. Tight Flow: Guard/Tackle Pull

Let me talk about run fits. If Sam covers the C gap and steps up to attack the blocker, Mike replaces Sam, and Will replaces Mike (Diagram #6).

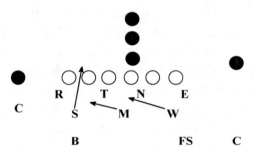

Diagram #6. Run Fit: Sam Replaced by Mike, Mike Replaced by Will

The same is true if Will steps up to attack the C gap. The Mike replaces him, and the Sam replaces Mike (Diagram #7).

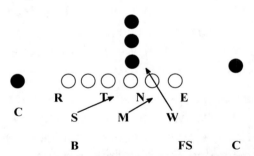

Diagram #7. Run Fit: Will Replaced by Mike, Mike Replaced by Sam

Against the option, if we are playing against a great quarterback, we can hit the quarterback. It does not matter if it is the zone read option, the veer option, and the quarterback is the best player, we must get our kids to believe we can knock him out of the game. We are not talking about illegal hits or dirty tactics. We are talking about going after the quarterback to force him to pitch the ball. We want to hit the quarterback on the pitch enough to force him to pitch the ball earlier, and our defense can react to the pitch on the option.

Let me talk about pass drops real quickly. I have gotten away from spending a lot of time teaching the linebackers to drop to a spot. We have gotten away from telling the linebacker to open up at a 45-degree angle and drop to a spot. We still do it some. We play some three-deep where we do it. We play some quarter/quarter/half where we do it. However, so much of our plays are matched up. We do not want to get involved in teaching something the players are never going to be great at doing. For us, we only have so much time to teach. For our linebackers we seldom drop to a spot. We are not going to drop to a depth of 12 yards and then turn around.

I talk to our linebackers about staying in their tilt when they do drop. I never want them to drop to a spot and then turn around with their shoulders square. You can only go fast in one direction, and that is the direction your hips are pointed. You can shuffle, and you can pedal, but if you have two equal players running, and one is running, and one is pedaling, the one who is running is going to win. We drop, and we point our hips toward the quarterback's eyes in the direction of the initial drop. If the ball goes back the other way, we open up.

We tell our linebackers that if they are blitzing, they really are becoming a defensive lineman. We spend a lot of time with our guys on pass rush. More than one third of the time, one of the three linebackers will be coming on a blitz. Last year, we ran the zone blitz about 35 percent of the time. If you do not work on the pass rush very much, I think you are cheating your players.

I will be around if you have any questions. I know we covered some of this fast, but I will be glad to answer any questions. Thank you very much.

DEFENSIVE SECONDARY DRILLS AND TECHNIQUES

University of Louisville

Thank you. It is great to be here today. We are a new staff at the University of Louisville. We are working hard to catch up with our recruiting. Coach Charlie Strong is committed to building the program at the University of Louisville back to what people expect it to be. I think we have had a good beginning for the short time we have been here.

We are working hard with the young men we have in our program, and the first thing we must concentrate on is the fundamentals of the game. Our indoor program is under way, and we are working hard every day. At the University of Florida, Coach Meyer told us that if we wanted to get good at anything, we had to put the time in and go back to the fundamentals. We are doing these things at the University of Louisville. We are teaching stance, get-off, proper footwork, and all those types of things to every position we have.

The thing we are trying to improve on right now is attitude. We won four games last year. In the eight games we lost, only one team blew us out, and that was Cincinnati. They were in every game they played. The reason they did not win those games is they did not know how to finish. We are working on finishing right now. We are learning how to finish.

We are teaching our team a lot of different things. We are teaching team competition, speed, conditioning, and the mentality of how to finish. We are teaching our team how to compete. What we are doing is all about effort. We have them matched by body size and position and have them going against each other. We are working on their attitude.

We are working on their attitude about winning and hustling in any drill we run. On Thursday, we have four different stations. We go though those drills and have a halftime break. We change the drills and start over. The types of drills we do are not important. What we are working on is competition and finish. If a player falls in the drill and jogs to the finish line, we are all over him. It is not about doing a particular drill; it is all about winning.

Finishing is how you win the close ball game. At Florida, we did the same thing, and it was a bloody mess. Those players got after each other and developed attitude. You have to develop an attitude among your players that you want to win. That attitude does not start at the beginning of the season or the beginning of two-a-day practices. It starts right now.

We use a rope tug-of-war as one of these drills. You may wonder what that has to do with football. It builds attitude. It is about competition, finish, and the fight you must have to win. When we have these drills, the coaches get excited. These drills take about 35 to 40 minutes. This forms the foundation and the attitude we are trying to bring to our team right now. If we can get their attitude right, we have a chance to win.

The players are starting to have fun, but they do not know what we are really working to instill in them. However, we are beginning to see the focus we are looking for. The drills we are doing are football-related, and they stress the fundamentals. We are working on their mental and physical toughness, discipline, and attitude. These intangibles in football help you win games. It is not talent alone; it is the will to win. Learning how to fight will give us an edge next season.

If you are interested in coming to our off-season program, we welcome you. We want you to be part of our family. You will see the players are starting to do the things they have not done in the past. We have to get back to that way of doing things for them to be successful. The off-season program is tough, but you can make it fun for the players.

I am not a clinic-type of coach. I have to be honest with you. The reason I went to clinics was to learn something to help with my coaching. I listened to a coach talk the other night. He talked about things that were not applicable to high school coaching because of the time restraints. What I am trying to give you is something that the high school coaches can do with their players.

Everyone has an off-season program because that is where you win. That is why we are working so hard to develop our program. The harder we work, the better chance we have to be successful. I can stand up here and give you some zone-blitz scheme, but do you have the time to teach them or the players who can run them? I want to make sure that when I finish, I have time to answer any question about the lecture you have. Otherwise, you came for the wrong reasons. I want to give you something to take back to your school and your players that you can use.

I am not up here just to talk. That is a waste of your time and mine. You are here to get better at what you do, and I am here to help you.

I want to get into some defensive back drills. I have been a defensive coach all my life. I have coached in high school, junior college, college, the NFL and back to college. The first thing I start talking about at all levels of football is stance. One of the biggest things a player has to do when he gets into a stance is relax.

I know most of the coaches spend time in the weight room. You know how to use the squat rack. We get the defensive back in a heel-to-toe stagger and put the hands up as if we are under a squat rack. We want to push the chest out and go straight down like we are squatting in the weight rack, keeping the knees straight. We drop the hands and roll the shoulders over. That will put him in a good defensive corner stance. For a cornerback, that is a simplistic way to get in a stance.

In the stance, we should have a 45-degree angle in the knees, hips, and ankles. In other words, the knees should be in front of your toes. The football position puts the defender in a position to tackle. It does not matter what position you play; the most important thing is to be in a position to tackle. This stance will put you into a position to tackle and attack.

The first drill is about the basic backpedal. The hands should hang right below the knees. Have the players concentrate on the first step. They push off on the first step. The second step is the reach step. The third thing is to stay focused on staying down and not raising up. Always keep a narrow base when you backpedal. If you come up, your weight will be behind you and you will be on your heels. That will slow you down when it is time to break and drive on a receiver.

When you are teaching backpedal, the biggest thing to consider is tempo. It is not how fast you go or how many times you can do the drill. The drill is about teaching proper technique with the right timing. It does not matter what position you coach; the first thing you need to look at is the stance. If you overlook the stance, you are already behind in the count. The players will be in a hurry-up mode to try to catch up. If the player starts off in a good stance, he has more of a chance to be successful.

The command for backpedal is: "Push, reach, and stay low." We constantly say that as the backs move through the drill. I watch the push foot, reach foot, and the back. The drill is not about speed. It is about tempo, technique, and attitude. It is about learning how to do things the right and proper way. That is how you get better. To do this drill, we align the back on a line and watch him backpedal. We use a 20-yard pedal drill.

The next thing we teach the players is backpedal, flip, and go (Diagram #1). The drill is the same as the backpedal drill, but we incorporate a turn-and-go technique. The coach aligns seven yards behind the defensive back. On the "go" call, the players start their pedal. Once they reach the coach, both players will open up to the coach. The key points are to open with the elbow thrusting down. This will keep the player's shoulders down and help get his head around. We can modify the drill by starting from the sideline. We set the drill up starting on the sideline, going toward the hash marks. The coach pats the ball, and the player starts his pedal. The coach turns the player on movement of the ball.

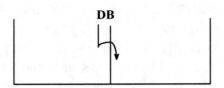

Diagram #1. Backpedal, Flip, and Go

It does not matter whether the player is a corner or safety; the skill is the same. The turn is all about body control. When the players get better in their technique, the coaches pick up the tempo of the drill. Too many coaches want to go fast all the time. If the player's technique is not great to begin with, we hamper him by forcing him to go fast. In coaching, the head coach is looking for a coach that can make his players better on game day. He is looking for a teacher.

I hear coaches say all the time that their players are not fast enough to play man coverage. You would be surprised how fast they can play if they have proper technique. I had a freshman play for me last year at Florida who ran 4.55 in the 40. That is not fast for a corner. The difference was he was a great technician. If you take the time to teach the techniques, speed will not matter.

If the coach can take the average player and make him a good player, his team will get better. That is what coaching the fundamentals and teaching them right is all about.

The next thing we do in the progression is to match the defensive back up with a receiver (Diagram #2). This drill is a combination of the first two drills. We put a receiver in front of the defensive back, running half to three-quarters speed. We stress the points in the push, reach, and stay down low. Once the receiver gets within three

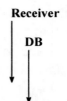

Diagram #2. Man-to-Man Backpedal

yards of the defensive back, he uses his flip-and-go technique.

We do a drill that I call a "wide weave" (Diagram #3). This teaches a defensive back how to move from side to side. The defensive back needs to stay square to the sideline and not turn his hips. He weaves at a 45-degree angle to the next line and pedals to the numbers. If you weave and stay square, you are in a position to tackle. If you turn your hips to change direction, you are not in a position to tackle someone running to your backside. We teach our players to go left and right, but stay in a good football position.

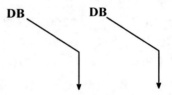

Diagram #3. Wide Weave

If you are a defensive football team and miss tackles, you are in trouble. In a four-year period at the University of Florida, we were 33-4 in games in which we had less than 10 missed tackles. The things that worked for us at Florida are what we are working on here at Louisville. Sometimes on Thursdays, Coach Strong would get our defensive team in a football position and make them hold it for one minute. You may not think that is not long, but it is because a football position is not a natural position.

That is all part of the foundation, stance, and technique. Those little things can give you the added advantage on game day. In the fourth quarter when both teams are tired, the team with the best fundamentals has the best chance of winning. You can get that done right now in the off-season. You can work on the little tidbits that will make your individuals better. If he can bring someone else with him, the team will get better. Everything right now is team-oriented. If we go as fast as we can go, we forget the little tidbits that make the individuals better.

When we do drills, we do everything on air first. If you do not, everything gets out of control. After we do the drills on air, I put a buddy with them. We do the drill again with the defensive back and his buddy working together.

From the wide weave drill, we go to a tight weave (Diagram #4). It is the same type of drill, except we weave back and forth across a yard line. This teaches the player to adjust his pedal by weaving and staying square. We set up two lines going toward the hash marks on a yard line. We are teaching tempo. We set the players into a pedal and begin to weave him across the line on your movement. We emphasize that the hips should stay square at all times.

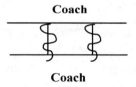

Diagram #4. Tight Weave

We follow that drill with the M/M weave (Diagram #5). It is the same drill, except the defensive back has a receiver in front of him. We want to work two lines at once. Have the defender five yards off the receiver on the left or right side. The receiver works on the yard line going toward the hash mark. Remember: you are teaching tempo. The receiver runs at half speed, weaving on and across the line. The defender must stay square in his pedal while weaving to mirror the receiver.

When you match up in the buddy system, you must be careful. If the defensive back and his buddy start to get into a competitive mode, the defensive back's technique will go to crap. He has pride, does not want to get beat, and speeds up the tempo. His technique suffers, and he goes backward in his teaching. We want a teaching tempo to teach the techniques.

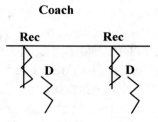

Diagram #5. M/M Weave

A coach once told me you never make a play as a defensive back in a backpedal. You make your plays coming out of a backpedal. Everything is about changing direction. You teach the linebacker to open up, break down, and react, but he makes plays coming forward. You have to teach a player how to get out of trouble. They will get in trouble on the football field.

To help the defensive back get out of trouble, we teach the 45 plant drill (Diagram #6). In the drill, two defenders will be seven yards in front of the coach and five yards apart. Both players have the outside foot back. On the coach's call or a movement, the players want to plant the outside foot and lead with the inside foot. This drill teaches a player how to break and drive off his plant foot.

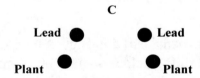

Diagram #6. 45 Plant Drill

The next thing is to add steps to the drop. We want to do the same drill at the end of three steps. The defensive back drops three steps and drives on his toes. We do not want him to stall the feet. He has to keep them moving. We want to keep the feet tight and not lead with the shoulder.

When you do the drill, you have to sell the players on what you are doing. They have to believe the drill will make them better. Otherwise, they will feel you are doing the drill to make them tired. Show them clips of pro players doing the same drills. That should let them see where doing the drill can take them.

After we work off three steps, we expand to the plant cone drill (Diagram #7). We want to work from the sideline. We set up four cones, two to three yards apart. The defensive back will start on the left or the right of the cones. He wants to break using his closest foot to the cones. You want him to work on both sides of the cones. The coach can give him a break call on any of the four cones. The defensive back plants and breaks at a 45-degree angle back toward the coach. This teaches a player how to break on his left or right foot.

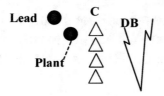

Diagram #7. Plant Cone Drill

When a defensive back breaks back on a receiver, he wants to break for the back hip like he is going to pick his pocket. If the receiver is making a double move, he will have to break through the defensive back. If the defensive back tries to come totally around the receiver, he gets himself in trouble.

The backpedal curl drill is done on the end of a route. We tell the defensive back and receiver that the pattern is a 12-yard comeback pattern. We do not want to run the defensive back to death when learning the technique. It is a way to teach the fundamentals of the technique. The receiver takes two steps and comes back to the ball. The defensive back plants and reacts back to the ball.

When you do these drills, the players start to understand you are doing the drills to help them achieve what they want to accomplish. If you can show the player footage of him doing the drill in a game clip, he will buy into what you are teaching.

We all have done the W drill (Diagram #8). I do this drill different from a lot of other people. If you do the drill only between the five-yard lines, that is not the way the game is played. I do not put the cones on the five-yard lines. I stagger the cones in depth. The first cone may be five yards, and the second one will be three yards. The next one may be six yards from the base line. If you put the cones five yards from the line, players get into a rhythm and do the drill mindlessly. I want them to think when they do the drill.

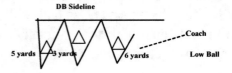

Diagram #8. W Drill

The defensive back begins his backpedal straight back. Once he gets past the cone, he plants with his outside foot, drives to the sideline, and repeats the drill through the cones. The coach is at the end of the drill, throwing a low ball at defenders. I throw the ball right at their knees. I want them to bend down and focus on the ball. This is not a race; we work on technique.

Sometimes, we make our players act like robots, and they do not think. On game day when you are not on the football field with them and something you did not work on happens, what is he going to do? If you never give your players a chance to think, learn, or grow, they cannot adjust. It is our job to teach them how to develop and grow. I am constantly trying to think of ways to challenge my players and make them think and grow. That will let them go out on game day and have success.

We do a lot of change-of-direction drills and break drills. That goes for the safeties as well as the corners. It does not matter where they play. They still have to break, and any wasted steps means a completion.

You have to make up drills to teach what you need. I used to call this drill the comeback drill (Diagram #9). I set the cones up for a 15- to 18-yard comeback pattern. We set up four cones in a straight line. The first cone was the starting point. The second cone was five yards from the start line. The third cone was 8 to 10 yards from the second cone. The fourth cone was five yards to the outside of the third cone. On the coach's command, the defensive back backpedals to the first cone. One he gets to the first cone he uses the flip-and-go technique. He sprints to the next cone, but he must drop his hips and plant with the outside foot and break inside the cone. A coach is at a 45-degree angle, throwing a low ball at the defender once he breaks. This will help the defensive back on deep out or comeback routes.

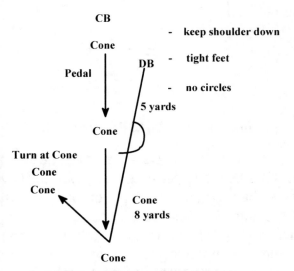

Diagram #9. Comeback Drill

For anything that is going to happen to your players on game day, you have to find a way to drill it. If you want to be a good coach, you have to work at it. The best coach I know is my father. He was one outstanding defensive coordinator. He worked at it, and that is what it is all about. When you leave here today, you should be a better coach. You have to challenge the players to get better, and you have to improve every day. If your coaching is not working on a player, you need to find something to get him going. I can go recruit another player. You cannot go get one. You have to develop what you have.

The coaching points to look for in this drill are critical. We want to keep the shoulder down as he breaks. We want his feet tight, taking short steps on the break. That prevents him from falling. If he takes long step, he is likely to fall. We want no circles on his break or flip.

A defensive back has to learn how to catch. Twenty-seven years after I left the University of Texas, I am still fifth all time on the pass break-up list. I could not catch. That was a problem, and I have to be honest about it. I was looking at the green grass, thinking about taking the interception for a touchdown. I had 41 pass break-ups in my career. I could get there and make a play, but I could not intercept the ball. Now that I am a coach, I make it a point in the grading sheet for our backs to catch the ball. A dropped interception is a minus on my grading sheet. It goes in the stats book as a pass break-up; however, he is going to get a minus because technically he did not finish the play. The small details will make you a good football player or an average one.

The double move drill is one you have to work (Diagram #10). This is one of those drills where you work on the little things. The double move is play recognition by the defensive back. The things that you work on in practice will pop up on you during the season. The double cut teaches the defensive back to break, drive, and use his hands on the receiver. The coach stands in a position to represent a quick out pattern by the receiver. The defensive back uses the coach's upfield shoulder as his aiming point. The defensive back backpedals and breaks on the coach's call. If the coach points up or uses the ball movement, the defensive back breaks up, defending the go route.

Diagram #10. Double Cut

This next drill I got from a buddy of mine with the Tampa Bay Bucs. It is a deep-ball drill (Diagram #11). The purpose of the drill is to teach the defensive back to locate the ball without turning his shoulders too soon. If he turns too soon, he slows down as he runs down the field. The defensive back starts on the command, jogging down the field. He will turn his head, looking outside, inside, and back outside. The coach throws the ball when the defender looks outside the second time. The defensive back must locate the ball at its highest point.

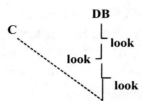

Diagram #11. Deep Ball Drill

The hardest thing for the young defensive back is finding the ball when it is thrown. When he turns his back to the football, he has trouble locating the ball when he turns to look. We work on that. Sometimes, we forget and think they should know that. When I got to the NFL, I was amazed at what the coaches do not teach anymore because they do not have time.

I coached college football before I went to the NFL to coach. I coached at the University of Michigan the year we won the national championship. I taught our defensive back how to find the ball. I had a freshman playing because I took the time to teach the fundamentals. I went to the head coach and defensive coordinator and asked for more individual time before we went to the team drills. I had some good players, but I gave them the tools they needed to be successful. I coached the only defensive back to ever win the Heisman Trophy, Charles Woodson. He was recently named defensive player of the year in the NFL.

I told Charles I was going to teach him three techniques and he needed to become a good technician. I told him if he got outside those techniques, I would coach them again. I sent him out to play. When you get a good player, it is your job not to screw him up. Teach him the fundamentals, and let him go play. Do not take the playmaking ability away from him. He is the guy who will make the great play and help you win the championship. You have to find out who those players are, and let them go play.

After we do the deep ball drill, I go to a completive M/M press fade drill (Diagram #12). I do this drill a little differently. We want the defensive back to fade into the hip of the receiver, get his chin up, and become the receiver if he is on the upfield shoulder of the receiver. We have a quarterback throw the ball. We start the defensive back on one side of a yard line and the receiver on the other side of the line. That gives the receiver the advantage at the beginning. We put the defensive back in a defeated position. That teaches the defensive back how to get out of trouble. The defensive back wants to get to the receiver's hip. Once he is in this position, when the receiver looks, the defensive back can now look. The key point is to have him look up, not back.

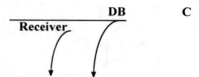

Diagram #12. M/M Press Fade Drill

One coaching point is to never let the defensive back trail directly behind the receiver. You have to remember the heaviest part of the body is the head. If the defender looks back, it causes a separation immediately. If he looks up, his shoulders drop and he moves into the receiver. In the fade drill we also teach playing the hands of the receiver. We want to drive to the inside hip of the receiver and not behind him. We play the hands of the receiver, using our inside arm. If he is beaten and the pass is completed, he plays the receiver for the strip.

In the competition drill, we teach defenders to fight for the ball. It is a simple drill. Two defensive backs align next to each other, facing the coach. On a command, both start to pedal away from the coach. On the break call, both defenders break back to the coach. He throws the ball, and they try to catch it. It is okay if they interfere with each other. The key is not to let the other defender catch the ball. If one defender catches the ball, the other tries to strip him of the ball. This drill is not about technique. It does not matter what they do to one another. One of them wants it more than the other one. It is competition.

We want them to fight and scratch because that is the way it is on game day. They use their athletic ability and technique to get to the ball, but after that it is a free for all.

The strip drill is to prevent the receiver from catching the ball (Diagram #13). We have two players with the coach standing to the inside of them. The defensive back aligns inside the receiver. The receiver has the ball in his outside arm. On the command, they both start jogging down the field. The receiver puts the ball up as if he is trying to catch it. The defensive back then tries to strip the ball.

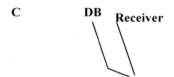

C   DB   Receiver

Diagram #13. Strip Drill

Next season in Louisville, we are going to play a lot of man coverage. We are going to get after people and play aggressive defense. Offenses throw patterns on time. We want to get up on the receivers and disrupt their routes. We want to destroy their timing.

I have to tell you a little story. When I played in Chicago with the Bears, we had a player who wore number 25 as his jersey number. He signed for 25 million dollars. After three years, he was cut and is penniless now. He did not take care of business and did not pay attention to the details and fundamentals of playing the game. His technique was poor. The money came, and it went. He could not do the little things that would have made him a better player.

Playing defensive back is not all about pass coverage. You must be a great tackler. That is the biggest skill in defensive football. You can teach these drills in junior high school.

The first thing we teach is the giant lift. The purpose is to teach the fundamentals of making contact and running through the ballcarrier. You have two players facing each other. The defender will get into a fit position. He starts with the right foot up in his stance. He should have his knee in front of his ankle. He needs a 45-degree bend at the waist with his back straight. On set, the ballcarrier jumps over the defender, putting his hands on the defender's shoulders for balance. The defender rolls off his front foot and runs through the ballcarrier. The defender must have his hands on the ballcarrier's waist.

The next step is the rhythm of making contact. The ballcarrier aligns five yards in front of the defender. The defender gets in his tackling stance as he did in the giant lift. On command, the ballcarrier will walk to the defender and jump over the defender, putting his hands on the defender's shoulder. The defender will contact the waist, push off of the up foot, and run through the ballcarrier.

The next part of the procedure is entering the contact. This the same as the second step, except the ballcarrier does not jump, and both the tackler and ballcarrier walk toward each other. The defender wants to make contact with the same shoulder and foot while putting his hands on the ballcarrier's waist. He wants the knee in front of the ankle with a 45-degree bend in his waist and his back straight. The drill is all about getting into a football position and making contact.

The next thing we do is the single-move open-step drill. We put the players five yards apart. The ballcarrier goes to the defender's right. The defender will open-step, making sure he does not cross over with his feet. He wants to keep his shoulders square. When the defender makes contact with his left shoulder, he wants to be on the left foot. He finishes in a fit position.

We continue the drill by backing them up to the depth of 10 yards. The tackler starts the drill by walking toward the ballcarrier. He walks straight at the ballcarrier. The ballcarrier comes straight at the tackler and makes an angle cut. The tackler repeats what we did in the first angle drill. He must remember to always use his inside shoulder.

This drill is also a good drill for reroute technique in the passing game. We play some cover 2 in our scheme. This is the same type of technique you play to reroute the receivers in a cover-2 roll.

The next part of the sequence is the double move. The tempo of the drill is still walking. The procedure is the same as the single move except the ballcarrier opens left and then opens to the right. The defender has to open twice and finish the drill in a lift position.

After we do a double move, we go to a stutter move. The procedure is the same as we have already talked about. When the ballcarrier stutters (runs in place), the defender accelerates and closes the cushion. If the defender breaks down and stops his feet when the ballcarrier stutters, he gets into trouble. The ballcarrier when he stutters is waiting for the defender to break down so he can make his next move. If the defender quickly closes the cushion, it surprises the ballcarrier.

After we go through those drills, we go back to the giant lift. We align the players five yards apart. The defender is in a tackling position. On command, both players walk toward each other. The defender wants to make contact with the same shoulder and same foot. He puts his hands on the ballcarrier's waist with his knee in front of the ankle, waist at 45 degrees, and his back straight. The defender finishes the drill with the giant lift technique.

We do the same drill with the open step and lift. We start them 15 yards apart. The defender starts the drill. Once he gets five yards from the ballcarrier, he must drop his hips and shorten his stride. That is what we call "coming to balance." After three steps, the ballcarrier will open at 45-degree angle. The defender will open step and use the giant lift technique with contact on the same shoulder and foot.

When it comes to defense, tackling is the name of the game. Tackling in space is the name of the game for the defensive secondary. You have to teach your defensive backs to tackle low. If you have small defensive backs, you should not expect them to take on a tight end high. We have to tackle low and get them on the ground. The sole purpose of a tackle is to get the man down. In the fourth quarter, those kinds of hits are just as painful. Not everyone can be a nose-up tackler. You have to teach your defensive backs that type of tackling to give them a chance to be successful.

One of the biggest excuses I hear from coaching about fundamentals is they do not have enough time. We do not have time because we are poor managers of time. Coaches waste more time than anybody in the world does. Think about the time you waste. Structure yourself, take the time, and get it done. I firmly believe I got married for a reason. I am going home to see my wife. We want to do our job and go home at night. If my wife is happy at home, I am going to do a great job of coaching. If my wife is mad at home, I am in a bad mood all day.

You have to find ways to structure yourself to get your job done. That way you can teach your kids and coaches. You will be a better father, and your staff will be better coaches. They will do a better job with your football team, and you will be successful.

I never knew anything about losing. In high school, I lost one game. The last year in high school, we were 15-0 with a state championship. After that, I went to the University of Texas, and we won big there. I thought that playing football was all about winning. When I became a coach, I found out I did not know it all. I thought I could coach anybody, and we would win. I learned the hard way and went 1-11. Since then, I have learned my lesson and have gotten back to winning.

I have two national championship rings and have coached in the NFL. I also learned if you lose, it is not the end of the world. You have to come back to work the next day. When things go bad, get back to the foundations and fundamentals of the game. I have to constantly do that with my players.

I have had fun today, and I hope you got something from those defensive back drills. I appreciate your time.

REFLECTIONS ON COACHING FOOTBALL FOR 57 YEARS

Florida State University

In the introduction, a comment was made about sons Terry and Tommy speaking here before. Terry Bowden is now the head coach at North Alabama. My son Jeffrey also coaches there. Last summer around July, Terry wanted to have a "Bowden Day" at North Alabama to raise money for the program and to get some enthusiasm for the program. I flew in from Tallahassee, and Tommy flew in from Clemson. Therefore, we had four Bowdens at the event. They had all four of us on a panel. We were sitting at a table, taking questions. We had the press present. There were reporters from all over the country.

When they introduced us, they told something about each of us. "Tommy has coached for so many years, Terry has coached for so many years, Jeffery coached so many years, and Coach Bowden coached so many years." They went on to say all of the Bowdens have coached a total of X number of games, and they have had only six losing seasons combined.

Tommy got up to talk first. The first thing he said was, "Which one of you had a losing season?" He had never had a losing season in his career.

Next, I got up to speak. I asked, "Which one of you have not been fired?" All three were fired at one time or the other. Of course, I might as well been fired at Florida State. I survived, but the alternative was not much better for me.

I am from Birmingham, Alabama. I coached at West Virginia University and Florida State University. I have 22 wins from junior college that have not been added in my total number of wins in my career. Let me assure you, I am counting those 22 wins. If the NCAA can take away winning games from my record at FSU, I am going to count the junior college games.

I got married very young in life to a young lady from Birmingham, Alabama. We had six children. We have 21 grandchildren, and three great-grandchildren. Of course, all of our kids are gone from home now. Therefore, Ann and I live by ourselves. When I speak in an area over 50 miles away from home, I fly to the area. If I speak close to home, within 50 miles, Ann will go with me, and she will drive. She drives all of the time. I just sit there and hold the wheel. I think we all have faced that when we reach a certain age.

While Ann is driving me around, she often makes this statement: "You like football more than you do me." I am sure some of you have heard that statement before from your spouse. We all catch that if we are in coaching long. When she makes that statement, I ask her, "College or Pro?"

I was born in 1929. That was when the Great Depression hit the country. It looks like we may be sneaking up on it again, here. Naturally, I did not remember a lot about the Great Depression because I was so young. My mother and dad told me all about the hard times.

During the Depression, most everyone lost their jobs. If you think people are losing their jobs now, it was nothing like the Great Depression. My grandfather built courthouses down in Alabama and Florida. His wife had died, so he lived by himself. He was doing very well, financially. My mother told me that when the Depression hit, my grandfather went to the bank to get his money out of the bank, and they did not have any money to give him. All of a sudden, he had nothing. Back in those days, when something like this happened, your relatives would move in with you.

My dad kept his job during the Depression. I had one sister at home. My dad kept his job, but he did not make a lot of money. My grandfather moved in with us. My grandfather and I slept in the same room for 15 years. We did have twin beds.

I had an uncle who lost his job, and he moved in with us. He had two young kids. Then they slept in my room. I had an aunt whose husband lost his job, and they moved in with us. By this time, I had four people sleeping with me. I never slept alone until I got married. All coaches know exactly what I am talking about on this one.

During the Depression, we all wore hand-me-downs. I had four sons and two girls. As soon as our oldest son grew out of his clothes, they were handed down to Tommy. After Tommy out grew them, they went down to Terry. When Terry out grew them, they went to Jeffrey. We all wore hand-me-downs in my family. It was the same thing when I was a kid. I wore hand-me-downs for 15 years. The thing about it is this: all I had was an older sister.

I was at West Virginia University for 10 years. I love West Virginia. There are great people who live there. They are proud people. They are blue-collar people. It is one thing I like about West Virginia people.

Then I moved to Tallahassee to coach at Florida State University. In football, they had gone 3-8, 1-10, and 0-11 in the three years before they fired the coach. They hired me to change things. At the time, the stadium seated 41,000 people. Now it holds 85,000 people. When I went to FSU, they were only averaging 17,000 people. Everyone knows you must fill the stadium. The football receipts paid all the bills. I would bet our football receipts pays 90 percent of all of our athletic department expenses at FSU.

In those days, the head coach received 10 complimentary game tickets, and the assistant coaches received four game comp tickets. You could do anything you wanted to do with those tickets, but you were not supposed to sell them. I had taken my 10 tickets, distributed them to my family and close friends, and I ended up with two extra tickets. I had two tickets, and I could not find anyone who wanted them. I had tried to give them to the janitor, but he did not want them.

That Friday, I had to go down to the Tallahassee Mall to get a haircut. I decided I would get rid of those tickets. I parked close to the barbershop and got out of my car. I took those two tickets and placed them on the outside of my car. I put them under the wiper blades on the front windshield. I knew someone would take those tickets. I went in to get my haircut.

I came out of the mall in one hour. I could not wait to see if the tickets had been taken. To my surprise, I found six game tickets on my windshield. At that time, I knew we were facing an uphill battle. However, we did make progress and improved the program over the years.

We have been with Nike for over 30 years at FSU. We were about the third school to sign up with them. Each year, we do a clinic for the Nike Coach of the Year Clinics. It is a privilege to do the clinics and to meet the people in different cities. I told them I would go anywhere, but I did not want to go north. I do not like the cold weather. This is my last Nike Clinic lecture, and I have made it to Connecticut. It is a good clinic, and I feel privileged to be here.

I was looking for my notes that I use when I give a lecture, and I had a hard time finding them. I had a secretary for 57 years, and when I needed something, I just asked the secretary to get it for me. I do not know where anything is now that I have moved out of my office. I do not have a secretary now, so I am on my own. I did find my clinic notes, so we are okay. I have a lot of subjects written down here. They are things I have learned over the years, and things that have meant a lot to me in coaching. I am going to go over these points as long as I have time. I hope that I will touch on something that will help you in your coaching career.

Let's say we play a certain number of football games each year. We play a certain number of teams we can beat no matter how good or how bad we are. We have those teams on the schedule each year. There are certain teams that you are just better than they are.

Then, there are certain teams that are going to beat you no matter how good or how bad you are.

That leaves the games that can go either way. They are games you must win. You may lose a game, and only one play separates you from winning that game. We all go through those types of games. I am talking about a team we are playing that is a toss-up. We need to win that game.

I believe in two intangibles. If I could do these two things, we are going to win that close ball game. The first intangible is persistence. Several coaches think persistence may be the best virtue you can have. Persistence is just saying, "I am not quitting." Persistence is saying, "You can't make me quit. I will fight you until the last second of the game."

Each year, I would take a game where I told the players about persistence. "Men, that team has a breaking point. We are starting the game off, and the score is 0-0. We must break their will. They have a breaking point. We have to fight them until we can break them. It would be nice if it happened early. It could take 60 minutes to break them. One of them is going to break. We have to break their will." That is persistence. If I have the kind of player who will not quit, that is as important a virtue as one can have.

Nothing can take away persistence. Talent will not. Nothing is more common than unsuccessful men who have talent. How many players have you coached who had great talent, but you could not get much out of them? They are not willing to pay the price. I have had so many players like that over the years. Talent is not the answer; it is persistence.

Being a genius isn't the most important thing in life. Education is not going to overcome persistence.

If I have players who are persistent, then I must have enthusiasm. I must have players with enthusiasm. Nothing great is accomplished without enthusiasm. It is a great spirit who can say, "I can, I will, and I must, in spite of the odds." You must have enthusiasm.

The first time I heard anyone talk about enthusiasm was Woody Hayes. I was at a coaching clinic, and he was a speaker. Most of you have heard of Woody. When I was coming up in the coaching world, he was a talented person. He told us at that clinic the word enthusiasm comes from the Greek work enthios, which means full God, which means God in you. If you have God in you, you have spirit. Do not be afraid to say that, men. You are just trying to get these people to be the best they can be.

I remember when I was coaching at West Virginia. I had used the term enthusiasm several times during the week of a big game. I had one coach who was always uptight. We were getting ready to play on Saturday afternoon. That morning, he was in a cold sweat. He was rubbing his hands and was nervous as a cat. I asked him what he was worried about. He replied, "I just hope I have covered everything. I have covered this, and I have covered that." I looked at him and said, "It is too late to worry about it today. It is too late to worry now. All you have to do is to be enthusiastic. You just act enthusiastic, because it is catching." He told me he did not know if he could be enthusiastic. I told him, "How about faking it? Fake the enthusiasm."

These two words are very important, especially when everything else is equal. I used those words often.

THE SIX COMMANDMENTS TO VICTORY

For 32 years of my coaching career, I made it a point to meet with my team the night before a game. We would go over some thoughts related to the game the next day. I would go over the points I thought it would take to win the game the next day. I called this meeting to make sure we knew what we expect from our players the next day in the game. It is what I call "The Six Commandments to Victory". Men, everything I cover here is what I got from somebody else. I have used the same points for those 32 years. The only thing is some of these points are older than you all.

"Boys, if we do these things, we will win." Most of us know, at this point, there is not much you can do to control the outcome of the game. You have already done your coaching and preparation during the week. Once they kick off, all you can hope for is for your boys to carry out what you practiced.

The six commandments I am giving you, as coaches we can control them. I used six commandments, but some other coaches may have used more and some coaches may have used less. These commandments are basic to the game of football.

Allow No Breakdowns in the Kicking Game

When everything else is equal, this is probably where you are going to win or lose. We have a good offense, and our opponents they have a good defense. We have big kids, and they have big kids. The kicking game is where you are going to win or lose the game

Be sure you have your punt team perfect, your punt rush perfect, your punt-return team perfect, your kickoff coverage and kickoff-return teams perfect, and your field-goal and extra-point teams perfect.

Allow No Missed Assignments

The second commandment is "Allow no missed assignments." Now, men, these commandments I am giving you are things you can do something about. You can train, practice, and prepare your kids to handle these things. You need to practice daily by stressing "No missed assignments."

I used to go watch Green Bay practice when Vince Lombardi was coaching. He always said that football consisted of two things: blocking and tackling.

When we put in a play, we put it on the blackboard first where we can see it. Then, we explain it to the players so they can hear it. Then, we have a walk-through. Next, we walk through it versus dummies. Then, we try to simulate it the best we can.

During the season, we practice at three speeds. One is at full speed. In the early part of the season, we get a scrimmage in when we can without jeopardizing our football team. Once the season starts, we are afraid to scrimmage. We do not want to beat our players up.

Play Great Goal-Line Offense and Defense

We always practice for a while at the goal line. We go full speed a lot of time because we do not get many players hurt when practicing on the goal line. No one gets a long running start at anybody. By goal line, we mean from the three-yard line to the goal line. Every day in spring practice, we finish with goal line situations for five minutes.

We put the ball on the three-yard line, on the left hash, and tell them it is third-and-goal. They get three attempts at running the ball. They may run a play-action pass, a sweep, or another play. If they do not make it, they can still kick a field goal. After that, we put the ball on the one-yard line on the left hash mark. Now, the situation is fourth-and-one for the touchdown. The offense needs to get the ball in the end zone. The defense needs to stop them. In this type of scrimmage, it is a defensive advantage. You can turn 11 people loose on defense.

Then, we go to the right hash mark and repeat the drill. The kids have a lot of fun. The defense may beat them four straight series. If they do, you can bet that next day the offense will score. You need to win on the goal line.

Allow No Foolish Penalties

This usually occurs in the kicking game. "You would have won that game if you had not roughed the kicker. When you roughed the kicker, you gave them a first down, and they went on to score."

Another situation may occur when your opponent is fixing to kick a field goal. One of the defensive players lines up offside. Now, they score seven points instead of three, and you lose the ballgame. Those mistakes will get you beat. We say, "No foolish penalties allowed."

This is the way I view penalties. We are the most penalized team we play. When we play, we always get more penalties. We try to prevent this, but we have not been very successful. Here is the thing about that situation: If you want to stop penalties, cut out your aggressiveness, and quit hitting people. Is that what you want? You check the conferences; the most victorious teams are the most penalized. If you are an aggressive team, you will get penalties called on your team. We tell our players "Just don't get the foolish penalties." Foolish penalties include lining up offside, jumping offside, hitting the opponents in the mouth—those are the foolish penalties.

Allow No Long Touchdowns

Men, you can coach that aspect of the game. You ask how we can prevent the long touchdowns. Back up. When I was in high school a long time ago, my coach told me, "If you cannot find the ball, back up." That is still true today. Do not let anybody get behind you. That was the first thing I really learned as a player. "If you do not know where the ball is, back up." They are probably trying to fool you, so get deeper.

If I am playing defense, if you cannot get a long pass against us, and you cannot get a long run on us, how are you going to score? If I play great goal-line defense, how are you going to score? You are going to have to kick to score on us.

Keep Fumbles and Interceptions to a Minimum

How do you keep kids from fumbling? We do a good job on this aspect of the game. We teach them how to hold a football. The fingers go over the end of the ball. At the other end, the ball is under the arm, and the elbows are down. There should be no daylight in the cavities. We stress both hands over the ball when the runner is going down.

Every time we do 11-on-11 or skeleton drills, we tell the defense to knock the ball out of the arms of the ballcarrier. When they go for a touchdown, we keep trailing them until they slow down, and then knock the ball out. Invariably when we have skeleton drills, a player will catch a ball and start running for a touchdown. Before he scores, he will get the ball knocked out of his hands because he relaxes too soon. We tell him to not let up on that ball until he scores. If he does let up, we will have someone knock the ball out of his hands.

SLOGANS AND QUOTES

I have a list of thoughts that I have collected over the 57 years I have coached. Some of these things are very important to me. I want to go over them with you. Some of these are slogans and famous quotes. I think it is worth going over because I have used these over the years. I have saved these for years. We may hang these signs in the locker room.

You Do Not Win Games; You Lose Them

Look at the games you lost last year. What did you do? Did you have an interception? Did you have a fumble? Did you have a player who missed a block? Did you let the opponents run a kickoff back for a touchdown? You do not win games; you lose them.

I know this sounds negative, doesn't it? Nevertheless, it is true. I could take every game we lost last year and say, if we had not made one mistake or the other, we could have won the game. You have to keep from losing first.

Get Mentally Tough, or Get Out of Coaching

If you are not mentally tough, you are not going to make it as a coach. You are not going to win all of your games. You are not going to make everyone happy. It is impossible to make everyone happy. If you win by 10 points, fans will say it should have been by 15 points. If you win by 15 points, they say it should have been by 20 points. You must be mentally tough, and do not let anyone take that away from you.

I always told my sons this. When something bad happens in coaching, I tell them it is just the nature of the game. If you can't stand the fans getting on you, it may be time to get another profession. I do not care how good you are, you are going to be criticized. Remember: you are not going to win all of your games. I hope you do win them all, but it is tough.

Don't Lose Your Convictions, and Don't Lose Your Guts

Have a plan, and do not let anyone talk you out of the plan. "This is the way we are going to attack the season. These are our goals for the season. This is the way we are going to go about achieving those goals." Do not let anyone talk you out of that. If that is what you believe in, you stay with it.

All of these points are things I have used with my staff down through the years. I made it a point to write them down.

Carry Out Your Plan Regardless of the Criticism: You May Be Wrong, But You Are the Boss

Don't forget this. You may be wrong, but you are the boss. You better believe you are right. Don't be wishy-washy if you are the boss.

If You Can't Stand The Heat, Keep Out of the Kitchen

We all have heard this before. President Truman made that quote.

Don't Listen to the Fans, or Soon You Will Be Sitting With Them

Isn't this the truth? Don't listen to the fans. However, I did not listen to them and I am still out of a job!

The Greatest Mistake Is Making the Same Mistake Over and Over Again

All of these points I am going over are things I wrote down when I was having a problem and I needed something to boost my morale. This next point is one that I wrote down when I was having a hard time. This is what I found out when I researched the situation.

Great leaders have had great losses and have had a hard time gaining success. We could name Churchill, Lincoln, Lombardi, Paul Brown, Nixon, Edison, and several others. They had setbacks, but they overcame them and shook them off to go on to greatness. At times, they were downright losers. It is hard for me to picture any of those men as losers. However, at one time, they were losers. Lincoln lost many elections, yet he went on to become one of the greatest presidents of the United States.

I have always liked the story I heard about Thomas Edison. He lived down in Fort Meyers, Florida. This was back before we had electricity. He was working late one night, trying to harness electricity. He worked all night long trying to get a light bulb to work. It was about 3:00 a.m. when he finally got electricity to work in a light bulb. It was the first time the light bulb had worked for him. He ran upstairs, woke his wife up at 3:00 a.m. He turned the light on upstairs in his bedroom and woke up his wife. He yelled, "Look!" She rolled over and said, "Turn that darn light out, it is 3:00 a.m." I know you do not believe that story, either.

Team Rights Supersede Individual Rights

The way kids are nowadays, this is important. Today, it is a "me" world. They want to know how many times they are going to get to carry the ball, or how many passes we are going to throw to him. The mommy and daddy are going to call and ask the same thing. They must realize the team comes first. You must sell your players on this point.

Responsibility Without Authority Will Get You Beat

This is important in coaching. If you are on my staff, and I give you a job to do, I expect you to do the job, and I will give you the authority to carry out the responsibility. If I give them a job and have to tell them how they must do the job, if I want to give them a task and tell them how to do it, then it is not giving them the authority.

When I was coaching, I hated if someone gave me a job to do, and then told me how to do it. They had a right to tell me how to do it. If you give a coach a job, give him the authority to get the job done. That is what I have done with all of my coaches. I tried to keep them out of my office.

He That Have Knowledge, Spare His Words

The person who is smart does not say much.

Even a Fool, When He Holdeth His Peace, Is Counted Wise.

If a fool does not say anything, you do not know he is a fool. Be careful how much you talk.

If Two Partners Always Agree All of the Time, It Means One of Them Is Not Necessary

I have always encouraged my coaches to speak up. If they did not agree with what I say, that is fine. I still went by the principle that I may be wrong, but I am the boss. I stayed with that point. When someone criticizes what you are doing, it makes you think, and it makes you look at what you are doing. You want to make sure you are doing things right. I never did want yes men. I want to hear their point, and then I can make the final decision on the discussion. I encouraged the assistants to say what they think, and I did not want them to be afraid to differ with the head coach. After we go outside, we all must be together on the field.

I have always believed this point: the best steel must go through the hottest fire! "We had the game won, and we blew it!" Then, when you start looking for a friend after that happens, it is tough to find people to support you. We all must go through tough times. It will make you a better coach.

A head coach is only a problem-solver. That is all you are, at the Division I level. If you cannot solve problems, where are you going to work? A person who can solve problems should make millions of dollars. Guys who can't solve problems do not get anywhere. As the head coach, or a CEO, you are a problem-solver. That is your job. That is part of the job.

Good steel must go through the hottest fire. You are going to make mistakes. You must learn from those mistakes and you will get better. You cannot prove your character unless you have been under fire. If everything goes as it should go, they cannot check your character.

If a Dog Can't Do What I Am Teaching Him, I Will Teach Him What He Can Do

This is very similar to coaching football. Let the players do what they do best and what we can teach him to do. I got this quote from a guy from

Valdosta, Georgia. That is a great football town. The man came to see me. He raised hunting dogs. He gave me the statement, and I wrote it down many years ago. That means to play the players at the right positions. If the player is not a good receiver, do not play him out wide. Put him where he can do his best. If you have a player on defense who will not hit, put him on offense. That may be where he can do his best.

When you are coaching, and you get a team that just does not have it, what are you going to do? Here is what we say you should do:

If You Get a Lemon, Make It Into Lemonade.

It Is Better to Fail in a Cause That Will Ultimately Succeed Than It Is to Succeed in a Cause That Will Ultimately Fail.

Football Is a Priority In Life, But It Is Not the Priority

This I believe in strongly. I am not sure if most coaches do believe this is true. I am not afraid to stand up here and tell you that my number-one priority is God! My number-two priority is my family. I am not going to let football get ahead of those two priorities. I think you would be wise if you did the same. If you are not careful, you will lose your family. If you are not careful, you will lose your soul. Yes, football is a big priority. When I coach, I am going to give it all I have, and I want to win as much as anyone, but, I am not going to put football ahead of those two things. Men, I think this is good advice.

When we are young, we all get wound up in winning. When I was young, I had a hard time with that point. When I got older, I became wiser. Don't let football be your God. You see all of these young coaches who "burn out." They may have their priorities out of place. Make football a priority, but not the priority.

The Number-One Quality You Want in a Coaching Staff Is Loyalty

Without loyalty, you will not be able to reach the goals you want for your program. This has been true throughout my coaching career. It is difficult to have loyalty when you cannot hire your own coaching staff. It is difficult if you do not have the authority to demand loyalty from your staff. The coaches must know they must be loyalty to the head coach and the rest of the staff.

This Too Shall Pass

There are times when your players are going to get into trouble. You walk the floor and ask what we are going to do. "This too shall pass." I can remember when I wrote this point down on my list of things to remember. It was in 1980 when several of our players got into trouble, and it posted across the country in all the newspapers. That is when I said, "This too shall pass!" Now, it is 30 years later, and I still remember this point. Keep this point in mind for your own peace of mind.

Do It Right, Do It Hard, or Do It Again

Football is a game of reps. We told the players to do it right, and to do it hard, or to go back and do it again. That was how we coached. Football is a game of reps.

Hire the best men possible, and have restraint enough to leave them alone to do their job. If they do not do their job, hire someone to take their place.

We must judge performance and not potential. I wrote that statement down back in the 1950s when I heard Ara Parsegian make that statement at a clinic. It is performance that counts, not potential. How many times have you played a person in whom you saw a lot of potential as a player and you waited and waited but the potential never came out of the person? If you have a player behind him who will fight and scrap, you are better to play him. Put performance first.

Another important point is to treat each coaching job as if it is the last coaching job you are going to have. If you want a better job, prove it. We all have seen coaches who are always looking for another job. They think the the grass is always greener somewhere else. You should take the job you have, and do the best you can possibly do. If you do that, good things are going to happen for you.

We are created equal in one regard. We can all give our very best effort. That is one aspect where we all are created equal.

That is 57 years worth of coaching experience talking. I hope I have given you something that will help you in your coaching career. Thank you for your attention.

OFFENSIVE LINE PASS SETS AND DRILLS

University of Maryland

It is a pleasure to be here. This is not the same scheme we ran when we went to the Orange Bowl. The game is constantly evolving. It is always changing. I was taught to block a long time ago—we were taught to get our fists on our breastplates and our elbows up. Today, we are aligned in four wide receivers, no huddle, spread offenses, and two-point stances.

What I am going to talk about today is our pass-protection technique we use at the University of Maryland. I am not going to talk schemes. I want to keep this meeting informal. How many big skill coaches do we have in here today? When I say big skill, I am talking about the offensive line.

Here is the deal: If you are in a team meeting and the head coach tells the skilled people to go to one side of the room and the offensive linemen to go to the other side of the room, we do not practice. The team does not move if the offensive linemen do not do their job. You are not going anywhere without the big guys up front. Learning how to block is a skill.

The offensive line is hard and hard to coach today. If you find yourself a couple of good offensive linemen, you need to nurture them along and make them feel special. I coach the big guys at the University of Maryland. I know a guy who did a bit of research on football. He did a five-year study. He figured in a normal football game there would be about 72 plays run. He broke it down further. He said there were 44 normal plays, 12 off-schedule plays, and 16 third-down plays. Off-schedule plays were plays involving a penalty—it was a team jumping offside or the play being called back for a penalty.

Of the 44 normal plays, there were 26 runs and 18 passes. I am in charge of the goal-line offense. I did the stats on our offense that year, and we had 850 snaps during the season. Of those 850 snaps, we had 25 goal-line plays. The point I am trying to make is that your practice time should be proportional to the occurrence of those types of plays in a game. The goal-line plays we ran that season were less than three percent of our offense. I spent more time practicing them than I should have.

I know the plays run in the goal-line situation are important because they lead to touchdowns, but do not get carried away with the time you spend in that situation. If it is three percent of your offense, it does not deserve more time in practice than that.

I want to talk about the game plan. "If you fail to plan, you plan to fail." In the first 10 plays of a football game, you are looking for something specific. I want to go unbalanced. I want to run the formation into the boundary as well as the open field. I am going to show a wing set or any special set I have. There are things I want to find out about the defense and how they are playing us. You do not want to run random plays. You want to set things up in a sequence so that later in the game you can use that to score. If you do not have a plan of how to set plays up, you are in trouble.

On your game plan, you need situational plays, but you also need a place for halftime adjustments. We want to list momentum-changing plays, formations to be used, best deep passes, best percentage passes, and plays to use in the no-huddle. You need a section on your game plan for the last plays of the half or game. If you have one play to end the game, what do you call? You cannot be caught short when the game is on the line. You cannot wait until the pressure of the game falls on you to think about what to call. Make a list so you have a choice. Do not be a coach that says, "I wish I would have thought of that play." Write it down on the game plan. Do not be caught short with the game plan.

The last thing we do on Thursday is run our last plays of the half or game against air. On our game plan, we have five plays. We set them up according to the position on the field. We have one play we run from the +45-yard line, +35-yard line, +25-yard line, +15-yard line, and +5-yard line. You are going against air, but if it ever happens in a game, you have practiced it.

You need a plan for short-yardage and goal-line plays. We start with the third-down situations and list the plays we want to run with one to three, three to six, and seven plus yards in the third-down situation. We make a list of red-zone formations and plays. We cover each down with those situations. On the sheet, we have two-point conversion plays. One of the most important items is the off-schedule plays. Off-schedule means you are behind in the down-and-distance count because of a penalty or a bad play. Another thing to have on your short-yardage sheet is coming out plays. That situation is being backed up and needing to get off your goal line so you can punt the ball.

The offensive line is made up of players who cannot play defense. We get the players who are not fast enough or quick enough to play on the defensive line. What we do in the off-season to develop these players is essential to the offense. You have to find ways to make your players the best athletes you have. I am going to give you a couple of things we do that will help you.

When you come to our weight room, we have a separate segment in our program for linemen drills. Every day that we lift, we do 5 to 10 minutes with linemen-related weight drills. One of the drills we do is *plate punches* (Diagram #1). We take a 45-pound plate and hold it in front of us with both hands. We get in a good two-point stance with the weight at waist level. We do the drill with the inside foot up in our stance. The lineman steps with his outside foot to the outside and punches with the weight. He is

simulating the punch in the blocking sequence of a pass block. We move him 10 yards in one direction and return. With each step he takes, he punches with the weight.

Diagram #1. Plate Punch

Punching with the 45-pound weight will get heavy after awhile, but it is a great drill. It is a very easy drill that you can do in the off-season. We also do jump rope, ladder drills, and drills that develop grip. We do not *hold*, but we have great *grip*. When we do this drill, we let them use the amount of weight that they can control. All we do is grip the edges of the weight plates. We grip the weight between the fingers and the thumb of each hand. We have them walk 10 yards gripping and regripping the weights as they walk.

We do *towel grips*. The lineman takes two towels and drapes them over a chinning bar. He grabs the towels with his hands. He pulls up in a chinning position and holds. He does not go up and down. He pulls up and holds for 15 to 20 seconds. These are some of the things you can do in the off-season.

During the season we have drills we do daily. One drill we do every day is a *four-point punch drill* (Diagram #2). We do this drill before we stretch. We do this drill twice a week during the season and every day during the pre-season. The drill is a simple drill. You start out with two players on their knees facing one another at arm's length. That puts the players' knees and toes in contact with the ground. Those are the four points we are talking about. In this drill, we emphasize the hands in a pass drop.

Diagram #2. Four-Point Punch

When we punch, we punch with the thumbs up. Every technique I talk about is the way I do it. If you do it differently and it works, continue to do it. Coaching is what you believe in and what you can teach. It is not what *we know*, it is what *they understand*. We have to teach the tackle. He has to block the monster coming off the edge in the third-and-eight situations, so he better know what he is doing.

The reason we teach with the thumbs up is because of what it does to the elbows. With the thumbs up, the elbows come in tight to the body. It allows the blocker to use the correct muscle groups in the punch. We want him to use his pecs, triceps, and lower back muscles. In run and pass protection, the block is all about who has their hands inside. It is not about who is more athletic, it is about who gets their hands inside.

In this drill, we are not teaching initially to punch. We work on bringing the hands and arms up and rolling the hips. The blocker is not pushing forward. He is lifting his hands from the ground into the defender, and, at the same time, rolling his hips. When you watch the drill, you should see the blocker's hips go forward, which gives a lifting action to the hands. It is not a push-and-shove drill. You must see the arch in the back and a drop in the tail as the hips go forward. The arch is referred to as the *reverse C*. The hands come up and are placed on the breastplate. That gives us hand placement on the target.

The hand placement leads us into the next drill. From the same position, we do a hand-combative drill. It is called *punch and reset.* When you play a bull rusher, you may have to do this several times in one blocking sequence. The first player punches into the chest of the other player. The player being punched knocks off the hands of the puncher and recovers a hand position inside on the other player. He does that by coming up from underneath the opponent's arms with his hands or knocking them down from the top. As soon as he has inside hand position on the opponent, the opponent repeats the drill by gaining inside hand position. This drill teaches

the blockers how to reset their hands if the defender gets his hands inside on the blocker.

The coaching point is to watch the hips each time the player resets his hands. He should work the hip roll each time he resets the hands. Make sure the hands come from the sides up and do not go behind the hips before he shoots them up. If he tries to load his hands back first, the defender will be into his body.

The next thing we do is called a *wall-sit drill* (Diagram #3). We do this drill in pre-season. Have your linemen put their backs against a wall and assume a sitting position with their backs against the wall. Get their hands up in a ready position. The angle in the knees should be a 45-degree angle. They sit in that position and simulate the punch. We hold them in that position for 15 to 20 seconds.

Wall

Diagram #3. Wall-Sit Drill

After we sit on the wall and simulate the punch, we match up with a defender. With the player sitting on the wall, we work the punch into the defender. In this drill, we also teach the shoulder punch. If you are playing guard, you will get the double-hand punch into the chest of a pass rusher. However, the tackle will not get a pass rusher down the middle too many times. The defensive end turns his shoulder and does not present a square surface for the offensive tackle to place his hands. He has to learn a different hand placement.

He is placing one hand over the other on the shoulder of the pass rusher in his punch. The defender charges outside and not into the blocker. The blocker does not have a surface to place both hands. He has to readjust his hands to hit the surface he is facing. If the defensive end tries to bull rush and run over the tackle, he can get his hands into the chest.

The coaching point in the punch is the timing of the punch and the angle of the arms. We want contact made with the hands, with the arms at a 45-degree angle. After the initial contact, the blocker extends his arms to a lockout position.

The defender leans into the blocker. He is square sometimes and leans in with his shoulder at other times. The blocker hits the target, whether it is the chest or the shoulder. He hits the chest with both hands and the shoulder with one hand over the other.

The next drill we do is an active *hand-target drill* (Diagram #4). One partner holds a hand shield on the wall. The blocker gets into his football position as if he were going to pass block. We have a number of commands for this drill. We are targeting the dummy at different positions. If we give them a high-right-to-low-left command, the blocker punches the dummy on the high right with both hands and proceeds to the low left with two hands. He hits the target as rapidly as he can but must maintain good balance and form.

Diagram #4. Hand-Target Drill

We can tell him to go around the clock. That means he punches the dummy on the outside rim going in a clockwise direction. We want rapid hand movement. We use a machine gun technique while doing this drill. We alternate punches with both hands punching one hand at a time. He is punching with the right hand and then the left. We go as fast with the hands as we can.

In pre-practice, we have a *step drill* (Diagram #5). We line up an offensive line facing the coach. Behind them is another offensive line. I stand in front of them and tell them what type of block they are to execute. They take their first three steps in the execution of that block. Everyone goes at once. We work on the steps to the reach, down, base,

fold, or whatever block you want. This is a footwork drill in which we teach blocking. I stand in front and give them direction and plays. They go through their first three steps that fit that play. I am looking for a perfect stance, perfect start, and a three-step movement versus air.

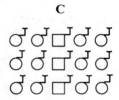

Diagram #5. Step Drill

I may call *inside set* or *outside set* and give them a cadence to get off. I could call G, T, pull and the guard and tackles go through the first three steps of their pull technique. You get massive reps in a short period of time.

I believe your linemen should align in a right-handed stance on the right side of the ball and a left-handed stance to the left side of the ball. That type of stance gives the offensive blocker a hard shoulder to the inside and allows him to step with his outside foot to the outside. If you put your players in a right-handed stance to the left side of the ball, their outside foot is up in their stance. That means for them to get into a pass set position, they have to reverse their feet on the first step. If you are a passing team, you have to put those players on the left side of the ball in a left-handed stance.

The next problem is what type of stance you use on a third-and-ten situation. Do you use a three-point, four-point, or two-point stance? Do not put your lineman in a disadvantaged position when you throw the ball. Put your left tackle in a two-point stance so he has a chance to block the speed rusher coming off the edge. Everyone in the stadium knows you are going to throw the ball, so put your player in a position to execute the block. I have no problem with the lineman looking straight at his blocking assignment in that situation.

If the offensive lineman blocks inside, he "posfsteps" with his inside foot. He moves the inside foot first and stomps to the inside. In all movements inside, he keeps his shoulders square. The outside foot is back, and he slides it as he gets inside movement. If he is on the left side of the ball in a left-handed stance, his inside foot is up and his outside foot is back. That is the way he is going to move his feet as he blocks inside. The reason we move with a sense of urgency going inside is because the ball is inside and we have to protect inside gaps first. We must have the hard shoulder and a postfoot to the inside.

It is the opposite when moving outside. There is less urgency because the ball is inside and the defenders are moving outside. We can take longer to get to the block. Having the outside foot back allows you to get depth and width in your pass drops. That foot position is what you need moving in that direction.

We do a *cone drill* to teach both movements to the linemen (Diagram #6). We use nine cones. We place the cones three yards apart on a yard line. We place three more cones at the same distance five yards down the field. The third set of cones is between the yard lines. We align the right side players to the outside of the first cone on the right and the left side players to the outside of the cone on the left side.

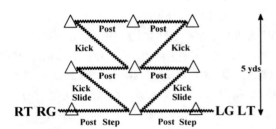

Diagram #6. Cone Drill

On the command, the player on the right and the player on the left use a poststep to get to the cone to their inside. Once they reach the cone, they kick-slide to the outside cone in the second line. When he reaches that cone, he poststeps to the second cone on the inside and repeats the drill through the third cone.

The coaching point on the kick-slide is to never allow the inside leg to get straight. It must always

be bent. If the blocker straightens the inside leg to get off the line of scrimmage fast, he can never regroup if the defender goes to the inside. It is all about balancing the weight. If he straightens the inside leg, he puts all his weight to the outside and is off balance. He cannot change the momentum to get back inside. On each step the blockers take, they simulate the punch.

The next thing to be concerned about is the body position of the blocker. We want the head back and the back arched. I want to tuck the chin to the neck with the elbows tucked tightly against the sides. The hands are moving and active. I do not want the hands up or down. I want them in the chest area and actively moving. We do not want the shoulders forward or leaning to the front because that is a balance problem, and it makes them susceptible to the swim technique and other moves.

We use a shuffle drill to teach proper footwork. The secret to the shuffle movement is the distance the feet are apart. We do not want the feet too wide or too narrow. If you are too wide, you have to lean to the outside to shift your weight. The most important asset of an offensive lineman is balance. If the feet are too narrow, you have no base. In either case, you are off balance. The feet have to stay under the shoulders to maintain balance. I never want my offensive linemen to do bag drills where they step over them or jump over them. That is not what we do on the offensive line. We do not jump in the execution of a block.

When we teach the shuffle drill, we call it a *mirror drill* (Diagram #7). I set up two cones and align two players facing each other in the middle of the cones. The cones are five yards apart. When I do the drill, I do it with a cast of four people. I want two doing the drill and two watching. I do not want them going in the drill back to back. If they do, you get a bad effort on the second set. I want quick movement. When I start the drill, I have the offensive blocker get in good body position and put his hands behind his back.

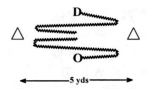

Diagram #7. Mirror Drill

The defender shuffles back and forth and the offensive blocker mirrors his movement. He wants to stay in front of him and square. The offensive blocker focuses his eyes at the base of the defender's inside number. You teach blocking with your eyes. The blocker has to ignore the head and shoulder movement and concentrate on the inside number.

We expand the drill and let the offensive blocker start with his hand on the defender. The problem the blocker has is the position of his body. He has his hands on the defender, but his body may not be in front of him. You cannot stop a pass rusher with your hands outside the framework of the body.

After we have done the hands on the defender, we let the defender spin as he moves. We want the offensive lineman to keep his hands on the defender as he spins. He moves his hands from the chest to the back as the defender spins. He cannot lose contact with the defender. He moves his hands with the rotation but keeps contact with the defender.

The next drill is a form of the *mirror-shuffle drill* (Diagram #8). The cones on the line are three yards apart. We set a cone three yards ahead of the line. That is where the offensive blocker starts. The defender is head-up the blocker. On movement, the defender tries to get across the line between the two cones. He uses any pattern of attack he wants. He can fake or run to either side of the blocker. He cannot run through the blocker. The blocker has to use his hands and feet to keep him from crossing the line.

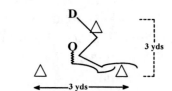

Diagram #8. Shuffle Drill

You can do a simple drill and work your entire group of linemen together. You align them on a cone five yards off the sideline. They poststep to the sideline and kick-slide back to the cone.

Another 1-on-1 drill is the mirror drill done as a *retreat drill* (Diagram #9). The linemen start out with their hands behind their backs and progress from there. In this drill, we have an inside and an outside. The two players line up facing each other. They are one yard apart. We use a cone to designate the ballside of the blocker. On the command, the defender moves inside or outside. If he moves inside, the blocker uses the poststep to get inside. If the defender goes outside, he uses a kick-slide step. The defender moves right and left and tries to get around the blocker. It is the mirror drill, except the blocker is retreating as he works on his footwork.

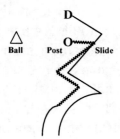

Diagram #9. Retreat Drill

To block a defender, the blocker has to get out of his stance and get into the defender. He has to use footwork to do that. We teach three steps to contact. To get out of the stance, we teach an inside step, half step, and outside step. The method of step depends on the alignment of the defender. The offensive guard's rule is to outside step when the guard's outside foot is in the crotch of the defender. We want to cover the defender up.

If the defender aligns with his inside eye on the outside shoulder of the guard, we are in good position to protect the inside gap. However, if the defender makes a hard outside move, we do not have much surface on the defender. Therefore, we do not take an inside step because that opens the outside even more. We take an outside step.

If the defender aligns head-up the blocker, the blocker's step cannot be the same as on the outside shoulder. As the blocker sets up, he must take an inside step to shut off the inside. If the defender gets on the inside eye of the blocker, he has to accelerate his poststep and get inside quickly. In those three examples, the offensive blocker has to take three different sets to be in sound protection position.

The tackle's set is a different set of problems. He has an angle rusher coming from a distance outside. There is space as well as angles involved.

To drill these techniques, we align the linemen in a three-point stance. We try to work with four or five linemen at once. On the first sound, they break their stance and get into a set position. On the second sound, they take their inside poststep.

We drill the set and reinforce the point of getting the hands up quickly. We take a defender with a shield or dummy. He stands to the right or left of the offensive blocker. The blocker gets into his stance. On the command, the offensive lineman breaks his stance into a set position. The defender, on the command, swings the dummy and tries to hit the blocker in the face. These guys are not wearing helmets. They have to get their hands up and punch the dummy. Obviously, the defender is not trying to hurt the blocker, but he is swinging the dummy on the movement of the lineman.

After we work on the set individually, we put them into a group and do the same thing. I give them a formation set or an *outside* set (Diagram #10). I place a cone in front of them to indicate the alignment of the defender. I want them to have an idea of what type of set they need to take. We use the outside set versus a tight alignment on the outside of a lineman. The guard uses an outside set when he has a tight 3 technique aligned on him. The thing we are watching is the balance the linemen have. We do not want them to lean to get outside. They have to be balanced at all times with their feet under them.

Diagram #10. Outside Set

If the guard has a wide 3 technique aligned on him, he has to kick out to get into a pass set on him. He cannot simply pick up his foot and put it down. He has to kick outside to get into position to execute the pass block. If the defender keeps jumping into the gap and making it hard on the guard, there is a remedy for that. We tell the tackle to get foot to foot with the guard. If there is a defender in the gap, there is no gap. Close off the area and you do not have a gap.

I move the cone to a head-up position on the lineman, and they take their set steps on commands (Diagram #11). With a man head-up, their step is inside to protect against the inside move by the defender.

Diagram #11. Inside Set

Finally, I move the cone inside of them and make them make the fast, hard inside post (Diagram #12). They must get inside and take the leverage away from the 2i or 1 technique.

Diagram #12. Inside Speed Set

The center with a 0 technique has a unique problem. He has to snap the ball with one hand. That means he has one hand to get on the defender at the beginning. He cannot rely on the guards to help him. He must single block, but he may get some help. If he is a right-handed center and the nose goes to his right hand or shades that way, he uses his left hand as he snaps the ball. He crosses over with his left hand and gets it on the inside shoulder pad of the nose. After he snaps the ball, his right hand comes outside to the nose player's chest.

It is easier for a right-handed center to handle a defender on his left shoulder or moving that way. His free hand is to the left, and he can get it up immediately to make contact with the nose. Going the other way, he is defenseless for a time with his hand between his legs snapping the ball. That is why he has to use his left hand as the immediate hand.

If we face a team that runs many twists in their scheme, you have to learn to vertical set with the tackle (Diagram #13). If you tell the tackle to kick-slide for width and depth against teams that use the T.E. (tackle-end twist) stunt, you are asking for trouble. The defensive end starts upfield, and, on his third step, he breaks hard to the inside over the guard. The defensive tackle takes a hard charge into the B gap. They are hoping to free up the defensive end coming inside.

Diagram #13. T.E. Stunt

The problem in the stunt is the defensive tackle in the gap. If the offensive tackle takes a kick-slide step for width, he cannot stop the tackle coming to the outside. He can make the block, but it is hard. He has to work for an inside position. The guard is in position to take the end coming around inside, but the tackle has no leverage on the defender in the gap.

The solution is the vertical set. This is an ideal set if you have strong offensive tackles. The problem in the vertical set is the bull rusher that can overpower the offensive tackle. The offensive tackle has to have the width in the pocket to have some give room before he is in the quarterback's lap. If you have a strong offensive tackle that can hold off the bull rush, use this technique. Instead of taking three kick-slide steps to the outside, he takes one kick-slide and goes straight back. He gets depth instead of width. He has restricted the size of the pocket, and he cannot be forced into the quarterback by a bull rusher.

The guard can help the tackle on this stunt. When he sees the defender go outside, as he release him, he shoves him as hard as he can to get

him wider in his charge. He wants to launch him onto the block of the tackle. By shoving the tackle, he changes the direction of the charge and knocks him off balance.

The way we teach the *vertical set* is to align the tackles on a sideline or yard line (Diagram #14). The offensive tackle takes one kick-step across the line. The blocker kick-steps with his right foot, and his left foot should hit on the line. He drops straight back from that point. The tackle kick-steps over the line, and he backs up on the line. That gets him going straight back instead of at an angle.

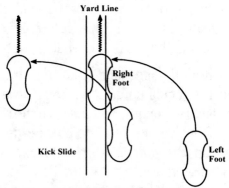

Diagram #14. Vertical Set

As the tackle vertical sets, he checks the shoulder of the defensive end. If the shoulders turn inside to the tackle, he goes and gets the defender. He wants to meet the force of the rusher with force of his own.

In the five-step passing game, the tackle takes three kick-slides to get his width and depth. The reason he needs to know the depth of the drop is his shoulder turn. He cannot turn his shoulder to the defender until the quarterback has the ability to step up. If the tackle turns his shoulders and the quarterback is still dropping, we will have a sack.

If the drop is a three-step drop, the tackle takes on the defender immediately. He uses a jump step and goes at the defender. He wants to attack the defender. If the guard has a 3 technique aligned on him, he steps with the outside foot and aims at the inside shoulder. If the 3 technique spikes inside, we have him. If the defender is head-up the guard, he steps with his inside foot because that is where the target is. He is still aiming at the inside shoulder. I do not like linemen throwing and chopping defenders on the three-step game. If anything happens, my lineman is on the ground and cannot help anyone.

If the tackle uses the jump set, he kicks out one step and goes after the defender. The tackle can change up his sets. He needs to give the defender a different look from time to time. He can vertical set, jump set, or kick slide.

In the dropback passing game, the tackle has to know where the quarterback is setting up. If we have a five-step drop and the blocker is inside, he has a yard in depth to play with. If it is a seven-step drop, we have a yard and a half.

When we teach the punch, we start off on the knees. We work against the shield first. We progress from the knees to the stance and punch. We get into a stance, break the stance, and punch. The lineman breaks his stance with his hands up and ready to strike. When the bag moves toward the lineman, he punches it.

The *two-man punch* is a good drill (Diagram #15). In this drill, we have two bag holders. The lineman is in the middle of the dummies. He poststeps to the inside and punches the inside dummy. After he hits the inside dummy, he kick slides outside and hits the second dummy. He repeats the drill and retreats for five yards. He is doing the cone drill, except he is punching along with the footwork. He is zigzagging and punching.

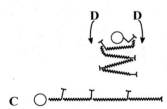

Diagram #15. Two-Man Punch Drill

We also do a *three-man punch drill* (Diagram #16). We align three defenders with bags in a line facing the blocker. The blocker sets and punches the first bag holder. The bag holder drops to the side, and the second bag holder attacks the blocker. He punches him and gets ready for the attack of the third bag holder. The bag holders are about three yards apart.

Diagram #16. Three-Man Punch Drill

The next thing we do is *punch down* the line (Diagram #17). We line up five bag holders. The blocker starts down the line using a poststep. As he reaches the bag holder, the bag holder will extend the bag and the lineman will punch it. I stand to the side and watch the technique. I find the linemen lose their technique toward the last bag holder. They start to reach back to punch, lose their posture, or start to unbend their knees.

Diagram #17. Punch Down the Line

After I do that, I stand behind the linemen and point to the bag holders. If I point to a bag holder, he does not offer the bag to be hit. That keeps the linemen from getting in a rhythm and punching without seeing. If they punch at a bag that does not come toward them, they tip forward and are off balance.

Every player is different with their punch. We do not want to punch from too far or too close. If our arms are extended before we reach the defender, we have no power. If the defender gets in too close on the lineman, the punch is ineffective. You have to be a coach and fit the punch to the player. You cannot have your players lunging at the defenders. The defenders will simply use a swim technique and be on the other side.

You must have a counter for the push/pull moves. We work on it constantly. We put the defender in a fit position. He grabs the outside shoulder and pulls down on the jersey. The blocker counters that move by punching with the hand to the side of the pull and moving his feet in that direction. We lock out the shoulder and skate in that direction. This is a violent movement drill, and I want to hear T-shirts ripping. That will defeat the pull on the shoulder.

We also do a *push/pull drill*. I have two players lock up in a fitted position. We do it without helmets. The defender puts one hand over the shoulder of the blocker and one on his opposite side. He grabs cloth so he can attempt to move him. The offensive blocker has his hands behind his back. I stand behind the offensive man. I give the defenders directions. I either point away, which means he pulls on the lineman in that direction. If I give him a motion toward me, he pushes him back to me. The defender tries to pull the offensive lineman or push him. This teaches body lean and balance. If I point to one side or the other, they attempt to pull the lineman in the direction I point.

To counter the bull rush, you must replace the hands one at a time. If the rusher gets his hands inside, the blocker replaces one hand by using a windmill motion to take his hand from the outside to the inside on the rusher's chest. It is the same drill as the hand-replacement drill I showed you earlier. He comes up and under the arm of the rusher in a windmill motion. He does that with both hands and recaptures his inside hand position. Once he gets his hands inside, he hops back with both feet and gets another bite on the rusher. Getting another bite means he lowers his hips regrips with his hands, and stabilizes his base.

To counter the swim move, you start out like the counter to the shoulder pull. When the defender grabs the shoulder of the offensive blocker, the blocker punches into the shoulder of the defender to the side of the grab. He works his feet to that side. When the defender brings his arm over for the swim, the blocker uses his inside hand and punches the defender under the arm and drives him.

The counter for the rip starts out as the same technique for the swim and shoulder pull. The defender grabs the shoulder of the blocker. The blocker counters with his hand and punches the shoulder area of the defender to the side of the grab. When the defender sets the rip, the defender uses his inside hand and pushes hard on the inside hip of the defender.

When I teach these counters, I fit two players in position. They both are locked up with their hands on the other player's chest. I stand behind the offense and tell the defender what move to use. The defender uses the move and the lineman counters it.

In 1981, I was at William and Mary College. I never made a home visit where there was not a mom or dad in that household. I went to Maryland in 2001. When I made some home visits, it was hard to tell who was living in the house. The role of coaches has grown more and more. To many of these players, you are the only male figure in their lives. There is no one else. That is the responsibility we take on when we decide to coach.

You have to be available on the good days and the bad days. My hat is off to you because you do not get paid for the hours you put into the business. You are in the trenches and hall doing what you do. Take care of your players. They need you. If I can ever help you, please call. Thank you very much. I appreciate it.

INSIDE TEXAS LONGHORNS FOOTBALL

University of Texas

It is a pleasure to be here representing the University of Texas. I have been lucky in life. I have been a college football coach for 37 years. I only coached a year or two in high school. I have been a head coach for 26 of those years. Not all of my experiences in those 37 years have been good, as you can imagine.

In 2005, we were going to play the University of Southern California in the national championship game. It was interesting because I was playing for a national championship as a head coach. Life is grand and funny. What do you do and how do you handle that situation? Southern California was good. Pete Carroll was a great coach, and we were playing in Los Angeles at the Rose Bowl.

You would think if you win all your games, you would be happy. In 2005, we won 13 football games and ended up in the Rose Bowl playing for the national championship. I did not think a little boy from Cookeville, Tennessee would ever make it to the Rose Bowl.

Last year when we played Alabama, I do not think we handled the loss of Colt McCoy very well when he got hurt. Things were going well and we had gotten a couple of turnovers. When Colt got hurt, he ran to the sideline with his arm dangling at his side.

Now that I have my preaching out of the way, let me talk about the topic. I am going to show you what we do in our program.

LEADERSHIP

Alarming Statistics

- Six thousand teenagers become alcoholics every day.
- Three million teens are problem drinkers.
- Thirteen teenagers commit suicide every day.
- One million teens attempt suicide every year.

What you do as a coach can help these numbers. Coaches have to know their players and parents. It amazes me when I go into schools and ask coaches what the players' parents do for a living and they do not know. The players are at home more than they are with you. You need to know what they are doing and where they are when they go home. The coach has to be influential in the players' lives.

If you are not doing that, you are probably not winning and not helping the players on your team to a point that you are not doing your job. At the end of the day, it is not going to be about the number of games you won. There are two of our former players here today. I love the fact that players we coached stay in touch and we know what they are doing. We had 35 NFL players that have played for us in the last 12 years with us at the Rose Bowl. That tells me our coaches are doing a good job with our players because they want to come back.

After practice, the coaching staff only watches half of the practice films because I want them home to have dinner with their families. We start early in the morning. We start at seven in the morning. You cannot tell me that coaching is so hard that you have to start at seven in the morning and stay there all day until 12:00 that night.

We went to the Middle East last year and spent eight days. If you ever get a chance to see what your military is like or how our soldiers are fighting, it can be life changing.

Middle East Tour

- The purpose of the trip was to show gratitude to our troops.

- It was reinforced that teamwork, passion, work ethic, and family make it all work.
- Everyone must buy into a common purpose.
- You need people who trust each other and want to be there. I think those are key reasons we've been a consistent winner at Texas.

The purpose of the trip was for us to say thank you, but I got a lot more out of it than I gave. The general told us he believes in the same things we believe in. He believes in discipline, teamwork, integrity, toughness, and winning. He believes in getting a hold of land. He told us there is one difference in what we do as coaches and what he does as an Army commander—every day that our guys leave, they have a chance to die.

I asked if it would be dangerous for me, and they told me it would be no more dangerous for me than driving to work in Austin. I got to the base north of Baghdad and was outfitted with an armored vest and helmet. There have been days going to work in Austin when I thought I might get shot, but I never wore armor to work. They told me that about every seven days there are incoming missiles.

It was 113 degrees there and the sand was blowing. We went in to eat and I met a cute little girl with a machine gun in one hand and a pistol in the other. She laid the machine gun down and said, "Hey Coach, give me a hug." That is a different world than we are used to. We can coach and come to these clinics because those kids are fighting for us every day. If you are a coach who prays, before you go to bed at night, say thank you to our soldiers.

When I go through airports today and pass one of our soldiers, I never miss the chance to stop and say thank you. Every morning they get up, they could be living their last day. Think about that for a moment, and then think about their wives and children at home.

When we talked about teamwork and passion, we asked one of the officers what happened if one of his guys in his group was not ready to play. He said they do not play. He said that leaders in the military cannot have bad days. I asked about drugs. He told me they do not have that going on. He said they could not afford to have someone next to them on drugs because they will die if that happens. They must have trust, belief, and a common purpose.

Developing Leaders

- Do we recruit leadership, hope it happens, or do we teach it?
- How do we prepare our youth for the tough road ahead?
- We teach leadership and grow leaders.
- We have a responsibility to grow leaders on our team, in our school, and in our community.

The other thing the general said was that the worst guy on your team may be your best leader. He will ruin your football team if you let him go unchecked. You need to get the player with the worst attitude on your team in your office and try to flip him to your way of thinking. Even if he is not on your team, he may be affecting your team and your players. Saddam Hussein was a great leader in a bad way. Think about your leaders and develop them.

You have to prepare your youth for the tough road ahead. If you are good, you will have three or four close games that you must win in the fourth quarter. If you are bad, you will have to fight every week.

Never hand the ball to a player who cannot make a play. Every time one of your players touches the ball, he should have a chance to score. If he does not, you should not hand him the ball. However, if he is the principal's son, put him at fullback and give the ball to him twice in a season. Do not throw the ball to a player who cannot catch it. If the quarterback and receivers cannot throw and catch against air, it will be hard when there is a defense. That is a simple concept, but that is the way it works. Always think about what kind of talent you have on your team, and do not ask them to do things they cannot.

This is one thing I make our players keep in their pockets. It is the creed of Texas football:

Leadership is not an option; it is essential. It is essential for motivation and direction. It is essential for evaluation and accomplishment.

It is the one ingredient essential for the success of any program on any level; from sandlot to the NFL. Take away leadership and it isn't long before confusion replaces vision.

One of the reasons we win is that we have great depth. We do not have as many great players as everyone thinks we do. We have a lot of good players who want to play. We change the depth chart every day.

Different Ways to Lead

- *Leadership is the art of getting someone else to do something you want done because he wants to do it. —Dwight D. Eisenhower*
- *The ultimate measure of a man is not where he stands in moments of comfort and convenience, but where he stands at times of challenge and controversy. —Dr. Martin Luther King Jr.*
- *Pressure is something you feel only when you don't know what you are doing. —Chuck Noll*
- *There is no such thing as failure. There is only giving up too soon. —Jonas Salk*

When your team is doing everything right, they do not need you. They need you when you lose someone on your team to a serious injury. They need you at halftime when you have given up 24 points like we did in the championship game. When you are in trouble, the team is looking at you to see what your body language is like and to see if you think you have a chance to win. Body language is so important. You must have a swagger when you walk into the locker room at halftime. If your defense does not get excited about sudden change because they have a chance to stop the opponent, you probably will not stop them.

If your offense does not have a goal to score 45 points, you will not do it. If you get mad and act like a fool every time something happens, the players are going to ignore you. I do not like to be cussed at, grabbed, or demeaned; so why would we think a player would like that? We are not going to do that to our players. We are going to talk to them. I will hold them by the arm, pull them over to me, and tell them that what they did is not going to work. After

that, I send them to the bench until they grow up and start playing harder. I am not going to embarrass them in front of their teammates or on national television.

I am always amazed at coaches who scream, shout, and embarrass a player that is doing poorly. They can make him quit football or, at the very least, perform worse. I used to tell our coaches they should treat their players as if they were their children. But, you cannot do that because your children are different. So, what we tell them now is to treat their players how they would want their children to be treated. How many of you who use this kind of behavior would like your child to be treated like that? You cannot motivate through fear. If they are not playing hard, we put them on the bench.

I had a leadership program this summer. The guy that conducted it was Jon Gordon. He addressed the team because we try to teach leadership to them.

Jon Gordon Leadership Training Notes

- Choose faith over fear
- Focus on the get to versus have to
- Too blessed to be stressed
- Invite the other guys on the bus
- Empower the passengers on your bus
- As a leader, take time to communicate
- Love your passengers
- Drive with purpose

When you choose faith over fear, it means to believe in something rather than fear it. We want to focus on the *get* to rather than the *have* to. We work on that point in spring practice. You want your team to be excited about what you are doing. Make it fun and competitive. Every time we have a drill in the fall or in the spring, we have a winner and a loser. It can be the simplest thing. It could be pickup basketball or a tug-of-war, but, whatever it is, there is a winner and a loser. Your players need to compete in those games. When they know someone is keeping score and they have to win, it carries over to the team.

We want to empower the passengers on the bus. I talked to Roy Williams, the head basketball coach at the University of North Carolina, this past year after he won the national championship. He had a bunch of good players. I asked him how he got his players to play together. They lost their first two conference games of the year and then won the rest of them. He told me he empowered the seniors within the team. He said they took things that they felt were unimportant and asked the seniors for advice on them—things like what color shoes they should wear.

At Texas, we had been worried about our defensive end Sergio Kindle's leadership during the summer. He came in before we played the University of Oklahoma and asked if the team could put something on our bodies about swagger. I want us to walk in that stadium with swagger. We want Oklahoma and everyone in that stadium to know that we are going to win the game. I came up with dog tags with "Texas Swagger" on them. You would have thought we had given them a Rolls Royce. It was unbelievable, but it was their idea, and it came from within the team. They had the power to choose.

One Sunday morning, a player called and asked if the team could do something for breast cancer awareness week. Our university does not typically get involved with charities, but I called the athletic director and the president to see if we could do something. I said the team wanted to do something, and they agreed to let us. We put pink ribbons on our headgear. We did not let them go crazy, but we did something simple. The point is that the players had input into what we did as a team. Figure out how to let your seniors and your best players have input into your team. You have to love the other passengers on the bus and drive with a purpose. We call our bus the "energy bus."

How does your staff get along? I have always been told if your staff fights among themselves, you will have problems on your team. If you and your wife fight, you will have problems with your children. They do not have to see it or hear it; they just know it is there.

As a head coach, we are unfair if we do not tell a coach what we want. Be direct with your staff. Be direct in your meetings, and when you walk out of them, give it up. I do not stay mad. We do not have fights in the meetings. We have discussions and then we have decisions.

HOW WE BECOME WINNERS: STAFFING WITH SHARED VALUES—"WHO EARNED THE RIGHT"

Coaching Staff

Our coaches must do the following things:

- Be passionate about coaching and winning
- Believe in themselves
- Be positive role models
- Have discipline, pride, and unselfish attitudes
- Contribute to the good of the team and staff morale
- Have a high level of energy
- Have extensive knowledge of their jobs

On your coaching staff, you want coaches who are passionate about coaching and winning. If they do not like football, they ought to quit. This is a hard job. I get paid too much, and you do not get paid enough. Regardless of the salary, it is a hard job. Coaches have to be positive role models. It is hard to get mad at one of your players who drinks too much if you do the same thing. If you are arrested for a DUI, what kind of message does that send to your team?

After we lost our starting quarterback in the Rose Bowl, it would be easy to walk around and say we would have won if he had not been hurt. That is an excuse. We should have prepared to take the pressure off the younger quarterback when he came in. We were not prepared, and we will learn from that.

It is amazing to me sometimes the way coaches challenge their players to play with energy but are lazy themselves. They run the same drills all the time because they have not researched enough to change. It is easy to get into trouble running the same drills. You have to change up what you do in practice. The kids today are using some form of electronics seven hours a day. They are faster than we were. They are not smarter, but they have more information available to them. You have to continue to challenge them and not give them the same old drill every day.

Players (Recruits)

Our players and recruits should do the following things:

- Smile (Do you like him?)
- Be confident and happy
- Be smart (3.0+ GPA)
- Have good family values
- Have ability
- Come from a winning team; be well coached; be a winner
- Exhibit leadership skills
- Be tough and competitive
- Be passionate

We want our players to *smile*. If they are not smiling, they are sending a message to you that something is wrong. I told my coaches to smile in the hallway and smile on the field. If they cannot do that, I will fire them. It is amazing how many of them start smiling. We try to sign players who are 3.0 or better in the classroom. That means they are in at night, going to bed, and doing their work. We have been successful 97 percent of the time with players who are 3.0 or better in their core classes. They take pride in what they are doing.

They need family values and they need to know the difference between right and wrong. We want our recruits to come from winning teams. The players we have taken from losing teams come in, will not participate, and do not care about winning because they are not used to it. It is amazing how players from winning teams want to win. They know how to win and what they have come to you for. We want to know if the recruit is a leader on his team, in his school, and in his community. They all have to be tough and competitive. If he is not competitive, he will lay down on you. That is why

you compete in everything you do so you can figure who will compete for you. They must be passionate like you are. They have to love the game.

I asked Pat Dye from Auburn University why most coaches get fired. He told me, "Most coaches bank on potential. Potential means the player has not done it. The player we want is the one who is doing it on the field. You can work with the one with potential, and he may come around, but do not get fired over potential."

No matter what comes up, it is the job of the head football coach to stay away from excuses and find a way to win. That is your job as the leader of your coaches and team. As coaches, we can talk about football, but what you see on the video is what you are teaching. If you cannot tell me something and show me on video that your players are doing it, it is a reflection on you. When my team does not play hard, that is me not playing hard.

It all comes down to the fact that players win games and coaches lose them because you are responsibility for them. If you blame a player for a loss, you are the reason because you coached him. When he plays good, you have helped, but pat him on the head and give him the credit.

Who earned the right? is an important concept to your program. For a player to play at Texas, he has to earn the right. If he does not earn the right, we do not play him. If you do, it sends a message to the rest of the team that you are letting a player play who does not hustle. That is why we go through the depth chart every day. We make a decision every day about who moves up and who moves down on the depth chart. We base it on production. No player is assured of his job the next day.

We build a foundation for our team with a *family atmosphere*. There is a 60-percent divorce rate in our country today. A number of our players do not have a stable family life. Our team becomes their family. We are going to be direct and positive with the players. If someone has a problem, we are all going to pull around him and help him.

Communication

It is the province of knowledge to speak and it is the privilege of wisdom to listen.
—Oliver Wendell Holmes

- Listen. Truly get to know your kids and staff.
- Make a decision you feel is right based on the feedback and input from assistants.
- Clearly state what is important.
- Make sure all parties understand the defined description and task at hand.
  - ✓ Ask kids to repeat instructions.
  - ✓ Understand that there is a difference between what you said, what you think you said, and what they've heard you say.

Believe nothing of what you hear and only half of what you see.

Part of the success in building the family atmosphere is to have *communication*. If your players will not talk to you, you have no chance. What I am talking about now is something I did not understand early in my career. If your players will come in and tell you one of their teammates is smoking dope, you have a chance. If your players will come in and tell you they are worn out, you have a chance. If they will not talk to you and are running around scared of you, you will never get them.

Trust and Respect

The mark of a man is how he treats people that can never do anything for him.
—Darrell Royal

- Janitors, trainers, managers, and walk-ons are as important to our family and team goals as our stars (our bench's attitude has won a bunch of games).
- You completely control your integrity, your honesty, and your attitude. Always do what you know to be right.
- Always treat people the way you want your family to be treated.
- If you can't say something positive about someone, don't say anything.

- Embrace cultural diversity (socioeconomic, race, and education).

If you cannot get your players to communicate with you, you cannot build trust and respect. Trust is so important to any football team. If your players will not talk to you, they will never trust you. A player who does not respect himself, his teammates, his coaches, his parents, or his family name will not make it. That means he will not respect his opponents.

In trying to build trust and respect, I have told my team what I have done in my life. We now ask them to stand up and do the same. Coach Dick Tomey came into our meeting and told me we should do that with the team. I thought it sounded like kum ba yah around the campfire. I thought it was the dumbest thing I had ever heard in my life. We had the players stand up and talk about the things in their lives. It was amazing what these players told. They told who they were, what they were, and what they faced at home. The respect from one player to another was unbelievable. It was simply amazing, and we now do it with the incoming freshmen.

Once a year, we take a team we are playing against and make it a *dedication game*. Each player on the team picks someone who is important in his life and dedicates the game to that person. Each player picks a person and has to call that person and tell them they are dedicating the game to them that week. If you want to talk about a team playing their tails off, it is in the dedication game. We have never lost a dedication game.

The MACK 8 committee is a committee made up of the staff. It includes the strength coach, trainer, and anyone outside our coaches. They talk to the players and come back to me with any concerns.

The *no depth chart or starting lineup* is another aspect of our program. It is better if you have 17 starters on defense. Every mom and dad wants their son to be a starter. We have 17 starters on defense; however, we do not send them all out to start the game. Do not make them mad by telling them they are a second teamer. Make them all feel good about themselves if they have earned to right to play.

Common Purpose

- During the week of the Rose Bowl, I asked each member of the team to find something he could do to help us win. It is what it is.
- Coach Royal told our guys, "To be a team, you must play as *one heartbeat*."
- We are in the *education business* during the week and *show business* on the weekends, where our goal is not only to win, but also to produce revenue for our athletic department.

This last point is easy to say and hard to do. It is like the military. You must have a common purpose. A common purpose is to win all the games, let the players have a great experience, and let them move on in their lives. It is not trying to get you another job or promoting a particular player; it is trying to win every game.

The power of one is the chain. The chain is only as strong as the weakest link. When we play good together and with passion, we usually win. At Texas, we are good enough to win all the games. When we lose, it is generally because of what we did instead of what the other team did.

Practice Winning Every Day

As coaches and as parents, we can only teach our kids that life is a series of options, just like football. If you make good decisions, you are likely to succeed. Once a decision has been made, do not look back. It is our job to make the decision work. Do not second guess.

We put a lot of these slogans up around our building. The players have to practice winning every day. If they do not practice at game speed in practice, they are not helping themselves. If you have a different tempo in practice than you do in games, you cannot turn the switch on and off. That is particularly true when things go bad. You must prepare for the bad days.

We do things weekly to motivate our players. When we played Baylor, we put little bears on every locker. We told them if they lost to Baylor,

the bear had to stay up all year. We have a theme every week. An example of the theme is: *This is the battle for Texas. Come and take it. Remember the Alamo.* We put the slogan up and tell the opponent to come and take it in our house. In 2006, our theme was *live the dream.* Our goal was to win the conference championship, and the dream was to win the national championship.

Handle Big Wins

- Don't get complacent.
- Don't eat the cheese.
- Don't sit in the shade.
- If it is not working, change it.
- To conserve game-day energy and legs, we now fly to Dallas to play Oklahoma instead of busing.
- Look complicated; be simple.
- Be known for something.

After we win a big game, we coach them extremely hard because they feel too good about themselves. In 2005, after we beat the University of Kansas 66-14, we had Texas A&M University the next week. I played for Coach Parcells at the Florida State University, and he called me the next day. He told me my players were getting ready to eat the poison cheese. He said, "The rats like that cheese and will be sick as they can be after they eat it. You better get their minds on Texas A&M and nothing else. Work them hard and get after them because they are going to feel too good about themselves after Kansas."

We put little lumps of cheese on everyone's lockers. In the first half, we did not play very well. At halftime, I told them they must have eaten the cheese because they were playing as if they were sick. Use things that are visual, and they will understand.

Complacency is a killer. We are constantly putting up messages to remind them of the message of winning. We put numbers up in our building. We have won four national championships, and they are on the wall. Find out what your school has done well, and make sure you promote it.

Promote the coaches who have been there. Make your place special so your kids will come out of the halls and onto the field. You have to differentiate your program from your opponents so the talent from the community comes to you. Make it a fun place where it is exciting and special. However, if they do play and do not feel special, they will not play hard.

We had an inspiration for this season. During last year's Super Bowl game with the Giants, I saw Lieutenant Colonel Greg Gadson on the sideline without any legs. He spoke to the Giants and was very inspirational for them. I asked our coaching staff if anyone knew anything about him. Our defensive coordinator Will Muschamp's brother played with him at West Point. I wanted him to come speak to our team. He was hit with a roadside bomb in Iraq and was a double leg amputee.

His message was simple. You do not always get to decide what circumstances you get. You decide how you must handle them and then turn them into a positive. He was the only person hit in a battalion of 250 men. He could give up or try to influence people not to give up. He chose to try to help people through their problems. He talks about losing his legs and overcoming it.

Corey Borner was a young high school football player at DeSoto High School in Dallas. He broke his neck and was confined to a wheelchair. During spring practice, I visited him to try and cheer him up. He could barely move at the time, but he told me he was going to find a way to get out of that chair. I used that message with our team in the form of a wristband that said, *I will find a way.* It is easy when things are going well in your life. It is tough when they are not. Find a way to fix what is wrong. I text Corey before every game and tell him to "find a way." He texted me after the championship game and said, "Coach, you found a way, you just ran out of time."

The following passage is in all of our players' pockets:

This is the beginning of a new day. God has given me this day to use as I will. I can waste it or use it for good. What I do today is very important because I am exchanging a day of my life for it. When tomorrow comes, this day will be gone forever, leaving something in its place I have traded for it. I want it to be a gain, not a loss; good, not evil; success, not failure in order that I shall not forget the price I paid for it.

Every one of us every day gets better or worse. Our teams get better or they get worse.

I want you to think tonight, as a coach, if you are doing the best that you can do. Are you influencing your players? Are you being positive with the other coaches on your staff? Are you influencing people within your community with your team? Are your players lucky to be playing for you? If you are walking around with a swagger and good body language and doing all the other things, you will be a winner. If you are not winning and you conduct yourself in that manner, you will begin to win because the players will start believing in themselves.

The second thing is whether you are happy or not. It is so easy to say you have a bad job. If the job was bad before you got there, change it. That is a cool thing to have a bad job and change it into a good one. I have always liked winning at a place that "cannot win" instead of maintaining a program that was winning. We have won 10 plus games for nine straight years. We won 13 games last year. Next year unless we win 14 games, it will be a bad year.

Fellas, it has been a pleasure being here tonight.

A 4-PRESS COVERAGE FROM THE UNDER DEFENSE

Marshall University

I am proud to be here today, representing Doc Holiday and Marshall University. This is my 34th year of being at this clinic. I came as a high school coach and a college coach. I have probably spoken at this clinic six or seven times. In this state right now, there are four new coaching staffs. If you count Marshall, which is across the river from Ashland, Kentucky, there are five new staffs. I know Joker Phillips, Charley Strong, Chris Hatcher, and Willie Taggart. They will welcome you coaches. New coaching staffs like to get to know the high school coaches in their state and area. It is also your opportunity to get to know them.

I want to tell you I have the distinction of playing at Fort Campbell in high school and the University of Kentucky in college. I have coached at two high schools in Kentucky at Paducah and Fern Creek. In addition, I have coached at four universities in this state. I coached at Western, Morehead, Kentucky, and Louisville. I have a feel for football in this state. Football has improved tremendously in this state.

In 2003, I arrived at the University of Louisville from University of Illinois. Bobby Petrino had been the coach for one season. They had won nine games and were third in the nation offensively and 98th defensively. My job was to install a new defense. He told me to start over and add new terminology along with everything else.

The defense I am going to talk about today is what we installed that year. The principles I am going to talk about is an under defense. We play a shade 59 to the tight end with quarters press coverage.

The first thing I am going to talk about is the principles of a 4-press defense. In this defense, we have a four-man rush scheme, with three underneath, and a four-deep secondary. The four-man rush comes from the end, tackle, nose, and rush end. The three-underneath coverage is the Sam, Mike, and Will linebackers.

The four-deep secondary has a field and boundary corner with a strong and free safety. In the base alignment, the Sam linebacker and defensive end align in a 9 technique and 5 technique to the tight-end side (Diagram #1). The nose aligns in a shade on the center to the tight-end side. The tackle and rush end align in a 3 technique and 5 technique to the openside of the formation. The Mike and Will linebackers align in a 30 alignment on the outside shoulder of the guards.

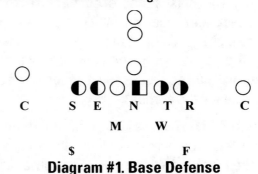

Diagram #1. Base Defense

The first principle of four-deep press coverage is maximum coverage on deep routes. In a three-deep secondary, the offense attacks with four vertical pass routes with two receivers running down the sidelines and two running down the seams of the field. The quarterback reads the single high safety and throws accordingly.

When I was at Louisville, we had a free safety who now plays in the NFL. Anytime we played three deep, the quarterback would look to one side of the field and throw to the backside vertical seam. He could not make those plays. By playing quarter coverage, we had the corners taking the receivers down the sidelines and the safeties taking the receivers running down the hash marks.

The other pattern the offense likes to run against three-deep coverage is a deep scissors route. The outside wide receiver ran in front of the inside receiver. He ran a deep post cut to pull the corner into the post. The inside receiver ran the corner pattern underneath the post pattern. Quarter coverage worked very well against the deep scissors route.

The second principle of 4-press coverage is quick run support. In 4-press coverage, we tell the safeties they are linebackers aligned at eight yards deep. If the safeties make a mistake, I want them coming forward rather than backing up. That gives us quick run support and allows us to play with eight and nine defenders in the box.

The third principle of this defense is to eliminate the short passing game. If the corners are aligned seven to eight yards off the wide receivers, the quarterback throws what we call a "now route." The now route is a one-step pattern for the quarterback and receiver. When the defender is seven to eight yards off the receiver, the one- and three-step patterns are the quarterback's staple. They throw the hitch route and it becomes an open-field tackle for the corner.

Coach Petrino made a living with the three-step hitch route. If the corner made a tackle for a five-yard gain, that was a good job. If the corner missed the tackle, the five-yard gain becomes an 80-yard touchdown. By pressing with the corners on the receivers, we eliminate the hitch, stop, and slant routes.

The fourth principle allows the defense to double the boundary or single receiver. The corner and free safety to that side can double on the curl, post, and dig routes to the backside. To the tight-end side, by reading the tight end we end up with double coverage on the outside receiver to that side.

The fifth principle of the 4-press coverage is coverage disguise. By playing the corners in press position and the safeties 8 to 10 yards deep, it shows the offense a two-high safety look. That allows the coverage to become a man-free scheme with almost no effort. You can drop one safety into the box as a linebacker and roll the other safety into the middle of the field as a free defender. We like to press the corners up on the outside receiver and blitz the boundary corner. I cannot tell you how many times we have had the boundary corner hitting the quarterback from the blind side.

By using a bail technique by the corner, we can accomplish the sixth principle. The route the offense throws against pressed corners is the fade route. We press the corners and bail out. We tell the corners when we use the bail technique, the quarterback is throwing him a ball. All he has to do is go get it. It baits the quarterback into throwing the fade.

The evolution of quarters coverage came with the option game. The object was to get quick run support to the strongside by reading the tight end with the strong safety. If the play was the veer pass to the tight end, the strong safety played that route. However, if the tight end blocked, he was an additional defender on the option.

By playing the two-deep alignment, it allows us to get to the seventh principle of the 4-press coverage. The coverage can easily become a three-deep zone. It allows us to invert the safeties and get into three-deep coverage. We can invert the strong safety into the alley and roll the free safety into the middle third of the field. If we roll the strong safety down to the strong side inside the Sam linebacker we call that a "curl drop." If he is outside the Sam linebacker, it is a "sky support" with the strong safety playing as a curl/flat defender.

The eighth principle is what we call "quarter-quarter-half coverage." The coverage is disguised by the alignment of the four defenders. The corners press the outside receivers, and the safeties align at 8 to 10 yards. This gives you a good jam on the wide receiver into the boundary and gives you two defenders over one receiver on a pass release.

I want to talk about some techniques of the defense. In the under defense, the Mike and Sam linebackers, the end, and the nose always travel together. If we give a directional call of left or right, those four defenders go to the side of the call. The tackle, Will linebacker, and rush end go opposite the call.

During my first year at Louisville in two-a-day practices, we had to start from square one. I had been there for 15 days, and the defensive players had never heard any of the defenses before. The players had three defensive coordinators before I arrived. We started with this plan, and I told them how easy it was to learn.

Occasionally, teams played with two tight ends or no tight ends. The defensive linemen wanted to get aligned and would end up on the wrong side of the defense because they did not wait for the direction call. That was not a good thing to happen under Bobby Petrino. When they ended up on the wrong side, the heat came back to me. I told the defensive linemen if they did not wait for the call, I would make them hold hands.

Our opening game that year was with the University of Kentucky. They came out early in the first quarter and aligned with no tight ends. One defensive lineman aligned to the wrong side. The play gained eight yards. I was in the press box, but I caught the wrath of the head coach. I told the defensive line coach to have the defensive line hold hands. That prevented them from moving before the call was made.

On national television, our defensive linemen were holding hands. Mike Tirico was the announcer for the network. He told the viewer that Cassity's defense was showing great camaraderie and were holding hands.

If we are shaded to the field side, we call it "under Falcon." The corners align with a slight inside leverage of the wide receiver. The field corner aligns as close to the receiver as possible. He has to be careful not to line up offside. That can happen with the Z-receiver who is aligned two yards off the line of scrimmage.

The technique we use is like an offensive tackle in a pass set. Mike Summers, the offensive line coach at Kentucky, and I have worked together before. When he teaches his tackles to pass set, they use a kick-slide technique. I use the same technique with the corners. The corner walks up on the receiver with his outside eye on the inside eye of the receiver. His inside foot is up, and his outside foot is back in his stance. He is in a low stance with a flat back, and his hands ready.

On the snap of the ball, the defensive back kick-slides with the outside foot like an offensive lineman. We do not want them to sit on the heels like the offensive linemen but we want them to separate from the receiver. As the receiver releases, the defensive back wants to disrupt his route. He punches him with his hand and gets on top of the route. The receiver should not be able to run the fade route because the defender does not allow the receiver to get even with him.

The defensive back punches and runs with the receiver. Any stop, hitch, comeback, or curl route is played as man-to-man coverage. The key coaching point comes on a slant route. If the receiver runs a slant route, the defender uses his outside hand to punch and rotate to the quarterback. If the receiver is running the quick slant, the quarterback will throw on the third step, and the defender reacts to the ball.

However, if the pattern is an in route, the corner releases the receiver and zones back to the outside. It is not man-to-man on an inside route. I tell the corner he cannot depend on having help on the post route by the outside receiver. That is particularly true to the backside of the defense. If the receiver runs a post cut, the defender runs the post with him.

The object of this technique is to disrupt the route of the receivers. Teams that throw timing routes hate the hands of the defensive backs on the receivers. The corner has to play man-to-man on all vertical routes, hitches, outs, and slants.

The key of the corner is the wide receiver to the quarterback. His responsibility is man-to-man on that receiver allowing nothing over the top. I tell them I want them to kick-slide, kick-slide, punch, and run with the receiver always staying on top of the route.

The strong safety aligns two yards outside and eight yards deep off the tight end. On some alignments, we are 10 yards deep. We initially teach the alignment at eight yards. I coached it for years as a break-in-the-knees and a flat-foot read. I taught that for 15 years. I now teach this alignment at 10 yards with his outside foot up and his inside foot back in his stance.

On the snap of the ball, he steps from 10 yards down to nine yards. That is his read step. We want him to read-step forward. On his first step, if he reads the tight end blocking, he comes to the party. His key is the release of the tight end.

We play the Sam linebacker in a 9 technique on the tight end with a slight stagger in his outside foot (Diagram #2). If the tight end attempts to reach the Sam linebacker, the linebacker maintains the integrity of the defense and stays outside. The strong safety fills inside the Sam linebacker.

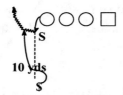

Diagram #2. Reach Block Fill

This type of block occurs on the toss sweep. The worse thing that can happen on a reach block is the strong safety fitting outside the Sam linebacker. That leaves a big hole in the alley.

If the tight end blocks down, the Sam linebacker squeezes to the inside and the strong safety becomes the contain players (Diagram #3). This type of play would be a power off-tackle type of play with someone kicking out the Sam linebacker. The Sam Linebacker steps and squeezes the hole and bounces everything wide.

The third type of block is the base block on the Sam linebacker. If the tight end fires into the breastplate of the Sam linebacker, he fights to keep

outside leverage. We do not want the read on a base block to be gray. The strong safety's fit on a base block is inside the Sam linebacker. If the tight end releases outside the Sam linebacker, the Sam linebacker is the contain player.

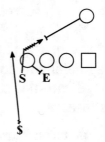

Diagram #3. Down-Block Fit

The strong safety reads the tight end, and on flow to him, he fits off the Sam linebacker's play. The Sam linebacker can never be wrong on his play. As the strong safety reads and starts up to support, at five yards he determines whether to fill inside or outside the Sam linebacker. If the Sam linebacker gets reached, the strong safety fits to the outside.

If there is flow away from the strong safety, he shuffles to the inside and is responsible for the backside B gap (Diagram #4). The nose is the A-gap player, the end is the C-gap player, and the strong safety has the B gap on the cutback run.

Diagram #4. Flow Away Fit

The pass coverage for the strong safety is the inside quarter of the field. He reads the release of the tight end and reacts accordingly.

The pass coverage is the reason I want the corners to press the wide receivers (Diagram #5). If the tight end runs an arrow release or runs to the flat, the strong safety takes his read step. He sees the tight going to the flat and looks outside at the outside receiver. If the wide receiver runs the curl route, the strong safety plays robber coverage under the curl. If the wide receiver runs a post, the strong safety uses a baseball turn and brackets the wide receiver with the corner.

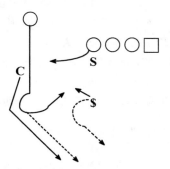

Diagram #5. Tight End Flat

If the tight end releases vertical, the strong safety read-steps and gets into a backpedal. He cushions on the tight end, and after 10 yards, he plays the tight end man-to-man.

The way teams try to control quarter coverage is with the pattern of the tight end. They ran him up the field to the depth of 11 yards and ran an option route with him. They took the tight end past the area in which the strong safety began to play man-to-man and flatten his pattern. They were trying to freeze the strong safety in coverage and throw the post over the top to the wide receiver. I coach the strong safety that 10 yards is not a hard-and-fast rule. We sometimes allow him to run 12 yards before we start to challenge his route. That is decided by game plan. However, after 10 yards, if the tight end runs a corner route, the strong safety has him man-to-man.

The third thing the tight end can do is inside release going across the field. If the tight end goes under initially, the strong safety zones back to his area. He gets his eyes to the outside and helps on the wide receiver. The coaching point to consider in this technique is not to be in a hurry to turn back to the outside. Teams will take the tight end to the inside for three steps and release him straight up the football field. The strong safety has to take his read step, zone his quarter, and get back to the wideout. He cannot get in a hurry to help on the

wide receiver. He has to be sure he knows what the tight end is doing.

The key for the strong safety is the tight end to the football. His responsibility is the inside quarter of the field and to make the Sam linebacker correct in his read.

The free safety's alignment to the weakside is two yards outside the tackle and 10 yards deep. If the free safety is aligned at eight yards, he uses the break in the knees and flat-foot read. If he is at 10 yards, he steps to nine and reads. He either comes downhill or back up after the forward step.

There is no inside receiver who can get down the field. Most of the time with a single receiver side, the free safety is a double cover defender to the single receiver. I tell the free safety if the play is not a run, do not be in a hurry to do anything. If the play is an outside run, the free safety is sky support. In sky-support, the free safety is the pitch defender against the option. If flow goes away from the free safety, he is the cutback defender in the backside A gap.

I want the safeties to have linebacker mentality instead of defensive back mentality. We want the safeties to support on the run. On the backside, the free safety has a robber technique on the split end or X-receiver. His key is the offensive tackle to the ball.

From this alignment, we can get into man coverage. We lock the corners on the wide receivers and drop one of the safeties down into man coverage and play the other safety in the middle of the field in a man-free scheme.

There are no secrets in football, but when I coached at Louisville, I was sworn to secrecy on our adjustment on twins. This scheme came from the NFL. Not only was Coach Petrino a good offensive coach, he gave me great ideas defensively of what created problems for an offense. Offenses like to use motion to see if the defense is in man or zone coverage. When teams see both corners to the same side on the twins set, they think it is man coverage.

Adjustment: Treo vs. Twins

Principles:

- Show quarterback man-to-man
- Play strong zone rotation
- Corners over: both corners align or motion to the same side
- Maintain great run support
- Corner back shoot
- Partner twin to pro or pro to twin
- Eliminate double pick bubble screen flare screen
- Keep it simple

Teams aligned in the twin set to see if both the corners went to the same side. If they did, they ran patterns with rubs and picks to free receivers. We have all seen those types of patterns. It is illegal, but it is never called. "Treo" to us is a zone coverage check (Diagram #6). We are showing the quarterback man coverage by bringing both corners to the same side. What we are playing is a strong zone rotation. That is an extremely important point. The offense reads the defense as man, and we are playing zone.

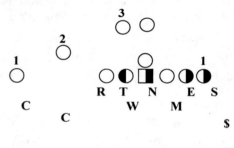

Diagram #6. Treo Alignment

We tell the corners, if the offense aligns in a twins set or motion the flanker into a twins set, the corner follows the motion receiver as if it were man coverage. The "treo" call means there are three defenders over two receivers. The corner on the outside receiver is in a press position. The inside corner aligns three yards off the line of scrimmage. He does not take his alignment on the receiver. It is on the line of scrimmage. He has outside leverage on the receiver. If they motion the receiver across the set, the corner comes with him and ends up in that

alignment, which is three yards off the line of scrimmage with outside leverage.

If the slot receiver goes in motion, the corner goes with him. If he ends up in the pro set, we are back into quarters-press coverage. If they start in pro and motion to twins, we check to treo. What this does is eliminates the double pick plays, the bubble screen, and the flare screen. The most important thing it is very simple to adjust.

When I said it was three defenders on two receivers, it is actually three defenders on one receiver. It is the corners and free safety on the inside slot receiver. We number the receiver from the sideline to the inside. In this set, the wide receiver is #1, the slot receiver is #2, and the fullback in the backfield is #3. The outside corner takes the #1 receiver man-to-man and eliminates his patterns. The inside corner keys the #2 receiver to the #3 receiver.

If the #2 receiver runs an outside cut, the inside corner takes him (Diagram #7). If the #2 receiver runs vertical and #3 comes out of the backfield, the corner snaps off his coverage of #2 and takes the #3 receiver. If the #2 receiver is less than 10 yards, the Will linebacker takes him. If he is over 10 yards, the free safety takes him.

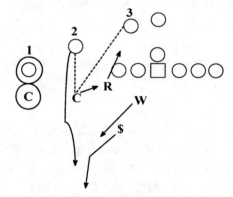

Diagram #7. Treo Coverage

The offense thinks the fullback is covered man-to-man by the Will linebacker, and they intend to rub the fullback off the patterns of the outside receivers and defenders. What happens repeatedly is the inside corner steps up and blows the running back to pieces. It is tremendously good when the offense uses motion. When the corner comes with the motion, the offense is sure the defense is man-to-man. If the slot goes inside, the Will linebacker takes him, and the inside corner zones back to the outside.

The inside corner reads the #2 receiver to the #3 receiver. If the #2 receiver goes vertical and the #3 receiver does not come out, the corner is looking to support or work in a double-team mode. Because the inside corner is reading #2 to #3, you get great support on a running play.

The free safety plays coverage as he did on the press corner. He reads the #2 receiver and reacts to what he does. If he runs to the flat, the inside corner takes him and he looks to the #1 receiver. If the #2 receiver comes vertical, he takes him up to the 10-yard limit. After he passes 10 yards, he has him man-to-man. If he is less than 10 yards, the Will linebacker has him.

If the #2 receiver goes inside, the Will linebacker picks him up, and the free safety works with the outside corner.

There are reasons why coaches say they cannot play this coverage. Coaches will tell you that they do not have enough skilled players to play this type of coverage. This coverage is a simple coverage, which requires no more teaching than any other coverage you may run at the present time.

They will tell you they are too slow to play man-to-man coverage. The defenses that teams run today require that you use man-to-man principles in a zone coverage scheme. Playing press-man coverage is easier than playing an off-man coverage. This defense allows you to keep the quarterback guessing and can disguise the coverage.

They will tell you it is too complicated for them to implement in their system. This is an easy answer. The coverage requires the defensive back to count from one to three. If they can count and recognize the split receiver and count from there, they have a lot of the teaching done.

My favorite excuse is the head coach will not buy this type of coverage. The last of the excuses is

we do not have the time to coach it. All of you in here have more time than I do.

To teach this coverage, you need to learn to react through repetition. When coaches do drill work, there are some things I think they should do. Never do a drill for the sake of having something to do on the field. All drills you do should be football-related to the position that you teach.

Before you do the drills, go over them with your players in a classroom setting. Explain what you are going to do and what you expect to get from the drill. Let them know your expectation and how the drill will help them. Show them the drill in film study, and point out the drill in game films. When you show them films, be position-specific. Show them how the drills you do in practice are what they do in the games.

If they think they will get better, they will try hard in the drill to improve. Do not do drills as conditioning drills. You are teaching a skill, and you need their attention and concentration. When you get on the field, do not give a clinic on the drill. You want to get repetitions. Do the clinic off the field before you come out to work.

When you are involved in a team or group drill, do your coaching on the run. Do not stop the drill for individual instruction. Coach every phase of the drill and technique, and do it while the drill is going on. Coach them going to and from the huddle.

Do not wait until you are into the drill period to set up the drill. Have the managers set up the drill before you are ready to do it. If the managers cannot do it, set it up before practice begins. You have only a limited time to work. Do not waste it trying to explain the drill or set it up.

When you run these drills, coach from the positive side. Make your players want to do the drill. Do not make fun of them or be too critical of them. You can make your own drill tape, which will help the players perform.

When you are coaching, use trigger words to emphasis what you want. Use words like stance, separate, punch, disrupt, lower, and eyes to emphasize what you want the player to work on.

I want to start out and talk about the kick-slide drill. The corner aligns with his inside foot up and his outside foot back. In the drill, the corner will kick back his outside foot and slide with the outside foot. I will talk about this more in a minute.

For the defensive back to backpedal, it all starts with his stance. People talk about shoulder-width apart for the feet; that is not what I teach. I teach four to six inches between the feet with a toe to instep stagger in his feet. He can have a toe-to-heel stagger but never more than that. The weight in the stance goes on the big toe of the front foot. I want the front foot slightly cocked.

The defensive back wants to pull with the back foot and push with the front foot. Too many times, they want to step forward before they go backward. On occasion, I stand on their front foot so they will not step forward. I want them to bend in the knees and ankles and have the hands relaxed.

I do a potato-chip drill. I have them hold a potato chip in their hands. They have one in each hand between the thumb and middle finger. In this drill, we practice the first step in the backpedal. The object is to make the step and not break the chip. I want the hands relaxed in their stance and movement. After we do several repetitions stepping with the right foot, I reverse their feet, and they step with the left foot.

When we start to do the drill, I use one of those trigger words I told you about. I tell them to get their elbows higher. When you lift your elbows, your shoulders move forward. Another common mistake defensive backs make in the pedal is they get too low in their bend. I want their chest up, and I want them to be relaxed as their pedal. Too many times, their base is too wide. I use the trigger, "Narrow your base."

When we do our drills, we do them from the sidelines to the hash marks. I use the yard lines as reference points in the drills. Before we start to teach the pedal, I line four defensive backs five yards apart on a yard line. I tell them to get on the line as if they were walking a tight rope. That means they had both feet on the line with one in front of the other. I have them walk backward and kick their heel each time they step. This is a drill to teach them to stay narrow in their stance.

The next things I do is put them in a stance and make them walk backward, pumping the elbows and kicking the heels. Believe it or not, that is a lot harder. The next progression is to do the same thing, except this time I give them a direction to the right or left. When I point, they flip their hips and break at a 45-degree angle across the next yard line.

Before you can expect the players to be proficient, even at the college level, you have to start from the beginning and progress. Another drill I do is called a backpedal weave. The back gets into a backpedal and weaves from side to side without coming out of the backpedal. The purpose of this type of movement is to be able to pedal with a receiver who is stemming inside or outside. The movement keeps the shoulders and hips square as the back continues to maintain inside or outside leverage on the receiver. When we finish the drill, we have the back do a zone turn and run out of the drill. We never just stop the weave; we turn and run as you would in a game.

This next drill can make an average defensive back into a great one. The drill is the "break/drive." The break/drive is a transition from running backward to running forward. The backs will not run forward; they run at an angle. When the back breaks, he breaks on a 45-degree angle.

In the backpedal, if the back wants to break to his left, he plants his right foot. He gets his left foot on the ground and breaks at a 45-degree angle. Let me explain the mechanics of the break/drive. If the back wants to break to his left, he has to stop his momentum with his right foot. He does not use his toe. He uses the entire sole of his cleat. When he plants, I do not want him to stop on the toe or turn the hips to the boundary. I want the right foot to come down within a two-foot circumference of their body at a 33-degree angle.

When I teach them, we walk in a backpedal. When I say "Plant," they pick up the right knee and plant their right foot on a 33-degree angle within a two-foot circumference of their body. After the plant comes the 45-degree-angle step. I have them point at a 45-degree angle with their finger to the sideline. The command for them to pick up the left foot and place it under their arm at a 45-degree angle is "point." The left foot should be under their arm. When they put the left foot down, it should be as close the other foot as possible, but not in front or behind the right foot.

The coaching point is to not let them put the left foot behind their right foot. If they do, they will round off their break. The last command is "drive." That is the transition step. When we put it all together, I give them the commands as they walk backward. I say, "Walk, walk, plant, point, drive." After we have done that, we work to the right. We start out walking.

After we get the footwork down, we do the drill with the backpedal. When they get good at the drill, we do a reaction drill. They stand in place and stomp their feet. When I give the command, they do the steps on the break. When I say "Drive," they step off in that direction. What this drill does is get an interception or a pass break-up instead of coming close.

The hip-flip drill is a movement drill we do. The back aligns on the yard line and backpedals. I give them a direction, and they flip their hips and run. I want them to run, not side run. I look for a smooth transition from the backpedal to the flip and run.

When we run the man swivel drill, we align at one yard inside the receiver and eight yards deep. The receiver breaks off the ball, and the defensive back pedals. When the receiver breaks the cushion on the back, he flips his hips and runs with the receiver. The back wants to hold the pedal as long as he can, but when he flips to run, I want him on top of the receiver.

We expand the drill to encourage the back to move the feet into the receiver. I do not want the back to use his hands in this drill. He moves his feet to get into the receiver so he can feel him. We do this drill in three parts. The first part is the flip, the second part is the feet movement into the receiver, and the third part is where we use our hand to impede the receiver and feel him with the hands.

In this part of the drill, the back wants to have his hand on top of the receiver's hands. If the receiver starts to run by the defensive back, he takes his hand off the hands and bumps the hip of the receiver. That will knock him off stride and slow him down. I want them to feel the receiver with their hands.

Gentlemen, I am out of time. If you even need us at Marshall, be sure to call on us.

DEFENSIVE CONCEPTS AND COACHING LINEBACKERS

Louisiana State University

It is an honor for me to be here to share some thoughts with you. It has been a couple of years since I have spoken at a clinic. As a young coach, I enjoyed every opportunity I got to attend a clinic. I was sitting where you are now, and I enjoyed it as much as anything.

This year was a different deal for me. It was the first time in 20 years that I changed my address. I have the same cell phone because I did not know whether I could remember another number. It was a totally different experience for me. I had been the defensive coordinator at the University of Tennessee for 15 years, and we ran the same defense in all that time. We tweaked the system every year, but the foundation of what we believed made us a good defense remained the same.

I wanted to take that same philosophy to Louisiana State University. We have talent and some great athletes to work with. We wanted to put that philosophy to work again. This year, we made some strides in the right direction. What I am going to do today is talk about philosophy and teaching the defense.

It does not matter whether it is offense, defense, or special teams—it is all about *communication*. You have to communicate a plan. There are a lot of great plans in today's football. There are many ways to play defense. What I have to do is take the plan and communicate it to the players. The 18-, 19-, and 20-year-old players have to go on the field and execute what you have taught. I think that is what coaching is all about. It all starts with building a relationship and earning the trust of your players. I think that is important.

When I went to LSU, I had to put together a staff. I had the opportunity to hire a young man by the name of Brick Haley. That name may not mean anything to you, but it does to me. When I was a 23-year-old coach, he was one of the first players I coached. After I coached him, I have no idea why he wanted to be a coach. He is the defensive line coach. I hired Ron Cooper as the secondary coach. Together, we are putting in this plan. We want the plan to be rock solid. The players and coaches have to buy into the plan.

When I left Tennessee, we were the number three defense in the nation and the number one defense in the SEC. This plan will work anywhere. I want to start talking philosophy geared toward linebackers.

LINEBACKER PHILOSOPHY

The primary goal of defense is to obtain the football for the offense. The three simplest ways to obtain the football are three-downs-and-out, cause a fumble, and take interceptions. I love working for offensive coaches. Coach Miles is a great coach to work for. It was an enjoyable year because all that those coaches want is the ball. If you get the ball for them, it will make them happy.

The first of the ways to get the football is *three-downs-and-out*. We want to chart them and sell our players on three-and-out. When the defense goes on the field and has a three-and-out, they have a chance to turn the field position. We want to give our offense the ball with great field position.

The second and third ways to get the ball are turnovers. You can cause a fumble or intercept the ball. We focus on turnovers in our preparation. We had a chance to watch the Super Bowl. Gregg Williams is the defensive coordinator for the New

Orleans Saints. He is one of the finest coaches I have ever had the opportunity sit down and visit with. I talked to him about football. The Saints are the best at creating turnovers. It won them a bunch of football games, and we did the same thing last year.

Creating turnovers is not something you write down on paper. You start out with those ideas on paper, but until the players buy into the plan, it is just words on paper. You have to communicate it, put it to work, and go out on the field and make it happen. If you do, it will make a difference in your football team.

You are judged by your team performance, not the victory itself. This phrase means we want to have a great performance. We want to win, and that is what we prepare for. We expect to win but the performance is what we want to make happen.

PRIORITIES

- Team first. Do what it takes to make the team as good as it can be.
- Play aggressive, attacking defense.
- Take one play at a time.
- Force turnovers.
- Force teams into making mistakes.
- Be a great tackler.
- Score on defense.

The team has to come first; I can give you many examples to illustrate that. I am going to give you one that happened recently. When I went to LSU, we had a starting safety who was a pro prospect by the name of Harry Coleman. Our linebacker corps was so thin I did not think we could get through the SEC without more depth. We looked at our personnel and we were deep at safety. Harry was and a senior and the starting safety from the year before. I called him into my office and asked him to make a change to linebacker. He did not bat an eye and told me whatever he had to do for the team was fine with him.

That is the kind of attitude you have to look for. That is the approach we are going to take. It is the team first. There is no individual. It is not about offense or defense. It is not about what position you play. It is about the team. The game of football presents a great opportunity. It is an opportunity to be part of something special. Being part of something that is bigger than you is what being part of a team is about. Harry Coleman understood that when he made the switch.

When he went to the Senior Bowl this year, he played both positions. He played at safety and linebacker. It enhanced his opportunity to go to the NFL. Some teams are looking at him as an every-down linebacker. They will not have to put the nickel back in to play for him.

You need to play aggressive and attacking defense. How are you going to do that? The biggest key is to get the players to understand what you want them to do. They have to have technique and understand responsibility before they can play. To be successful, you have to play aggressive, attacking defense.

That does not mean you have to blitz every down. We are going to do it by coming off the ball with our down defenders and putting pressure on the offensive line. That is the mentality of our front. Our 3-technique and 9-technique players are going to get off the ball and penetrate. We want to play on their side of the line of scrimmage. When we do blitz, we will understand how to pressure the offense. We will understand the type of blitz we are running, and we will strip at the football every opportunity we get.

You have to take one play at a time. The most important play in the football game is the one you are about to play. That statement is never more evident than a position such as cornerback. We put our corners in many 1-on-1 situations, and we do not expect them to get beat. However, we know sometimes it will happen. When it happens, he has to forget about it and get ready to play the next play because that is the most important one for him. We have to play that play like it is going determine the game.

How many times have you graded the film after a loss and say we played great? You cannot say that because you lost and gave up 21 points. However, if you have two of those plays back, you played great and only gave up seven points. You never know when those plays are going to happen in a ball game. You have to be ready and play every play like it is the most important play.

We talked about turnovers earlier, but you have to have a head coach that will work with you in this aspect. You play like you practice, and it is important that we play aggressive in practice. It is important to know how to strip the football and when to do it. Obviously, you do not want to put another player in jeopardy, but you must practice stripping the ball. Once they understand how to strip the ball, it will happen in the games.

I thought we did a good job of stripping the ball until I went down and watched the Saints practice. It was unbelievable. There were some players on offense who did not like the way they did it in practice. However, I bet they liked the Super Bowl championship ring they got. They forced many turnovers this year, and it did not happen by accident.

How do you force offenses into mistakes? You do it by being aggressive in your scheme. You also do it by changing your scheme. You have to do things that they do not expect you to do. You want to show the offense the same looks and do something different from those looks.

You cannot play defense if you are not a great tackler. There has not been a single day that we have been on the field that we do not practice tackling. Even if we are in shorts, we will practice the fundamentals of tackling. I believe there are two things that coaches do not spend enough time working on. One of them is tackling, and the other is blow delivery. That happens because we do not have enough time to cover it all.

The last item is to score on defense. I want to show you how big that play was by using this example. We played the University of Washington in our opening game of the season. They had a new coaching staff and a good quarterback. On the first series, we made a mistake and they scored to go up 7-0. On our first series, we went three-and-out and punted the ball back to them. In their second series, they tried to hit a quick pass. Our linebacker made a great break on the ball and intercepted it. He returned it for a touchdown, and that completely reversed the momentum in the game.

Accomplishing Priorities

In order to accomplish team priorities players must do the following things:

- Be in excellent playing condition
- Eliminate mistakes; make daily improvements
- Achieve great execution and second effort
- Maintain poise and confidence at all times
- Have love and respect for their teammates (we play for one another)

If you want to accomplish your priorities, you must be in excellent condition. We talk to our players all the time about this point. Tommy Moffitt is the strength coach at LSU, and I think he is by far the best strength coach in the country. Our players have bought into his system and work in it all year. They do a tremendous job. Our players will be in shape. The players have to accept that responsibility.

We are multiple in our schemes and we will make mistakes. The simplicity of our scheme will be techniques. We may teach a player 10 different techniques. When we get multiple in our scheme, we use numbers to tell the players they are playing certain techniques. We do not want them to learn the entire defense. We want them to understand technique. We want them to play those techniques aggressively. You will make mistakes on defense, but we want daily improvement—eliminate those mistakes.

The first thing we do when we grade a film is to grade effort. We want our players to grade their effort because we want them on the same page as the coaching staff. In our first scrimmage this past spring, we had 137 loafs as a team. That is a lot of

40s to run after practice. If we tell them we are going to run 40s or do up-downs for each loaf, that is what we are going to do.

Players will buy into that because they want to play hard and fast. Sometimes, they do not understand that they are not pushing themselves. They do not understand they are not giving 110 percent. You have to ask that from your players.

Your team has to play with poise and confidence all the time. At Tennessee in 1998, the year we won the national championship, we were in trouble in the Arkansas game that year. We were down 21 points in the second half but had come back to be down four points with time running out in the game. The offense had a fourth and short in the last minute and 30 seconds of the game. They did not make it. I was thinking to myself how this could happen to us.

We had one time-out left. As the offense came off the field, one of our defensive tackles told the quarterback not to take his helmet off because they were not going to be out there long. When he made that statement, it made me realize that he thought they we were going to win the game. I needed to think we were going to win the game. He knocked the guard into the quarterback, caused a fumble, and we went in to score. The confidence that he showed is what you are looking for.

When you are part of a team and they are much bigger than you are, that is where it all starts. Your team must have respect and love for their teammates and play for each other. We want them to feel the bond and know the player beside them is going to give the same amount he does.

When we came to LSU this year, we had a problem right away. We were a new staff with no carryover from the previous year. We had to start anew and put in a new system. The first thing we had to do was introduce a new terminology to them. Terminology gets everyone talking the same language and gets everyone on the same page. That is how you communicate and call the defense. It may be the same thing they had done in the past, but it was not the same term.

When you put a new staff together, some coaches will revert back to a system they had been in before. It will happen, but you have to prevent it from happening. Every coach must use the same terminology. Along with terminology, there was a different numbering system for the linemen and different gap responsibilities.

The defensive huddle in college football today is almost nonexistent. We never huddle. With all the no-huddle offenses we see, we do not huddle. Our four defensive linemen stand on the line of scrimmage in close proximity to the ball. Our defensive line will be responsible for what happens. We should never get a ball snapped on us quickly.

The linebackers look at the personnel coming on and off the field. The Sam linebacker watches the sideline to get signals from the coaches. In some cases, we use wristbands and cards to call the defenses. The safety is the one responsible for letting our defense know the down and distance to go for the first down. The corners are always wider than anyone in the formation and do not come into the middle of the field.

We have to constantly change our signals because coaches will pick them up if we do not. We feel like with the offenses we are seeing, getting into a uniform huddle is not the way to go. We have a system in place with our calls. The words we send into the game tell us the front, blitz, and coverage.

We may send three different coverages into the game. The players understand based on formation what coverage they are to run. Within that coverage, we may have a check built in so that if the offense changes the formation, we change the coverage. Offenses show you one formation looking for a particular defense. If they do not get the defense, they start the cadence, back out, change the play, and run something else. We must have the ability to change the defense when they change their play. We have dummy calls built in to our system also. That lets the offense think we are changing the call when we are not.

We have three different ways to communicate that information to the team on the field. We do it with signals, wristbands, and cards. Each week, we have five live cards on our sideline. If we hold up a black card, the defense knows to what defense we are checking. If he holds up a red card, they know the defense that goes with that. All the cards do not change defenses. Some of the cards are dummy cards.

Our linebackers watch the offense to make the formation calls we need to make. The strength of our call is predicated on the tight end. There are other factors that determine our strength call. If there is no tight end, we determine the two-receiver side as strength. If the formation is a balanced formation, we declare the wideside of the field. If the ball is in the middle of the field and the formation is balanced, we go to the dominant hand of the quarterback. If he is right-handed, we declare left. If he is left-handed, we declare the strength right.

We also have the ability to call the defense into the field or the boundary. There are reasons you want to do that. If a team has a personnel group on the field and you are not sure where they will align, we pre-call the strength into the field or the boundary. That is particularly true with a team with two tight ends on the field.

The Mike linebacker makes the call that comes from backfield alignments by the backs. He has to not only call the backfield alignments but also how deep they are aligned in those positions. With offenses today, we know 75 percent of the time what is going to happen by the depth of the back in the backfield. If you know where the offense is going to go, give the information to the Mike linebacker and let him call it. Make him study what you have given him, and make him make the calls while he is watching films as well as in the game. The last thing we identify is the flanker position.

In our basic teaching, we start by teaching stance. That is true in regard to all positions. I believe the stance is important. I am not going to make our players robots, but I am going to get them into a position that they can be successful. As coaches, we need to give our players a chance to be successful. I also believe that 99 percent of the good plays that happen start with a good stance.

In the linebacker stance, we want the feet slightly wider than the shoulders. We want a balanced stance with the arms within the framework of the body.

There are three things in linebacker play that I think are important. They have to play with their eyes. The *eyes* have to see so many things. They have to see alignment, splits, boundary, and field. There are so many tips that will tell them what is going to happen. If the eyes can see that information and relay it to their teammates, they have the advantage.

The linebacker has to play with his *hands*. He must keep his hands within the framework of the body. If he gets his hands outside the framework, he cannot play with the hands.

The last thing is *feet*. I have been blessed to have coached some great linebackers. The one thing all those linebackers had was a great understanding of how to play the game. They also had great athletic ability, which I cannot take credit for that. Understanding the game is something we, as coaches, can perfect.

The next essential is *alignment*. Why would a 30-technique linebacker who is into the boundaryside of the field think about aligning wide? He should tighten down into a head-up position. If he is into the wideside of the field, he may be wider in his 30 technique. That is common sense with regard to alignment. Alignment is relative to down and distance and the position of the ball on the field. Those situations require some commonsense thoughts from the linebacker.

If it is first and ten, the linebacker should anticipate a running play and have the weight on the balls of his feet with the heels off the ground ready to attack a blocker. If it is third and long, the linebacker is in a flat-footed stance. The linebacker has to understand the alignment and all the elements that go with it. He cannot simply align on the outside shoulder of the guard. He has to adjust that alignment with regard for the ball position and down situation in the game.

The next element in teaching linebackers is their *keys*. We have basic keys that we teach, but I have learned something about keys in my career. I had three players who started for three years together as a unit. In their senior year, I asked them how much they relied on the key work we did in practice. They told me the only time they think about their keys is when the offense showed them something different. They said, "We rep the plays so many times in practice, we recognize them by the first or second step in the games. When the offense does something different, we go back to the keys we learned in practice."

At our level, there are four or five running plays you will see from each team you play. Of those four or five plays, there will be two or three you must stop. Once you know that, you rep them until they become second nature to the linebackers. There will not be a 20-play script of running plays you have to stop. There may be 20 formations they run them from, but there will only be two to three running plays you must stop. That forces teams into a pass game.

An important element for the linebacker is *initial movement*. It is important to every player on your defense. If the situation is third and long, I do not want the linebacker with his heels off the ground. I want him flat-footed. If he has his heels off the ground, his initial movement is going to be toward the line of scrimmage. It does not matter what the offense does, I do not want his first movement in that situation toward the line of scrimmage. The initial movement does not come only from what they are looking at but also the situation. Late in the game when the offense has to move the ball down the field to score, I do not want to see the linebacker up two yards from the line of scrimmage. They must have some awareness of the situation.

This next element is a difficult one to teach because of the way offense is played today. The *linebacker responsibility on the run* and the pass is difficult to teach. They have to understand when they are the cutback player and when they are the fast-flow player. As much as we change with our safeties, we have to rep our linebackers on their responsibility in the running game. The linebackers have to know if they have to hold their point on the backside or if they can fast flow. We roll the safeties down into the box to play the cutback lanes and allow the linebackers to fast flow.

We ask our linebackers to play four *techniques*. We ask them to play fill, scrape, cutback, and force techniques. If they can play those techniques, they can play the running game. I will teach them those four techniques, and if they can execute them, it does not matter what the defense is—they can play the running game. When we make the call, there will be a call within the defense to tell the linebacker what technique he will have to play. If the linebacker has a safety rocked down behind him, he knows he is not the cutback player. He can forget the cutback and play fast to the ball away from him.

This next area is one we do not do a good job of teaching. Since we are a multiple front, we do not get to teach to *disengage* as much as we need to. There are essential elements to any defensive football team. They have to deliver a blow, disengage, pursue, and tackle. If you cannot do those things, you cannot play defensive football. A big part of what I am talking about is getting back to the basics of fundamental football. If you can teach your players to do that, you can put him in a scheme in which he can be successful.

When we teach the linebackers, we use a number of drills to help them. The more foot movement and change of direction we can use, the better they are. This first drill I want to talk about is the *W drill* (Diagram #1). We start the linebacker on a yard line, have him backpedal for five yards, and then sprint forward at a 45-degree angle back to the line. He tilts at a 45-degree angle to the third cone and sprints back to the line.

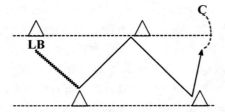

Diagram #1. W Drill

When we do this drill, I do not want to see the feet stop. I want them to accelerate out of each cut when they change direction. I want them to accelerate out of the cuts whether it is forward, backward, or on the angle. In the drill, we can incorporate an *Oskie drill* or *intercept drill*. We throw them the ball. We want to catch the point of the ball and reach out for it. We do not want to trap the ball to our bodies.

When we teach our linebackers to drop into their zones, we teach a three-step crossover drop. We play a number of coverages. We have some match-up zones, man-to-man schemes, and true zone coverages. The only thing that will take us out of the three-step crossover is a three-step drop by the quarterback. In that case, we break off the drop and react to the throw. The W drill helps us in our zone drops. I want to see the linebacker's hips open and drive out to his drop. When the quarterback takes his front hand off the football, I want to see the linebacker break on the ball. He has to anticipate the throw and make the break. The linebacker, when he drops, has to play with his eyes, hands, and feet.

We use a *key drill* daily (Diagram #2). The initial set in the drill is what we refer to as a *step-and-gather* step. We are reading through the guard to the backs. We step and gather and gather information as we fill out gaps. The formation will tell the linebacker something about what to expect. The down and distance will also tell him. In the drill, we process the information as we move. He keys the running back's flow and shoulders to know whether the play is an inside or outside play. We start out teaching angles to their responsibility against air. We add to the drill as we go. We add backs first and later linemen in the drill. It is a simple drill which I am sure all of you have done.

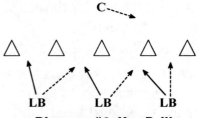

Diagram #2. Key Drill

When we start out, we do two step-and-gather steps to read and process what has happened. After the initial steps, the next steps are attacking downhill steps. Those are the steps after we have processed the information and we are pressing the line of scrimmage. We work all three of the linebackers in the key drill.

We do tackling every day. We start out with an elementary tackling drill. We put two players two yards apart (Diagram #3). It is a form tackling type of drill. We want to watch their footwork. We want to make sure they are not taking false steps. We want the head in the proper position. We want to strike across the bow with our eyes. We want the contact of the tackler on the backside shoulder. We want to hit the ballcarrier heavy and have our whole power line in place. The power line is the ankles, knees, and hips. If any of those areas open up, it takes away power from the tackle.

Diagram #3. Form Tackling

We have done studies on tackling. We found out that 93 to 95 percent of the tackles made in a game will be angle tackles that will end up in the position we use in the drill. We are a good tackling team because we do a great job of teaching the mechanics in this drill.

We want to get the proper eye placement and hand placement. We want to keep the hands and arms within the framework of the body. I do not want him to reach for the tackle. I want him to club with the arms as he makes the tackle. He brings his hands and arms up through the tackle and clubs the ballcarrier. We club with the arms to try and create a turnover in the initial tackle.

We want to club in the initial tackle. If the ball comes out, we get after it. If it does not come out, we encircle with the arms and grab cloth on the back of the ballcarrier. We want to pull the ballcarriers back to the tackler and run on his toes. When we do the drill, we lay a dummy behind the feet of the tackler. That prevents him from taking any false steps.

When we teach blow delivery, we start in a six-point stance (Diagram #4). The six points in the stance are the hands, knees, and toes in contact with the ground. From that position on the ground, we want to drive the belt buckle toward the target. We work our hand placement into the breastplate of the target. The target could be a sled, dummy, or body. On the hand placement, we want our fingertips slightly outside but the thumbs turned inside. If we keep the thumbs in, the elbows will stay tight to the body. That keeps the arms within the framework of the body.

Diagram #4. Blow Delivery

If we strike a good blow with our hand placement, we can control the blocker with our hands. We want to strike with the big muscles in the body. We want to strike with the quads and hip muscles. We start to teach the blow delivery from the six-point stance. From there, we progress to the two-point stance in a close position. After we go at the close distance, we back them up and do the same thing from an off distance. As the distance gets greater, we want to maintain the discipline of the technique. You would be surprised at how many of your players cannot get their hips involved in the technique until you perfect the drill.

The next stage of the blow delivery is the escape or disengagement. We have to separate by pressing the blocker away from the body and ripping with the backside arm. We can also crossface or swim.

I am going to stop right here. Coaches, it has been an honor to be able to come in and share some things with you. I hope I have given you something that will help your players get better. If there is anything I can do for you at LSU, do not hesitate to give me a call. The biggest thing for me is fundamentals. I enjoy talking schemes, but if you want to get your football team better quicker, concentrate on the fundamentals.

YOU GET WHAT YOU EMPHASIZE

University of Wyoming

I want to thank Nike for the opportunity to speak. I appreciate the partnership that Nike Clinics have with the Marine Corps. We have that type of commitment at Wyoming with the United State Special Forces. It is important for the average citizen to understand the importance of our military and what they do for our country.

I have sat in the seats you are sitting in before. I went to my first clinic in Washington State. I remember sitting out there, listening to all the coaches talk about their programs and their ideas. I have been very fortunate in my career. I got into this business hoping to be one of the 120 Division I head coaches in the country. I have coached at all levels from high school to where I am now.

I never knew where my career was going to go or where I would end up, but I was always planning for the next step. I was not looking for another job, but if I were an offensive line coach, I wanted to be the coordinator. For the past 25 years, I have tried to prepare myself for a head-coaching job.

I went to clinics and listened to coaches share their ideas. I was not looking for 50 new ideas, but if I could come up with one or two things that could help, the clinic was successful. Over the years, I have built up quite a file of ideas.

I am going to talk about how we rebuilt the Cowboys football program. I am going to talk about things that helped us rebuild the program, and I hope when I am finished I have given you some hope.

When we took over the program at Wyoming, it was in shambles. When I tested our players, I found there were two senior offensive linemen who could not bench 300 pounds. I challenged them. I told them I was 49 years old with a torn rotator cuff, but after of month of training I could bench 300 pounds. We had to change the mind-set of the program.

In 13 games this past year, all of those teams had better personnel than we did. I walked on that field 13 times, and I would have traded our personnel for the opponents every time. We played 12 true freshmen and started eight true freshmen. Our kicker was a non-recruited walk-on from Pennsylvania who showed up and tried out for the team.

We did not have much talent, but we never used that as an excuse. We were going to put in a system and a program that we believed in and find a way to win. No matter where you are, or the amount of athletes you have, there are things you can emphasize and find a way to win. We were fortunate enough to do that this year.

Whatever it is, if you emphasize it enough, you will get it done. The year before we came to Wyoming, they turned the ball over 36 times. We were non-athletic, and people thought I was crazy to take this job.

I thought it was important that we start to change the program from day one. At our first team meeting, I set a level of expectation for winning with that team. I had a meeting with the media from the area and told them the same thing. I told the team we expected to win. We expected to compete for the conference championships. In addition, we expected to go to a bowl game. We had a senior class that had never been to a bowl game in their entire college career. I told them I was not expecting to do this two or three years down the road. I told them I expected them to do it next year. When we came to the meeting, we introduced three core values, which our program would be built around.

THREE CORE VALUES

- Academic integrity
- Social responsibility
- Competitive excellence

The first thing we talked about was academic integrity. We told them that for every player who comes into our program, if he stays, he will graduate with a degree. We will make sure they go to class. We will have a study table, and they will be on time for everything they do. They had better be early because every second they are late will have stern consequences. We are going to have academic success. I tell players we recruit; if they do not want to get a degree, they do not need to come to Laramie. Our players are going to go to class and graduate. Academic integrity is going to first and foremost in our core values.

The second thing is social responsibility. Laramie is a small town. I do not want to get phone calls in the middle of the night on our players. There is going to be strict discipline in place, and they have to act accordingly in their community. It does matter whether they are at home or at school, they are going to do the right thing socially.

The third core thing is competitive excellence. That goes back to our expectations for the team. We expect to win, compete for the championship, and go to a bowl game.

The next thing I talked to them about was attitude. Everyone in our program is going to have a great attitude. He may have a bad day, but if it affects the football team, that is a bad attitude. It does not matter who the person is; if he is part of our program, he is going to have a great attitude. It could be the janitor sweeping the hall or a trainer or a secretary; all of these people are going to have a great attitude to be involved with our program. We are all part of one team.

Every meeting room we have has the same sign hanging in it. If a player has an issue, we have them come into the office. We give them a copy of the sign and have them read it. We had one player write what was on the sign for 30 straight days before he got it straight. He got an attitude adjustment. The sign reads:

> The longer I live, the more I realize the impact of attitude on life. Attitude to me is more important than fact, more important than the past, education, the money, circumstances, the failures and successes, and more important than what other things they are doing. It is more important and inherent than giftedness and skill. It will make or break a company, church, home, or a team. It is a remarkable thing that we have a choice every day of the attitude we will embrace for that day. We cannot change our past. We cannot change the fact that people act certain ways. We cannot change the inevitable. The only thing we can do is play on the one strength we have, and that is our attitude. Life is 10 percent of what happens to you and 90 percent of how you react to it. The one hope we have is that we are in charge of our attitude.

The next thing we talk to our players about is no excuses. The basic thing is this: I do not care what the excuse is. It is not important to me that you were late to a meeting because you overslept. That is not important to me. You were late for the meeting. My coaches do not give me excuses, the players do not give me excuses, and I do not want any excuses from my secretary. We accept no excuses, and you get no excuses from me. That is how you run a great program. You have a great attitude and have no excuses. That is how we do things, and they are very important in our program.

We want to pay attention to detail. We have detail in everything we do. We have very detailed plan in every phase of the program. If a coach draws up a scouting report, I want it done well enough to be published. If he draws a diagram on the board, I want it perfect. Our players are not allowed to run into the line and stop. They must run three steps past the line. Everything we do throughout our entire program is done in detail.

Dick Vermeil, former NFL head coach, had this to say about detail:

I'm a detail man to the point where I am called a workaholic because I put so much time into detailing everything and making sure everything is organized in preparation.

That is what many coaches have a hard time doing. We want to make sure every detail in our program is in line for our success. That is an important part of our program.

You need to have a comprehensive plan for every phase of your program. Nothing will happen in your program by chance. We have a comprehensive plan for the following areas:

- Academics
- Recruiting
- Player development
- Leadership building
- Offense, defense, and special teams

We want to develop an edge in each of these areas to have chance of success in our program. We are not blessed with the greatest talent in the world. In 12 of the 13 games we played, we were the underdog, but we found an edge in a number of different areas, and it gave us a chance to win.

In all these areas where we have a comprehensive plan, we have achieved what we are looking to do. After each season, we critique all the areas and see how we have done. In our academic plan, we have achieved our goals every single year. We finished our recruiting Wednesday. On Thursday morning, we will sit down as a staff and critique everything we did in relationship to recruiting.

In our player-development area, we completed that in the first part of January with four hours of meetings, going over everything we tried to achieve in that area. We reviewed everything we did to try to make our team better. I will talk in detail about that part of the program later.

When you build a program, you must have some general principles. When you take over a program like we did, you must have a plan for what you want to do.

GENERAL PROGRAM PRINCIPLES

Two-Month Plan
- Hire staff.
- Meet support staff.
- Recruit.
- Evaluate the current team.
- Begin to implement player-development program.
- Set goals for expectations.

Competition
- In everything we do

Player Policy Manual
- General principles
- Standard of conduct
- Compliance
- Policy (locker room, training room, etc.)
- Player evaluation
- Grading system

Discipline Policies
- Academic
- Non-academic

Player Development Program
- Strength development M/W/F
- Winning-edge program T/Th 6:00 a.m.
- Testing program
  - ✓ Strength testing—Game day in the weight room
  - ✓ Friday testing
  - ✓ PR program—Goal boards in coaches' offices

Hiring a staff is the most important thing that a head coach does. You have to put the right people together. We did not win the games we won because of me. It was because of the people I hired. I was fortunate at Wyoming to hire anyone I wanted. I have my own trainer, strength coach, activities coordinator, and my personal assistant. I hired every coach on my staff. I hired great people. That is how you achieve success. You surround yourself with the absolute best in your profession.

When you come into a job, you must retain a certain amount of people that will work in your program. You have to meet your support staff and let them know your expectations for the program. You have to hold them accountable for what they do to meet those expectations. When I came to Wyoming, I had to retain a trainer. We worked for a while until he made a decision, and now he is gone. You have to respect their decisions, but they must get on board with your program and do the things your way.

We came into the program and immediately started to recruit. We had to evaluate the team we had to work with. We did that almost immediately and put in place our player-development program. We had to set goals for our expectations in the program. All these things had to be done in the first two months we were at Wyoming.

In our program, we want our players to compete in everything they do. We are going to teach our players to compete because that had not happened before. When we got there, the first competition was in their academic roles. We want all our players to strive for high grades. We do not allow our players to take short class loads. They all take 16 hours a semester because we want them to all graduate in four years. If they get that done earlier, they can go to graduate school.

We want them to compete in the classroom and the weight room. Every day they are in the weight room, we want them to compete. We want them working for their PRs (personal records) as well as with each other. Obviously, we want them to compete on the football field.

I have two other things I read to the team. One of them is entitled, "The Psychological Profile of a Wannabe." The other is entitled "The Psychological Profile of a Champion." When I first took over at Wyoming, we had many "wannabes" on our team.

Profile of the Wannabe
- No pride
- Do not care whether he wins or loses
- He goes with the pack
- Know-it-alls and resistant to new ideas
- Grippers

- Makes excuses
- Complainers
- Looks good against teams that are not high-caliber
- Looks bad in big games or when competition gets tough
- Quits at the end of games we are losing

I took the "Profile of a Champion" and posted it on every player's locker.

Profile of a Champion
- Coachable: Takes advice and is easy to coach, eager to learn, easy to approach, follows rules
- Aggressive: First-place-belongs-to-me attitude, exerts himself, great competitor, and dying to be the best
- Leadership: Shows the way and sets a good example, respected by his teammates, others follow his examples, and takes advice
- Physical toughness: Develop toughness by hard work, keeps training rules, trains the year round
- Mental toughness: Never-give-up attitude, ignores heat, cold, and pain, no excuses

We had to change the thinking of the football team to get them to think that way.

The next thing we did was to put together a player policy manual. I gave this to the players, and it has everything about our program. It had a section of general principles. It had a section on standards of conduct. It gave them an idea of how we expected them to behave around the facility and in the community. It dealt with compliance issues and discussed what was legal and what was not. It had policies dealing with the locker room, training room, and weight room. It told them what was expected in all those areas.

I had a section dealing with player evaluation. I told them about the grading system and how they were to be evaluated after each practice and each game. Every one of the areas in the player manual, I covered every day in two-a-day practice in the fall. The coaching staff does the same thing in the spring. Twice a year, we go through the entire policy manual so they know what our expectations are of them.

We want to make sure they understand every area in the manual. Sometimes, we have players come into the office with questions about the manual. We want to make sure the players know exactly what the expectations are.

We have discipline policies in place on our team. I do not think you can have any success at all if you do not have great discipline. In this day and age, you do not have a chance to run a successful program without discipline. We have a discipline policy for academics and non-academics. If a player misses a class or study table, that was strike one. The player had to come into his coach's office for a two-hour session. If you came into the coach's office for some non-academic issue, that was strike two, and you had to do some type of running. Strike three was for a problem, and the player had to come in with everyone who plays on his side of the ball. Bringing a whole group into the discipline area because of one player's behavior puts peer pressure on the offending player.

I meet with each player after the season to talk about the program. They expressed things they liked and things they did not like. The major theme throughout these interviews was they were tired of running because some other player screwed up. I told them to take that issue up with the player who is screwing up. They did not know they could do that.

The policy for a strike one academically is a study hall in the coach's office. They come in on Friday night from 9 to 11 p.m. for the study hall. The next morning, the player comes back and does up-downs outside in the stadium. It does not matter whether there is green grass or three feet of snow. That is the strike-one discipline.

Strike two is Friday and Saturday night study halls from 9 to 11 p.m. in the coaches' office. They come back Saturday and Sunday mornings and do up-downs in the stadium. If it gets to strike three, they get two full weeks of that activity.

For a non-academic issue, there are no study halls. They meet with their coach for five straight mornings outside on the turf. If they miss any of the

five days, the five days start over. If the players are dumb enough to screw up to where they have to come in and do this stuff, they get what they deserve. Each coach has one weekend that they have to be in town so they can take charge of the discipline. With two weeks as a penalty in the program, we do not have many screw-ups.

I want to talk about our player-development program. That is a number of different phases for us. We have a strength-development program we run during the off-season on Monday, Wednesday, and Friday. Our strength coach and every coach in the room are working on football-related exercises. We have a long way to go. I go down to check on things that are going on. I keep all the numbers and paperwork, but I do not get involved with what is going on in the room.

During the season, we lift on Sunday and Wednesday. We have some players do dynamic training on Fridays. When we start spring football, we lift two days a week. Our "winning edge program" starts this coming Tuesday. We work Tuesdays and Thursdays in this program. Our entire staff is involved in this program, and we start at 6:00 in the mornings. This is our in-door program. We work for an hour-and-a-half. We have a mat section, agility section, and form running section. We start out with a warm-up, and afterward we go to the different stations. This program was the reason we came from behind in five of the seven games we won. We pushed them to that level doing this program.

In our strength-testing program, we test three times a year. We test a one-rep max in bench, power clean, and squat. When we have our testing days, we post big signs outside the weight room that read: "Game Day in the Weight Room." This is an entire week's worth of activities. We want a lot of enthusiasm along with music going on in the room. Every time someone achieves a personal record, we blow the whistle. The entire team stops and gives a cheer for the player. We want great enthusiasm in the room. This active is just like game day during the season. We do these three times a year.

We also have Friday testing. Every Friday for a five straight weeks during the indoor program, the players will come in and test. It starts at 12:30 and goes to around 3:30. They can come in anytime with their group to test. We time them electronically in the 40 and one or two agility tests, which changes every week. We do the shuttle test as one of the agility test. We time them three times in the 40. We do the vertical jump and the lone jump also. The testing protocol has to be accurate so we can evaluate our program.

We emphasize personal records in the indoor testing. We test in the indoor program throughout the off-season. We test in speed and agility. What we want to see is a personal record every time the player tests. We do not like it when a player comes in and does not get a PR. We want one every time he tests. We are not looking for huge gains in his performance. We are looking for improvement every time he tests. If we can get 95-percent of our team to get a PR, our football team will continue to get better.

We become stronger, faster, and more agile in our skills and become better athletes. We have a goal board in each position coach's office. Across the top of the board in red are lists of athletic standards. Those are the numbers to be an All-Conference player. We take those standard numbers from the NFL Combine. Every coach has his players listed and their PRs for each test they take. When they achieve a new PR, they go into the coach's office and change the board. We make a big deal about increasing their PRs. We emphasize that point. We want to constantly compete in everything we do to get better.

SPRING PRACTICE

- Coaching philosophy
- Cowboy toughness
- Competition: keep score on every drill
- It's all about the ball!

When we go to spring football practice, the first thing we touch on is our coaching philosophy. We coach aggressively on the field. I do not want a clinic on the field. On every rough draft of our practice schedule, I want a coaching point listed. I want my coaches running through the action the entire practice. Coaches are just like players: they do not walk on the football field. We run everywhere we go. If I have a punt team punting the ball, I want a coach chasing them down the field, coaching them. We coach that way at our place. There is no standing around and watching. There are no folded arms or hands in the pockets with our coaches.

The thing we had to get back to at Wyoming was "cowboy toughness." The people of Wyoming are hard-working, tough people. They did not like to see teams that did not show the toughness they were used to in everyday life. The people of the state of Wyoming are "cowboy tough." I put together film clips of violent hits at Wyoming. I show that to the players and emphasize that is the kind of toughness we are looking for. We want to be like Christians. It is better to give than to receive.

We had our spring game in April last year, and the weather was good. We had 18 players miss the spring game because of injury. You cannot be physical if you are not physical in practice. We had players knocking the crap out of each other. We were physical in the spring. In the spring, we go hard in practice. We had 18 players miss the spring game, but that had to do with poor conditioning, and not very good athletes who were not used to hitting. We played Fresno State in the bowl game, and I had two players miss the game. We changed the toughness of that football team from the spring when we got there to the bowl game.

We compete in every drill we have. There is a winner and a loser in every drill, and we keep score. Following is an example of our score sheet. We are going to have competition in the drills, and at the end of practice; there is a winner and a loser. The "winner, winner, chicken dinners" get to watch the loser and their coaches do up-downs. The winners get the dark jerseys for the next practice. Before we got there, these players did not know how to compete. Now, we compete from the start of practice to the end.

Example Practice Competition Score Sheet

1-on-1

Goal: Defensive backs and wide receivers, completion/incompletion

Scoring: Defense 2, offense 1

Note: (An interception for a TD is double points for the defense.)

7-on-7

Goal: 3rd down—Conversion, stop 1st, 2nd; 5 yards

Scoring: Defense 3, offense 2

Note: (An interception for a TD is double points for the defense.)

Inside Run

Goal: Offense 3 yards for more, defense less than 3 yards

Scoring: Offense 2, defense 1

11-on-11

Goal: 3rd down—Conversion, stop 1st, 2nd; run +3 yards, pass +5 yards

Scoring: Offense 1, defense 1

1-on-1 Pass Rush

Goal: 3.4 seconds

Scoring: Offense 1, defense 1

When we took over the program a year ago, they had 36 turnovers in the previous season. That was the only stat Wyoming led the country in. It goes back to what you emphasis. We were not very good athletically, we did not have any explosive players, but we did protect the football. In 13 games, we had 14 turnovers. It is all about the ball. It does not matter how bad the player is; you can coach ball security. You can coach that into your players. We had T-shirts printed that read: "It's all about the ball." That became a point of emphasis for us. That made the difference in winning and losing. When you have a plus number in the turnover margin, you have a chance to win. Every player in our program knows to carry the ball high and tight. People who can only get the ball through a fumble or interception know to carry it high and tight.

We have strip drills every day. We have a turnover circuit we go through defensively. I had one coach put a boxing glove on a long stick and went around jabbing the ball. We emphasized that point. We are constantly working on fumble drills and ball security. You can do these types of thing regardless of the talent you have. It will make a difference.

People were telling me the defense looked good. It looked good because we did not give the ball to the opponent 36 times. They had to score on their own this year without our help.

Summer Program

- Making sacrifices
- All returning players stay in Laramie.
- All freshmen are in Laramie for four weeks.

Every one of our returning players spent the summer in Laramie last year. Everyone of our incoming freshman came into school for four weeks. We put them in a dorm. Everyone on our football spent part of the summer in Laramie. All the returning players were there all summer. The freshman came for four weeks and went home for five weeks before returning in the fall. That helps them with homesickness. They are not helping the football team while they are gone for five weeks, but it keeps you from losing too many players because they want to go home. We lost only two freshman players who did not return in the fall.

There are not that many football players in Wyoming, and we have to go outside the state to get players. If you keep a kid in Laramie from June until December, he will be one homesick cookie.

I asked our players if they wanted to win and be a championship team. If they did, they had to be here in the summer time. Every night we give them a sheet with a practice plan, and the players went out and practiced. There were no coaches there, but they practiced for an hour-and-a-half. The strength coach and trainer are allowed on the field with them. You must have players who are willing to sacrifice their summers for the team.

In pre-season, we were picked to finish dead last in the Mountain West Conference. All the media outlets picked us to finish last. We were picked where we should have been. I told the players we have 12 opportunities to earn the respect and creditability for the program. I told them it was up to them to do something about it. If they did not like where the media picked us to finish, do something about it. That is where we are. You do not give respect; you earn it. I thought they did one hell of a job and went to the field and played their butts off every week.

Fall Camp First Season

Plan to Win

- Play great defense.
- Win the turnover margin.
- Play great special forces.
- Eliminate mental errors.

We did not win every game, but we competed every week. When we went to fall camp, we knew we had to play good defense. We did not have too many players coming back on offense, and we were going to start a freshman quarterback. We knew we had to win the turnover margin. I knew we would win the turnover margin because we had a great coaching staff. We knew we could gain an edge if we played great special forces. We used our best players on our special teams. As in any program, to win you must eliminate the mental errors.

Team Bottom Line

- Be enthusiastic.
- Be a six-second competitor.
- Know your assignment.
- Play cowboy-tough and physical.

The bottom line is this: We expect to see these four things every play. It does not matter about the ability level. Every player can be enthusiastic. If they go to practice and are dull and uninspired, I get their coaches to get the enthusiasm going. We went to practice one day, and it was terrible. After 45 minutes, I could not stand it anymore. I stopped practice. We went to the end of the field and started practice over. That was the last time I had to do that.

Six seconds is the average length of each play. We want our players to play from the snap of the ball until the whistle blows on each play. The ability and talent does not affect their ability to give all they have for six seconds.

It takes no talent to know your assignment. You may not execute it correctly, but know what you are supposed to do. The last thing is to play physical and be cowboy tough.

In our first season, we had to find a way to win football games. We felt we could win with our special forces emphasis. I wanted it to be a special honor to be on the special teams. When we traveled, they got their individual seat on the bus or plane. They got snacks and drinks on the bus and did not have to wait in line at dinner. They went to the front of the line at all eating functions. At the end of the year, any player that started the whole year on special teams came to my house for a steak dinner.

We have a point system and a special forces player of the week and year. We used the term special forces for our special teams. I got a letter from Brigadier General Michael Respass, who is commander of all Special Forces. I posted it on the wall in our football building. It reads:

Dear Coach Christensen:

I understand your special teams are known as "Special Forces." We expect that these collegiate warriors will perform without fear and with distinction. We do not expect mercy from our opponents and give none in return. We have men of uncommon valor and character in our ranks, and we expect no less from your players who bear our name.

Sincerely,
Michael S. Respass
Brigadier General, U.S. Army

We had to get special permission to use the name and some of the honor we give to our players. It has become an honor for the players on our team to play on these teams.

The one thing I cover on a weekly basis is the Pyramid Objectives. It is 13 weeks of comparisons on a chart, which we post for our players to see. It gives our statistical ranking in the conference. We had five blocks on the top and six blocks on the bottom. The categories on the top blocks were turnover margin, offensive turnovers, defensive takeaways, penalties, and win the fourth quarter. On the base of the pyramid were six blocks with the special teams' rankings. The categories were: win the kicking game, house team, ranger team, kick scoring, net punting, and kickoff coverage. The house team was the kickoff-return team and the ranger team was the punt-return team. The bottom of the pyramid was our offensive and defensive statistics.

We cover these charts every week so the players on those teams know the importance of them. We were not perfect on all things, but when you consider field position, the punt-return team and our punt team changed field position. The turnover margin meant we were not giving the opponent the short field, which gave us an advantage. Those two factors alone were the reason we were able to win seven football games. We had no business winning the number of games we won. We emphasized the things that were coachable, and that led to a successful season.

I had a late-season meeting after a tough three-game stretch. We had just finished playing Air Force, BYU, and Utah. We competed but lost all three games. I told them they were "All in or all out!" If they did not like the way things were going, "When we leave this meeting, go into the locker room, take your stuff off, and leave. The coaches will be out on the field waiting for the people who want to play." That was the turning point for our team. We had three games left. We went to San Diego State and won in the fourth quarter. We played TCU, and they beat us. We finished the season against our rival at Colorado State, and we won that game by one point. That win got us into a bowl game against Fresno State.

Five of the seven games we won, we came from behind in the fourth quarter to win. We did all the little things right. The coaches "coached up" the things they could control. The result for us was the opportunity to go to a bowl game and win.

FUNDAMENTALS OF DEFENSIVE LINE PLAY

Towson University

Thank you. I am excited to be here. I am going to talk about defensive line techniques and play. I want to get right into the talk. The basis for any line techniques goes back to the fundamentals of football.

The defensive line serves as the foundation of the overall defense. It is imperative that the line functions in the realm of their responsibility because, in order to have a sound defense, you must have a solid foundation; it all starts with the people up front. It takes a person with innate tenacity and aggressiveness to play defensive line. He must possess the size, strength, and power to go against, generally, the biggest players on the football field: the offensive line. But, he must also have speed and quickness to get off blocks, pursue and make tackles, and rush the passer. It takes a dedicated and determined individual to work constantly on the techniques that are necessary to become a defensive lineman.

MASTER OF RUN DEFENSE

We have six essentials that the defensive linemen must master in order to have a good run defense:

- Stance and alignment
- Key and initial movement
- Target
- Block recognition
- Separation and escape
- Pursuit and tackle

For a defensive lineman to play, he must have a good *stance*. I am not too particular about the stagger in the stance. I do not want him stretched out in his stance. I want a balanced stance with his feet under his body.

Stance and Alignment

The techniques for run defense are:

- Flat back with weight distributed between the balls of the feet and hands
- Feet shoulder-width apart, no more than a toe-to-heel relationship
- Shoulders parallel to the line of scrimmage
- Down hand is three inches in front of the head; off arm and hand are in a ready position; head is up in a bull-like body position cocked in a position ready to explode
- Proper bend in three great levers: knees, ankles, and hips
- Concentration

If he has too much stagger in his feet, I do not like that. If he spreads out wide, I do not like that. I want the lineman to be comfortable in his stance. If the lineman can take off and move from his stance, I will not change his technique.

We align in both right- and left-handed stances. When we get down, I want the inside hand on the ground. When the inside hand goes on the ground that means the inside foot is back in the stance. The off hand is not dangling or resting on the off knee—I want it cocked and ready to go.

When the lineman gets down in his stance, I want his cleats in the ground. I do not want him up on his toes. It is like a race car. They have big, wide tires on those cars. They have those types of tires to give the car better ground traction. I want the defensive lineman with his cleats in the ground so he can push off. The most important thing for the defensive lineman to do is get off the ball. Every drill, we work on takeoff. We have to work hard on the getoff in practice. I want the defensive lineman out of his stance and off the ball. That is the focus of the drills. I want to work on stance and start.

In our *alignment*, we have a vertical and horizontal alignment. In their vertical alignment, I want the defensive linemen as close to the ball as they can possibly get. I know you have all heard about being able to run a credit card through the defensive lineman's hand and the ball. That is what I strive for. We want to get as close to the ball as we can.

When I talk about *horizontal* alignment, I am talking about the alignment on an offensive blocker (Diagram #1). We use the numbering system that has been in football forever. In our defensive scheme, we align in a shade on the center, 2i, 4i, and 6i techniques. Those are the inside positions on the guard, tackle, and end. The head-up positions are 2, 4, and 6 techniques. The shoulder positions are 3, 5, and 9 techniques. We replaced the 7 technique with the 6i technique. Those positions give us our horizontal alignments.

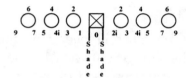

Diagram #1. Horizontal Alignment

When you work with a young lineman, you should back him off the ball. That gives him a chance to read the offensive lineman.

Key and Initial Movement

The next aspect of defensive line play is the *key*. Keying gives us a quick indication of what the play is. We will react to our primary key by making an initial reaction. A correct reaction to your primary key is a vital part of whether you can make the play or not. You should see and react to your primary for two steps while expanding your vision to your secondary key.

When I teach keys, I start with a key progression (Diagram #2). The primary key for the defensive lineman is the offensive lineman he is aligning on. In the key progression, the defensive

lineman has three keys that come from the primary read on the offensive lineman. If the offensive lineman fires out at the defender, we know we are near the point of attack and we play accordingly. We want to protect our gaps in that case.

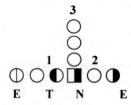

Diagram #2. Key Progression

If the offensive lineman goes away from the defender, he has to react in a different way. He has to make contact and look down the line of scrimmage for a trap. The third part of the key progression is to look into the backfield for an offensive blocker.

To play on the defensive line you must *move*. If you play on the defensive line, you must have quick hands, quick eyes, and quick feet. The defensive lineman must play with his hands. If he tries to play with his forearms, he cannot play defense. When I first look at a player, I want to see what he is doing. If he has a bad stance, he probably has bad feet.

With initial movement, a player must:

- Maintain peripheral vision on the football and move on ball movement
- React to ball movement, not sound (no gifts, and no mental errors on cadence)
- Attack his man with fast eyes, hands, and feet

Target

- Half of the man on
- Outside hand to near shoulder; inside hand to breastplate
- Tight hands, elbow tight
- Fast hands
- Get-Off
  - ✓ Power-pack step with the hips, not the feet
  - ✓ Shoot hand
  - ✓ Let feet follow

When we work against the offense in practice, we want to get a jump on the ball. If the quarterback calls the cadence and does not go on the first sound, we are going the next time he opens his mouth. He is not going to snap the ball on three. If the ball is not snapped on the first sound, we are going on the second sound. That gives us an advantage on the get-off. That is particularly true on third and long. We are going to get a good jump and go.

When the defensive lineman attacks the offensive lineman, he attacks half the man. When the defensive lineman comes off the ball, he wants his inside hand to be down the breastplate of the offensive blocker. He wants his outside hand on the near shoulder pad.

When he attacks, he wants to attack with tight elbows. As he attacks with his hands, he wants his thumbs up with his fingers flared outside. That brings the elbows inside. He wants to get his hands on the offensive blocker as fast as possible. The offensive blocker is going to try and get his hands on the defender. The one who gets his hand inside has control. If the offensive blocker's hands are outside the defender, he has no power or control over the defender.

When I was playing, the coaches taught us to take a six- to eight-inch power step. Every time I taught that type of movement, the player would stand up and play too high. I do not emphasize that anymore. What I emphasize now is to shoot the hands as fast as possible. If I can shoot my hands and get them on the offensive blocker, the feet will follow.

I want to shoot the hands and roll the hips. If I can do that, the feet will follow in the technique. I do not teach the six-inch power step. I teach shooting the hands, rolling the hips, and keeping the back flat.

We do a 1-on-1 drill every day which teaches everything I want the defensive linemen to do. We work with the bags and without the bags. We work from our knees to start with and shoot the hands into the linemen. We shoot the hands and bring the feet. We work on shooting the hands, bringing the feet, and shedding the blocker to one side or the other.

When we do this drill, I want the defender's hands above his eyes. The eyes have to see the target. The eyes cannot be looking for the football. They must see the target, shoot the hands, gain control, and then look for the football. When he shoots his hands, I want to see him grab cloth. I want his elbows in tight and the thumbs up. As he comes off, we want a good body lean into the offensive blocker.

When we play head-up an offensive blocker, both hands go to the breastplate of the lineman. If we play an odd or shoulder technique, the inside hand goes to the breastplate and the outside hand goes to the shoulder.

When we are working this drill, I want the defender to get his hips into the technique as much as he can. I do not want the hips lagging behind. I want him to get them rolled and into the offensive blocker.

Block Recognition

The defensive lineman must be able to recognize what type of block the offensive lineman is using. If the offensive lineman fires out on the defender and tries to cover him up, we know that is a *base* block (Diagram #3). The first thing the defender wants to do is come off the ball, get his hands into the blocker, and get a vertical push. The thing he wants to do is stay square to the line of scrimmage. I do not want him to turn one way or the other. He has to have a two-way go once he recognizes where the ball is going.

Diagram #3. Base Block

If the offensive blocker tries to reach the defensive lineman, I coach them not to run away from the reach (Diagram #4). I do not want the defense to do what the offensive lineman wants him to do. I do not want to turn and run outside to keep from being reached. I want the defensive lineman to get in contact with the offensive lineman and get a vertical push into the backfield. If the offensive lineman reaches the defender, it will be three yards deep in the backfield, not on the line of scrimmage. If he gets penetration three yards into the backfield, he is allowed to get reached. The thing that kills the zone play and a reach block is *penetration*. On the reach block reaction, I do not want the defensive lineman to turn and run. I want him to keep his shoulder square to the line and work for depth.

Diagram #4. Reach Block

If the offensive blocker *down blocks*, the defensive lineman's key goes away from him (Diagram #5). The 3-technique defender is playing man-to-man defense on the guard. If he tries to go down and get up on the linebacker, the 3 technique is not going to let him get inside. He gets his hands on the guard, works flat down the line of scrimmage, and then he gets off and pursues. As he plays inside with the guard, he keeps his shoulder square to the line until he finds out what is happening or finds the ball.

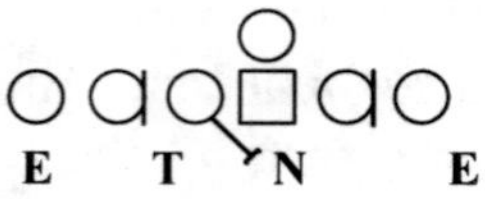

Diagram #5. Down Block

If the defender encounters a *double-team*, we want to split it (Diagram #6). I was taught if we were double-teamed to fall on the ground and create a pile. We do not teach that technique. I emphasize splitting the double-team. The double-team will start out as a base block by the man the defender is aligned on. When he feels the double-team coming, the defender wants to beat the shoulder of the drive blocker and get a vertical push up the field. He should be starting the vertical push on the post man because that is the way we play the base block. When the guard comes down on the shade technique, he wants to get his hat in front of the shoulder and work for penetration up the field.

Diagram #6. Double-Team Block

The next block we play is a *chip block* (Diagram #7). That is a form of a double-team. The defender will encounter two blockers but be blocked by only one of them. In the chip block, someone other than the blocker the defender is aligned on will end up blocking or passing him off to another blocker. It could be the center trying to overtake the shade technique with the guard getting up to the linebacker. The defender attacks the center the same as he did on the base block. He wants to stay square to the line of scrimmage and dip his shoulder into the guard until the guard leaves. After the guard leaves to go to the second level, the defender reappears in his gap and does not let the center overtake the block on him.

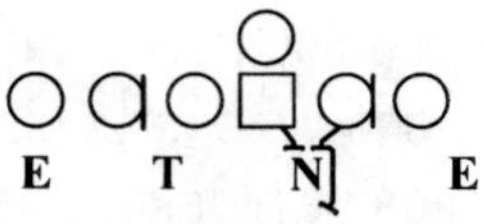

Diagram #7. Chip Block

The *slip block* is similar to the chip block (Diagram #8). The offensive guard will try to push the shade-technique defender onto the center's block or hit him so the center can overtake the offensive guard's block. The guard's responsibility is someone on the next level, and he wants to slip after the hit. He is helping the center get a block on the shade-technique defender. The nose defender wants to make sure the guard cannot get to the next level. I coach the shade-technique defender to play the center and snatch the slip blocker. He grabs the slip blocker and prevents him from getting to the linebackers. We call that holding the *jump through*.

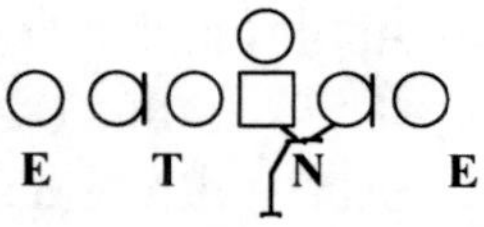

Diagram #8. Slip Block

We face the *power O* all the time. The offense will block down on the defenders and kick out at the point of attack. I coach the 3 technique to fight the pressure and get vertical. If he cannot get vertical, he fights the pressure and gets across the blocker's face. If the defender gets out into space, he can turn his shoulders and pursue. When he is playing blocks on the inside, he has to stay square and play the blocker. Some coaches teach the 3 technique to play from the backside of the block. I feel that 99 times out of a hundred, the defender will not get in a position to make a play.

The next type of block we have to recognize is the *turnout block*. When the offensive blocker turns out and tries to drive the defender to the outside, the defender squeezes down inside. I want him to squeeze but keep his shoulder square to the line of scrimmage. We want to get into the middle of the blocker and squeeze him down.

The *lead block* is like the turnout block in some ways. This becomes a spill technique for the defender. We want to wrong arm the blocker. The thing I do not want to do is run down the line of scrimmage. I want to spill the play as deep in the backfield as I can get. I want to go through the inside of the block but at the same time get up the field.

When we teach block recognition, we use 1-on-1 drills, including the mirror-read drill (Diagram #9). In the 1-on-1 drills, we work on the base, reach, and cutoff blocks. In the 1-on-1 drill, we are working on mirroring the offensive blocker. The players align in three-point stances. The blocker squats down with his hands to his side. He lets the defender get his hand into the breastplate. The coach standing behind the defense will point to the defender's right or left shoulder or chest, or he'll show a pass set to direct the blocker as to what type of block to show. The coach gives the snap count to the blocker.

Diagram #9. Mirror-Read Drill

We go to a 2-on-1 drill (Diagram #10) and work on the chip and slip blocks. After that, we go to a 3-on-1 drill and work on double-team, down, trap, and lead blocks. We can work on a scoop scheme in this drill. We want to work on schemes we will see in the game.

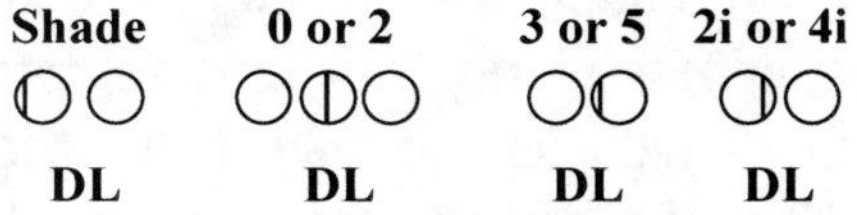

Diagram #10. Key Read Drill (2-on-1 or 3-on-1)

Separation and Escape

Key Elements of Separation

- Get eyes into the V of the neck
- Hands into breastplate
- Elbows in, thumbs up
- Good bend into knees, ankles, and hips
- Be able to explode, hands above eyes, and hips in front of feet

Key Elements of Escape

- Push/Pull technique: Initially the gap hand is the power hand and the cover hand is the trail hand. Push with the power hand and pull with the trail hand.
- Arm over (swim)
- Underarm (rip)
- Shrug

After we recognize what the block is, we have to play it. In all cases, we want to try to get penetration. However, to make a tackle, we have to get off the blocks. We must learn how to separate from the block and escape. That goes back to using your hands. To get into position to separate, we must have our hands above our eyes and our hips in front of our feet. You cannot separate from a blocker if your hands are below your eyes.

To escape, one of the techniques we use is a *snatch and shrug*. We have to snatch and shrug at a 45-degree angle to the side. What happens many times is the defender will snatch the offensive block and, instead of pulling him at an angle, he will pull him right back onto himself. We want to shrug him to the side and escape at a 45-degree angle.

Besides the shrug, we use the *arm-over* or swim technique. We want to punch the offensive blocker, gain control, grab the outside shoulder, and bring the inside arm over and across the face of the blocker and outside shoulder. We also use the underarm rip technique. When we rip, it is important to get the inside arm as high as you can under the outside armpit and shoulder of the offensive blocker. If you do that, it allows the hips to stay in front. The higher the arm gets in the rip, the further the hips are in front of the blocker.

We also use a *push/pull technique.* The way I want to perform this technique is to push with the outside hand and pull with the inside hand. We attack the outside shoulder and push hard on it. When we pull with the inside hand, it turns the shoulder of the offensive blocker. You cannot escape from a block until you get control of the blocker. Using the push/pull technique lets us get control.

We can drill the push/pull technique. Fit two players in a pre-locked position with both players facing one another in a square position. The defender places his hand on the offensive blocker's shoulders while the blocker's hands are at his side. On the coach's command, the blocker takes a step to the right or left, simulating a reach or cutoff block. The defender power presses the shoulder of the blocker upfield while pulling the other shoulder in order to turn the blocker. Repeat the drill several times and then switch.

Another drill we use is a *separation-and-shed drill* (Diagram #11). We fit two players in a pre-locked position with the offensive blocker's shoulder square to the line. On the coach's command, the blocker tries to reach block the defender. The defender locks out the upfield shoulder of the blocker and pulls the other shoulder in order to turn the blocker. After he has turned the shoulders, he uses one of the three escape moves:

- Underarm: Rip arm underneath the armpit and shoulder of the blocker.

- Over arm: Pull the outside shoulder down, and bring the inside arm over and across the blocker's face.

- Shrug: Use the blocker's momentum to jerk his body sideways. The coaching point is to never try to escape until you have control of the blocker.

Diagram #11. Escape

Once you get off the block, you have to pursue. We do pursuit drills all the time.

Pursuit and Tackle

Pursuit does the following things:
- Eliminates a long touchdown (the big play)
- Discourages your opponent (especially the ballcarrier)
- Helps to cover any possible mistakes in your defense (helps your teammate)
- Makes us the best defensive team in the country

What it takes to pursue:
- Pursuit, first, is a mental process (if you want to, you can)
- Visualize pursuing and making great plays (be a big-play guy)
- Physical condition is necessary so you can have great pursuit every play
- Speed (think fast and quick)
- Get-off blocks-get to the ball If on the ground, get off the ground quickly using only the hands and feet then proper pursuit angle

How to pursue:
- Play your responsibility
- Take correct course to ball (near hip of the ball), then adjust to the angle of the ball
- Wanting to get there (mental)

We do all kinds of pursuit drills to fit the scheme we have to face. One pursuit is a *sprint-to-the-receiver drill* (Diagram #12). The purpose of the drill is to teach get-off, pass rush moves, sprint to the quarterback, then hustle to the receiver to make the tackle. The drill starts on the movement of the ball. The defender rushes the quarterback then sprints to the cone where the quarterback throws the ball. Set the cones to represent a swing pass to the back or a downfield pass to a receiver.

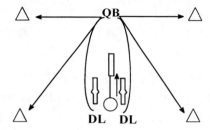

Diagram #12. Sprint to the Receiver

We work on *screen pursuit drills* (Diagram #13). The defensive linemen align in their positions. We throw the ball to the outside as if there was a jailbreak screen. The defensive linemen get off the ball, go through their initial steps, and pursue to the ball. You create the pursuit drills that fit what you want from your defensive linemen.

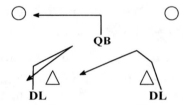

Diagram #13. Screen Pursuit Drill

We have a *sight* and a *pressure* key. The pressure key is the man the defender is aligned on. The sight key is the offensive linemen to the inside of the pressure key. If the defender is aligned on his pressure key and goes to the inside, he does not want to be flattened and washed down the line of scrimmage. As he steps inside, he has to get his outside hip back to square and get a vertical push up the field. If he can get his hip turned square to the line of scrimmage, he can get up the field.

We drill the movement in a simple 1-on-1 drill (Diagram #14). I put two trashcan barrels about five yards apart. I put the defender in front of the barrel. The blocker will be directly behind the barrel, slightly turned inside. On ball movement, the defender will slant, dip his shoulder, rip into the blocker, and get his hips going upfield. The blocker will try to push the defender flat down the line of

scrimmage while the defender leans into him working his hips upfield. Put a cone five yards up the field between the two barrels. The defender does not want to be driven inside past the cone.

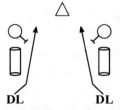

Diagram #14. Slant Drill (1-on-1)

The next drill we do, slant and read (Diagram #15), involves the sight key. The defender does the same thing he did in the slant drill. However, in this drill, he reads the sight key. If the sight key steps toward him, he gets vertical up the field. If the sight key moves away from him, he continues flat to the inside and locates the football. If the sight end shows a pass set, he gets vertical and rushes the passer.

Diagram #15. Slant-and-Read Drill

The next thing we do is expand the drill and add the second offensive lineman in the drill (Diagram #16). We have the pressure key and the sight key in the drill. It is a repeat of the two drills. This time the defender is reacting to both his pressure key and his sight key. If he cuts inside the pressure key and he tries to block him, he gets vertical up the field. If the pressure key goes inside, he focuses on the sight key. He plays the technique the sight key gives him. If the sight key comes to him, he gets vertical. If the sight key goes away, he flattens, continues down the line, and locates the ball.

Diagram #16. Two-Man Key Drill

The coaching point to all these drills is to concentrate on the defender getting his hips square as he cuts inside. If he cannot get his hips square, he has no power. If his hips are going inside, he will continue inside, get flattened and washed down the line.

The next thing I want to cover is the *pass rush*. I do not teach pass rush moves anymore. If you spend all your time teaching a pass rush move and the player never uses it, you have wasted your time. What I teach now is the leverage side of the pass rush and the techniques of the pass rush. The defensive end lines up on the offensive tackle in a tight alignment. However, after the offensive tackle gets in his stance, the defensive end may widen his alignment. Those are the coaching points I help the defensive linemen with.

We run many defensive line games in our scheme. I have the defensive linemen fake moves before the ball is snapped. We fake as if we are going inside when we are really going up the field. It is like I told you earlier, if the ball is not snapped on one, we are going on the next sound. We have a pass rush progression.

PASS RUSH PROGRESSION

Have a Plan

Predetermine your move. Picture what you are going to do before the ball is snapped. That will aid your quickness. You should be:

- Confident
- Coiled
- Concentrating

Take-Off

Explode on the snap. Gain ground on each step. Keep good body angle until you make contact with the blocker. Get inside hand placement on the blocker as soon as possible by:

- Grabbing in a vice-like manner
- Having the eyes strike the chin simultaneously with the hands

I teach the defensive line a pass rush stance. In that stance, we want the lineman to narrow his base and get more weight on his hand. That means he gets his tail higher and increases his stagger. He looks like a track sprinter in his stance. The biggest advantage the defensive lineman can get in the pass rush is the take-off. We want to get on the offensive lineman before he can get set. We want him to be scrambling to get to his set-up point. We want to get our hands on the offensive blocker as quickly as possible.

The next thing I talk about is *hand placement*. The defensive lineman wants to get his hands on the blocker as *soon* as possible and keep them on him as *long* as possible. The one thing I tell the pass rushers is to move their hands and feet. If they stop their hands and feet, they will not be good pass rushers. They have to have busy hands and feet. If they stop their feet, they are dead as a pass rusher.

If the defensive lineman is a contain rusher, he contains the quarterback. He does not contain an offensive lineman. If the defender is supposed to contain, he needs to stay outside and contain. If he goes inside, he may look good, but everyone else will look bad when the quarterback escapes.

We contain the quarterback, but we do not rush past him. We are no good running behind the quarterback. We have two targets in our pass rush scheme. The targets are the front shoulder of the quarterback and the back shoulder of the quarterback. The contain rushers are targeting the back shoulder of the quarterback and the interior rushers are focusing on the front shoulder.

When you rush the quarterback, you do not have time for four or five moves. You have time for one move and a counter off that move. The pass rusher must have what he is going to do in his mind. His first move is not going to work all the time. He has to know what his counter move is going to be. If that does not work, he becomes a bull rusher to the quarterback. If he feels he cannot get home, he gets in front of the quarterback and gets his hands up. The pass rusher wants to use the offensive lineman's technique against him. We do the following things:

- Keep feet moving. Do not lunge.
- Stay in lanes. You need to keep a balanced rush on the quarterback; watch for draw.

- Contain rusher; force the quarterback up inside. Rushers force the quarterback back.
- Do not allow the quarterback to step up or roll out.
- If you can get no push, get your hands up.
- Do not rush behind the quarterback.

You have no more than three seconds to get to the quarterback. You do not have time for three or four moves.

Be undaunted. By a missed move, be ready for the counter move. Keep working, and get penetration.

Use His Technique Against Him

- If the blocker is giving ground, use a power move.
- If the blocker is meeting the defender on the line, use a quick move.
- If the blocker set takes your original move, counter with another.
- Move.
- Take advantage of anything the blocker gives you.

We use a number of drills to teach pass rush, and most of them emphasize the get-off. The first drill is a *see-and-touch hand drill* (Diagram #17). Align two players facing each other one yard apart. The defender aligns in a three-point stance and the blocker is in a two-point stance leaning over at the waist. On the coach's command, the defender will come out of his stance toward the blocker. The blocker will move his hands in unison to various positions around his body as targets for the defender to touch with two hands. This makes the defender concentrate on where the blocker's hands are.

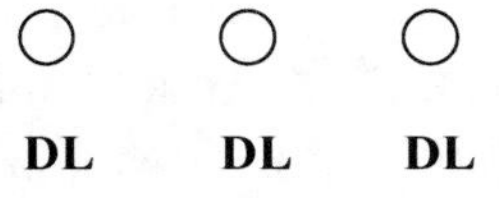

Diagram #17. See-and-Touch Hand Drill

The next drill we use is a *close-the-cushion drill* (Diagram #18). Have the blocker start two yards from defender within a 10-yard mark area. The defender will start on the line. The blocker will backpedal as quickly as he can to the 10-yard mark. The defender will get off on the blocker's movement and close the distance from the blocker as quickly as possible. The defender will try to touch the blocker's shoulders with both hands before he can reach five yards. The second time, have the blocker start at three yards, and the defender must touch him before he can reach seven yards deep.

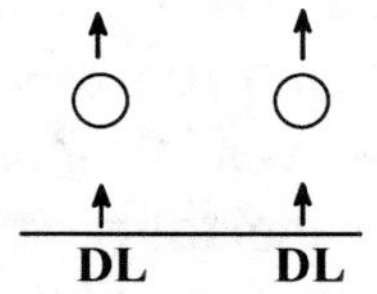

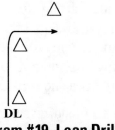

Diagram #18. Close-the-Cushion Drill

The last drill I want to show you is the *lean drill* (Diagram #19). This shows the ability to get off on the ball, to run and lean in non-parallel lines, and to burst and close on the quarterback (timed between 1.1 to 1.5 seconds). The defender aligns with his inside shoulder outside of the first cone. He gets off on the ball movement and sprints to the set point (second cone), then dips the inside shoulder, and sprints underneath the last cone, which simulates the quarterback. You can also add to the drill a towel on the ground inside the second cone so when the player turns around the second cone, he will pick up the towel to emphasize dipping the shoulder.

Diagram #19. Lean Drill

I have reached the end of my time. Do you have any questions? If you are good, I appreciate your attention.

DEFENDING THE TRIPLE OPTION

University of Connecticut

Thank you. I appreciate you being here. It is a pleasure to be here so I can spend some time with you. My topic tonight is: defending the triple option. I am going to take you through defending the option as we would from the 4-4 and 3-4 defenses. We have played Navy, who run this attack. We have defended the option well in some years and not so well in others. The important thing in defending the triple option is not to wait until the week before you play that team to start preparing. If you know you have an option team on your schedule, you need to start preparing in the spring.

When fall practice starts, you must work a little each week in preparation for that type of offense. If you wait until the week before you play them, there is too much teaching to put on your players. Another thing I found, which was effective in defending the option, was practicing the offense with no ball in the drill. That makes your defense go through their responsibilities every time.

If you hand the ball off all the time, the perimeter people will not get the type of reps they need. Using no ball makes every player go through his responsibility on each play. To stop an option attack, you have to play the dive, quarterback, and pitch. You must have discipline within your defensive team so they will play assignment football. That is first and foremost to stopping the option attack.

In addition to being disciplined in playing their responsibility, the defense must be disciplined in taking angles to the football. You do not need a number of schemes to play the option. You have to execute what you want to do. You must be prepared to make adjustments and changes during the game. Their coaches are going to do things at halftime to

help their team. We have to be ready to counter anything they do.

The first defense I want to talk about is the 4-4 defense (Diagram #1). In this defense, we play with a Bandit and a defensive end. They play the 5-technique positions on the defense. On the interior, we play with a nose and a defensive tackle. The inside linebackers are the Mike linebacker, who plays on the strongside, and the Will linebacker, who plays on the weakside.

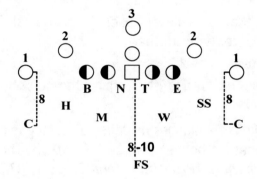

Diagram #1. Base Defense From 4-4

Our third linebacker (or Rover back) is called the Husky. In the secondary, we play with two corners and two safeties. The strong safety will become an outside linebacker in this scheme.

In this defense, our free safety is going to be the alley player to either side of the defense. The corners are playing a 1x8 alignment on the split ends. They will take inside leverage and basically are playing half the field. We are not thinking pass from this offense. Most teams that run the triple option are not looking to throw the football.

The thing the corners have to be aware of is the play-action pass. Triple-option teams will lull the defensive backs to sleep. They will run the ball in all situations, downs, and distances until the defensive back gets careless. When that happens, they throw the ball over the top with the play-action pass. Generally, if they catch you napping, it is a touchdown.

We play with an end and a Bandit. They are basically the same position, but we do some different things with our Bandit that we do not do with the defensive end (Diagram #2). We want both the defenders to play in a heavy 5 technique on the outside shoulder of the offensive tackles. A 5 technique for us is the inside foot of the Bandit on the outside shoulder of the offensive tackle. In a heavy technique, we want the inside foot in the crotch of the offensive tackle.

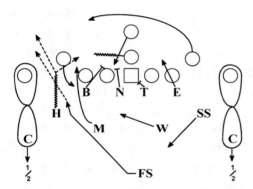

Diagram #2. Run Responsibilities

Their responsibility is to squeeze and reroute the tackle so he cannot get up to the linebacker or free safety. If the tackle tries to release across the face of the 5-technique defender, he cannot allow the tackle to get inside. If the offensive tackle tries to block out or loop to the outside of the 5 technique, he fights pressure or closes down.

The nose and defensive tackle are A-gap defenders and play the center the same way. They align on an inside shade of the offensive guards. They are not going to allow the center to get off the line of scrimmage to block the backside linebacker. The tackle and nose want to make sure the backside linebacker can get over the top on plays away from them.

The linebackers align in a 30 alignment in the B gap. The Husky and the strong safety are aligned on the slotbacks. The Husky is our third linebacker.

They align at four yards and read the release of the slot. If the slot releases inside, they sit and hang in their position. They play the quarterback to the pitchman on an inside release of the slot.

If the slot arcs off the line, the strong safety or Husky will play the pitch. As the slot comes on the arc block, the Husky wants to play through his outside shoulder and push him back if he can. He does not want the ball to get outside of him. However, he wants to keep the running lane inside of him as tight as he can. They want to attack the arc block before the slotback can get his shoulder turned square to the line. If the Husky hits the back before he can get square, he can run him backward. The back has no power or push while he is running sideways.

If we get a dropback pass with no motion, we are playing a man-free concept in the secondary (Diagram #3). The corners are playing the wide receivers man-to-man. The Husky and strong safety have the slot players in man-to-man. The free safety is playing free in the middle of the field. The linebackers have the remaining back. If he releases to the right, the linebacker to that side takes him. If he goes the other way, the other linebacker picks him up. One linebacker plays the fullback, and the other linebacker is freed up. That is how we play the pass if it is a dropback pass.

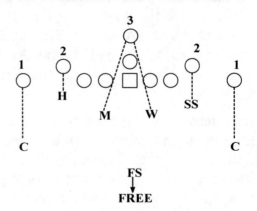

Diagram #3. Dropback Pass

The Husky and strong safety are playing with outside leverage on the slotbacks. If the strong safety gets a play-action pass to his position, he is a flat defender. He buzzes the flat and pushes to the

#1 receiver. He plays a zone on anything coming from the inside for flat/curl. The corner is man-to-man on the #1 receiver and does not allow him to get into the post area. If it is play-action pass away from the strong safety, he retreats through the middle third of the field, heading for the post.

If there is a play-action pass, the free safety is responsible for the #2 receiver to that side on a vertical pass (Diagram #4). If the slot and split end go vertical, the corner takes the split end, and the free safety takes the slot. The safety or Husky buzzes the flat/ and the Mike linebacker takes the hook/curl area.

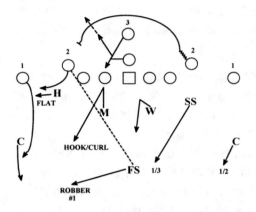

Diagram #4. Play-Action Pass

The Mike and Will linebackers are the playing the veer or dive. If the offensive-tackle blocks out on the Bandit or end, the linebackers are the B-gap players and attack the diveback. If the offensive tackle tries to release around the defender, that is the same as blocking out on the defender. If the linebacker sees that, he fills on the diveback immediately.

If the offensive tackle veer-blocks to the inside, the linebacker plays over the top of that block. The Bandit closes with the offensive tackle, and the Mike linebacker comes over the top, playing from the inside-out. From that position, he plays the quarterback to the pitch. If there is a pass, he has the back if the back comes his way. If the back goes to the other side, he is free. On a play-action pass, the Mike linebacker is the hook/curl defender.

The free safety is a player who must be disciplined and have great eyes. He plays 8 to 10 yards

off the line of scrimmage. As he reads, he keys the quarterback's flow and depth. When he sees the quarterback on the line of scrimmage, his eyes go to the slotback on that side. If the slotback blocks inside, he runs for the pitch. The Husky's responsibility with the slotback inside is a quarterback to pitch player. If the slot picks off the linebacker, the Husky plays the quarterback, and the free safety runs for the pitch. If the wide receiver cracks on the free safety, the corner replaces him in the run scheme and goes to the pitch. The safety will not play with as much depth as he normally does.

The corners cannot think of themselves as pass defenders. We told them they had half the field to defend, but they will have only one receiver to be responsible for. Offensive coaches want to make the corners make plays. If you use the safety in run support, the offense will crack-block on the safety and make the corner come up and make the tackle. You have to coach your corners up so they are physical enough to come up and make plays. If there is a play-action pass to the corner, he is playing a cheap half field. He cannot let the #1 receiver get to the post. He must keep him out of the middle of the field. He has to protect the post.

I have told you the responsibility of each player on the defense. The scheme works off the block of the tackle and the slotback. If the tackle blocks out, the Mike linebacker steps into the B gap and plays the diveback (Diagram #5). If the slotback arcs on the Husky, the Husky comes up and plays through the outside shoulder of the slotback to the pitchback. The free safety reads quarterback on the line and reads the slotback. When he sees the slotback arc on the Husky, he knows he has the quarterback. We call that a robber technique for the free safety. If all goes well, he will not be alone on the quarterback. The Will linebacker from the backside should be coming over the top and will assist on the quarterback. When we play the quarterback, we hope to have half a defender on the inside of the quarterback and half a defender on the outside of the quarterback. As the free safety plays the quarterback, he is playing on his outside half. The inside half player will be the frontside linebacker, nose, or backside linebacker.

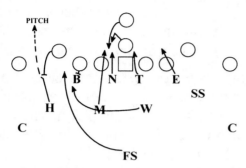

Diagram #5. Out Block/Arc Block

The next situation is the offensive tackle veer-blocks inside, and the slotback goes inside (Diagram #6). The defensive end makes the play on the diveback. Since the slotback went inside, the strong safety's responsibility is quarterback to pitch. If the linebacker gets over the top of the veer block and slot crack, he helps on the quarterback. If the strong safety has to take the quarterback, the free safety runs for the pitch because the slot blocked inside.

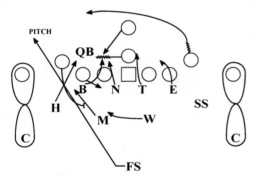

Diagram #6. Veer Block

The coaching point on this play is to make sure the end does not let the tackle get up on the linebacker or the free safety. The tackle and nose have to do the same thing to the center inside. They cannot let him cut off the backside linebacker. Technically, the inside linebacker should be a half man player on the quarterback. However, he has to play the veer back first. The corner has to replace the free safety, if the wide receiver cracked on him.

You know when their coaches see the free safety running to support on the quarterback or the pitch, they will crack him. You have to work to get the corner to replace the safety. You have to convince him he is not going to play pass all day and not have any run support. He has to be an active member of the support team.

We want the offense to pitch the ball. We feel the back receiving the pitch will have to run the hump to get outside. The longer he runs east and west, the better chance we have of stopping the play. To the short side of the field, the sideline is another defender we can depend on. We do not want the quarterback or the diveback to run the ball. We want the quarterback pitching the ball. When you pitch the ball, someone has to catch it. That can lead to a fumble.

We want the defense running from the inside-out on the option. The free safety runs from the inside-out in the alley. He has to know whether he is fitting inside or outside. If the slotback arcs, he is fitting inside on the quarterback. In a perfect world, the linebacker will be over the top, helping on the quarterback. If the tackle and nose can keep the center from getting up on the backside linebacker, we will gain an extra half man from the backside.

The option is based on having more blocker than you have defenders. They feel the quarterback, by reading the 5-technique defender and the pitch key, can gain an advantage. They think the quarterback reading the defense is like him blocking two men. That is why the half defender coming from the backside is important to the defensive scheme.

Both sides of our defense play the triple option the same way. It is a mirror image. The Bandit and end are playing the same techniques. The nose and the tackle are doing the same thing to and away from the action. They will get a down block or a combination from the center and onside guard. They have to make sure the guard cannot get off on the backside linebacker. If the offense attempts to reach with the center, the backside A-gap defender must penetrate and be a factor. The backside A-gap defender cannot let the center get out or be blocked by any type of scheme coming from the backside guard. If the center tries to cut off the backside linebacker, the backside A-gap defender has to stop him from getting upfield. We do not want the backside guard to scoop or chop the A-gap defender.

A triple option is constantly watching the perimeter defenders to see how they are getting to their responsibilities. If the slot arcs for the free safety instead of the strong safety, the strong safety has to play the pitch. The slot may pick off the free safety, but there is no one to block the linebacker.

We want the inside linebacker to play the outside half of the quarterback. We would like to have the backside linebacker to play the inside half of the quarterback. That gives you a half man to each side of the quarterback.

On a dropback pass, we are playing man-to-man on the slots and split ends with the free safety in the middle of the field playing free. If the fullback does not release, both linebackers are free. We could use one or both of them in a blitz scheme, but that would be decided by a game plan. We like to drop the free linebacker into the low hole in the middle of the field. He is the free player in the underneath area of the field, and the free safety plays in deep middle free.

On a play-action pass, the free safety is playing robber coverage (Diagram #7). When he sees quarterback on the line of scrimmage, his eyes go to the #2 receiver, which is the slotback. When he reads the release of the slotback and sees the quarterback leaving the line of scrimmage, he plays

pass. If the #2 receiver has gone to the flat, the strong safety or Husky will have him in that area. He turns his attention to the #1 receiver. The corner will keep him from running into the post, but the free safety can help on the dig or curl route.

If the play-action pass goes away from the strong safety or Husky, they retreat through the middle third. He could easily pick up the backside slot trying to get down the middle. The backside corner has play-action pass away from him and zone off the backside half of the field. If the split end tries to get to the post, he plays him all the way.

In the 3-4 defenses, the defensive tackles play the same technique as they did in the 4-4 defense (Diagram #8). They align in a heavy 5 technique. They must reroute the offensive tackles and keep them from blocking the inside linebackers or the safety. If they reroute the tackle inside, they will be in position to take the diveback. When the 5 techniques come down inside with the offensive tackle, the defensive tackle has to stop the diveback.

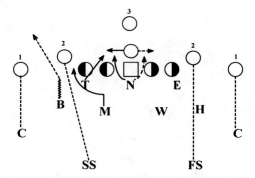

Diagram #8. Base 3-4

The nose must be a two-gap player. He reads the center's head and gets into the frontside A gap. He needs to work frontside and stays on that course. He wants to close off the frontside A gap. He has to be help on the diveback in the B gap. The backside linebacker plays off the course of the nose. If the nose gets into the frontside A gap and has control, the linebacker plays the backside A gap (Diagram #9). If the nose gets reached, the backside linebacker plays over the top into the frontside A gap.

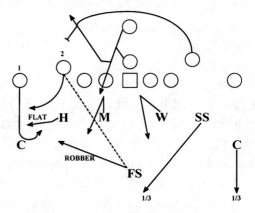

Diagram #7. Robber Coverage

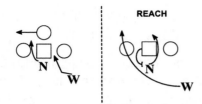

Diagram #9. Nose Linebacker

The Husky and Bandit play on the slotbacks and will read the release of the slots. They play the same techniques that the Husky and strong safety did in the 4-4 look. If the slot goes inside, the Husky and Bandit sit and hang. His responsibility is to play the quarterback to the pitch. If the slot arcs, the Bandit and Husky play the pitch using the same technique as I discussed previously.

The difference in their techniques occurs when the ball goes away from them (Diagram #10). If the ball goes away, they have to be the cutback player on the backside. The backside linebacker may have to play across the nose to the frontside. If that happens, the Bandit or Husky is the player that fills the gap created by the linebacker.

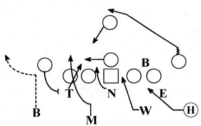

Diagram #10. Cutback Gap

In the secondary, we play quarters coverage (Diagram #11). The Bandit and Husky are flat players. If the slot releases to the flat, they take him. The free and strong safeties are reading the #2 receivers for their keys. If the #2 receiver goes to the flat, they play the robber technique under the #1 receiver. If the #2 receivers go vertical, the safeties will take them deep. The safeties support the corners on the #1 receiver, if the slot goes to the flat. The safety plays over the top on the smash route by the spit end and slotback. He support on the inside verses the post, curl, or dig route from the #1 receiver. Teams that run this type of offense do not make their living throwing the football. Their passing game is coming off the play-action pass.

The Mike and Will linebackers are veer-read players. If the tackle blocks out on the defensive tackle, he is a B-gap player and takes on the diveback. If the offensive tackle releases inside, the linebackers scrape to the outside and play quarterback to pitch. If we get dropback pass, the Mike linebacker is a middle-hook player.

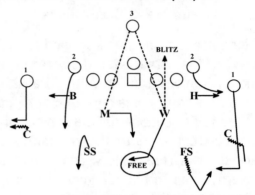

Diagram #11. Quarters Coverage

On pass, the Will linebacker becomes the low-hole player in the middle of the field or the fourth rusher on the quarterback. Since we have only three rush linemen, we would probably blitz the Will linebacker.

The corners are playing their 1x8-yard alignment on the split ends. When the corner does not expect support from the safeties on the #1 receiver, he will have an inside leverage position on the split end.

The safeties are aligned on the slots at eight yards deep. They read the #2 receiver, which is the wingback in the set. If the wingback goes inside, the safety is the pitch player. If he arcs, the safety is the alley runner.

The most important thing the corner can do in the run game is crack replacement (Diagram #12). When the offense finds out how the safeties are involved in the support scheme, they will crack-block them with the split ends. If the safety gets blocked, the corners have to replace the safeties in the running scheme. The coaching point for the corner is not to replace the safety until the crack occurs. If the split end releases inside and runs to the safety, the corner cannot release the split end and head for the line of scrimmage. That is the offense's favorite play. They release the split end on the safety, then break him back on a flag route into the corner of the field.

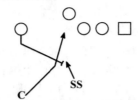

Diagram #12. Crack Block

The corner can help the safety on a crackback block. When the corner sees the receiver headed into the crack-block area, he yells, "Crack!" to the safety. If the safety hears the "crack" call, he cannot try to get outside the crack block. If it is a fake block and corner route, the free safety will not be cracked. If it is a crack-block, and he attempts to fight over the top to the outside he will screw up the corner path to the pitch.

He needs to stay inside and fight back outside. If he tries to get outside the crack block, he forces the corner wider, and it opens up a big running lane if they pitch the ball. The corner needs to come off the hip of the crack blocker to get into the pitch area. The backside safety is a late alley runner in the run-support scheme.

In their pass coverage, the corners have the #1 receiver man-to-man. They are to stop all short routes, but they will get help on the deep patterns from the safety as long as the #2 receiver does not go vertical. The corner, in a quarters coverage, must read from the #1 receiver to the #2 receiver. If the #2 receiver is vertical, the corner will get no help on a deep ball to the split end. He refocuses on the #1 receiver and plays him accordingly. If the #1 receiver cracks, the corner is in the run-support scheme as a safety.

To stop the triple option attack, it is imperative that you stop the dive. In this defense, the noseguard or the backside linebacker have to be active players on the diveback. If the nose beats the center into the A gap, he helps on the diveback. If he gets reached, the backside linebacker plays over the top and helps on the dive. If the dive is stopped by the 5 technique, the nose or the backside linebacker becomes the inside half player on the quarterback. The onside linebacker plays the outside half of the quarterback.

That gives us three defenders on the diveback. If we cannot stop him with that kind of scheme, my advice is not to schedule them. I am not kidding. I was in a rules committee meeting the other day and the ACC coaches were up in arms. They laughed at everyone else having to play triple-option teams. Now that Georgia Tech is in their conference, they are not laughing anymore. When you have to prepare for Georgia Tech and have only a week to do it, that is hard. That is why the service academy runs this offense. It gives them a chance against teams that do not play it.

When you see the offense only one time during the season, it is a cultural shock for your players. Everyone is running spread offenses, and no one is pounding you every play with running plays. These teams have four backs who can run the ball. Their feature back is always the fullback. The kid they had at Georgia Tech last year was a bear. The quarterback was not too shabby of a runner, either. The wingbacks are generally fast and really pressure your perimeter people to make plays in the open field. It is hard to get ready to play them in a short amount of time. That is why, if you have to play them, you better spend some time in the off-season working on your schemes and simplifying what you do.

In this offense, we are not going to force the ball to be pitched quickly. We want to give the safety time to get to the pitch. If we force the quarterback to pitch, there is a chance the offense will get to the corner. The safeties are coming from eight yards deep to the pitch. That makes the safety play too fast and leads to mistakes in his reads. When we see the step motion they use with the wingback, we can get downhill somewhat.

When the outside linebackers see the arc block by the slot receiver, they want to attack him right away. They do not want him to get his shoulders square to the line of scrimmage. If they hit him before he can get his shoulders turned, they can control him with no trouble.

An adjustment we made from our robber coverage was on the split of the wide receiver (Diagram #13). If the offense wants to get a crack on the safety, they like to cut their wide receiver splits down. If we found that happening, we rolled the coverage into half coverage over the top and brought the corner down to play the safety's responsibility. The safety played over the top to handle the corner's area. If the split of the wide receiver stayed wide, the danger of the crack was not a threat.

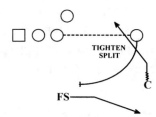

Diagram #13. Roll Coverage

The defender who plays the quarterback does not want to attack him. He wants the quarterback to come to him. However, he does not want to run away from him and open the inside for the quarterback to duck inside. He wants to squeeze the lane and slow play. The longer the quarterback holds the ball, the better off the defense is. He never wants to turn his shoulders. He has to keep his shoulders square to the line. If the quarterback tries to make a play on the defender responsible for him, the defender drills him. If he starts inside, the defender hits him hard. If the quarterback pitches the ball, the defender has an opportunity to take the proper angle and make a play on the pitchman. Pursuit angles against a triple-option team are tremendously important.

One thing I want to mention is about the free safety in a 4-4 scheme. Make sure you put a tackler into that position. You do not need pass coverage against a triple-option team. You need a safety who can run and who is a sure tackler.

When you play a triple-option team, you have to find ways to get the extra man to the point of attack. However, you have to remain sound in your pass coverage because of the play-action passes. If you can force them to pass when they do not want to, you are way ahead of the game. You do that by getting ahead in the game. They do not play catch-up that well. What you have to do is get the ball. They are going to dominate the time of possession if you cannot stop the dive.

The worst thing that you can do is to do too much against a triple-option team. You have to execute what you plan to play. You have to remain sound at all times and not gamble too much. Blitzes and stunts are not the thing you want to do all the time. In fact they want you to blitz. They want you to get your linebackers off the second level. If you blitz the linebacker the wrong way, he cannot pursue the ball. You need more people in pursuit, not less. The thing you have to do is play fast and aggressive defense.

If you played a 4-3 defense against this set, it would be a combination of both defenses I have shown you. In a 4-3 defense, the line adjustment would be the same as the 4-4 defense. The secret is which defensive back you wanted to roll down into the outside linebacker spot. You can play the strong safety at five yards to the side opposite the Husky. He is close enough to the line to read and react to the keys I just showed you.

Thank you very much. I appreciate your attention. Our practices are always open. If we can do anything for you, do not hesitate to call on us.

THE FIVE- AND SIX-MAN PASS PROTECTION

University of Maine

We are going to talk today about five- and six-man pass protection. We are going to start off with some fundamentals and techniques. In 2008, we were like Georgia Tech. We ran the ball, and it did not matter how many defenders the defense put in the box. They could put six, seven, eight, nine, or ten defenders in the box, and we still ran the ball. This year, we had injuries and lost our two top running backs before the season started. Our running game kind of shuddered. This year, we were like Texas Tech University. We threw the football all over the place.

We had injuries in the offensive line and had to start three freshmen. The center, right tackle, and left guard were all freshmen. We threw the ball 444 times this year and had 20 sacks, which is not bad with three freshmen in your starting lineup. That amounts to 1.8 sacks per game.

BASIC PASS PROTECTION

I want to go through the basics of our pass protection and how we teach it.

Pride

- Unit and individual: We want to be the best on the grass.
- No one touches the quarterback (keep him upright).
  - ✓ The offensive line and the quarterback need to be on the same page.
- Limit quarterback pressures and hurries; never allow a sack.

These are things we talk about. We have to deal with individual pride. I want my players, when they come on the field, to be the best on the grass. I do not want choirboys. I want players who will take a risk if they need to. I want some mean players.

Nobody touches the quarterback, and that is something we pride ourselves on. We chart sacks, hits on the quarterbacks, and pressures. Anytime the quarterback gets hit, somebody has to pay.

Knowledge

- Where is the quarterback's set point?
- Do you have help and where is it coming from?
- Where are the safeties?
- Where is the spot?
- What foot does the defender have back?
  - ✓ Outside foot: Move on the third step.
  - ✓ Inside foot: Move on the second step.

The quarterback and the offensive line have to be on the same page. The defense will determine our slide. That has to be communicated. The players do a lot of film study. Our players are required to watch three games on Sunday night. On Monday, they can do our scouting report for us. I want my linemen to look at every defensive player he will face and know his positives and negatives. They go through the film, put a list together, and present to our team on Tuesday morning. The offensive line does the defensive line. The running backs do the linebackers. The wide receivers do the secondary players.

I tell my players I do not know many millionaires who only work eight hours a day. We must put in the extra time and know the players on the defensive line. In 2008, I had an All-American center. He was awesome. If he saw a slight difference in a defender's stance, he could tell you what the entire defense was going to do.

When you play in the offensive line, you have to be smart. The center and two guards have to be willing to put the extra time into learning the defense. If you ask my center what time it is, he'll tell you how the watch was made. The guards have to pick up the defensive stances and know what is going on.

There are a number of things the offensive line has to know in a pass play. They have to know where the quarterback is going to set and launch the ball. If the line does not know the set point, they cannot protect it. They have to know if they have help and where it is coming from. The offensive line has to see the safeties and know what they are doing. The safeties will tell you where a blitz is coming from.

When I refer to the spot, it is the point where the defensive lineman turns his shoulders toward the quarterback. The spot deals mainly with the rush of the defensive ends. If the offensive lineman knows where the spot is, it will help him in his pass protection. In football, you are either proactive or reactive. We want to be proactive 95 percent of the time. There are a couple of ways to help the linemen decide where the spot is. We read the feet of the defensive end. If he has his outside foot back, he makes his move on the first or third step. If his inside foot is back in his stance, he makes his move on the second or fourth steps—that will help them in their pass sets. In our set, we do not use the kick-slide much. We use the jump set most of the time. We want to get on the defender right away.

Balance

- Weight is centered between the feet
- No excessive body lean
- Stay off toes (susceptible to being pulled)
- Jeet Kune Do footwork; ability to move front, back, left, right, and at angles
- Pass protection = Constant battle of balance

Football is *balance*. It is also *martial arts*. You must have great balance, and we want it centered between the feet. I do not believe in a drastic body lean. We do not want to be on our toes. If a lineman

is on his toes, the defender will grab him, pull him forward, and he will end up on the ground. We want the weight on the inside part of the midfoot.

People are finding out if you jam the inside foot in the ground, it takes longer to pick it up to reset the foot. If you play with the weight on the ball of the foot, you can shuffle quicker. I do not like to use the word *shuffle*, but that is almost what it is. We do not teach pounding the foot in the ground. *Jeet Kune Do* is a martial arts movement. We use that type of footwork to move forward, back, right, left, and at angles. If you want to see an example of great balance in pass protection, watch a pair of sumo wrestlers.

Toughness

- Violent mentality and killer instinct
- Take the fight to the defense
- Must do a great job striking defenders
- Never quit on a rep
- Compete for seven seconds

When you play in the offensive line, you must have a *violent mentality* and a *killer instinct*. I do not like it when people say, "He is a good offensive lineman but he does not have that defensive mentality." We want to *strike* people. We want to strike them hard and fast. We give points to our offensive line for strikes.

I do not want choirboys. I want them to be violent with a killer instinct. We want to take the fight to the defense. The business of the offensive line is balance, striking people, and breathing. We have to excel at that. We punch everything. We punch janitors. We will even punch the AD if he comes into our meeting room. We do a great job of punching. We punch dummies and medicine balls. Anything you can do to help your linemen strike defenders, you should do it.

I never want our guys to quit. I want them to go through the echo of the whistle not stop on it. If I do not have the referee come to the sideline and tell me that he is going to penalize us if we do not stop on the whistle, we are not playing hard.

Quickness

- How fast can you go from a three-point stance to a two-point stance?
- Quick hands and feet
- Recover ability
- Jeet Kune Do principle; economy of motion
  - ✓ Simplest things work best
  - ✓ Conserve both energy and time

It takes quickness to get from the three-point stance to the two-point stance. We do power sets and kick-slides with bungee cords in resistive and assistive pass work. At the beginning of the off-season workouts, we time the linemen in a three-step kick-slide. We time them again at the end of the off-season, and they should have improved if they are doing the right stuff.

The linemen must have the ability to recover from a bad position. The *economy of motion* means the simpler the technique, the better it will work. We are not going to spend time on a bunch of adapted techniques. We are going to spend time working on proven, simple techniques. Using simple techniques allows us to conserve time and energy.

Effort

- Do not lean on your hands after contact.
  - ✓ Use your legs and posterior chain to provide power and strength.
- When not covered, put your head on a swivel.
- Cover in the direction the pass is thrown in case of an interception.

The first point in effort is never lean on the hands after contact. That is a balance issue, and you are not using the power muscles of the body. We want to use the legs, back, and butt muscles in blocking. If the lineman is not covered, he has to get his head on a swivel and look to help someone.

We always cover in the direction the ball is thrown. We do not do conditioning after practice. We do it in the drills. When we have a pass drill, the offensive linemen must sprint 15 yards downfield on each pass. They have to sprint past me. If they do not, I am all over their butts.

Three-Point Stance

- All movement originates from this position
- Put yourself in great biomechanical position for success
  - ✓ Toes straight ahead
  - ✓ Feet staggered (toe to instep relationship)
  - ✓ Slightly wider than the shoulders (about two feet apart)
  - ✓ Weight on the midfoot (below the balls of the feet)
  - ✓ Place your hand directly outward from the shoulder
  - ✓ Place all five fingertips on the ground
  - ✓ The back is arched in the stance with the tail tucked
  - ✓ The offhand will rest on the knee with the elbow on the thigh
  - ✓ Positive shin angles (keep the cap inside the ankles)
- Offensive linemen in an athletic position play that way

The offensive line and defensive back are the only two athletic positions on the field. It is difficult to punch moving backward. The offensive line and defensive backs have to work in that position. They have to punch without allowing the shoulders to come forward.

Two-Point Stance

- Vertical maintenance of the pre-snap stance
- The inside foot is up, and the outside foot is back
- Forearms will rest on the thigh boards
- The back will look like a banana and the chin is tucked
- The weight is evenly distributed between the feet
- We move off the midfoot in two step combinations
- If you are too far in the backfield, lean forward to make the helmet break the center's belt

When we do our step combinations, we always want to be in even steps. We want to step two, four, six, and eight. The reason is the kick-step. The kick is one step, and the blocker wants to slide to come back to balance. I got my butt chewed out by the head coach. He told me to get the linemen up on the ball. I want the linemen as far off the ball as I can get them. I talk to the head linesman before the game and ask him to warn me when they start to get close to being in the backfield. At that point, I tell them to make sure they lean forward to get their hats on the center's belt.

THE FIVE COMMANDMENTS OF PASS PROTECTION

Head Out

- Always keep your head out and back when you set

The reason you keep the head out is so the body will not follow the head into the defender. If the defender grabs the head of the blocker and spins it, the entire body will spin. If you keep the head out and back, you maintain balance and control.

Hands Up

- Keep your hands up and see your target through your fingers
- Arms are a factor of time
- Longer arms = More time to create time and recover from lost time
- Short arms = Must have great feet (smaller recovery window)
- Always know where your hands are

You want to get the hands up and see the target through the fingers of the hand. You work better when you look at something through your field of vision. In practice, I overexaggerate the hand position, and in the games we carry the hands lower. We want the elbows in tight to the body. If we miss the punch and the defender leans on the blocker, he has a natural base to work from.

The arms are a factor of time. If the blocker can touch the defender and lock out his arms, he is in great position. The first one-and-a-half seconds of the pass rush is a street fight. In those three yards, anything goes. Linemen with longer arms can create more time to recover a block and get the defender locked out. His feet do not have to be as good if he has long arms. Linemen with shorter arms must have better footwork. They have a smaller window for recovery when they get beat. If the blocker has his hands knocked down by the rusher, he has to know where they are to recover.

Spine Back

- Get upright ASAP
- Shoulder blades need to be pulled together
- Don't lean and lunge

Take the Defender on With Your Feet Apart

- Equal weight distribution between your feet
- Keep your feet apart
- Set with tight feet
- Feet need to hug the ground
  ✓ Grab the ground with your toes

When we pass set, I want the feet in contact with the ground. We do not do drills where we pick our knees up. We want their feet tight to the ground in all their movements. In the summer, I sent my linemen outside and they did pass protection with no shoes on. They could grip the grass with their toes. They were anchoring themselves to the ground.

Set for Cover

- Always set to a slight inside target on the defender
- Put the stripe of your helmet on the defender's inside eye

When you set to cover, the lineman needs to put his helmet on the inside eye of the defender. That puts him slightly inside. If you set too far inside, it gives the advantage to the rusher.

BASICS OF PASS SET

Tempo

- Set up in one motion.
- Set on the defender's movement.
- Set up based on the defender's alignment.
- Establish your position; be proactive.
- Set with speed and quickness.
- Beat the rusher to the set point.
- Be in a position to take away a straight line to the quarterback.

Target

- Get your head and eyes on the target.
- Get big eyes on the defender.
- Keep the hands up and see through the fingertips.
- Banana the back, tuck the chin, and keep the head out.
- The eyes must lead the body.
- Draw the eyes into the target with hands up.
- The eyes must see the hands contact the numbers.
- Maintain an inside position on the defender.
- Honor inside moves.
- Dishonor outside moves.

Offensive linemen must have big eyes. They have to focus on small targets. When we pass block, I want them to see the top of the inside number or some other small area. The eyes have to see where the hands strike the defender.

Footwork

- You must either kick slide or power step.
- Keep your feet underneath your hips.
- Be a knee bender.
- Keep demeanor (keep your hands up, shoulders square, and take an even number of steps).
- Cover the defender.

The offensive lineman wants to be toe to toe with the defender with his helmet slightly inside. We want to cover him up.

Punch

- Pre-shrug the shoulders prior to punching.
- Keep the arms at 70-percent extension.
- Punch to 90-percent extension.
- The punch should come from your upper back and triceps.
- Deliver the hands up and under for leverage and lockout.
- Snap the wrists on contact.
- Think about pushing yourself away from the defender.
- Strain to keep the head out.
- Force the rusher to restart, redirect, and reseparate.
- Patience and timing is everything.

I changed my vocabulary from *punch* to *strike*. When I used punch, I got too many people leaning and not striking. When we strike, I want to shrug the shoulders and get the arms at a 70-degree bend. When we punch, we extend the arms to 90 degrees. We do not want to lock the arms all the way because of the force it puts on the elbow. It is hard to stop someone's momentum and control them with the arms straight. You have to keep a little bend in the elbows.

If the lineman is facing a fast speed rusher, he should think about pushing himself away from him. Do not ever punch a defender twice. That means after the blocker punches the defender and sets his hands, he cannot punch him again. If he does, he will lose the defender. He has to stay on the block and keep his elbows tight to his body.

You can set, throw the hands, and pull them back quickly. We try to get the defender to chop at the hands and get off balance or open up his chest. But once the chest has been captured, do not try to release and reset the hands.

Finish

- Never shorten the corner.
- Play until the echo of the whistle.
- Never give up a sack.

If my linemen give up a sack, it is as if their girlfriend left them. I want to go over the footwork quickly. The outside foot is the kick foot, and the inside foot is the power or postfoot. On the kick-step, we keep the weight concentrated on the inside foot and leg. We want 60 percent on the inside foot and leg. The kneecap is inside the ankle, and the nose should stay aligned with the crotch. The lineman never wants to be in a position where he is twisted or out of balance.

The power step is a flat, aggressive inside step with the power foot. It is intended to take away an inside rush lane. When the lineman power steps, he cannot let the head go past the midline of the body. A line goes through the center of the body. The left hand stays on the left side of the body, and the right hand stays on the right side. If the head crosses the center line, you are out of balance. The slide-step is the sliding motion of the back foot in a kick-step.

When we talk concepts for different alignments, there are only four we talk about (Diagram #1). They are wide, normal, head-up to inside, and tight/gray area.

WIDE   NORMAL   TIGHT/ GREY AREA   HEAD UP/ INSIDE

Diagram #1. Alignment Concepts

On the *wide alignment* the tackles use a *jump set* and the guards use a lateral set. They are the same moves. The lineman takes one kick-step with the outside foot. He wants to get the instep of the inside foot in the ground immediately. We use a technique called the *duck-demeanor* steps, which are short, choppy shuffle steps toward the defender. We want to close the distance as fast as possible. We attack the defender from the inside out with the aiming point on the inside shoulder and sternum. We want the inside hand on the sternum and the outside hand on his shoulder.

If we *vertical set*, we kick-step straight back with the outside foot. We want to drag the inside toe and retreat straight back. We are thinking three kick-steps. We want to pump the inside arm and carry the hands high. The eyes are on the target at all times. We carry the inside hand low so if the defender comes inside, we can punch.

We also use a *kick-sink* set. When we do this set, we kick the outside foot at a 60-degree angle while dragging the inside toe straight back. This is the same thing as the kick-slide except it gives a little more width. We are thinking slight width set. We drag and pump the inside arm and carry the hands high. When we use this set, we are proactive with it.

On the *gray alignment*, the defender is in an area where we do not know where he is going. He could go inside, outside, or bull-rush the blocker. We use a *short* set for this alignment. We take small steps with the inside foot. We slide the outside foot for balance. We want to protect ourselves in case he comes inside. We set to an inside target with great balance. We want to get the second step down as fast as possible. We play heavy with the hands. We do not try to kill him—we only want to disrupt him.

On the *head-up to inside alignment* we want to *power set* or *short set*. We power step with the inside foot and drag the outside foot. The target is an inside target. We use the same techniques I talked about in the power set. The thing we want to remember is that we want to move the feet before we put out hands on the defender. We want leverage before we try to put our hands on the defender. When we get our hands on the defender, we want heavy hands. On the *normal alignment* we use the *kick-sink* or *jump-set* technique.

EXAMPLES OF DIFFERENT SETS

Center (Snap Then Stab)

- Set to an inside target.
- Always bring your second step.
- Be ready and think recovery.

Guards (Depth of the Pocket)

- Block defender as close to the line of scrimmage as possible.

- Set to a slight inside target (cover).
- Bring heavy hands.

Tackles (Width of the pocket)

- Block defender as close to the line of scrimmage as possible.
- Set to a slight inside target (cover).
- What type of rush are you getting?
  - ✓ Top pass rush move?
  - ✓ Top counter?

The tackles have to know the defensive end's top rush move and his top counter move. We want to find the best move he has and work on it. However, you cannot get beat by his counter move. We want to define the type of rush we will see.

DEFINE THE TYPE OF RUSH

Speed Rush

- Make the defender commit outside.
- Turn the inside toe slightly, force the defender to widen, and push him past the quarterback.
- Are his hips even with your hips?

Inside Rush

- Flatten the defender (trip defender with the inside foot).
- Keep inside leverage/FBH (feet before hand).
- May need to grab and lift defender with inside hand.

Bull Rush

- Both hands will enter your field of vision.
- Drop and pop; then hop, hop, walk.
- Break the bridge.

When the blocker gets the speed defender past the quarterback, his job is not over. He has to stay on the defender because they will retrace their steps or stop and try to come under back to the quarterback. You have to block him for the full seven seconds. On the inside rush, we want to move the inside foot before we try to get the hands on the rusher. The FBH means *feet before hand.* On the inside move, the blocker may have to grab and lift the rusher with his backside hand. He may miss with his punch.

In the bull rush, *break the bridge* refers to knocking the hands of the defender off the blocker by coming from underneath with both hands or down from the top with both hands. If the rusher gets his hands inside, the blocker has to replace the hands one at a time to gain inside position with his hands.

We do a drill to teach move recognition. I put a block and defender in stances in front of each other five yards apart. On the first hut, they come out of their stances. On the second hut, the defender shows a rush move. The blocker has to call out the move he sees. The key to the bull rush is both hands in the field of vision. We start the drill out at five yards and move to three yards. When we move closer, the blocker has less time to react. The defender works the move and the blocker moves his feet. After we go at three yards, we move the drill to one yard and they do the same thing. Since we have been doing this drill, we are getting much better in the games.

The *swim move* is a technique we have to learn to counter. If we have a great punch that is so effective that the defender misses the grab, we can avoid the swim. If the defender gets the grab, we press hard with the hand to the side of the grab. As the opposite arm swims over the blocker, the blocker must punch the armpit of the swim arm and push hard, working for a lockout with the arm. We keep the foot and body moving in the direction of the swim move.

The next move we have to counter is the *rip.* When the defender tries to set the rip, clamp and trap the rip arm in the armpit. The blocker drops the center of gravity (with the rip arm trapped) to prevent the rusher from completing the rip. With the offhand, the blocker pushes on the hip of the rusher to widen him. He keeps the feet and body moving in the direction of the rip to shut off the rush lane to the quarterback.

The last counter is the bull rush. The rush starts as a speed rusher. When the rusher gets to a spot, he makes a transition to the bull rush. When we see both hands coming, we want to "bull the buller." We drop the center of gravity and react quickly to drop and pop. We mule kick the feet back on contact while dropping the center of gravity. We put the helmet in the defender's throat, roll the hips, and punch a hole in the defender's chest. We keep the feet tight and give ground grudgingly. The last-ditch effort is to break the bridge with a high or low break on the defender's hands.

We call our six-man protection *60*. That is made up of the five offensive linemen and the tailback. The last digit will tell us the direction of the initial slide. If it is 60 protection, the slide goes to the right—the code word for that is *New York*. The *61* protection is left or *Los Angeles*.

The concept is half man and half slide. We slide the front to the most dangerous man (MDM). We zone or man the backside of the slide depending on film study. If we have a 3 and a 5 technique, we may zone the backside.

Offensive Line Rules

- Big + most dangerous man (MDM)big = Any defender in a three-point stance at the line of scrimmage
- Any secondary defender (linebacker or defensive back) covering an offensive lineman
- Example: Bear defense with "mugged" linebackers

Big is classified as any defender in a three-point stance, any defender covering an offensive lineman, or any secondary player that has broken the heels of the down linemen (Diagram #2). In the 4-3 defense, the protection scheme is the four down linemen and the Mike linebacker.

The most dangerous man in most defenses is the Mike linebacker. We can designate any player as the most dangerous.

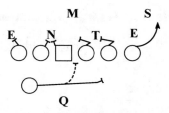

Diagram #2. 61 Protection vs. 4-3

Who Is the Most Dangerous Man?

- The Mike linebacker with no blitz look
- Defender with blitz demeanor
- Safeties rolled to one side pre-snap
- Any specific look based on film study

The center will point out the most dangerous man, but the quarterback could come to the line and change that call. He could change it two or three times on the same play. I do not like that, but it can happen. The center comes to the line and makes the front call and calls the jersey number of the MDM.

The playside tackle has to locate the Sam linebacker and strong safety. He points them out. We read the safeties to get clues to what the defense is going to do. With two high safeties, we feel that is a coverage defense. If there is one high safety, there may be a blitz coming. If there are no high safeties, buckle it up because they are coming.

The backside tackle finds the free safety and the Will linebacker. The quarterback comes to the line and double-checks the center's calls and makes any adjustments he feels are necessary. He gets everyone on the same page.

Tailback Rules

- Work opposite of the offensive center's call
- Work inside out with a scan mentality
- Responsible for the next linebacker or defensive back backside to perimeter

With the tailback, we can go to the call or away from it. In our protection scheme two years ago, we always put the back away from the call. We got every zone blitz in the world to that side. We put him to the call and away from it and let him scan back to the backside of the protection.

Playside Tackle, Guard, Center, Backside Guard

- Alert to call (slide to call and block outside gap)
- Covered
  - ✓ Block big
- Uncovered
  - ✓ Slide to call
  - ✓ Drag dual technique

Backside Tackle

- Block big

The *drag dual technique* is the defender at the break of the slide. If the backside guard has a shade defender between the center and him, he is going to block that shade if he comes to the backside B gap. If he goes to the other side of the center or engages the center, he slides. That takes care of the twist stunt between the nose and defensive end. The backside guard has to know that a defender that comes from the zoneside back to the manside is his responsibility. He is the last man in the slide and has to take that defender.

The tailback works opposite the quarterback's call (Diagram #3). He works inside out with a scan mentality. He has freedom to work both sides; however, he has a blocking assignment. He is responsible for the next linebacker to defensive back from the backside perimeter.

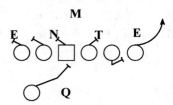

Diagram #3. Protection Scheme 60

Hot Situations

Hot situations are blitzes that bring more rushers than we have blockers. There are two ways we handle these situations: wide receiver sight adjustments or built-in hot throws.

The five-man protection is exactly the same technique and rules as the six-man scheme. The only thing that is different is the way we call it. If the call is *50*, that is a right slide protection—the code name is *New Jersey*. If we slide left, it is *51* and the code name is *Oregon*. This is a protection scheme with all the backs and receivers in the pattern. We have the same rules as the six-man protection. We are sliding and blocking the backside with a man or zone scheme.

There are questions that we want to answer during the week of practice. We have to know what type of blitzes we will see and address how to block them. We want to know if they have some kind of exotic or unconventional blitz scheme. Your linemen have to know the blitzes they will see. While everyone is kicking the ball and doing their special team assignment, we work on blitz pickup. We do not have to go full speed but we do it. I stand behind the offensive line. The center IDs the front and I tell scouts where to blitz.

We try to handle the line movement with the cadence. We go on first sound, long cadence, fake cadence, sideline control, or ice them to see if they will jump and give away what they are doing. We can go no-huddle and fast cadence. There are a number of ways to help the offensive line.

If there is anything I can do for you, call. Thank you for having me.

OFFENSIVE LINE BLOCKING RULES VERSUS PASS RUSH

University of Tulsa

Thank you. It is good to be here today. For you to get an understanding of what we do, you need to have an idea of what we are trying to accomplish. Two years ago, I left West Virginia University and went to the University of Tulsa to coach. I was co-offensive coordinator with a coach by the name of Gus Malzahn. He had been at the University of Arkansas. What we ended up doing was taking the best of the things we were doing at West Virginia and what he was doing at Arkansas to come up with an offense.

From West Virginia, we took the inside and outside zone plays along with the play-action passing game. Gus was running the gap dive, counter, and power O game. We put together what we thought was a good package. The first meeting we had with the team, we told them we were going to be the number one offensive team in the country. If you took an exit poll when those players left the room, there was not a player in the room that thought we could do it. In 2007, we led the nation in total offense. In 2008, we averaged about 570 yards a game in total offense.

For two years, we had a lot of success offensively. The players won the conference and had a swagger about them. It has become a tradition for us. There are some misconceptions about our offense. People think we are a spread team. We are a two-back run, play-action team. We are going to run the football, and that is what we are going to be talking about for the next couple of hours. We are going to talk about the shotgun running game. We want to put constant pressure on the defense and their coaches by accomplishing these six goals:

- We are a no-huddle that runs our offense on a two-minute pace. That will physically and mentally wear out the opponent.
- We want to have a balanced attack.
- We want to use misdirection in the run and pass game.
- We want to stretch the field both vertically and horizontally.
- We want to throw the book at the defense with specials, fire alarms, and the Wildcat package.
- We want to present the option in a variety of different ways.

We feel that running our offense at this pace will wear the defense out both mentally and physically. We sell our players on that point. We sell our players that the core center of our program is the training we do.

We want to have a balanced attack. In 2008, we averaged 270 yards rushing, which was fifth in the country. We averaged 301 yards passing the football, which was ninth in the country. The balance in running and passing is the key. If you are running the ball for 400 yards a game, that is great. If you throw for 400 yards a game, that is outstanding. However, we strive for a balanced attack—that way you can take advantage of all the different skills your players may have.

In our running game, we want to run the counters and reverses to give the defense a misdirection attack. A play-action pass, to me, is misdirection. When the linebacker steps up on a play-action pass, the offense has created doubt in that player's mind.

We want to make the defense defend the entire width and depth of the field. We want to stretch them so they cannot concentrate on any one area. You can stretch the width of the field with formations and alignments. We make the defense defend the depth of the field because we will get vertical in our patterns. We go into each game trying to figure out how to throw the ball down the field 10 times a game.

That is something we track during the course of the game. We want to know how many times we have challenged the defense vertically. That is one reason we want to run the ball well. If we can get the safeties to creep into the box, we can play-action pass over the top.

When we talk about *specials*, we are referring to trick plays. We go into every game with four or five trick plays. If we run one in a game, we take it out of the rotation for four or five games. We want to show them and make defenses defend them. The players like to run them and get excited about them. On the first day of spring practice we install the inside zone play. We also install a flea-flicker off that play.

In our first scrimmage, we got to the end of the scrimmage and threw the flea-flicker for a 70-yard touchdown. The defensive coordinator looked at me like, *I cannot believe you did that on the first day*. That is who we are. That is the way we play. We rep these plays repeatedly as if they are part of the offense. The specials are not something we pull out of the hat. We work on them and rep them so they are part of the offense. We may put a special in the first week of camp but may not run it until November. By the time we run the play in a game, we have done reps on the play hundreds of times.

Fire alarm is a way to control tempo. We are a no-huddle team, but occasionally we change the tempo with a fire alarm. We huddle, burst out of the huddle, and run the play as quick as we can. We call that a fire-alarm play. When we do this, the defense will not be aligned. We run a blocking scheme that is totally area in fashion. We come out in an unbalanced line and run a perimeter play or a play-action pass using slide protection.

You are not trying to come out in a fire-alarm situation and try to block a man blocking scheme on an isolation play or throw a five-out pattern. We want to run something where all we have to do is secure a gap and catch the defense napping. It gives them another thing to think about.

The Wildcat is nothing more than a quarterback run. When I got to Tulsa, I told them we ran the Wildcat at West Virginia—his name was Pat White. It is not like another offense. It is putting the play into the context of how you want to use it.

I spent the first 10 years of my career coaching defense. The thing I did not like to see was the option. Against an option team, the players played slower. On every snap, they had to go over in their minds what their option responsibility was. We want to present the option in a zone-read option or a speed option.

In order for us to accomplish all those things, we have to keep things relatively simple. That is the key to functioning at a rapid tempo. The offensive line must have confidence in what they are doing. You cannot have confidence if you have doubt or questions in your mind.

At the first offensive line meeting before spring practice, I draw on the board how we identify fronts. I show them six different defensive concepts. Within those six concepts, you will be able to interpret about 90 percent of what your players will see during the season. I am not worried about the 10 percent I do not cover because that 10 percent will not get your butt beat. Every week of practice, we practice against all six fronts. You never know what you will see. The six fronts are the even 4-4, odd stack 3-3, Eagle, even stack 4-3, 3-4 defense, and Bear.

The first defense is an even look with no Mike linebacker in the middle (Diagram #1). The even front concept, for us, is a single-safety look. If I walk out receivers to each side and get into the shotgun, the Will linebacker and the strong safety will move out into coverage but the box defense does not change. They still are a 4-2 stack defense inside with no defender head-up the center.

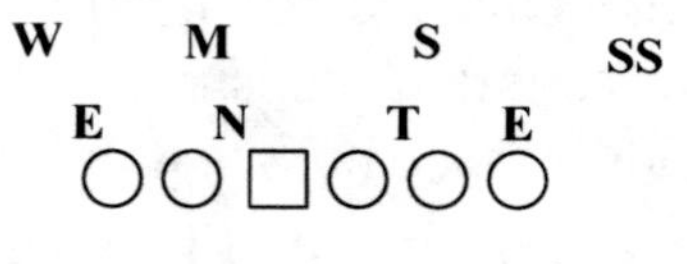

W   M   S   SS
E N   T   E
○ ○ □ ○ ○ ○

Diagram #1. Even 4-4 Concept

If we run the inside zone, we will handle the backside end by reading him. That gives us a hat on a hat in the blocking scheme. It is a four-down front. It does not matter where the defensive tackles align. They can be in a shade and 3 technique and it does not matter to the line. The only difference is how we work the combo blocks inside. We have a different combo for the shade technique than the 1 technique. When the center is going to work with the playside guard in a combo block, we call *ace combo*. If the guard works with the tackle on a combo block, that is called a *deuce combo*. If the tackle works with the tight end, we call it a *trey combo*.

The even stack is the same concept except there is a Mike linebacker in that defense. When you have a Mike linebacker, it changes our thought process with relationship to the combo blocks.

The odd stack is the 3-3 front. We run that defense. It is a stack defense as opposed to a simple odd front. We are starting to see more 3-4 defenses, where the defense is trying to keep two safeties down in the box with some kind of quarter coverage. With the odd stack, you have three down linemen and a true Mike linebacker.

The Eagle front is a combination of two fronts. If you look at it from the tight end side, it looks like an odd front. If you look at it from the openside, it looks like an even front. We have to decide how we want to attack it as an odd or even front.

We see the Bear in a lot of short-yardage situations. Anytime the center and both guards are covered, we treat that as some kind of Bear front. In addition to our blocking schemes, the protection is tied into the front recognition also. As soon as the center comes out, he has to make a front declaration whether it is a run or pass.

In our combo blocking against the even front, the tight end is going to work out of the box (Diagram #2). He is responsible for the overhang on the outside. That will be the outside linebacker or strong safety. The frontside combination block between the center and playside guard is to the first linebacker in the box. On the backside, the

guard, tackle, and tight end (if we have one) work the cutoff scheme. If there is no tight end to the playside, the slot receiver is still responsible for the overhang. We either block the linebacker with the slot or run a bubble off him. One way or the other, the wide receiver has to handle the overhang.

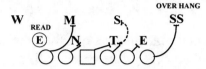

Diagram #2. Zone Blocking vs. Even

The zone read by the quarterback off the defensive end varies in technique from team to team. Your alignment has to be correct to give the quarterback the right timing. If you are aligned too tight, the end is there too quickly. You have to give the quarterback a chance to read it correctly. When the defensive end comes off the ball, the quarterback looks for his facemask or the earhole on the helmet. If the quarterback sees the facemask of the defensive end, he gives the ball to the back. If he sees the earhole, he pulls the ball.

One simple way to run the play is to ask the quarterback if he can get outside the defensive end. Depending on the ability of the quarterback, you may not want him to pull the ball. If the quarterback has any chance of getting around the defensive end, he pulls the ball. If the quarterback is dangerous in the open field, we want him with the ball. However, if you have a stud running back, you want to leave the ball with him. Decide who the money player is and give him the ball.

If the defense is a stack even front, the center cannot work the combination for the first linebacker in the box (Diagram #3). If there is a shade on his backside, you cannot ask him to work a backside combo to the Mike linebacker because his angle is bad. He has to work with the playside guard in a combination block for the Mike linebacker. When we do that, the tackle and tight end have to block in the box. They will run the combo block on the 6- or 7-technique defender to the first linebacker. It does not matter whether the tight end splits to the slot position or aligns in the backfield—

he is responsible for the Sam linebacker. He has to block the first linebacker to that side in the box.

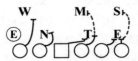

Diagram #3. Zone vs. Even Stack

The odd stack is an eight-man concept and the tight end works out of the box (Diagram #4). The playside guard and tackle work the combo for the first linebacker in the stack over the tackle. The center and backside guard work the combo for the nose and Mike linebacker. The backside tackle has the cutoff in the B gap on the Will linebacker or a spiking defensive end.

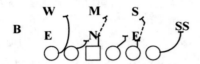

Diagram #4. Zone vs. Odd Stack

There are some coaching points for the backside tackle's block. The read key for the zone read usually aligns on the outside shoulder of the tackle. The backside tackle has to cut off the Will linebacker. However, if the Will linebacker walks out between the tackle and the slot receiver and aligns outside the read key, he has to use a different technique. He has to determine if the Will linebacker is in a position to make a play. If he feels the linebacker can fold back into the play, he uses a *sit technique*.

The offensive tackle is on the inside shoulder of the read key. He keys the Will linebacker. If the Will linebacker comes back inside, the tackle blocks the linebacker. If he stays outside in coverage on the slot receiver, the tackle turns back on the read-key defender (Diagram #5). The quarterback is on the same page as the tackle. He sees the Will linebacker in a walked-off position and knows the tackle will turn out on the read key.

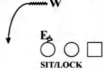

Diagram #5. Sit/Lock

He gives the ball because the end will not be able to close on the back. If the Will linebacker walks up on the line of scrimmage outside the read key or presses the slot receiver, the Will linebacker is not in a position to make a play. The tackle uses a lock call. Now he turns out on the read key and blocks him. Because the Will linebacker left the box, we have a hat for a hat on everyone in the box.

With the odd front, we have a hat for a hat on the box players. The tight end is blocking the Sam linebacker in or out of the box. If the tight end splits and the Sam linebacker goes with him, he blocks him. If the weak outside linebacker walks out on a slot receiver, the tackle uses his sit or lock call to the backside.

Against the Eagle front, we handle the play to the tight end like an odd-front blocking scheme. If we run the play to the Eagle side, we handle it like an even-front scheme.

You can run the zone against the Bear front, but you better have a stud at the backside tackle position (Diagram #6). He has to cut off a defensive tackle aligned in the 3 technique. The backside guard and center run the combo for the nose and Mike linebacker. You have a hat on a hat to the playside. The tough block is the backside tackle's block on the 3-technique defender.

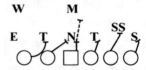

Diagram #6. Zone vs. Bear

Sometimes you just have to run the ball even if it is a tough block. That goes back to what I said earlier about being balanced in the run and pass game. The key to being balanced is not only running or throwing the football when you *want* to but running or throwing the football when you have to. That is when you know you are balanced in your passing and running game. We can run the ball against the Bear when we want to run it. However, we can run the ball against the Bear when we have to run it.

When the guards align, I want them to take a two-foot split from the center. If they do not keep their splits, it wipes out your inside running lane. I never want the split closer than one foot. If the backside tackle has to cut off a 3 technique, he can cut his split to 14 inches. If he gets closer than a foot, he cannot step without stepping underneath himself because he has no room to work his feet. On our alignment, we try to get our guards and tackles as far off the ball as we possibly can.

When the guard puts his hand on the ground, I want it aligned on the center's shoelaces. That allows the guard's head to break the plane of the center's butt and that makes you legal. The tackle puts his inside foot on the guard's inside foot. I want them squared up to the line of scrimmage. I do not want them bowed back as we go to the outside. If we get into short-yardage or goal-line situations, the guards move up and put their hand on the back of the ball. The tackle always aligns on the feet of the guard.

The backside tackle can widen his split. If there is an open B gap, he can widen his split. Instead of two feet, he widens to two-and-a-half feet. When he widens his split, he takes the read key wider and gives the back and quarterback more time.

The quarterback, in the shotgun, is set at five yards deep. The tailback aligns at seven yards deep. His inside foot aligns on the outside foot of the guard. Our tailback alignment changes depending on some plays. People think they can key the back's alignment and know what play is coming. We move the back around from seven to five yards. In fact, we use the alignment to sell a fake. It is good clinic talk but hard to see in the games.

If you are a good offense, you will have tendencies. You do what you are good at doing. That fact builds tendencies. If you are good at something, do not mess with it. Keep on doing it. If you are good at something, there is no reason to add anything or change something because it looks good.

The aiming point of the back is the near hip of the center (Diagram #7). He comes into the quarterback, receives the ball, and tracks for the near hip of the center. The big runs on the zone play do not happen in the playside A gap. They generally happen in the backside B gap. If he tracks to the guard, he has a hard time getting to the backside B gap. We do not care what the down linemen are doing. What we are trying to do is get the linebackers to fit into a seam. By hitting tighter to the center, the linebacker will still move and it lets the back have a chance to get out the back door.

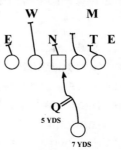

Diagram #7. Tailback Track

When we go into a film-study session, the first thing that comes out of my mouth is, "What is the front ID?" I want every one of them to know that. It is the center's job to call out the front, but they all should know what they are looking at in the alignment of the defense.

On the inside zone play, we want to get vertical displacement. I want to move the defensive linemen off the line of scrimmage. I want to double-team them every chance I get. The longer the guard can hold onto the double-teams, the better the play will be. The play may get only two yards, but second-and-eight is better than second-and-thirteen.

On the backside of the play, if the lineman is moving to a second-level defender, I want him to cover the linebacker up. I am not worried about the position of his head. I want the lineman to cover up the linebacker and let the back make the break.

In the even front, the center may have to change his combination block. If the nose aligns in a backside shade on the center, the center may give a call to the playside guard to base block because he is not going to combo with him. If the nose is in the gap, he normally turns him over to the backside guard. If the noseguard is closer to the center than the guard or is a good player, the center may combo with the backside guard up to the first linebacker. That allows the backside tackle to track to the backside linebacker.

The backside tackle, when he tracks the linebacker, is not trying to get a position block on him. He is trying to cover him up and get a body on him. He lets the back make the cut off his block instead of trying to give him a seam to run into. All he wants to do is get a hat on the linebacker and square up.

Based on the scouting report, we adjust our blocking scheme off the defensive tendencies. If we know what the defense will do when they align in a particular position, we adapt. We change the blocking scheme from an odd to an even concept. We played a team that every time they brought the outside linebacker to the line of scrimmage, he was coming. We changed from an odd concept scheme to an even concept scheme and blocked the tight end out of the box on the outside linebacker.

The playside tackle on the inside zone play knows the ball will start over the center/guard gap. If he has a 5 technique aligned on him, he will base block on the 5-technique defender. If the 5 technique tightens down in his alignment or the linebacker walks up on the guard, the guard tells the tackle to protect himself. That tells the tackle not to take the zone step to the outside. If the 5 technique slants across the tackle's face as he takes the outside zone step, he is in danger. Instead of zone stepping the 5 technique, he lead steps, which prevents the 5 technique from spiking inside and blowing the play up.

If the tight end is to the read-key side, he arc blocks for the inside linebacker. He does not go for the outside force player. On an option play, there are two keys. You have a read key and a *pitch key*. In the blocking scheme, you never block the keys. The quarterback reads the first key and pitches off the second key. The tight end turns back inside and looks for the flowing linebacker or the first defender inside the pitch key.

The offensive line is blocking the inside zone play, but the backfield action gives a different look to the same play. We can go to an empty set and run a quarterback zone play from that set. We put a back in speed motion in front of the quarterback. He fakes the jet sweep to the back and runs the inside zone play. Nothing has changed for the offensive line. We still run the inside zone, but we present it in a different way to the defense. However, on this type of play, there is no read key.

On the inside zone, the back has to see what is happening. The first thing he sees is the frontside A gap (Diagram #8). If that is open, he takes the ball into the A gap. If the A gap is not open, we do not want him to make a decision right away to go somewhere else. We want him to press the heels of the offensive linemen before he makes a cut. The biggest problem the back has in his track is being too wide. If he is in the gap or behind the playside guard, his track is too wide.

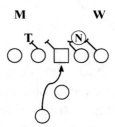

Diagram #8. Back Read

The second mistake he makes is to cut before he presses the heels of the offensive linemen. This is not a bend-back play. He has to press the heels to get the linebackers to move. If he does not force the linebackers to move somewhere, we have no play. He presses the heels and makes his cut based on the first down lineman to the backside.

In the 4-3 look, the Mike linebacker is a playside A-gap defender; the Will linebacker is the backside B-gap defender (Diagram #9). You have to make them defend their gaps. In this situation, there is a 3-technique defender to the backside of the play. The backs whole thought process is directed to the 3 technique. The backside guard and tackle have a combo working on the Will linebacker and 3 technique. The back has to know if the 3 technique is cut off from the A gap. The playside guard posts the inside hand on the 3-technique double-team and stays on it as long as he can. At some point, he has to snap off for the linebacker. If we can cut the 3 technique off, we can split the defense. If we have the 3 technique cut off, the back bangs the ball into the A gap. However, if the 3 technique is being washed inside, the back has to bend the ball behind him.

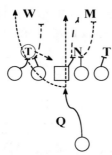

Diagram #9. Backside 3 Technique

From a three-step read standpoint, you have to give your back some direction. I would run the football at the 1 technique all day if I can get the 3 technique cut off (Diagram #10). If there is a 1 technique to the backside, the running back looks at the block on the 3-technique defender. If the guard has him cut off, his key is the first down lineman to the backside. If we have him pushed and cut off, the back runs into the A gap. However, in most cases, the 1 technique gets washed to the frontside and the running back takes the ball behind the 1 technique.

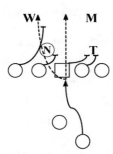

Diagram #10. Read vs. 1 Technique

The track takes the back to the frontside, but his read takes him to the backside. He bangs the ball into the A gap or bends it behind the backside key.

I want to talk about the outside zone. Once you understand the blocking rules and hat responsibility for the inside zone play, the rules do not change for offensive line when we go to the outside zone. The aiming points, tracks, and techniques will change,

but the rules of who to block remain the same. On the outside zone play, the quarterback and running back change their alignments. The quarterback aligns at five-and-a-half yards and the running back aligns at five yards. The running back aligns behind the tackle to his side, five yards off the ball.

The reason for that is so we can stretch the defense. If the running back aligns even with the quarterback, on the exchange, the running back automatically gets pushed downhill toward the line of scrimmage. When the quarterback aligns at five-and-a-half yards, the thing he has to avoid is moving his back foot. If he does that, he forces the running back downhill. We want the running back coming straight across and pressing his outside read.

The aiming point and track for the running back is to chase the outside hip of the playside tackle. We tell him to do that so he moves and gets the defense to stretch. On the inside zone, we wanted a vertical displacement of the defenders. We wanted to knock them back. On the outside zone, we try to get lateral displacement. We want the defense to spread out on the line of scrimmage. The object is to stretch the frontside and get a cutoff somewhere on the backside to split the defense. If you can do that, you have a chance for a big play.

In the offensive line, nothing changes as far as the defenders they are responsible for. Against the even front, the guard and center have a frontside combination block to the first linebacker in the box. The backside is working to cut off the backside linebacker. We still read the backside end on the outside zone.

Nothing has changed in their responsibility. What has changed is their *technique*. The steps for the lineman on the inside zone play are different from the outside zone. On the inside zone, the playside tackle's first step is a lateral step, and his aim point is the inside V of the defender's neck. The playside guard has the same step. He aims for the inside V of the 3 technique's neck, and he tries to knock him off the ball.

When we run the outside zone, the aiming point for the playside tackle is to put his hat on the outside

V of the defender's neck. If the tackle has a 5-technique defender aligned on him, then on the first step, he opens his hips. He has to give ground so he can gain position on the defender. He does not step in the bucket so to speak. It is a stretch step. He gains ground and position on the first step. He opens his toe, which helps open the hips.

The offensive tackle wants to make the 5 technique defend what he is defending. His coach has coached him to avoid getting reached. The tackle tries to reach the 5 technique and makes him defend that movement. The tackle does not necessarily want to reach the 5 technique. He is concerned with making the 5 technique stretch to keep from being reached. In a perfect world, the tackle would not give up any penetration and would move the defender down the line of scrimmage to the sideline. That would be a perfect block for the tackle.

The tackle has to know if he is working with someone else or alone. If he is working with someone, he has to know what second-level defender he is working for. His technique on the block changes based on whether he has inside help. If the center and guard are working an inside combo, the tackle is alone on the block. The worse thing that can happen to him is for the 5 technique to beat him across his face and get penetration.

The tackle uses a *drag hand technique*. As he takes his stretch step to the outside V of the neck, his backside hand placement is the thing that will slow him down enough to catch the 5-technique defender if the defender slants inside. The aiming point for the drag hand is the backside pec of the defender. That movement will stop the penetration of the defender inside. The tackle cannot come off the ball with no concern of the defender slanting inside. He uses the drag hand to catch and hold the defender so he cannot penetrate.

If the defender stays outside, the tackle has threatened his technique. He has threatened his leverage with his helmet placement. The defender will move to keep the tackle from reaching outside leverage on him.

If the lineman has inside help with the combo block, he can come off the ball and be aggressive on the defender (Diagram #11). The lineman takes his stretch step for the outside V and fires his backside hand into the sternum of the defender. The guard does not worry that the 3 technique may spike because the center is combo blocking with him and will pick up the inside movement of the 3 technique.

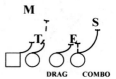

Diagram #11. Combo and Drag Hand

If we have an *ace combination block* to the callside, the tackle is alone on his block. If he sees the Will linebacker cheat to the outside, he probably is facing a slant-scrape stunt off the edge. He makes a *pull call* to the guard (Diagram #12). The call pulls the guard into a combination block with him and off the inside combo with the center. The pull call pulls all the blocks toward the tackle.

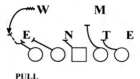

Diagram #12. Pull

That is the way the line blocks the play. The play will work if the backs are disciplined in their read progression. In the inside zone play, the backs had to be disciplined getting to the line of scrimmage. Once they got to the line of scrimmage, they could go to work. The aiming point of the back is chasing the outside hip of the tackle. His first read is the first down lineman on or outside the tackle. His second read is the next down lineman inside the tackle.

As the back goes through his progression, there are a few things that can happen. The first thing that can happen is the defensive end gets reached. We do not necessarily want that to happen. We want the ball to bang or bend. We do not want it to bounce because the back will move laterally. You do not want that situation, but you have to teach it in this progression for it to make sense to the back.

If the first read is reached, the back *bounces* and goes outside. Here is an important point (Diagram #13). If the first read is reached and the back does not bounce the ball, you need another back. The only thing the offensive lineman wants is to be right. I coach the back to make the linemen right. Do not put the offensive line in a bad position. If the first read is reached, the back bounces the ball to the outside and gets what he can.

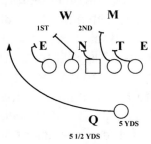

Diagram #13. Bounce

The tackle reaches the defensive end, but instead of the back bouncing the ball, he dances and takes the ball inside and the tackle gets called for holding. The back put the tackle in a bad spot because he was not disciplined enough to go through his read progression. Crap runs downhill pretty fast. The tackle gets called for holding and I get my butt chewed out. The fault lies with the back.

The next part of the read progression is when the first read is not reached (Diagram #14). If the first read is not reached but is stretched and running outside, the back looks to the second read. If the next down defender is reached, the back runs a *bang*. The back secures the ball, plants his outside foot in the ground, and gets the ball north and south immediately. Once the back makes his decision, he cannot dance, make a double cut, or fake anyone. He bangs the ball outside the reached defender to the inside.

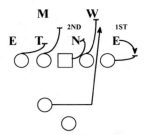

Diagram #14. Bang

The last progression is the *bend*. The bend occurs when the first and second read are both stretching and running outside (Diagram #15). For us to get a bend run, someone on the backside must get a cutoff block. You have to cut a defender down and split the defense. What I can do to the backside to split the defense is to block the guard back on the 3 technique and fold the tackle around for the linebacker. That stops the 3 technique's pursuit and puts a hole in the backside for the back to bend the ball.

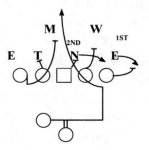

Diagram #15. Bend

When you run this play from a two-back set, this is one of my favorite plays (Diagram #16). When we run the outside zone from the two-back set, the fullback is tracking for the fourth defender to the weakside. That is his blocking assignment, but he will insert himself into the blocking scheme as if he were running the football. He goes through the same read progression as the ballcarrier. If the first read is reached, the fullback goes outside. If the second defender is reached, he bangs into the B gap. If the first and second defenders are not reached, he bends to the backside. He always blocks the first opposite-color jersey as he turns back.

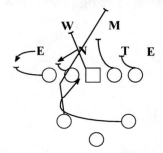

Diagram #16. Two-Back Zone

If the fullback bounces the play to the outside, he blocks the first color that shows. If the defender is attacking the play, the fullback kicks him out.

However, if the defender remains on or back of the line of scrimmage, he works to stretch him to the outside. If the defender is on his grasses, we stretch him. If he comes on our grasses, we kick him out.

Here is a coaching point for the offensive line. The frontside tackle, as he stretches the defender, is aware of when the back will cut. Through repetition and timing with the back, the line knows when he will make his cut. After the tackle runs four to five steps to the outside stretching the defender, he locks the backside hand. That prevents the defender from putting on the brakes and falling back into the play from the outside. Once we get them outside, we do not want them to be able to fall back inside and help on the back. That has to do with the trust the linemen have for the running back. They trust he is going where he should be.

The guard does the same thing. He has his inside hand on the sternum of the defender and works to lock out the inside hand. If the defender fights to get back inside, the guard locks out the inside arm and works the hips upfield.

The entire line must understand the timing of the scheme. As the tackle takes his first step and has the defensive end reached, the back has not gotten the ball. That is why the line must be patient, and you have to teach them that. You can tell when they have gotten the timing of the scheme. If you watch this play, all the linemen are taking the exact same steps in unison. It almost looks like a choreographed dance. The back is doing the same thing. He is taking the same steps that they are.

One of the rule changes in football effected this type of play. A guard used to be able to post up a 3 technique on the backside and the tackle could cut him down. That is illegal now. That is the chop-block rule. If the defender is in contact with one blocker, the second blocker cannot cut him. The pull call the tackle makes to the guard effects all the blockers back to the backside guard.

Normally, the backside guard and tackle would combo on the 3-technique defender to the linebacker. When the tackle gave the pull call, the backside guard gives a slip call to his tackle. That means he is not going to touch the 3 technique and is going straight to the linebacker. In that case, the backside tackle can cut the 3 technique legally. That is all part of the communication between linemen. If the guard puts his hand on the 3 technique and the tackle cuts him, that is a 15-yard penalty.

When we run the outside zone play, we like to run it to the 1-technique and 5-technique side. We feel it is a better play that way. We are not always able to do it that way. I tell the offensive linemen to change up the way they cut off the backside. I do not tell them they have to use a particular technique. I tell them to change up what they are doing. We may slip cut the 3 technique and linebacker on one play. We may block back with the guard and fold the tackle for the linebacker. We can use the slip call and chop the 3 technique. They have to change up the way they do things to keep the defense guessing.

Thank you for your kind attention.

SPECIAL TEAMS MANAGEMENT IN PRACTICE

Purdue University

In my introduction, it was stated that I followed Coach Joe Tiller at Purdue. I was very fortunate in that I was able to come to Purdue as an assistant coach in Coach Tiller's last season. It is very important to be able to spend one year in transition before taking over as the head coach at a major college. I had worked with Coach Tiller three different times. I first worked for him at the University of Wyoming, then at Purdue, and a second trip back to Purdue in his last year.

At Wyoming, we were on the cutting edge of the spread offense. We brought that same offense to Purdue in 1997. We had a blast with that offense. Drew Brees was our quarterback. I left Purdue and went to Eastern Kentucky University as the head coach for five years. I came back to Purdue and worked with Coach Tiller his last year.

It was a great experience to sit down with the coach I had worked with three different times and review the different phases of football during our experiences together. We were able to come up with a master play for Purdue football. I was able to sit down with someone whom I trusted and cared about. We looked at every phase of the program and talked about the changes made and why they were made. We came up with an academic and athletic game plan, and a recruiting game plan that we felt would give our team a chance to reach the championship level.

First, I want to talk about the academic part of the program. Some of you may be not believe I am going to come here and talk about academics. We are taking the same approach that I took to Eastern Kentucky University when I became the head coach. We have a goal for our football team to carry a cumulative grade-point average of 3.0. We told the parents of the players we were recruiting that we want our players to maintain that 3.0 grade-point average. We hung our hat on that primacy.

Our thinking on the academic aspects for our athletes is this: I do not think we can win games at Purdue if we only recruit players who are average students. We do not want players who only want to work hard enough academically to remain eligible. We do not feel we can beat the teams we play every year if we surround ourselves with average student-athletes. We have a goal for our football team to carry a 3.0 GPA. This is a master plan for our program, and it is not just lip service. It is critical; if we want to build a championship program, we feel we must maintain our high academic standards.

Let me give you some information on Purdue. We have about 40,000 students, and about 16,000 of them live on campus. Purdue is one of the top academic schools in the country. We feel it is the best combination for big-time football and big-time academics in the country. In the last 11 years, Purdue has been in the top-10 college teams in producing players to go on to play NFL football.

When I look back at my career, the thing I feel lucky about is the fact that I have worked with and for some great coaches. My first coaching job was at Manatee High School in Bradenton, Florida. I worked for Joe Kinnan. He won about 90 percent of his games there in 30 years. That was back in the 1980s. I was there four years, and we were 44-4. What a great start in the coaching profession.

Next, I went to the University of Louisville as a GA. The next year, Howard Schnellenberger hired me as the offensive line coach. He is an outstanding football coach. Coach Schnellenberger had worked for George Allen, Bear Bryant, and Don Shula. What a great opportunity to work with Coach Schnellenberger. He is still coaching and is at Florida Atlantic University.

Then, I was lucky enough to work for Joe Tiller at Wyoming, and later at Purdue. I played at Eastern Kentucky University for legendary Coach Roy Kidd. I was lucky to work for those great head coaches, and that has been the difference-maker in my life as a football coach.

I have learned three or four things over the years that have impacted my life as a football coach. You go into coaching for two reasons. You go into coaching because you cannot live without the game. The second reason to go into coaching is because you want to be around young people. If those are not the two reasons you are motivated to go into coaching, then you are in the wrong profession. I can assure you, a coach is not as cool when he is 50 years old as he was when he was 25 years old to the young people. If you do not love the game, and if you do not love young people, after a while it will wear on you. I think it is important to love the game and to love young people.

I talk with young people who are thinking about going into coaching often. I ask them if they would be satisfied if they never were able to coach beyond the high school level, if they could be content. If the answer is no, then they do not need to go into coaching. I promise you, those are the two main reasons to go into coaching.

When I went to coach for Coach Tiller, he had a marching order. I followed his same procedure in this area. At Purdue, the assistant coach is responsible for the academic and athletic performance of the players you coach and recruit. I want to repeat that marching order. As an assistant coach at Purdue, you are responsible for the academic and athletic performance of the players you coach and recruit. If you are the offensive line coach, and you have a soft offensive line, you may be a soft offensive line coach. If you are a receiver coach, and your players do poorly in school, it may be because you are not disciplined enough with your players. We hold our assistant coaches accountable for the players they

work with. That is a tough marching order, but it has a lot of merit to it.

I coached with Coach Schnellenberger at the University of Louisville for 10 years. In 1990, we went to the Fiesta Bowl and played Alabama. We beat Alabama in the bowl game. It was a huge win for the University of Louisville. It was a fantastic year for Louisville.

It was a miserable year for me. We did not have a very good offensive line, and I was the line coach. I was a struggling young coach. I tried to decide on what I should hang my hat on as a position coach. The first thing I considered was the "want to." I wanted to know how important it was to the players. You should never have to question how important it is to your players. When they ran sprints, I wanted them to try to be first. When I gave them something to do, they could jump on it and do it at will. "Wanting to" is one of the most important parts of football.

As a head coach and as an assistant coach, I want to see a team with a burning desire to win. When you watch your team practice and perform, and watch them prepare, if there is any question about how important winning is to them, you need to bring that to their attention immediately.

The second thing was tempo. We want to be the hammer and not the nail. We want to be the aggressor.

The third thing was "us." We wanted to be a close-knit unit, as a group. It could be the offensive line, linebackers, or the entire football team. "Want to" is how important to players. "Tempo" means we want to be the aggressor. Last but not least, we wanted to be "us" where we worked as one team. That is what we hung our hat on for years.

I like football practice. I liked it as a player, and I like it as a coach. Some people to not like football practice as a coach or as a player. It is the most important two-and-a-half hours in the day. In my mind, football players should practice fast, and they should practice hard. You must communicate what the tempo is to be in practice.

We have two tempos in practice. One is full speed, and the other is walk-through. We get out of our stance in full speed, and we can go game speed. We do not want to be caught off guard on Saturday.

Those are the only two tempos we have in our practice. We have full-speed tempo with shorts, or we may go in half pads, or full pads, and walk-through tempo. When we do walk-through tempo, it is detailed. When we do the walk-through, I want everything perfect just as we want it in a game. The only difference in full tempo and walk-through tempo is velocity. The details should be the same in my mind. This has helped us to practice up to game speed.

I think it is important to communicate what you want to accomplish in practice. We have a list of Keys to Victory each week. We list five or six things that cover every phase of the game. We talk about the keys to victory in practice. We talk about what we are going to emphasize in practice each day. It may be that we are going to change the snap count that week during the course of the game. We want to slow the defense down on the rush. We stress to our offense it is important to change the snap count, and we do not want to get caught offside when we do change the count. We let them know we are going to stress that in practice that day. I will talk to the team about this issue before we go out to practice. If we can stress a key to victory each day in practice, by the time the game comes up, we have a good idea what we have to do to win the game.

We believe it is important to be punctual. When you say practice is going to be over, it should be over. If we say practice is over at 6:00 p.m., we may run to 6:01 p.m., but that is about it as far as running over the time we said we would stop practice. When that whistle blows, it is "all up!" This is the reason we do it that way. If the players do not know when practice is going to end, how can they go full speed? If they think you are going to go longer in practice, they will hold back in practice. I do not like to practice in slow motion, and I do not like players to pace themselves. When we say practice is over at 6:00 p.m., you can bet it is going to end at that time. The players know this. I think you can get the

players to practice at a different speed and at a different tempo if the players know you are going to quit practice when you say you are going to stop.

We have done some things differently in our program. We train for a lot more specific position techniques in the off-season. We have done a lot of different technical things at each position. We do something different for each group each day. We have them work about 10 minutes on their own after they get through lifting weights each day. When we get into spring ball, it will not be the first time they have heard those terms and techniques.

We have spent some time on speed training. I worked for Coach Schnellenberger for all of those years. He had played football for Bear Bryant and came from the old school of football. We ran our players a lot during practice. The thing about it is this: it made the players tough, and it got them into condition, but it did not make them faster. When I went to Eastern Kentucky, I ran our team a lot. We could play 100 quarters if we had to. I do not believe anyone got any faster after all of that running. The running was to make them tough mentally and to get them into physical condition.

When I got to Purdue, I decided I would take about one fourth of the time we spent on running and spend it on form running and speed running to see if we could improve our speed. We used instructors who were experts in this field. We brought in some speed trainers to work with our team and coaches. We had them spend time with the athletes as well.

We still run the players to get them into condition. However, we also spend some time with our players in form running and speed running to try to improve their speed and athleticism. We do that rather than speeding their entire time running just to be running them.

I think it is very important to communicate our intentions to the player about what we are trying to accomplish in practice. I may tell them we are going to run them more today than they have ever run in their life. I explain why we are doing this running drill. We may end up playing a team, and the game will go down to the wire. The team that is in the best mental and physical condition is the team that will not quit. We may have to go to our limits, but we want to be the team that is still standing when we reach that plateau that separates the winners from the losers. If they know why we are running so much, they will give us a better effort because they will know it is because we are doing the drill to help us when we really need to be the superior conditioned team. When the game comes down to the team that quits first is going to be the loser, we do not want it to be us.

At one time at Eastern Kentucky, we had lost some games in the fourth quarter. In my mind, we were not conditioned enough to play tough in the fourth quarter. We practice three quarters of the time and then called the team together. We told them we were going to grade their performance in practice as if we were in a game in the fourth quarter. We worked them hard for three quarters, and now we were going to see who wanted to win in that fourth quarter. There is always a method to our practice, and we always communicate that to our players.

We had one heck of a season at Purdue this past year. We wanted to have a special season. We wanted to be able to play in the post-season and to shock the football world. We had some special moments, but we did not get to play in the post-season. We turned the ball over a lot earlier in the season. We led the nation in turnovers in the first few games of the year. We started the season off 1-5. The fans were not happy. A lot of people thought we were going to give up. We did a great job as a team of sticking together. We cared about each other. In the end, our team made a great run and finished the season with a great push.

We came on in the season, and got better as the season went on. We beat Ohio State, and they were a top-10 football team. At the time, they ranked seventh in the nation. It was the first time Purdue had beaten a top-10 team in 25 years. That was like getting a monkey off our back in a way. After that win, our team felt we could beat anyone. We felt we could beat anyone left on our schedule. All of this changed in about three hours. What a difference-maker that win was.

In our next game, we went to Michigan and beat them. It was a big win for us. It was the first time we had beaten Michigan at Michigan since 1966. Bob Griese was the quarterback the last time Purdue had won at Michigan. Then, we had a win against Illinois. We beat Indiana at the end of the season, and they are our archrival. We did not have a great record, but we did have a great team. Our seniors walked away feeling they had left some kind of legacy they could be proud of.

When I got the head coaching job at Eastern Kentucky, I felt I had a great plan. After I was there a short time, I realized I knew very little about special teams, and I knew nothing about kickers. I did what all head coaches do: I faked it. It did not take long for coaches to figure me out. After a couple of years, I decided this was not fair to the players.

I got on the phone and called a friend. I told him I was looking for a young coach to come to Eastern to be the special-teams coordinator, and to coach the kickers, punters, and snappers. He would also serve as the football operations coach. After a year, I promised I would hire him as a full-time coach. I hired Coach J. B. Gibboney. He did a great job as our special-teams coach, and he worked with our kickers. When I came to Purdue, I wanted to bring Coach Gibboney with me. I had a reason why.

When I was at Purdue in 1997, our spread offense was on the cutting edge. A lot of teams have changed to the spread offense, and it has changed some since that time. The spread offense was what we hung our hat on during that time. Now, we feel our special teams will be our cutting edge that makes a difference in our program.

We are different from most Division I schools. We do have nine full-time assistant coaches, as other schools have. Most teams have five coaches on offense and four on defense. We have four coaches on offense, four on defense, and one special-teams coordinator. I think this impacts our team in a lot of different ways. We have taken one coach and we have dedicated that coach just to special teams. It also allows our linebacker coach to be free from being responsible for one or two special-teams units. He can focus his time at coaching his position and players. He may have a player or two on special teams, but he can give more attention to his position if he does not have the responsibility of a special-teams unit.

As you know, recruiting occurs now during the season. How can you be a position coach in a Division I school, and coach your players, watch all of the films, deal with your players and their academics, and then be in charge of a special-teams unit, and recruit full-time? You have to do all of this during the season. If this is the case, we know something is going to give. When I was a position coach, I was in charge of the kickoff-return unit. I can tell you now; the kickoff return was second to the offensive line, which was my position to coach. I think my assistant coaches are the same as I was.

We have committed our special teams to a full-time coordinator. As the head coach, I get involved in all of the special teams. Coach Gibboney is in charge of all of the teams. He knows what we are doing on a daily basis. He can tell us why we are doing the drills, and he can give us all of the techniques, and all of the game planning. He and I go over everything together. We are on the same page on everything about special teams. I attend every special-teams meeting, and I am involved in every special-teams practice.

We have a practice plan that we think is conducive to giving us the best chance to win through our special teams. Like everyone else, we have a specialty period. We come out before practice and warm up. Our kickers warm up as well. Our coaches walk their groups through some drills. Then, we go to a stretch period. Everyone has a specialty.

We also have a special teams period just as everyone else has. We take a certain amount of time for the different units just as other teams have. We have special-teams scrimmages just as other teams have. We do a few things in our special teams that we feel may be a different from what other teams do.

We have a gold team. This is our special-teams scout team. Coach Gibboney has his pick of players for the gold team. It does not matter where a player is; if we call for the gold team, that player must report to Coach Gibboney in a hurry. The scout team or gold team is a group of players that are the fastest and toughest, and wide-eyes-open guys that do not play much on Saturday. They go against our special teams in practice, and they take a lot of pride in being on the gold team. We have players who will get up to introduce themselves, and they will tell you they are so and so, from a certain town, and they will state, "I am on the gold team." He will tell his friends and teammates he is on the gold team. They take pride on being on the gold team.

We also have what we call a Pearl Harbor team. No one knows when we are going to call for a special-teams unit in practice except for Coach Gibboney and me. We can be in the first-and-10 period, and I will blow a whistle. I will call for the first team "kickoff-return team" to report. The GAs will call for the gold kickoff team. Those 11 screaming maniacs come running to the kickoff area. They line up, and we have one minute to get the kickoff. We do it this way to keep them alert on the kickoff. If you only do kickoffs in a certain time frame of practice, it gets old after a while, it gets mundane, routine, and the players know what is going on, and they pace themselves during that period. If it comes during practice, the players must be alert, and they cannot pace their drills waiting for the special-teams drills.

CIRCUITS

When I came back to Purdue this time, they were doing something different in the special-teams period. We liked what they were doing, and we have continued the drill. We come out and stretch. Before we go to individual periods, we do a special-teams circuit period. It is a special-teams individual practice that lasts 10 minutes a day. We have the circuits scattered across the field and work on different phases of the individual special teams.

Later in practice, we have team sessions for our special teams, but in the circuit phase of practice, we are working on individual aspects of special-teams play. We do this just after we stretch. I think this makes a big difference for us.

This is how we set up the special-teams circuit working on special-teams individual skills.

Circuit #1

We work on point after touchdown (PAT) and field goals. This circuit is with the offensive line coach and the inside linemen. We check their stance, and have them go through their techniques. We rotate the players in to make sure we work everyone during the drill. We want multiple snappers during the drill. We want multiple holders and multiple kickers in the PAT and field goal session.

In the second part of Circuit #1, we work on the sky punt. That will be the last five minutes of the circuit. We work on the returns with the return men with their heels on the 10-yard line. Some teams line their return men up on the eight-yard line. The reason we go at the 10-yard line is because we do not want our return men backing up. We want to be able to use that 10-yard line as a landmark. We want to be able to work sideways, and he can see that 10-yard line.

We also work on our gunners sprinting down the field and locating the football. We want them to put the ball on their hips at the five-yard line to keep the ball out of the end zone.

In another area of the practice field, we have our return team working during Circuit #1. We have players set up to return to their landmarks and get ready to execute their shield blocks. They sprint back to the landmark, set up, and keep their eyes on their target. They are six inches apart and they work on the double-team block. Our man that is going to peel around the double-team block and execute his trap or ambush block must get around the double-team block in order to make his block.

We work against the pooch kick with our ends and upbacks catching the short kicks. We line the kicker up at the 30-yard line and kick the ball high. We give all the return men a chance to field the kicks.

If you are going to use the circuit drills, you must have a layout of the practice field. The coaches must know where their drill is located as well as the players. The worst thing in the world is for the whistle to blow, and you have eight kids come up to you and ask where they go. We post the map or diagram where all circuit drills are located. We post this in the locker room each morning, and the assistant coaches should let their players know where they are on each circuit for the day. We have a watch on our punter during this drill.

We work on individual techniques during the circuit sessions. It is not a full-speed drill. It is a time where we can stop the players and teach proper techniques. We work on all phases of the kicking game. We work on receiving all types of kicks with our return players. We work on all of the Circuit #1 drills on Tuesday.

Circuit #2

On Wednesday, we work on Circuit #2. Again, start with PATs and field goals. We work with the inside line on their techniques. We exchange the snappers to make sure everyone gets to work on their specialty. We are always looking at new guys on the special-teams players. We rotate players in and out of the circuit. We do not have players standing around in this session.

We will take a few minutes during this session to do some form tackling. We feel it is important to teach offensive skilled players how to tackle. We have speed on offense, but we are afraid to put them on special teams because we do not think they will tackle anyone. We take five minutes in Circuit #2 and work on teaching tackling to those offensive skilled players. We teach form tackling and sideline tackling.

Also during this session, we work on the spread punt with the punters, and the punt-return hold-up. We refer to this as a "crush" technique." We want to pin, lock, and trail the defender we are trying to hold up. We want to pin him as he comes off the line, and we want to pin him to the sideline. We lock on him and stay with him down the field.

When the whistle blows for the second phase of Circuit #2, we work on the punt coverage, our net drill, and our punters fielding bad snaps from the long snappers. The snaps are not always going to be perfect. We take five minutes during the course of the week and work on the punter catching those bad snaps. If the punter does have to move to field the ball, he is better off if he can land on his plant foot, so he can get the ball off. He does not want to land on the kicking foot. We work on the high snaps, low snaps, the dribble snap, and left and right snaps.

Circuit #3

In Circuit #3, again, we work on PATs and field goals. It is not the same drill every day. We work on a field-goal-block drill. We try to get the block on the fifth step. We use a sprinter's stance. We tell the defender blocking the field goal to lock his thumbs. The hands are underneath the eyes. By crossing the thumbs, it allows the defender to stretch out as wide as he can. We do not want the ball to go between the man's hands.

We also have a punt-protection drill during the first part of Circuit #3. In the second five minutes of Circuit #3, we work on PAT and field goals and our kickoff-coverage drill. We have a lot of kicking-game drills going on during this time. You must have the field laid out so everyone knows where to go during the drills.

We will do PATs and field goals later in practice as a team. Everyone comes together, and we run those kicks. We do not coach a lot of technique during this part of practice.

We do have a "block spot" that we work on when we are teaching our players to block the punts. We have a mat or pad we use to teach the block spot. It is the spot where the defensive man aims for when he is trying to block a punt. It is out in front of the punter's foot, where the ball is going to be when they get deep enough to reach the ball off the foot of the punter.

We are a spread punt team. Before I came back to Purdue this time, they used the traditional punt. Everyone would zone block and get into their normal splits. We had our line set with the outside foot up and the inside foot back. That looked odd to me because I coached the offensive line. This was just the opposite of the way we pass blocked. They had done a lot of research. Most of the players on the punt team were defensive players. We do not put the big offensive linemen on the punt team. We felt the defensive players struggled to stay square. They set back and zone blocked on the punt team. They had the outside foot back.

We changed that positioning and put the outside foot up. They would step back and keep their shoulders square to take the defenders on. They were defensive players, and we were teaching them how to block. If we are defending an offensive lineman, we do not want to keep the shoulders square. We do not use the traditional punt anymore.

We run the focus drill with our punt team. We want to find the flight of the ball. We do not give the "ball" call until it is on the way down. This makes the players flip around to find the ball, and then they can take a good path to the ball. This helps them find the flight of the football. He must flip around to find the ball once the call is given.

We do a cover drill from the sideline. We have different cover drills. We have an avoid zone and an attack zone. We are trying to recognize who is trying to block us.

We set the drill up on the sideline, where we do not have to run as much. We have two blockers and a ballcarrier. The two blockers are in the avoid zone. We want to avoid the two blockers and get by them (Diagram #1). Next, we go to the attack zone. We must get rid of the next blocker, or get off him, and force the ballcarrier to go one way or the other. It is a simple drill, but an important drill.

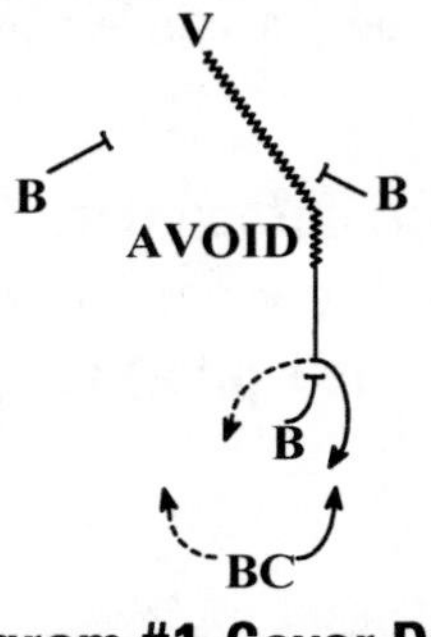

Diagram #1. Cover Drill

Circuit #4

Our Circuit #4 is very similar to the other three circuits. During the first five minutes, we have our PATs and field goals. We work on the punt block and our spread punt drill with our protection.

In the second five minutes, we work on our backed-up punt drill. We work on giving a safety during this period. We want to work on it in practice so if we do have to give up a safety in a game, the players will know what we are doing.

Also in this period, we are working on our "hands" team. We have two kickers so we can get as many reps as possible. We post the layout of the field for our circuits in the locker room each day. The coaches and the players know how the field will be set up and they know where to go for each circuit.

Our operation time for the PAT and field goal is 1.3 seconds or better. In high school, it comes out to about 1.4 seconds. The punt is 2.1 or better for the punt to be completed. In high school, it may be 2.2 or 2.3, depending on the kicker. The snap time is 0.8 or better. It will be about 0.9 for high schools. The snap is 1.3 to 1.4, based on the quality of your snapper.

Goals for our special teams are set at the beginning of the year. For the punt team, it is 40 yards net. We want to down the ball inside the 15-yard line. We want a hang time of 4.5 seconds or better. We want a net of 55 yards with our kickoff team. We are kicking the ball from our 30-yard line, and we want the ball down to the opponent's 25-yard line. We want a 4.0 plus hang time on the kick.

Our goals on our kickoff-return team include the following. We want to return all kicks. We want our average starting point after the return to be on our 35-yard line. We want to maintain possession on all returns.

Our goals for our punt-return team include fielding all punts. We want to average 10 yards on the return. We want a net of 130 yards per game.

Before we see the film, I want to let you know we did a lot of great things with our special teams this past year. We covered the things we do in our special teams management in practice. This week, we looked at all of our game film of our special teams from last year. It was a great thing for Coach Gibboney to sit down to look at all of the cut-ups. One thing I learned a long time ago is this: you cannot be too proud to admit you may have made some mistakes along the way. This is particularly true as the head coach. We did some great things with special teams this year, but we did find we made a couple of mistakes.

One mistake I made was this: we did not have a lot of depth especially on the defensive side of the ball, particularly in the secondary. We had four seniors in the secondary, and then we had a group of freshmen. None of the freshmen were ready to play in the secondary. I did not punt any of our top secondary players on our special teams. I was afraid if I got one of the starters hurt, we would have to play in the secondary with a freshman who was not ready to play. As a result, we took some lumps special teams-wise because I did not play the best players on those special teams. As a result, we will have better players on our special teams this year.

The other thing I look back on as a special-teams mistake was this: I did not feel the position coaches were able to utilize their coaching expertise enough. A lot of the techniques we use on our special teams are the same techniques we use on our offense or defense. There is no excuse for our players on our special teams not to know how to execute the techniques we use because they are the same as we use every day on our offense or defense.

My time is up. I will be in the breakout room, and we can go over anything you want to cover. Thank you.

FRONTSIDE/BACKSIDE/THREE-MAN COMBO LINE BLOCKING

C. W. Post College

Thank you. I would like to begin by thanking Chuck Rohe and Buddy Krumenacker for the opportunity to present here today. I have had the pleasure of speaking at the Nike Coach of the Year Clinic for the past six years. I feel these are the best-run clinics around. They always have a great lineup. It is an honor to speak at the same clinic with the great names here today. I also want to take a second to commend you guys who are here to become better coaches.

C. W. Post is coming off our second season in the prestigious Pennsylvania State Athletic Conference (PSAC). We finished the season at 6-5 after winning our last four games in a row and 5-1 in our last six games. While it is obvious that we struggled early in the season, our guys did a great job staying the course, and we were able to turn things around.

Highlights of our season include finishing first in rushing, fourth in total offense, sixth in scoring offense, and second in sacks allowed among the 16-team Pennsylvania State Athletic Conference. I am here to show you how we teach and drill our offensive linemen in the gun double and triple option. I want to give you a glimpse of our base play. I want to show you how we drill to answer the many variables a defense will throw at us. I will cover the run game drills for our frontside and backside two-man combinations as well as our three-man gang blocks. If time allows, we will cover our pulling techniques and drills for our big-on-big pass protections.

TERMS

First, I think it is important to identify some of the terminology I use in our teaching progression:

Stance: We are a two-point stance team. We feel this gives our best advantage in adjustments and vision, as well as the ability to depart the line of scrimmage in several different ways.

Splits: Two-foot base, adjusted to our advantage

Solo Block Terms

Angle of departure: The position descriptions of our first step off the line of scrimmage

Contact step: *Usually Step 2*

Firm knee: Knee of foot that took Step 2

Roll the firm knee: Describes the drive down of the knee over the toe of the second step. For example, if we would drill the tight reach, we would use these terms:

Angle of departure: Flat step right

Firm knee: Left knee

Roll the firm knee: Drive left knee down over the toe of the left foot.

Step 3: Made with right foot; should be short and drive this knee down to get Step 4 down.

Finish: Run the feet; heel replaces toe.

We will break up our blocks into one-, two-, and three-step progressions. We will drill the fit and finish, and we will work to put it all together. We drill all year long in this part/whole/part progression.

Combo Block Terms

Covered (man): Defensive line is shaded to head-up.

Uncovered (man): No defensive line shaded or head-up.

Frontside combination blocks

Linebacker Terms

Plus position: Shaded to point of attack.

Stack/Grey position: Stacked or protected by the defensive line.

Minus position: Shaded away from the point of attack.

BASE RULES

- If you are covered, block him.
- If you are uncovered, declare.
- Initial step is always with the callside foot.
- Position/angle of first step depends on the following:
  - ✓ Position of down man relative to the covered guy
  - ✓ Position of the linebacker (plus/stack/minus)
  - ✓ Point of attack
  - ✓ Who is carrying the ball

ANGLE OF DEPARTURE FROM THE LINE OF SCRIMMAGE

Lead Step

- Short jab step into line of scrimmage on fullback runs (Diagram #1).

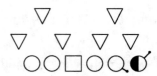

Diagram #1. Onside Tackle and Tight End

- Up and down step on tailback runs (Diagram #2).

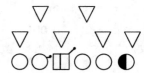

Diagram #2. Center and Backside Guard

Who: Covered

When: Any fullback run versus on/in alignment; any tailback run versus in alignment and linebacker minus point of attack.

Note: Uncovered linemen are never to be asked to lead step.

Flat Step

- Lateral step to the callside (Diagram #3).

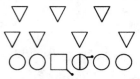

Diagram #3. Onside Guard and Center

Who: Covered

When: Defensive line head-up; linebacker minus to stack

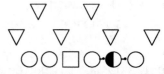

Diagram #4. Onside Tackle and Onside Guard

Who: Uncovered

When: Defensive line tight inside on covered man; linebacker in minus position

Drop Step

- Angular gap step that opens hips to help blocker attain proper position relative to the defender.

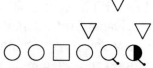

Diagram #5. Tight End and Onside Tackle

Who: Covered

When: Versus outside shade; versus head-up with linebacker in plus position

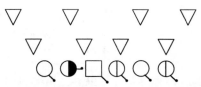

Diagram #6. Tight End and Onside Tackle / Frontside Guard and Center / Backside Guard and Backside Tackle

Who: Uncovered

When: When partner is covered head-up to outside

Coaching Point: The depth of the drop step varies with the width of the down defender. The depth of the drop step by the uncovered man is determined by the width of the down man. We want the uncovered man to step at the down man as if he is blocking him without help.

Since the technique is dictated as much by alignment of the defender as by the point of attack, we can spend the bulk of our time teaching the technique. How we handle our combinations actually becomes the scheme of the zone play.

Our teaching progression begins with two offensive linemen and one defender down man. We are constantly reminding our lineman that securing the down man is the highest priority. (Linebackers make tackles; defensive linemen make tackles for loss.) We also are trying to "trick" our players; we will talk it and walk it through before we go full tilt. Initially, we take a three-command cadence: Step 1/Step 2/finish. We always follow this step-by-step progression with a "full go" repetition.

2-ON-1 DRILL

Next, we are going to look at our 2-on-1 drill. We have three situations: inside, head-up, and wide.

Situation 1: Covered Inside

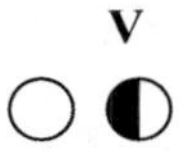

Diagram #7. Covered Inside

Covered: Lead step on fullback runs; up and down step on tailback runs.

Uncovered: Tight drop or flat step

Situation 2: Covered Head-Up

Diagram #8. Covered Head-Up

Covered: Flat step

Uncovered: Drop step

Situation 3: Covered Wide

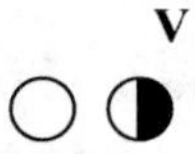

Diagram #9. Covered Wide

Covered: Drop step

Uncovered: Drop step

Next, we add a linebacker to the drill. First, the linebacker is in a minus to stack position relative to the point of attack. Then, we put the linebacker in a plus position. Our initial steps are consistent with the drills in our other three situations in the two-on-one drills. The variable here is hand placement or how much of the down man the covered lineman will take. Our choice are flipper, Rip, one-hand stab, one-hand read, and hand punch.

Let me give you the sequence we teach. We have the covered and uncovered positions on each situation. We use the following six sequences. Listed are the techniques we use in each situation.

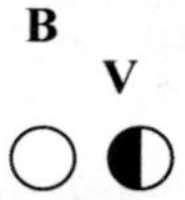

Diagram #10. Covered Inside Linebacker (Minus)

Covered: Flipper

Uncovered: Two-hand punch

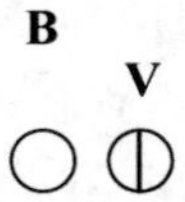

B
v

Diagram #11. Covered Head-Up Linebacker (Minus)

Covered: Two-hand punch to a one-hand stab

Uncovered: One-hand read to a two-hand punch

Diagram #12. Covered Wide Linebacker (Minus)

Covered: Two-hand punch

Uncovered: One-hand read to two-hand punch

**Diagram #13. Covered Inside Linebacker
(Gray to Stack)**

Covered: Rip to one-hand stab

Uncovered: Two-hand punch

**Diagram #14. Covered Head-Up Linebacker
(Gray to Stack)**

Covered: Rip

Uncovered: Two-hand punch

Diagram #15. Covered Inside Linebacker (Plus)

Covered: One-hand stab to one-hand read

Uncovered: Two-hand punch

These are initial hand placements. They will adjust according to the movement of the defense. We stress feeling the down man while seeing the linebacker.

From here, we add movement. We also do this in a progression. First, we will tell the offense exactly what is going to happen (Diagram #16). We will initially do these in steps, with two-command and three-command cadences to a full go (Diagram #17).

Diagram #16. Linebacker Outside

Diagram #17. Linebacker Inside

After we can pick up those moves, we do them on what we call blind movements. The coach standing behind the offensive line and puts the defense in random movements. All the steps remain consistent. The hand placement will be the area of greatest adjustment.

From there, we go to the backside movements. We spend a great deal of time on the specific techniques used on the backside of our double and triple option. Our backside is basically the frontside of the under-center dive and veer options.

Since we read the last man on the line of scrimmage for our give or pull read plays, we must drill at the possible paths the backside tackle will take to block the man who plays the quarterback, or his attack versus a traditional flow from the linebacker. Let me give you a few examples (Diagram #18).

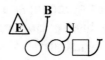

Diagram #18. Basic Backside Blocks

The linebacker will move in cooperation with the defensive end (Diagram #19). Here he goes outside.

Diagram #19. Linebacker Outside Movement

The linebacker goes inside and the end goes outside (Diagram #20).

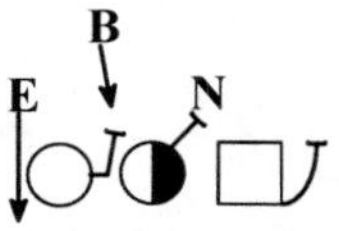

Diagram #20. Linebacker Inside Movement

As a result, we must drill these moves repeatedly. As with our frontside combinations, I will not try to fool the offensive players at first. I will call the movement out and let the player gain confidence in his path and steps.

The backside tackle must step flat into the B gap. I have three examples I want to cover:

- Time up his read (Diagram #21)
- Keep him square versus a downhill linebacker (Diagram #22)
- Answer the spike into the B gap by the noseguard (Diagram #23)

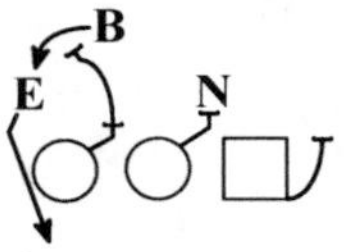

Diagram #21. Time Up Read

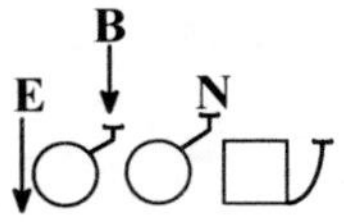

Diagram #22. Square vs. Downhill Linebacker

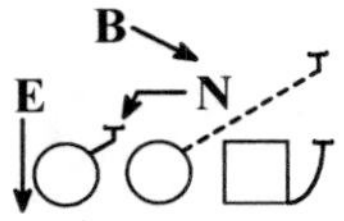

Diagram #23. Spike Into B Gap

We always want our first step (angle of departure) to be ready to handle all possible situations the defense will present.

The next big backside situation is when the defense aligns a 3 technique to the backside. This is different from the frontside combo in the way the linebacker approaches it.

The first situation the linebacker plays the traditional flow (Diagram #24)

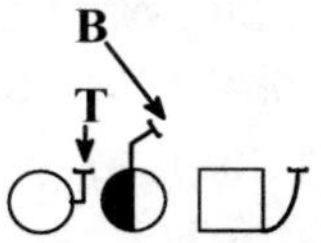

Diagram #24. Linebacker Traditional Flow

Backside tackle: Flat step right; snap defensive tackle if possible.

Backside guard: Up and down step right. Pull the defensive tackle if possible.

The other look is when the defensive end plays the quarterback on the backside (Diagram #25).

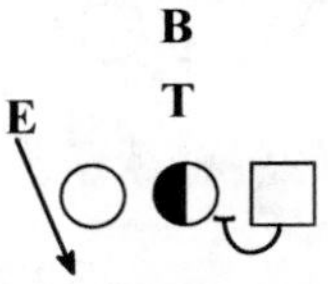

Diagram #25. End Plays Quarterback

We can use the same steps on the backside with the end coming inside or playing wide on the option play. The backside tackle can wash the pinch stunt or turn out on it if the inside linebacker comes outside on a pre-snap move.

Any time we feel that a two-man combination could get picked off on its way to the linebacker depth, we may pull another player into the combination. These game-plan calls are used against teams that like to slant their defensive line, or they will align in such a way that our rules for combos may be compromised.

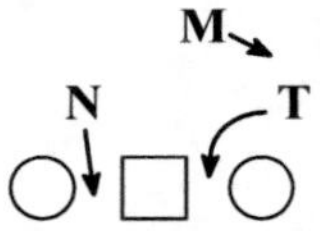

Diagram #26. Two-Man N & T Pinch

That block is no different from this pre-snap alignment (Diagram #27).

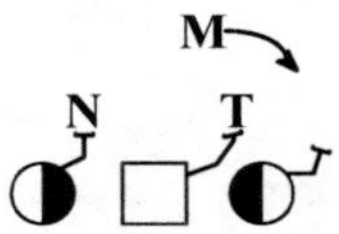

Diagram #27. Pre-Snap Alignment

We follow all our basic rules for potential frontside combinations with one major adjustment. The middleman in the gang will take a short one-two shuffle toward the point of attack and then take a tight drop step to take the spike or get on the proper angle to block the linebacker. Let me give you three examples (Diagrams #28, #29, and #30).

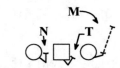

Diagram #28. N & T Pinch

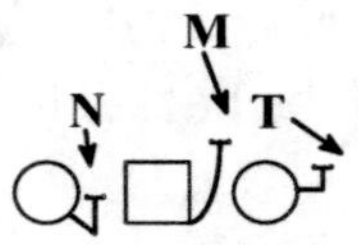

Diagram #29. N & T Slant Left

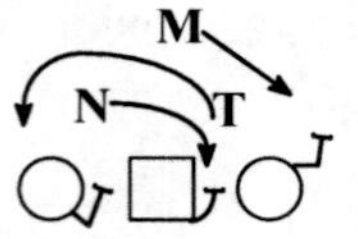

Diagram #30. N & T X Stunt

We block all possible three-man combos against all the possible looks for that week.

I hope this helps in your quest to answer all the looks a good defense will give you. Please do not hesitate to contact us at C. W. Post College if we can do anything to help your program. Thank you for your attention.

BASIC LINEBACKER DRILLS AND TECHNIQUES

University of Arkansas

Good afternoon, coaches. It is always a pleasure to come back to my second home. I was recruited by Coach Schnellenberger and came to the University of Louisville before it was popular to be a Cardinal. I was fortunate enough to finish my career here on an extreme high when we beat the University of Alabama in the Fiesta Bowl. I had an opportunity to come back in 2003 and work for Coach Petrino. I had the opportunity to coach in a BCS Bowl game, which the Cardinals won. Louisville has been a special place in my heart, and I consider this to be a second home.

Today, I plan on talking about some basic linebacker drills and fundamentals. The schemes do not matter unless you can accomplish the fundamentals of playing linebacker.

At a clinic like this, usually one of three things will happen. The first thing is that coaches will leave this meeting wondering how I ever got a college coaching job.

The second thing is that I will confirm something you are already teaching with your players. That will make you feel better about what you are doing. That will give you more conviction with what you are teaching.

The third thing is that you will pick up something small that can help your team become better at what they do. You can take it and add it to your repertoire and help you be a better coach. Hopefully, today it will be one of the latter two scenarios that will take place before you leave. In the next few minutes, I want to hit some general points and then get into the meat of the lecture.

You have to stress to your players that they are in a position of *leadership*. They continually interact with the front as well as the secondary. The linebackers have to be the playmakers on the team. They have to set the tempo and tone for the defense. Playing linebacker is all about setting examples for the team to follow.

I tell my players daily that they cannot talk about playing well—they have to *do it*. Do not talk it—do it. You must stress to them that they *lead by example*. However, they have to be vocal. They have to talk and encourage their teammates. If things are not going well on the field, we go to the linebackers to get things done. They have to encourage their teammates, but, at the same time, they have to be forceful with what they are saying. They are the team leaders when the coaches are not around. Leadership stresses the positive aspects of other players.

The next trait the linebacker must possess is *accountability*. Too many players these days want to point the finger at others when things start to go bad. If the linebacker is supposed to make a combo call to the safety and it does not happen, the linebacker has to be accountable for the mistake. The linebackers have to be accountable for everything that goes on within the defense. It is not only in football that the players have to be accountable. We talk about being accountable in the classroom and in all aspects of the player's life. It is part of growing up and becoming a young man. It takes a man to stand there and admit he made a mistake.

The linebackers have to take pride in being great *communicators*. Before the advent of the spread offense, the linebacker stood in front of the huddle and took control of what went on in the huddle. With the spread and no-huddle offenses in today's football, the huddle is a thing of the past. They must be vocal in what they see on the football field. They have to recognize formations and make adjustments, which requires great communication skills. They are the ones who must spread the word throughout the defense.

Communication skills go beyond the field. During time-outs and other breaks on the field, the linebacker has to communicate to the coach what is happening on the field. The linebacker has to be the coach's eyes and ears on the field.

The linebacker has to do his job first, but he must have a *working knowledge of the defense* and know everything that goes on around him. There is nothing more disheartening to a coach than having the defense misaligned. The linebacker must know where he aligns on a 31 defense, but he must also know where everyone else aligns. If we call a 31 defense and get two 3 techniques from the defensive tackles, that is the linebacker's fault. That goes back to communication skills, but the linebacker has to know what the function of the defense is. He has to know the strengths and weaknesses of the defense and of any particular call he makes.

We want our linebackers to be experts at what they do. They have to be experts at their position. That is especially true if they expect to be playing on Sunday in the NFL. They must master the *techniques* it takes to play linebacker. The NFL is not everyone's dream, but for those who think they can play at the next level, it goes back to techniques. If you have players who have the dream to play in the SEC or the BIG EAST, they have to do everything in their power to make it happen. Perfecting technique is tremendously important to achieving those dreams.

We think success is found in *preparation*. Everyone talks about being a fast and physical defense. You have to do everything necessary with your linebackers to make sure that is happening on the field. The linebackers must know the defense in regard to the mentality and scheme. Understanding the situations of the game is tremendously important. When I went to Louisville with Coach Petrino, we felt that part of the game was where the linebackers excelled. They studied and knew the situations of the game.

If the offense came out with a 21 personnel grouping on first down, the linebacker knew whether they were going to run or pass. They had done the preparation and studied those situations so that it became a strong focus for our team. They knew in second-and-short yardage what the offense was likely to do. They knew if that was a waste down for the offense or whether they would try to pick up the first down.

The linebackers coach has to understand the game plan going into the week so he can help his players in their study and preparation for the upcoming game.

The next thing the linebackers have to understand is *team and loyalty*. At our level, the media is always looking for a story. If they have to create the story, that is fine with them. They are constantly asking players to compare one player to another. They want the players to evaluate someone else's play. We discourage our players from getting into that type of discussion with someone outside the program. We want them to be loyal to their teammates. We simply tell them to say they are good players and great competitors and they look forward to competing with them on the field.

We do not want them talking about their coach or about calls made in a game. We want them to be loyal to their team and all personnel associated with the team. That aspect is huge for us.

The biggest thing I look for in a linebacker is *passion for the game*. They must play with passion. When you think about linebackers like Mike Singletary, those guys were excited about playing the position. They were excited about striking someone and kicking the crap out of them.

Every coach wants a linebacker who is bigger and stronger, but, for me, I want the linebacker who can run and will hit. If you have a linebacker who will run and strike, you will be alright. It all boils down to that youngster's passion, emotion, and enthusiasm for playing that position.

Linebackers have to be *tough*. We define toughness as never turning down a hit. If we can light your butt up, we will light you up. The linebackers have to be on the same page as the coach in terms of defensive philosophy. We are going to win with great technique, discipline, and pure hustle.

Our defensive priority is to stop the run and hit the quarterback. I have five basic areas that I have to work with my players on. We call it a "must list." On the must list is the skill we are trying to teach and the drills we need to use to work that particular technique. It includes a coaching point to help us achieve that goal. The five areas I have to work on are *movement, vision, blow delivery and block protection, tackling*, and *pass drops*. The passing game skills include drops, man coverage, and pass-rush skills.

The must list allows you to put your thoughts down on paper so you are organized as to what you want to do. It lets you identify the things you want to work with your players on—you have thought about them and written them down. After you do your must list, you need to put together a drill book. If you have already done that, you are ahead of the game. The drill book includes a list of all the drills you need to do during the entire season. If you have them listed and check them off when you do them, you will not leave out something important that you should have done. I did not start to do this until I joined Coach Petrino's staff. The drill book must marry your must list.

In a perfect world, I would have 25 to 30 minutes of individual time to work on those five areas. During the spring, we have the time to work individual drills in those areas. However, during the fall practice, we do not have enough time to do those things. I only get 15 minutes on any given day. I have to combine and consolidate drills to make sure I touch on those areas.

Everything, in terms of how I teach things, starts with *stance, alignment, key, responsibility, run toward*, and *run away*. Every spring, I start over with my players. I go back to gap responsibility and technique alignments. I do that every year because I want my players to talk the way I talk and think the way I think. I start over every year. They look at me like I am crazy, but that is the way I do it. You can never take for granted or assume they know it all. I assume they do not know anything. If a player comes to me as a freshman, he will get the same teaching four or five times. Any call I give a player, he has to give me his responsibility on run to, run away, and pass. If he cannot do that, he does not play. He stands on the sideline watching the game.

To play linebacker, everything starts with the *stance*. You want to be in the best position to move with no false steps. You do not want to dip or raise, and you want to keep as constantly pad level as you can. Everyone does not have the same level of flexibility, so the bend in the knees will adjust. We want the toes pointed straight ahead with the toes slightly inside. The weight is balanced on the inside balls of the feet. We want them to have good bend in their ankles with their pads over their toes. We want the hands in the ready position.

I cover these fundamentals of the stance with my players every year—that includes my fourth- and fifth-year players. The fundamentals never change, and I never deviate from them. You will have to decide what drills are best for your individual players. I use the drills listed in my drill book for my particular players.

When you put your drill book together, there should be a description of the drill and a diagram showing what should be done. The first drill we do in the spring is a footwork drill (Diagram #1). I do the drill to see good stances and proper footwork. I want to see a good bend, weight distribution, hands off the knees, and using good vision. After practice, we come in and watch the video of practice. I can make the corrections using the video to point out the flaws in their fundamentals.

Diagram #1. Step Drill

In the step drill, I am looking at their stances and their first step. The *shuffle drill* is almost the same drill. However, instead of stepping forward, we are shuffling up and inside (Diagram #2). We see a number of two-back sets in our league. This teaches the linebackers what to do if the ball is in the tackle box. If the linebacker can read the tailback's number or see any part of his front, they keep their pads square and are in a quick shuffle to the line of scrimmage. The play is probably an inside to cutback run.

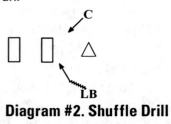

Diagram #2. Shuffle Drill

If the linebacker sees the profile of the running back, they can open their hips and run. What I am teaching in the shuffle drill is the tailback is in the tackle box. When we play isolation teams, we get our linebackers in a stack position and still are able to see the tailback and rock back into a gap. In both drills, I am teaching stance and first step.

After practice, we come into the film room and get immediate reinforcement of what they worked on in practice. You should see what you worked on in the individual periods show up in the group-work drills. The linebacker should be able to tell what type of play is coming by their first or second step.

In all the drills I do, there is some type of movement. The linebackers have to train their hips and feet to be like a defensive back. Any drill I do requires foot quickness, hip mobility, flexibility, knee bend, and good pad level. Most of the drills I do have those elements represented in the drills. You must have a variety of drills and some order of different combinations that you work.

The next drill I do is a down-the-line drill (Diagram #3). They align on the coach and open their hips and run down a yard line. This works on hip flexibility. This will point out the players who are stiff in the hips and have trouble moving. As they run down the line, I will stop them and have them break back to the coach. I also have them level and break at a 45-degree angle to one side or the other. I also have them break at a 90-degree angle off the line.

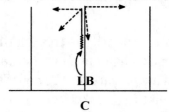

Diagram #3. Down the Line Drill

When you do these drills, put your thoughts on paper. Write down why you are doing the drill and the coaching points that go with the skill—that helped me grow as a coach when I started to do that.

You are not going to see too many revolutionary ideas today. I am sure most of you have done these drills. I believe in keeping things as simple as possible. I want my linebackers to play as fast as they possibly can. I do not want them thinking about how to move. I want them playing fast. I do not drill for the sake of doing something.

With the line drill, you can incorporate a ball drill with it. You can throw passes to them or roll fumbles to expand the drill. When your players see the video of the drill, they begin to understand and grow in their development.

We expand the line drill and go to an *angle drop drill* for the linebacker (Diagram #4). He aligns on the coach, opens his hips to 45 degrees, and drops to a pass-zone spot. You can use this drill as a ball drill also. We have the linebacker drop to his zone and throw the ball to make him move and react to it. We try to throw the ball so the linebacker has to break downhill to intercept the ball.

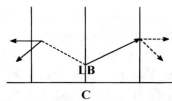

Diagram #4. Angle Drop Drill

The next drill teaches techniques used in the run game. This drill is a *run-shuffle-run drill* (Diagram #5). The linebacker and the ballcarrier align at their depth opposite each other. We have a number of cones on the ground to form a lane for the ballcarrier to turn into. On the snap of the ball, the linebacker presses the line of scrimmage. He keeps inside-out leverage on the ballcarrier. You are teaching the linebacker to maintain a position on the back hip of the ballcarrier while gaining ground toward the line of scrimmage. He runs toward the line and shuffles as the back moves outside on the cones. He has to alternate the run with the shuffle to maintain the proper pursuit angle to the ballcarrier.

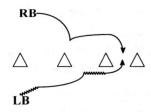

Diagram #5. Run-Shuffle-Run Drill

With every drill we do, we try to expand and use a combination of skills. In this drill, we have a form tackle at the end of the rep. It is a run-shuffle-run, but they are finishing the drill with a tackle. In this drill, you can also review the footwork and mechanics of the tackle.

To begin with, we make the ballcarrier go to the outside only. However, we expand the drill and let the ballcarrier pass a lane and cut back into it. That makes the linebacker keep his relationship to the ballcarrier. That makes the linebacker react to whatever the ballcarrier is doing.

In our league, you need to play with a good base in the tackle box. We play against a lot of 300-pound linemen. If you spend too much time shuffling in the tackle box, you will find yourself looking at the sky.

When we play blocks off the offensive line, we crossface in our technique. If the lineman is taking a radical angle as in a cutoff block, we tell them to be football players and beat the block. However, our hard-and-fast rule is to crossface the block.

One of the drills we use on the second day of pads is a *perimeter drill* (Diagram #6). It is an interesting drill. It is a live tackling drill. It is all outside running plays, bubble screens, hitch screens, and one-man screens to receivers. We take the defensive tackles out of the drill. That allows the offensive linemen to climb on the inside linebacker quickly. It is a live drill, which makes the linebackers play the lineman blocks as well as the cut blocks. They have to play the block, pursue to the ball, and make the tackle.

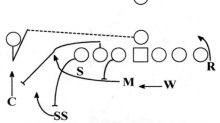

Diagram #6. Perimeter Drill

This drill forces the linebackers to run and make plays. It makes your linebackers take the lead in terms of energy and excitement in practice. However, the linebackers coach has to get involved in the drill and demonstrate the type of excitement he expects his player to show. The players will feed off the involvement of the coach. That means I have to get my fat butt out there and be enthusiastic about what is going on. They say the players adopt the mentality of their head coach. They do, but they also adopt the personality and demeanor of their position coach. If the position coach is on the field exerting energy and having fun, the players will tend to follow his lead. I think that is tremendously important. My point is the position coach has to get on the field and exert the type of behavior he expects from his players.

Everything we do as a linebacker is about *sight, movement,* and *contact.* You must be able to see it, move to it, and tackle it. Everything that happens in the game will not be pretty or look like a form tackle. The bottom line is to make plays and get ballcarriers on the ground.

We do countless numbers of bag drills. I am sure you have done them. We put one foot in each hole and then put both feet in the hole. We use bag drills to teach lateral shuffle, plant, and drive movement. All bag drills stress is foot quickness, movement, pad level, change of direction, and finish. In every bag drill, we stress all those points.

We use drills to simulate *play-action passes* (Diagram #7). We align the linebacker at his proper depth. We make him cover his run responsibility to his gap and retreat to his coverage zone. The linebacker bursts forward and shuffles before he recognizes the pass. He has to get to his spot drop, see the quarterback, and break on the ball.

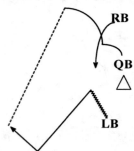

Diagram #7. Play-Action Pass Drill

In the week before we play a big play-action pass team, we do this drill. We do not do all the drills I have been showing you every day. We change up the drills and use the ones we think the game plan dictates. You tailor what you do in the drill based upon what you will be facing from the opponent that week.

Two years ago, I used to use the chutes. However, it is a pain in the butt to leave my defensive area to go to the defensive linemen area. They live under the chute. I did bag drills underneath the chutes, or I would use ladders. The chute is adjustable, and you can do the same drills under the chute. You can teach your wave drills, bag drills, and ladder drills under the chute. You are teaching pad level, flexibility, and change of direction, but it is a different way to do it. My linebackers hate to work under the chutes because they are always hitting their heads.

I have gotten away from using the chute and have gone to hurdles. They are four-foot tall hurdles and I use them because they are more mobile (Diagram #8). We had them made for us. We first used ones made from PVC pipe, but we tore them up too fast. They are now made of metal. By using hurdles, it makes the linebackers keep a constant pad level. As they come through the hurdles, if they are rising up out of one hurdle and ducking to get under the next one, they are not staying level.

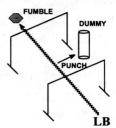

Diagram #8. Hurdles/Blow Delivery

We are still teaching the same things. We are teaching pad level, footwork, good knee bend, body mechanics, flexibility, and all that good stuff. However, we do the same drills we did under the chutes. Regardless of where I am working, a manager can grab a couple of hurdles and set up the drill anywhere on the practice field.

What you watch for when players work under the hurdles or chutes is their pad level. If they have to duck to get into the drill, their pad level is not right. When I work the drill in these areas, I have to combine what I am doing. We do not have the time to work any one technique. We have to combine the techniques in the same drill. While I am working under the hurdles, I can teach blow delivery, block protection, and tackling along with the footwork drills. I have to combine the drills because we only have 15 minutes of individual work on a great day—some days it is less.

At the end of the sequence under the hurdles, I will have a one-man sled to tackle. I could have a live body to tackle. I can have a player throw a cut block at the linebacker as he comes out from under the hurdle or chute. You can roll out a ball at the end and have a scoop-and-score finish. You have to constantly change up how you work your drills.

However you do them, you still get the same thing out of them. All I am trying to do is give you some different ideas about how to finish a drill. I hope some of these help you.

We use a see *drill*. A linebacker's vision is the most important trait in terms of linebacker play. If they do not understand what they are looking for or at, they will never get there. We read the offensive line to flow in our key progression. The offensive linemen are the primary key, and the flow is the secondary key. Based on film, that concept can be adjusted. The linebacker has to have great eyes and feet.

When we talk about keys, we talk in terms of *triangles*. You want to teach your linebackers about pictures and snapshots—that comes from constant repetition. They see the isolate play so much that they recognize the play from the picture. It is the constant repetition that puts the picture in the mind of the linebacker. What you want to achieve is play recognition by the first or second step the linebacker takes.

When we run an inside drill, I make all the young linebackers stand behind me. I stand behind the linebacker who is doing the drill. What I should hear from the younger linebackers standing behind me is what type of play they see. On the first or second step, I should hear the younger linebacker call *iso* or *power*. They are mentally taking reps while they are watching the drill. If you do not do something like that, they will not pay attention.

Play recognition is all about beating the blockers and ballcarriers to the spot. It is all about sight, movement, and contact. In the triangle, the linebacker sees the offensive lineman and running back. They have to understand that when they can see the back's numbers, the play is something tight and inside. They need to know the footwork involved with that action. If they see the profile of the running back, it is probably some type of outside run—it could be a sweep or option. They have to get on their horse and get to the outside.

You have to read offensive linemen because of the counter and pull plays. Those fat butts will take the linebacker to the ball. That keeps them from chasing decoys. The offensive line is the primary key for the linebacker.

On the running game, the linebacker has to get into the proper run angles and play downhill. He has to keep his pads square to the line of scrimmage. Let me emphasize again, when you do any drill work, write it up and draw it out.

When I do my drills, I like to use trash cans to teach run angles. We set the cans up to represent gaps of responsibility (Diagram #9). That gives the linebackers a target to angle to as they read. We start this way with the young linebackers with the coach giving the motion. When we start out, we put the linebacker over the trash cans at linebacker depth. The coach gives the movement and we watch his footwork. We progress from the coach creating the movement to the running backs giving the keys. This is all about training the eyes of the linebacker and letting him see what you want him to see.

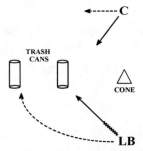

Diagram #9. Run Angles

The next part of the progression is to put a guard in the drill. The type of action we use in the drill is tailored to what we see in the SEC. We see two-back sets in our league. With the guard in the drill, the linebacker has to see through the guard to the running back. He reacts to what the guard does, but his keys are the same as the other steps in the drill.

If we play a one-back offense, the linebacker has to mirror the running back. In the drill, the linebacker reads the key, presses the line of scrimmage, and makes a form tackle on the ballcarrier. We work the drill with a cutback as well as a straight ahead run.

The next progression in the drill is to add the second linebackers. When you use film study, you can get good tips on inside zone teams and what they like to do. On the inside zone play, very few teams keep the ballcarrier on the frontside of the play. They want to cut the ball back. I coach the backside linebacker on the inside zone play to blow his gap. The frontside linebacker is pressing the line of scrimmage and working for the fallback moves of the back. That is not our standard rule but is based on the type of team we are playing and what they do offensively.

In our individual drill, I move the linebackers closer to the line of scrimmage to cut down on the amount of contact. If I feel they need to be at the proper depth, I will move them back. When I do that, we have more collisions in the drill. Regardless of the depth, they have to punch, use their hands, and crossface. Some coaches teach the linebackers to use the flipper. There is nothing wrong with the flipper, but in our league they have to use their hands.

I felt that using trash cans in these drills gave the linebackers the idea of having big bodies in front of them. I felt they grew faster in their knowledge of how to fit into the gaps. From the individual drill work, we go to a half-line drill.

When we teach the crossface, we start with two players about a yard apart. The blocker fires into the defender, and the defender punches him with his hands. We used to teach hat and hands but have changed that technique. With so much emphasis on concussions in football, we try to keep the head out of the technique. When we teach the technique now, we talk about hands, hips, and feet. The defender steps, punches, rolls the hips, and brings his feet into the offensive blocker.

The hand placement on the punch is to the breastplate of the offensive blocker with the thumbs up. The eyes of the defender should be below the level of the facemask of the blocker. If his eyes are above that point, he will end up on his back. He pulls with his gapside hand and rips crossface of the offensive blocker.

We play with a Sam linebacker in a 9 technique. He has to learn a *spill technique*. He keys the tight end to the near back. His technique is somewhat different because of his position in the defense. When we teach the Sam linebacker to play the fullback's block, we want him to attack the inside pad of the fullback and push vertical up the field. We do not want him to simply give up a body one for one. We want him to push up the field and create a problem for the running back. We play the same technique on the pulling guard. We attack the inside pad and push upfield.

Some of the things I am showing you are taught to the defensive linemen. We teach the same techniques in blow delivery. The difference in the techniques is the linebacker puts more weight on his hand so that it forces separation and helps him shoot his hips past the blocker. We use all kinds of releases to get across the blocker. We use the shrug release, rip, and swim release.

In the spring, we use medicine balls to work our punch. We get two players in close proximity to one another. One player holds the medicine ball and the other player punches it from his linebacker stance. If you want to burn the players' thigh muscles, this is the drill you want to do. What I am trying to get them to do is be physical when they punch the ball. The linebackers we play are going against players who are a lot bigger than they are. Our biggest linebacker this year was about 235 pounds, and the smallest was 218 pounds.

After they have done that a number of times, I take the ball away and have them strike the chest of the other player. When they finish the punch, they rip crossface. To progress in the drill, we put a ballcarrier behind the blocker. The defender punches, rips crossface, and tackles the back. We use these types of drills before we get into the key drills. We use a cut block as part of this drill also. That is expanding the drill to include more skills in the one drill.

When the offensive lineman comes off the ball, unless he is coming out on the linebacker, he does not have power in his movement. If he is zone stepping or reaching outside, his power is diminished. If the linebacker can get into the offensive lineman before he gets vertical, we can overpower them. The linebacker is going to get blocked; however, he cannot *stay* blocked.

When we teach how to play the cut block, we start from a fitted position because we want to target the hat and near shoulder pad. We want the linebacker to punch the hat, press down on the shoulder, and skate the feet away from the block. We start out working in the fitted position and go to the large medicine ball as part of the next progression. We have a big medicine ball and a smaller one (Diagram #10). We use both of them in the drills. We use the big medicine ball to represent a big offensive lineman and the small one to represent a wide receiver or running back. That makes the linebacker adjust his hand placement with the size of the ball. We roll the medicine ball at the feet of the linebackers, and they punch, push, and skate the feet.

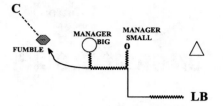

Diagram #10. Cut-Block Drill

The next progression is live blockers. We use two offensive blockers on the linebacker. He has to play the first cut block, get off it, and play the second one. We put our entire defense through this drill. The d-line, defensive backs, and linebackers go through this drill.

Against the live blockers, we want to punch the headgear to keep it from getting into the outside knee. We press on the shoulder pads to force the blocker to the ground. We skate the feet away from the blocker to keep him from getting into the feet.

Gentlemen, I appreciate your patience with me. Hopefully, Coach Browning will ask me back. If you have any questions, I will be around. Thank you very much.

RUN GAME BLOCKING PLAYS FROM THE SHOTGUN

Penn State

It is a privilege to be here. I was excited to come to Pittsburgh and speak. I think we are obligated as coaches at any level to give to this community of coaches the opportunity to exchange ideas and talk about football. I am true testimony of the benefits I received going back to my high school coach. I am indebted to him for the things he gave me. I have been blessed to be able to have coached at Penn State University for Joe Paterno for as long as I have.

I am going to start out tonight talking about some techniques that I think are important to offensive line play. There is no real genius in any of the things I am going to talk about. I think the guys who had the greatest influence on me were Dan Radakovich and Mike Morgan. They were very influential in teaching me a coaching style. They taught me mannerisms and the understanding certain principles that are important to be proficient in coaching the offensive line.

I am a better coach when I have better players. There is no coach who makes all the difference in the world. You must have some degree of talent to get the job done. I am going to start out with a simple talk about some things and principles that I think are important to line play. I am going to show you a little bit of technique. After that, I am going to show you what we do with our running game at Penn State. And finally, I will talk about the shotgun and the quarterback run game out of the shotgun. We are doing some unique things at Penn State that go back a number of years. The wildcat offense has become the favorite son in offensive play right now. It is in all levels of football. You can run that offense with a multitude of talent and athletic ability. I will show you some things that will demonstrate that to you. I will take you through the run game as it

exists out of the shotgun. I am going to give you the nuts and bolts of our running game. I will cover the draw, sweep, counter, and power. Those are our primary runs.

You would be surprised at the way we do things at Penn State. We played LSU in the bowl game. They were a good football team. We were disappointed because we wanted to be in the BCS Bowl, but the reality was Coach Paterno wanted to play LSU. It was the most intense I have seen him. It is unbelievable how energetic he is. On Thursday before the bowl game, we ended up our two-a-day workouts. The players thought we were going to have a walk-through then head up to Orlando to play the Outback Bowl®. At the end of that session, he blew a whistle and we went through about a 70-play scrimmage. He drove that team into the ground. When we went to Orlando, we were ready to play football.

He is passionate about everything he does, and we argue about everything we do. At 83 years old, he can still get in a three-point stance. The only thing about it is he puts his knuckles down on the ground.

I break everything down in our program in the run and pass game. I break them down into three phases. The approach phase as it relates to blocking is the stance and start. The reason they pay $64 for a ticket and sit 110,000 deep in Beaver Stadium is because football is the greatest game on earth. It is a game that has a beginning and an end. The beginning and end last from 4 to 6 seconds, which is the average length of a football play. An event happens for 4 to 6 seconds, and the crowd goes berserk. If you are lucky enough to have a seat, you get 165 or 170 of those events a game.

As a coach, it is critical that you teach a player to manage those 4 to 6 seconds. That is all he has to be concerned with. Great players learn how to manage their minds in the present tense. When it comes to blocking, we teach three phases, but it is all about a 4- to 6-second window. We work year-round in football, and it is becoming that way at all levels. The average game has about 70 offensive plays. That amount is a whopping seven minutes of actual playing time in a game.

At Penn State, our players have to master the three phases of football.

Approach

- Stance
- Power drive
- Shoulders
- Eyes
- Acceleration

Contact

- Principles of leverage
- Mechanics

Follow-Through

- Attitude to dominate
- Maintain
- Driver not a leaner
- Body control

Stance

- Base
- Feet
- Power angles
- Hand
- Shoulders
- Head and eyes

The first thing you have to do in a stance is establish a base. We want the toes pointed straight down the field. The mechanics of where you distribute the weight is all that matters in a stance.

As long as you put the knees in the proper relationship with the ankles, it does not matter what kind of problems you may have. If the weight is put on the inside soles of the feet, the knees are inside the ankles. If the knees are out, the muscle group you use is the groin muscle instead of the quads, hamstrings, and glutes.

The stagger will vary according to the body style of the individual. However, we work for a toe-to-instep stagger in our stance. In the stance, you must build powers in the stance. We want an angle in the ankles, knees, and hips. That is where the power is generating from. When we align the first day of practice, that is the only time Coach Paterno will allow an offensive lineman to use a line to line up. When we break the huddle and come to the line of scrimmage, the first thing you see is our linemen look down and check their feet. They are looking at the coaching points of getting in the stance.

In the stance, I want the knees over the toes and the heel slightly off the turf. We want the feet in contact with the ground because that produces the power angles in the ankles. If the legs are extended in the stance, there is no power in the stance. The legs have to have a 45-degree bend in the knees to have a power angle.

The shoulders have to be parallel. If one shoulder is higher than the other, you have to make an additional movement to get out of the stance. We do not want the head up in the stance. If the head comes up, the tail goes down. We want to look through our eyebrows. It does not matter whether you can see the defender's face. If I can see his knees, that is enough.

In the takeoff, we want the lead step to be short and direct. When we lead step, we have no weight on the lead foot. We have a heavy foot and a light foot. If we lead step to the right, all the weight is placed on the left foot. That is how we can move the right foot.

In the contact phase there are principles of leverage we have to consider. If you get nothing else from this lecture, make sure you get this.

Principles of Leverage

- Vertical
- Inside
- Lateral

The first principle of leverage is vertical leverage. That means being low. We obviously want to be lower than the defender every time. At Penn State, if my eyebrows are below the defender's shoulder pads, that is low for us. That can be at a different place, depending on the defender. The next point is inside, but I want to talk about that last.

The third leverage is lateral leverage. As a coach, every block we teach has to have a degree of lateral resistance. The point of resistance the blocker applies to the defender is the point at which we want the ball to go. If I am blocking a defender, and the ball is going outside of my block, I want outside leverage on the defender. The aiming point becomes the defender's armpit. If the blocker is trying to cut off a defender, his aiming point may be the inside gap. If we are executing an inside drill block, the blocker's aiming point is the inside number of the defender. The blocker applies resistance to the inside number as it relates to where the ball is going.

You should not have one block in your offense that takes the defender on the midline. It is the inside number or the outside number. Never take the defender on the midline. That gives the defender a two-way go on the blocker. If we block a down block, the target is the near shoulder. If we want to stop penetration, the hat goes in front of the defender. If we want to stop pursuit down the field, we put the hat behind the defender.

The last principle is inside leverage. It is the most important of the three. This all relates to the elbows. The game of football in the offensive and defensive lines is played in the number regions of the jersey. The player who gets his hand and elbows into the number area of the jersey wins. They will win the day 100 percent of the time. The defensive line is trying to do the same thing to the offensive linemen.

If you want to teach this, get yourself an inner tube and cut it into strips. Tie the strips around the player's elbows so he cannot flare them out. Make him hit the sled and play with the elbows bound, and the player will understand the difference between keeping the elbows in and having them out.

The next thing is the mechanics of the contact. The aiming point on the jersey is a point on the jersey that gives the blocker a direction to step toward. The object of blocking is to hit the point two to three feet behind the aiming point. The best way I can explain that is what happened to my son. When he was 20 years old, he came running down the stairs of my house. He stumbled and went through the glass storm door at the bottom of the stairs. He did not get a scratch. The reason for it was he exploded through the glass and did not stop when he hit it.

Blocking is the same theory. You have to explode through the plate glass door. You have to come at the defender and explode through the block. If you have ever done karate and broken a board, you understand. If you aim at the board, you break your hand. If you aim through the board, you break the board. That is the momentum. The blocker has to explode through the defender. If they aim at the defender, there is no pop, and the blocker stops. You can see it from the sidelines. When the defender's helmet rocks back, you know what has happened.

The next principle of mechanics is to work to the midline. We do not turn our eyes, head, or swing the hips. Everyone in this room has an imaginary line that bisects the body. That is called the line of symmetries. It is there because God loves football. If the nose turns to one side of the midline, the hips, feet, and tail will naturally follow that movement, and you will be able to sustain a block. If you start to swing the hips and tail, your ability to strike is diminished greatly.

The way you block a defender is to block him on whatever angle he is moving. We want to stick the nose in first and follow with the hat and hands. To hit the target, you have to use your eyes. That produces the battering ram we are looking for. The eyes, hat, and hands are the three-point strike.

After we do all those things, we get to the follow-through phase. That is the finish of the block. The first thing you must have is an attitude to dominate. I do not want to coach a player who just wants to be on the team. I want to coach a guy who wants to be the best in America. Blocking is the most unnatural skill on the planet. To maintain a block, you must have the hips down with leg drive. You want to be a driver and not a leaner. You have to keep your body under control and control the steps.

I want to move ahead to our offense and talk in detail about it. I want to talk about the single-back set. The shotgun set for a lack of a better way to describe it, with the quarterback carrying the football.

Why Do We Run the Quarterback?

- To combat teams that leave seven in the box versus spread sets
- To combat man coverage
- To open up the passing game
- To take advantage of an athletic quarterback

The game of football is math. If the defense has seven defenders in the box and you only have six blockers, they have you outnumbered. The quarterback run game gives you a chance to even the numbers. With the quarterback running the ball, we can get 7-on-7 in the box.

If you become effective with the quarterback run game, you move the defense to a decision. They either have to play the pass or commit another secondary defender to stop the run. That opens up your passing game. If you have an athletic quarterback, the offense takes advantage of his ability to make plays.

When we run the quarterback counter game, we run it to the open-end side of the formation most of the time. If we want to run the counter to the tight-end side, we call "Q Y Counter." The play to the tight-end side will be slightly different for the backs, but the line will remain the same. The primary formation we run this play from is a 2x2

tight-end set with the tight end into the boundary (Diagram #1). The R-receiver is to the boundary side with the X- and Z-receivers into the wide field. The running back sits to the split-end side with the quarterback in the shotgun.

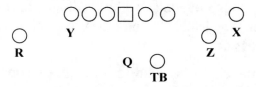

Diagram #1. Counter Formation

If we run the triple formation, the Y-tight end is into the field with the X- and R-receivers (Diagram #2). The Z-receiver becomes the single receiver into the boundary. The quarterback is in the shotgun, and the running back is toward the split end.

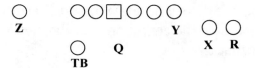

Diagram #2. Triple Formation

The play I want to show you is run to the left. I want to walk through the basic principles of the play (Diagram #3). The tight end (or Y-receiver) has a C-gap cutoff. He looks to sift through to the Sam linebacker if the tackle is uncovered. If the tackle is covered, he has an aggressive down block on that defender. If the right tackle is uncovered, he pulls and runs through the left C gap and climbs the Will linebacker. We want him to get an inside-out position on the linebacker. He wants to wall the defender to the outside.

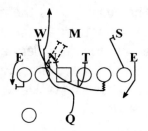

Diagram #3. Quarterback Counter

He uses what we call a "retreat pull." He backs off the line of scrimmage with an inside and outside foot step and gets depth off the line of scrimmage.

He shows a vertical set because we want the linebackers to stop and pause in their reaction. We want them to read pass initially. This also helps us with our draw play. After his vertical set, he pivots off the inside foot and runs downhill at the line of scrimmage, eyeballing the Will linebacker. He attacks the linebacker on the inside half and drives him outside.

The backside guard's rule is tied into our backside protection scheme. He has an inside rule. That means he has a block progression rule. The first rule is the man aligned on him, and B gap is second. If he has a man aligned on him, he pass-sets. We call it "set in your shoes." He does not give ground in his pass set. He does not go forward or backward. He blocks the defender on any angle the defender wants to go. He handles any B-gap defender. If there is no one in the B gap, and he is not involved with the center on a combo, he climbs to the linebacker.

The center has a backside A-gap rule unless he is covered. If he is covered, he has an "on rule." He handles the first defender to the backside A gap. The playside guard's rule is on/inside. In this diagram, there is a shade defender on the center. He blocks down in combination with the center and punches over to the Mike linebacker.

The playside tackle has an on/big rule. If he has a man aligned on him, he blocks him. We want the tackle to pass-set on the defender. If he has a defender on him and one outside of him, he blocks the widest defender. However, he has to communicate that to his guard. He tells the playside guard, "Big." The guard blocks the man aligned on the tackle, and the tackle blocks the widest defender. If he has two defenders aligned on him, generally the guard is uncovered. However, if the guard is covered, the pulling tackle will trap the man aligned on the tackle.

The back fakes the zone play and cuts off the first defender off the hip of the tight ends. The coaching point is to get tight to the line of scrimmage and block inside-out on the first defender to show. The quarterback fakes to the

running back, faces up with the pulling tackle, and works north and south.

In the over-front, there is a particular coaching point I want to make (Diagram #4). If the defensive end aligned in the 5 technique on the backside tackle and spikes to the inside, the guard blocks him. The guard rule is on/inside, but he is B-gap responsible. If the defender spikes inside, the guard blocks him. The tight end's rule sends him down on the 5 technique who covers the offensive tackle. As he comes inside, he sees the defender spike to the inside. He redirects his angle and replaces the guard's block on the Mike linebacker. The running back cuts off the Sam linebacker over the tight end.

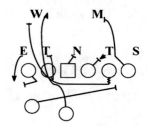

Diagram #4. Backside Spike

With the playside guard and tackle covered, the pulling tackle is thinking A gap for his turn up on the linebacker. He keys the outside hip of the center. If the playside guard is covered, he pass-sets and drives the defender in the direction he wants to go. The tackle turns up off his block. If the pulling tackle has a linebacker aligned on him, he pulls. If the linebacker blitzes through the C gap, the tight end will block him because he has a full-man cutoff rule.

He steps flat with his inside foot, crosses over with the outside foot, and runs up through the gap. He tries to get his head in front and rip up through the inside gap. I do not want the tight end to cut or chop block. If the defensive end spikes, the guard will block him, and I do not want the tight end on the ground trying to cut him. When the guard blocks the spike, the tight end is on his feet and continues to the Mike linebacker.

In the split look, the center has a backside shade stack on him (Diagram #5). The backside guard posts up on the shade nose with his inside foot. He still looks to the B gap for any threat coming into that gap. If the nose fights into the backside A gap, the center blocks him, and the backside guard either blocks the defensive end on a spike or climbs to the linebacker. If the center gets a soft play from the nose, he tries to punch him across the face of the guard and goes up to the linebacker. He has the best angle on the linebacker. The center and guard use a "you-me" combo to the middle linebacker. If the defensive end's spike takes the guard, the tight end blocks the linebacker.

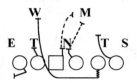

Diagram #5. Split Look

The thing this play does is to freeze the linebackers with the pass sets and move them with the run fake. That gives us a chance to get the hats in the right position to cut them off. That gives us an adjustment angle on the linebackers. When I draw my diagrams, I put a dot at the point I want the lineman's hat. That is the spot they are trying to put their helmet.

The next alignment has the 3 technique aligned to the tight-end side with the 1 technique to the field (Diagram #6). The Sam linebacker is not in the picture. The tight end has to cut off the 7-technique defender to his inside. The backside guard pass-sets the 3-technique defender and blocks him. The backside tackle pulls. The playside tackle has an "on" call and pass-sets on the defender. The playside guard has no "on" assignment. He goes inside with a hard post on the 1-technique defender. We do not want the defender to be able to split the combination block of the center and guard. The center has to make sure to check the backside A gap for a run-through by the backside linebacker.

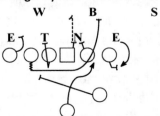

Diagram #6. Boundary 3 Technique

We would like the guard to knock the nose across the face of the center and let him make the block. If he can do that, he climbs to the second level for the backside linebacker. If the nose fights into the guard, the center climbs to the second level and walls the backside linebacker. The backside tackle looks for the hip of the playside guard in the B gap. If the tight end gets to the backside linebacker, the center or guard moves up to the next level, looking for a safety.

Every play we run has a tempo, which we coach. This play is a slow developing to a fast action by the quarterback. The linemen are not aggressively pursuing the defenders from the first step. If they do that, they cannot sustain their blocks that long. They would be on the ground by the time the quarterback got to the hole. They are showing pass and using the movement of the defenders to help them with their blocks. This play is a slow tempo to a fast action play.

In the double Eagle defense, we have two 3-technique defenders and a zero-technique defender on the center. If the defender to the three-man surface is aligned in a 4i technique, the playside guard has to treat that as a B-gap defender. When this happens, the center makes a "triple" call. We do the same thing in pass protection. The center and both guards will zone any combination of twists they get from the TNT defenders. They all pass-set and exchange any kind of stunt game. That keeps the lineman from trying to fan block on the defenders. That leads to penetration from the defense.

If the left 3-technique defender spikes the A gap, the guard blocks him until he runs into the center (Diagram #7). The center reads the loop going to the left and looks for the penetrator coming to the inside. He attacks the penetrators and yells "Switch" to the guard. The guard has his hands on the penetrator and delivers him to the center. He moves back and picks up the loop stunt coming to the outside.

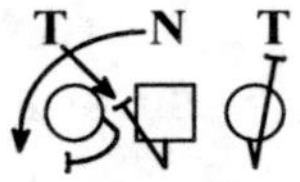

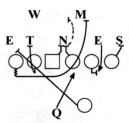

Diagram #7. Triple Call—Twist

In the Okie (or 3-4) front, the tackles are covered, and the guards are uncovered (Diagram #8). The tight end has to drive the 5 technique on the pulling tackle. The problem is to the playside because the tackle has two defenders outside of him. He makes the "big" call to the guard. The playside guard and tackle zone block on the defensive end and the Will linebacker. If the defensive end comes upfield on the tackle's pass set, the guard goes outside for the Will linebacker. If the defensive end spikes inside into the guard, the guard blocks the defensive end, and the tackle handles the Will linebacker. If the Will linebacker drops into coverage, they handle the defensive end. The center has an on block. He pass-sets and takes on the nose. The backside guard is uncovered. The guard pass-sets, checks his B gap, and climbs to the linebacker.

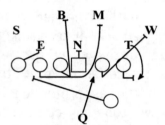

Diagram #8. Okie Front

This is how we get our quarterback involved in the running game. We can run the same play out of a two-back offense and a single-back look.

If we run the play run to the tight-end side, the entire interior blocking is the same. The difference is the rules for the tight end. We call the play Y counter (Diagram #9). We run it out of the same looks. We can run it from the 3x1 or the 2x2. Both of those formations are primary formations for us. In both of them, we set the tailback to the tight-end side. The tight end's rules change when the counter comes his way. He is responsible for the Sam linebacker or the support player to his side. He blocks the Sam linebacker on or off the ball.

Diagram #9. Y Counter

If there is no Sam linebacker and there is an inverted safety as the support defender, that is his assignment. If the tight end pass-sets and the Sam linebacker drop, the tight end attacks him. If the Sam is in man coverage on him, he runs him off and crosses faces him to get him walled off from the play. The tailback takes the fake and cuts off the backside. The quarterback fakes the tailback using the open hand and hits off the hip of the pulling tackle.

The sweep is the most productive run we have at Penn State. This can be run out of 3x1 set or a 2x1 set. We pitched the stretch out of the offense this year. We felt our tailback was more suited to getting the ball in his hands with the opportunity to make a play on the edge. The schemes we used I refer to as "shutting the water off." We went to a man system to get outside to the tight-end side for both the tailback and the quarterback sweep. When the quarterback carries the ball, we call the play a zero sweep or an 8 sweep. If the tailback carries the ball with a fullback or H-back lead, we call it 40 sweep or 48 sweep. If we run it out of the single-back set, it is a zero sweep or 8 sweep, but we have a check principle in the call. If the defense outnumbers us with the single back, we have to check out of the play.

On the sweep to the tight end, the blocking back will align to the tight end side in the strong alignment (Diagram #10). The tight end's rule is base. At Penn State, the blocking progression for a base block is "on, over, first linebacker to the inside." The tight end blocks the defender aligned on him on the line of scrimmage as his first rule. If there is no man on the line of scrimmage but a linebacker over him, he blocks the linebacker. If he has no man on or linebacker over, he blocks the first linebacker to the inside. The playside tackle's rule is inside. His inside rule is to block "down to on." If he has a defender in the B gap, he blocks him. If there is no defender in the B gap, he blocks the man on him.

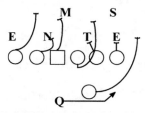

Diagram #10. Quarterback Sweep

The playside guard pulls for the playside linebacker. On this defense, the guard is responsible for the Mike linebacker. We call that a "mirror pull." He watches the Mike linebacker and mirrors his movement. If the Mike linebacker blows the gap, he comes back and blocks him. The back in the backfield is responsible for the Sam linebacker in this defense. He is responsible for the support player on the sweep. We block the center two different ways on this defense. He can bump the backside shade defender and get out for the backside linebacker.

If the shade defender is a load, and we are not sure the backside guard can cut him off, the center blocks back on him (Diagram #11). The backside guard folds around the center and up on the backside linebacker. That call will be made based on the ability of the player in the backside A gap. We did that a lot against LSU in the bowl game.

Diagram #11. Backside Fold

The backside guard has a cutoff rule. If he has no defender aligned on him, he is in combination with the center. He works on the shade defender for the cutoff or pulls around the center on the block-back technique. If he has a 3 technique aligned on him, the guard works aggressively through the A gap and tries to get up on the linebacker. He does not want to engage the 3 technique. The tackle's rule takes care of the 3 technique. He comes flat to the line of

scrimmage with his first step. He crosses over with the second step and rips inside the 3 technique. If the backside tackle gets to the Will linebacker, the guard or center is free to work to the next level for the safeties.

The defenders that stop our running game are the safeties. We can block the line of scrimmage. We do not have much luck blocking a nine-man box. Iowa is hard to run the football on because they commit their safeties to stop the run. We cannot account for that man in our blocking scheme. That is probably the reason the Colts lost the Super Bowl. Bob Sanders could not play, and that made all the difference in their defense.

In the base rule, the tight end very seldom gets to a first inside linebacker rule. He has a man on him most of the time. I want to make a critical point on this play: The most important block on this play is not the end man on the line of scrimmage. The most important block is the next block in. The most important block is the down block of the tackle and the mirror block by the guard. That is where the water has to stop. That is where you create the running lanes in the defense.

The over 4-3 gives a different look for the line. The nose is in the strongside shade, and the defensive end moves down into a 5 technique on the offensive tackle Diagram #12). The tackle's rule is "down to on." The 5 technique is the man on, and he has to block him. If the 5 technique aligns so wide that the tackle does not think he can reach him, he calls the tight end down to set the edge of the sweep. He pulls for the Sam linebacker aligned on the tight end. He executes a running roll block on the Sam linebacker. If the Sam linebacker hangs on the line of scrimmage, the tackle attacks and rolls him up. If the Sam linebacker penetrates, the tackle traps him to the outside. The quarterback or tailback follows the block of the tackle.

The center and playside guard have the same situation with a defender playing in the gap or 1 technique on the guard. The guard blocks down, and the center pulls around the guard for the linebacker. He takes the place of the mirror pull guard on the playside linebacker. Those blocks will shut off the water from the inside. If the center can make the reach on the nose in the gap, we leave him on that block and pull the guard. The thing you cannot do is to allow the shade to run down the line of scrimmage.

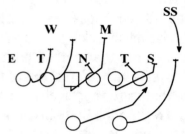

Diagram #12. Sweep vs. Over 4-3

That is the adjustment we make and the reason we make it. You may think you cannot teach this, but you can. It does not matter if you are in the I formation and toss the ball or are in the shotgun. The water has to stop in the B and C gaps if you are going to have any success running outside.

The tight end on his block has many options on where to drive the Sam linebacker. He can drive him straight back, outside, or inside. He cannot allow the Sam linebacker to penetrate. If the Sam linebacker gets into the backfield immediately, we have no play. If the Sam linebacker is in the wide 9 technique, the tight end comes on a 45-degree angle at the outside half of the defender. He is, in essence, covering the entire inside half of the defender when he executes that charge.

The last thing I want to show you is the draw. We can run the quarterback draw from all the formations I have showed you today (Diagram #13). We always let the blocker coming from the backfield be responsible for the Will linebacker. If the tailback runs the ball, the fullback blocks the Will linebacker. The playside tackle's rule is "on big." The playside guard's rule is "on over first inside linebacker." The center and backside guard have the same rule as the playside guard. The backside tackle's rule is "on big." The tight end's rule is "Sam linebacker or support defender."

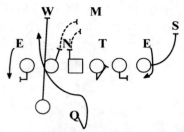

Diagram #13. Quarterback Draw

The center and both guards have the same rule. That means we are going to get the Mike linebacker. If the center has a shade defender, the guard to that side is going to zone to the middle linebacker with the center. If they are all covered, they block the "on call."

We use this scheme as one of our primary pass protections. If we align in the empty set, the quarterback is responsible for the Will linebacker. There is no back in the backfield to block him, so the quarterback must read him. If he comes, the quarterback has to throw the ball. We have a bubble pass always available for the quarterback. If the Will linebacker is in coverage, the coverage is sound because everyone is blocked.

What high school coaches do is critical. We do not get a chance to change men's lives. You guys are in the front lines, fighting the noble fight. You go 12 months out of the year. You have summer passing leagues. You have the weight rooms you are obligated to.

I am here to tell you that what you are doing matters. I am here today because of my high school coach. I tip my hat to you. We sit down there in the big stadium with big crowds every Saturday. However, what you are doing is the whole backbone of this game. You are so important to these young men you coach, and you do make a difference in their lives. If my head coach were here today, he would tell you there is nothing more important than the job you are doing. All the teachers in the school have a job to do, but no one impacts a young man's life as you do. I hope some of this was beneficial to you. I appreciate you being here.

DEFENDING THE WILDCAT OFFENSE

University of Illinois

On behalf of Coach Zook and the rest of the staff, I appreciate the opportunity to be here. I was at Kansas State University last year. I worked for Coach Synder for one year and learned a lot of football. In the Big 12, everyone runs the spread offense. We have been installing our defense at the University of Illinois, and we are putting in a defense to stop a two-back offense. We did not run this defense last year at Kansas State because we did not see any two-back offenses.

The spread offense in the Big 12 is the norm. The Wildcat is an offshoot of some of the things that were run in high school, which the Miami Dolphins popularized. When you play a team that runs the Wildcat offense, you have to account for the quarterback as a runner. Offenses that play with a conventional quarterback and play with a 21 personnel group, you should be able to stop them with eight defenders. If you put nine defenders in the box, there is one defender on the defense who is not responsible for a gap.

If you play a team that plays with a conventional quarterback and an 11 personnel group, you can stop them with seven defenders. Eleven personnel is an offense that plays with one tight end, one running back, and three wide receivers. If you count the gaps, there are only seven gaps to cover.

If the offense plays with four wide receivers and no tight end, the defense can stop them with six defenders in the box. If the quarterback is a threat to run the ball, the defense has to commit another defender to the box. If you are playing against 21 personnel, you have to add another defender to the box if the quarterback is a threat to run. Instead of playing with eight defenders, you have to add the ninth man.

If you are playing with nine men in the box, most teams have a high safety in the middle of the field. For all the offensive personnel groupings, the defense will have to commit an additional defender to the box to stop the quarterback run or what we like to call the *Wildcat*.

To be good against teams that run the quarterback, we started using a term called *nine-man surface* (Diagram #1). When you look at the defense, you will see it as a read-2 adjustment in the secondary. The corners and safeties are reading the #2 receiver to their side. They will be accountable for him. In our base defense, we play with a 39 alignment to the tight end, and a shade on the center, and a 5 technique to the openside. If the offense aligns in a 2x2 set with the tight end to the defensive left, the #2 receivers are the tight end to the left and the slot receiver to the openside.

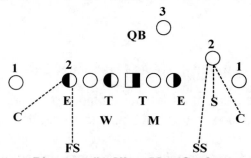

Diagram #1. Nine-Man Surface

If the slot comes in to block the Sam linebacker, the strong safety becomes committed to the running game. The corner is reading the slot also. When he sees the slot block on the Sam linebacker, he turns his attention to the #1 receiver. To the tight end side, the free safety and corner are reading the tight end. If he becomes a blocker on the play, the free safety is committed to the run. The corner turns his attention back to his #1 receiver. If the inside receivers block, we will have nine defenders in the box.

The Wildcat offense has a quarterback power, isolation, misdirection, and divide zone as the base runs from that formation. Most of them run the power, lead, and divide-zone plays. With the Wildcat, we feel it is a two-back offense. The fullback is the blocker and the quarterback is a runner. That is the way we approach the defensive scheme. In your defensive scheme, you must have an extra defender.

The simplest way to get the extra defender is to play a conventional over *front* and let the Mike linebacker be the extra defender off the fullback's action (Diagram #2). It is like playing an isolation team. The Mike linebacker is the fast-flow player reacting to what the fullback does. The fullback will always create another gap for the defense. The Will linebacker covers the backside A gap, and the Sam covers the frontside B gap. The Mike linebacker reacts to where the fullback goes.

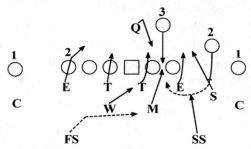

Diagram #2. Mike Linebacker Extra

It is basic math when it comes to covering the play. As long as you can count to three, you have a chance to play this defense. We had a player at Kansas State we called "Two Count." He could never get to three. I moved him to a place where he only had to count to two and that became simple for him.

If the backside flanker comes in motion to give the offense a trips set, we bump over in our coverage. I will show you that later. In most Wildcat offenses, the Wildcat is not much of a threat to throw the ball. However, if you have a team with a Wildcat who can throw, you have to play the pass from this defense. This defense is a good pass coverage scheme.

The safeties and corners are reading the #2 receivers. If the #2 receivers go vertical, the safeties take them. If they go to the flat, the corner sits and the defense becomes an *in-and-out, man-to-man coverage,* which is commonly referred to as read 2. That means if the #2 receiver goes out, the corner takes him, and the safety plays over the top for the #1 receiver. If he stays inside, the safety takes him and the corner takes the #1 receiver.

The coverage is a *quarters concept.* However, if the split between the #1 and #2 receivers becomes too wide, we go to *lock coverage.* The safety cannot go to the #1 as the #2 receiver goes to the flat because the split it too wide. In that case, we lock the coverage and it becomes four-across man coverage.

Another way to align against the Wildcat set is to kick the front to the back (Diagram #3). This creates some issues for the offense but it is harder to teach. This adjustment takes away the open B gap to the side of the back. We move the tackle from a shade on the center to the 3 technique on the guard. To the tight end side, the tackle moves into a 2i technique and the defensive end moves from a 9 technique to a 7 technique on the inside shoulder of the tight end. This gives you a good opportunity to stop the zone read play and the quarterback power.

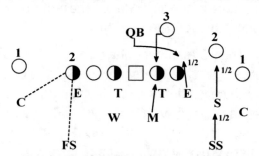

Diagram #3. Kick Front to Back

The most important thing to this adjustment is what the linebackers do. When we play the option, we want to have two defenders on the dive play. We need one defender to take the quarterback and one defender to take the pitch. We also have an alley player in the scheme. We need four defenders to cover the option at the point of attack. When we put the tackle in the 3 technique, he becomes a dive player along with the Mike linebacker. The 5-technique end plays a half-man responsibility. He is a half-man defender on the inside of the quarterback. If the offensive tackle blocks down on the 3 technique, he squeezes down and plays the dive to the quarterback. The other half player comes from the Sam linebacker or the strong safety.

Teams will read the alignment of the Sam linebacker and use him as a key. If the Sam linebacker comes off the #2 receiver and moves inside, the offense will throw the bubble screen to the slot receiver. The #1 receiver blocks the corner and they will gain six or seven yards if you can make the tackle. To keep the offense from running the automatic, we run a *robber scheme* (Diagram #4). The Sam linebacker aligns on the outside shoulder of the #2 receiver. If the #2 receiver goes to the flat, the Sam linebacker takes him, and the strong safety fills inside on the running threat.

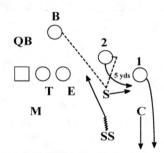

Diagram #4. Robber Scheme

If the #2 receiver goes vertical, the Sam linebacker reads the #3 receiver in the backfield from a wider position, and the strong safety will take the #2 receiver vertical. This gives you the half defender on the quarterback from either the strong safety or the Sam linebacker. The Sam linebacker in your scheme may be the nickel back. You can get away with this because the 3 technique allows the 5-technique end to be a half-man defender on the quarterback.

If we have a shade tackle and 5-technique end, the play is different (Diagram #5). If the offensive tackle blocks inside on a veer block, the 5-technique end has to become a spill player. The 5-technique end closes inside and squeezes the hole. He spills anything coming in the B gap. The Mike linebacker becomes a scrap linebacker coming to the outside.

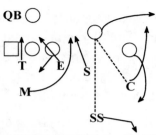

Diagram #5. 5-Technique Spill

When you play the 5 technique, it is hard to rob the coverage on the outside. The end is playing the dive instead of half man responsibility. The Sam linebacker has to be in a read-2 concept, which puts him inside the #2 receiver. He cannot play the bubble screen as we did in the robber coverage. The corner is aligned on the #1 receiver three yards off the ball. He reads the #2 receiver. If the #2 receiver runs the bubble screen, the corner has a *007 technique*. That is the James Bond technique, which is a *license to kill*. If it is not the bubble screen, the corner has set the edge on any running play.

The next thing I want to cover is the 3x1 formation (Diagram #6). We play the quarters concept to the #3 receiver side. It puts some pressure on the backside corner because he is on an island. If the back aligns toward the #3 receiver side we keep the same quarters concept. The corner, strong safety, and Sam linebacker are reading the #2 receiver. The Sam linebacker reads from #2 to the #3 receiver, which is the tight end. If the #2 receiver goes vertical, the strong safety takes him and the corner focuses back to the #1 receiver. When the #2 receiver goes vertical, the Sam linebacker looks to the tight end. If the tight end goes vertical, the free safety from the backside takes him. If he goes to the flat, the Sam linebacker takes him.

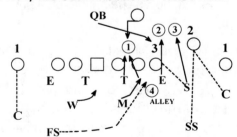

Diagram #6. Quarters vs. Trips

With the back aligned to the #3 receiver side, the defensive tackle to that side plays a 3 technique.

He and the Mike linebacker are the dive players on the option. The 9-technique end becomes the quarterback player. The Sam linebacker plays the pitch. If the tight end blocks, the free safety is the fifth defender in the alley to the #3 receiver side.

If the offense puts the back opposite the three receivers, we kick the line that way (Diagram #7). The Mike linebacker is the fourth defender to that side, and it is a hard play because of his responsibility to the B gap to his side. What we will do is bring the 7-technique end on a long stick into the B gap, which helps the Mike linebacker get to the backside. That may be an unsound way of doing things but it works. The 5-technique end plays his technique as he did with the 3 technique to his side. The other adjustment into the backside B gap is to bring the free safety down into that gap if the tight end blocks.

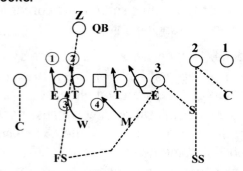

Diagram #7. Back Opposite Trips

One thing I have learned is that if you always do the same thing in every situation, the offense will burn you. You cannot slant the end every time, and you cannot cover with the free safety every time. You have to change up what you do. If you cover the backside B gap in the trips set with the free safety, they will beat him down the middle on a play-action at some point.

These next two things I am going to show you are a little bit reckless. In this scheme, we set our corner inside. We like to bring him from the boundaryside of the defense. It is not that difficult. The way I got to this point was by studying what Bud Foster does at Virginia Tech. I have tweaked it to look like something that he does. We disguise it on some occasions, and at other times we show it and do not come.

This is still a nine-man surface, but we are going to move the defense. We will bring the corner regardless of where the back aligns. We are going to tear up all the gaps with line twists and bring the corner off the edge. If you decide to play this type of defense, you must have a Will linebacker who can carry a #2 receiver vertical.

When the ball is snapped, the offense does not know who the support player is going to be. The corner and the free safety exchange positions, and the Will linebacker will carry the #2 receiver vertical. To play this technique, you cannot assign a gap to the Will linebacker.

When we played Iowa State University this year, they kept cracking on our free safety as he supported in the C gap. We used this blitz and it helped us tremendously.

To take the gaps away from the Will linebacker, we go to a three-man twist game to the tight end side (Diagram #8). Some people call it the *pirate game*. Monty Kiffin runs this type of scheme. The 3-technique tackle aims for the nape of the neck of the center. If the center goes away from him, he flattens out and pursues. If the center comes toward him, he works across his face. The 9-technique end does the same thing aiming at the guard. The nose wraps around the angles coming down and contains on the outside if it is a pass. We are trying to spill everything to the corner.

In the Super Bowl game when New Orleans went for the touchdown on fourth-and-short on the goal line, this is the stunt Indianapolis ran. The corner got blocked, but the Mike linebacker came over the top untouched and made the tackle.

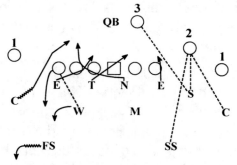

Diagram #8. Corners In

This almost looks like a corner blitz. We have made the free safety accountable for the #1 receiver. On this scheme, the corner keys the #2 receiver. If the #2 receiver is blocking, the corner is knocking. The Mike linebacker's pass responsibility is the middle-hole #3 receiver check-down route. To the backside away from the corner there is nothing new to teach. The 5-technique end closes inside and spills with the Mike linebacker scraping outside. The Sam linebacker, strong safety, and corner play the read-2 coverage and support pattern.

If we play the corner in against the trips set, we bring him from the single-receiver side (Diagram #9). We play an over defense to the tight end and run a two-man twist game to the corner's side. To the trips side, we play our normal defense like I showed you before. The 3-technique tackle is to the side of the back. The corner and strong safety play read 2 with the #1 and #2 receivers. The Sam linebacker reads #2 to #3 and plays like he did before. Since the free safety is playing the #1 receiver to the boundaryside, the Mike or Will linebacker will have to carry the tight end vertical.

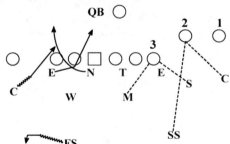

Diagram #9. Corners In vs. Trips

That is the same defense we played before with a slight adjustment to the backside surface.

If we run the corner in to the field, it is not as technically sound as coming from the boundary (Diagram #10). On this adjustment, the strong safety takes the #1 receiver and plays half-field coverage. However, it is really man-to-man coverage. The free safety has to carry the #2 receiver into the field vertical. Since we are bringing the corner off the edge, the 5-technique end slants into the B gap. The Sam linebacker reads the #2 to the #3 receiver and plays his technique.

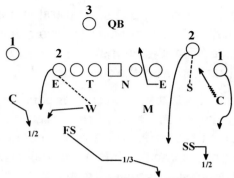

Diagram #10. Corners In From Field

On the backside, the corner is playing half-field principle but is mostly man-to-man. The Will linebacker to that side must carry the #2 receiver vertical. The obvious weakness is the boundaryside flat. Every defense has its weaknesses. If there was one perfect defense, everyone would be playing it. This is really Tampa-2 coverage because we have two half players and a third player carrying the middle of the field.

Against the trips set, it is the same type of defense (Diagram #11). We can run the three-man twist game if we want or a two-man slant game to the inside. What I like about this is the bubble screen. The corner reads the #2 receiver as he comes down. If the offense throws the bubble screen with the corner coming inside, it good for us.

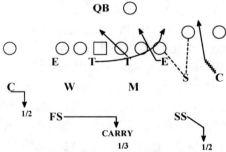

Diagram #11. Corners In vs. Trips

To run the corners in, you have to show it all the time. If you only buy your wife roses on Mother's Day or Valentine's Day, you are going to catch some heat. You have to show up in the flower store all the time to keep people from noticing you. You do not want to do things all the time because it loses its effectiveness. If you run it sometimes and show it a lot, teams will be uncomfortable running the bubble screen. The thing that makes it a bad play against the corners in is the ball is a lateral instead of a pass. That will be a turnover for the offense. You bluff it and run it sometimes because it deters people from throwing the quick bubble.

We did this last year and it was good for us. We can kick the linebacker over to become the fourth defender on the perimeter. I think you have to do that against spread teams. It is especially true against four-wide-receiver teams. If the Wildcat teams start to run power from that set, you must get your linebacker kicked over. When the offense pulls a player from the backside, they have added a block to the point of attack. The defense has to add a defender to compensate for that. The defense needs five defenders at the point of attack to counter the lineman pull. That is hard to do against a spread offense.

When the guard pulls, the center will block back. However, the center can also pull around for the linebacker. The linebacker has to read the center's pull. We teach the linebackers to read guards so it is no problem to teach them to read centers. The tackle trap is hard to play because linebackers do not read the tackle pull. Unless the player has grown up seeing a wing-T offense, players do not know how to read it.

When you play teams that pull the centers, you have to cheat and get the linebackers kicked over. If the offense is going to pull a lineman to the point of attack, we have to add the fifth defender to the point of attack. If the formation is the trips set with the back to that side, we play the same concept in the secondary with a tweaked adjustment. We play cover 2 with quarter-quarter-half coverage (Diagram #12). We play the strong safety over the tight end and slot receiver. We play the field corner in an apex position on the outside receivers. We give up the field flat, but the adjustment allows the free safety to sit on the backside.

It looks like zero man coverage. We call the coverage *zero* when the secondary zones off the fieldside. That means the free safety does not have to carry the tight end on a vertical route. We call that a *fish call*, which means the free safety is

inside. The free safety becomes the fifth defender on the pull play. This concept stays within our quarters scheme and allows us to kick our linebackers over.

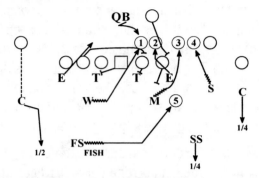

Diagram #12. Quarter-Quarter-Half-Fish

When we play man free, the linebackers will have the backs. We play a nickel scheme with this concept (Diagram #13). When we align, the corners have the outside receivers. The free safety and nickel play the #2 receivers. The strong safety is the free player. In this scheme, we take the strong safety, normally the high safety, and assign him to the remaining back or quarterback. If the offense runs a power with the quarterback, the safety is assigned to the fullback. When that back becomes a blocker, the strong safety is automatically added to the run game.

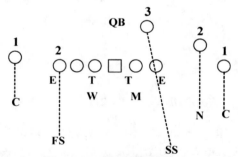

Diagram #13. Man Free

This is a simple way to get the additional defender to the point of attack. Wherever the fullback goes, the strong safety will be added as the extra defender. You do not have to read or adjust the coverage. You can do anything you want with the front and always have one more defender than they have blockers.

If you play this defense every time, the offense will run motion and run the fly sweep. You cannot do the same thing every time. You have to change up how you do things to keep the offense guessing. If you have to play the trips set with the man-free concept, the free safety will be the free player. The strong safety will have the tight end in man coverage, and the free safety will be locked on the fullback. He becomes the extra defender in the box.

We want to bring pressure to the fullback. We have primarily two pressures toward the back. We have a number of pressure schemes, but we feel the majority of the time the ball will go toward the back in the backfield. Joe Lee Dunn ran these types of pressures. He had a defense he called *mad and bad*. This is fashioned after those pressures.

On this pressure, the 5-technique end charges inside on a spill mode with the Sam linebacker blitzing off the outside (Diagram #14). They both are half players on the quarterback. The 3-technique tackle to the running back sticks across the face of the guard through the neck of the center. The backside tackle and end slant one gap outside. The secondary plays zero man coverage with the corners playing the #1 receivers and the safeties playing the #2 receivers.

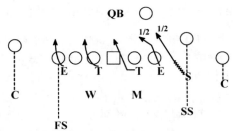

Diagram #14. Pressure to Back

If you do not stop the run, you cannot stop anything. If you try to stop the run and the pass, I think that is great. However, you have to stop the run first. You cannot simply stack up against the run and let the offense throw it all over the place. You need to stop what they do best. When you play with two linebackers in the box, it puts pressure on the secondary. You can run the same blitz and play the Will linebacker on the #2 receiver. That will let the free safety play as a high safety in the middle. That is somewhat safer against the pass.

If we bring the blitz away from the back, the tackles and 9-technique end slant toward the back and the Will linebacker comes off the edge (Diagram #15). The Sam linebacker aligns on the #2 receiver and cheats back into the box. The strong safety takes the #2 receiver. If you want to free up the strong safety, you leave the Sam linebacker on the #2 receiver and play the strong safety high.

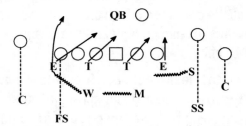

Diagram #15. Pressure Away From Back

The next thing we can do is switch the call. Joe Lee would call it *mad switch* (Diagram #16). On this blitz, the 5-technique end goes up the field and the Sam linebacker comes inside into the B gap. Their responsibilities are the same as the other blitz. Everyone else does what they did on the other blitz. It is the same concept. If the formation is a trips set, the free safety has the tight end to the other side. If you want to play man free, the Mike linebacker will take the tight end and the free safety is high in the middle.

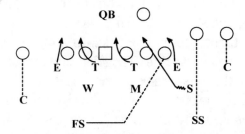

Diagram #16. Pressure to Back Switch

The switch blitz away from the back is the same blitz with the Will linebacker going through the B gap and the 5 technique going up the field. Everything else on the call is the same.

The offense will start to run the ball away from the back if you start to blitz toward him. They may shift the back from one side to the other late in the play clock. If you are trying to kick your front the other way, do you change your linebackers or change the blitz? It gets confusing. You are better off calling the blitz to one side or the other and running it. Once they see they cannot dictate to you what you are going to do, they will stop.

We had a player at Clemson University by the name of Gaines Adams. We would never let him play a spill technique on this blitz because he did not do that well. He was good at playing John Daly football. He could tee it high and let it fly. To his side, we always let him go high and the linebacker came inside to spill.

I went to Texas last year. It seems like everyone in that state is running the spread offense. I knew we were going to face those types of teams every week. I asked those coaches what they did not like to see teams play against them. I asked 30 of them and 28 said they did not want to see 4i techniques. They did not want to see walk-away defenders with two linebackers in the box. The walk-away defenders were in-between defenders. They wanted to play against a 4x1 box. They know how to play against that type of alignment. When the defense plays a five-man box with the bubble outside, that was hard for the offenses to handle.

To the tight end side, we play the 9 technique in his normal position (Diagram #17). The 3-technique tackle moves to a 4i technique on the offensive tackle. The shade tackle moves head-up the center. The 5-technique end moves into a 4i technique on the offensive tackle. The Will linebacker stacks behind the nose tackle, and the Mike linebacker moves to the outside behind the 4i defensive end. He is a walk-away defender, as is the 9-technique defender on the other side.

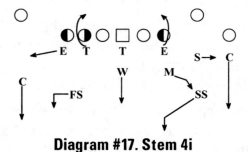

Diagram #17. Stem 4i

In the secondary, we can play normal quarters coverage or we can go to a five-under and three-

deep scheme. On that, the corners drop into outside-third coverage. The 9-technique end drops into the strong flat. The free safety rolls and plays hook/curl. The strong safety rolls to the middle third. The Will linebacker has middle hook. The Sam linebacker has the flat, and the Mike linebacker plays the hook/curl area. If you do that, the pass rush is not very good but you have eight defenders playing pass. You can always blitz the Mike and Sam linebackers off the edge and play zero man.

Playing this alignment makes it hard for the center or the tackle to pull because there are defenders aligned on them. If you are a 50 defensive team, this can tie into your system easily. We are not a 50 scheme and it becomes harder to do this.

One of the things we are going to do is run some 3-4 schemes. In our scheme, you will not see the zero nose or two 4-technique tackles. Anytime you run a weak Eagle defense from the under front, you are technically running a 50 defense. We use some different terminology because we add another linebacker. We have Bandit and Sam outside linebackers. At the Bandit position, I have coached five players who now play in the NFL. I have been lucky to have had good players at that position.

The Bandit is a 9-technique player to the tight end (Diagram #18). The tackle plays the 3 technique to the tight end side. The nose plays a center shade to the openside, and the defensive end plays a 5 technique. The Mike and Will linebackers are in a stack position behind the tackle and nose. The secondary alignment does not change. We are going to create a Bear defense from this front.

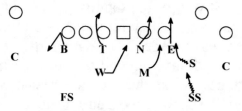

Diagram #18. 3-4 Defense

If the offense wants to run the quarterback power, they have to block back with the center on the 3-technique tackle. They cannot block the Will linebacker. The frontside guard cannot get to him because he has the nose in his inside gap. The Will linebacker can scrape over the center and be in the middle of everything. We still play a nine-man surface. If the #2 receiver blocks down, we can get six defenders to the point of attack.

There are some negatives to playing this defense. You do not have a contain pass rusher to the Bandit side. I coached DeMarcus Ware at Troy University. The first couple of years the Dallas Cowboys had him, they were dropping him outside trying to cover the #2 receiver. When we had him, we did not put him in coverage. We rushed him—that is why we did not play this defense that much.

If we need to get pressure from this front, we zone blitz and still play quarters in the secondary. Against a trips set, we run a blitz called *Pitt* (Diagram #19). The Mike linebacker runs a *fit blitz* on the guard. If the guard fans, the Mike linebacker becomes a 3 technique. He rushes and has to two-way goon the guard. To the trips side, we play two robber with the strong safety and Sam linebacker. We play the free safety vertical on the tight end. This gives us a four-man pressure package with the tackle, nose, end, and Mike linebacker. If the tight end blocks, the free safety plays a fish technique and fills inside.

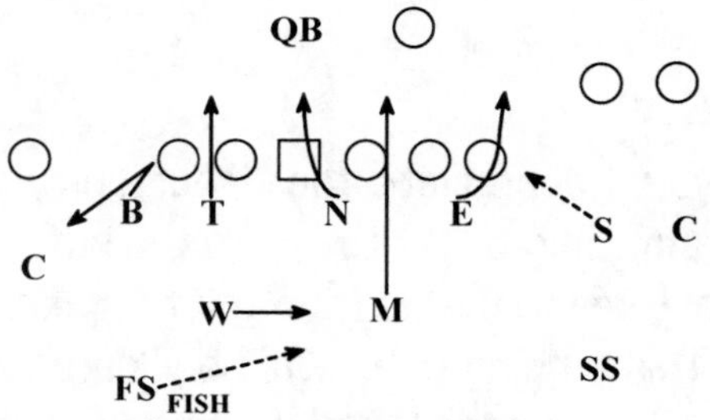

Diagram #19. Pitt

If it is a balanced set with two slotbacks, the Bandit walks out on the #2 receiver to his side. We play our quarter scheme with the read-2 concept.

That is all I have. If you have any questions, I will be glad to answer them. I appreciate your attention. Thank you very much.

OFFENSIVE LINE BLOCKING SCHEMES

James Madison University

Thank you. I appreciate the opportunity to speak today. I am going to try to get to the nuts and bolts of our off-season, when we try to make our guys better. This is going to be a laid-back presentation. I want it to be informal, and if you have questions, I want you to ask them. I cannot give you everything we do, but I am going to give you everything I can in the hour-and-a-half that I am here.

We are a spread option team. We run the inside zone, stretch, and the triple option. We have a very athletic quarterback, and he fits this scheme well. I coach the offensive, and I am probably the tallest guy in our group. I am 6'2", and it seems like all the linemen in our league are in that range. The Division I programs recruit all the tall linemen, and the 6'2" types end up at our level. However, if you have a 6'2" or 6'3" lineman, I want to talk to you.

My head coach is a defensive coach. If a player can play defense, our head coach wants him on that side of the ball. If he gets too slow or too big, he comes to me. This is what I call "everyday drills for success." After the season, you know what you have to do and what you have to fix. We start with these drills and try to improve and develop the players we have.

I am going to talk about offensive line run block progression. The first thing I am going to show you is a power step. The power step is a short first step, coming out of the stance. We want it to be short, where all the power angles in the hips, knees, and ankles are intact. As we look at the players in their stance, we look for the power angles in their stance. We look for the ankles outside the knee. If the player's knees are outside his ankles in his stance, he has no power when he steps one way or

the other. We want the stance to have the knees turned to the inside in a knock-kneed stance.

If the player overstrides with his power step, he has no backside V in his knee. When a player has no V in his knee, he has no power. When I talk about the V in the knee, it means his backside leg is too straight. We go through the power-step drill daily. We step with the inside and outside foot in this drill.

Doing the power step, I want the players free and relaxed as they come out. I want their eyes up and in a good football position. I want their thumbs to the sky and their elbows into their body.

We are a zone-blocking team in our schemes. The first step we teach is a half-bucket step. I want to lose ground to gain ground. On this step, we are doing more of a lateral step than backwards, although we are trying to get to the outside of a shade defender. We come off keying the knee of the defender in the onside gap. The blocker is expecting to see lateral movement into the gap. If there is no lateral movement into the gap, he is thinking of climbing to the second level.

We call the next step a jab pop. When I was learning how to block, my coach told me to power step on the first step. The problem was the second step. If I could not get the second step on the ground fast enough, the defender blew me up before I could get to the third step. When I took the second step, my foot was off the ground at contact, which gave a distinct advantage to the defender. I learned the jab pop from Coach Jim McNally.

We use this step with the guard to help post the 3 technique on the combination or double-team block with the tackle. On the step, the offensive guard takes a short step with the outside foot and gets a quick post step with the inside foot. His inside step is almost an up-and-down step with the inside foot. At the time he is taking his post step, he brings up his inside flipper on the 3-technique defender. That step does two things: it buys time for the tackle to catch up to the double-team, and it improves the timing of the double-team. Also, by using this step, the guard can pick up any lateral movement from the outside gap.

The next step we teach is the reach step. The reach block is a wide settle step. A settle step is a lateral step taken to get movement and not necessarily gain ground. I give the offensive lineman freedom to decide how far to step. If the target is wide, he takes a wider reach. If the target is tight, he takes a tight reach step. I tell them to step relative to the target. When we step for the reach, the knee to the side of the reach should be perpendicular to the line of scrimmage and not parallel to the line. We do not want the lead step in the reach to have the knee flaring out. When that foot hits the ground, we want the knee heading straight downfield, not opened or flared. We want the lineman to be able to reach and run to the outside on a train track. If he gets off the track, he is in trouble.

The angle drive is a step taken at the outside shoulder of an outside defender. In the step, we lead-step to the target. If the target is outside, we step with the outside foot directly at the target. If the target is inside, we do the same thing.

We drill our players on power walking. When I was a kid, they called this duck walking. This is used to train players to work on the line of scrimmage as well as the second level. You get your players in a good fundamental football position. I want the knees bent with the knees over the toes. The back is straight, and the arms are bent in a cocked position around the waist. You can go slow or fast, but all the steps are short, choppy steps.

Doing this walk requires the player to stay down in his fundamental position at all times. He pounds his feet as he moves forward. The arms are moved in unison with the pounding of the feet. The common mistakes big linemen make are they get on their toes, get the weight on the outside of their feet, and do not stay low. To do the duck demeanor drill, you are going to do the opposite of those mistakes. We want the weight on the inside of the feet and the feet close to the ground with the full foot making contact on each step.

DUCK DEMEANOR DRILL

- Get into a stance with the feet slightly wider than shoulder-width apart.
- Drop down like a linebacker with the chest over the knees, and weight on the balls of the feet.

Coach's Directions

- Right and left movement: When going right/left, the player will always lead-step and slide the back.
- Shuffle: The right foot moves six inches, and the left foot moves six inches.
- Carry hands high in front of the face, and look ready to strike a punch.
- When moving backward/forward, steps are power steps in duck-like fashion.
- Keep elbows tucked to the rib cage, pumping hand and arms in running form.
- Keep feet close to the ground. Always keep a good base, and do not let the feet click together.

The purpose of the drill is to keep all the power angles in the body intact. We want the hips, knees, and ankles to stay in the cocked power angle. When you think about power, you want to hear it from the stomp of the feet. If you cannot hear the feet in this drill, they are not generating power. The same thing is true of the arm movement. If they are moving the hands by swinging the elbows only, they are not doing the drill the way we want it done. I want them to swing their arms from the shoulders.

We drill the walk using a weave. Nothing changes in the walk except instead of going straight, we are redirecting forward with a sideways step. The feet and arms continue to do the same thing in the drill except we change our direction by stepping with the outside or inside foot in a lateral direction. We do not point the toe outside; we step over square. Everything is this drill is done with the shoulders always square to the line of scrimmage. The shoulder or hips are never turned on an angle. If we want to move at an angle, we use an outside or inside step to set the angle, and we continue to do the same movement. The shoulders are always square to the position we are moving. If we move on an angle right, the shoulders are square to that angle.

I call this drill the frame drill (Diagram #1). We have two players involved in the drill. One player holds a shield, and the other player is on his knees in front of the shield. The player holding the shield is standing and braced behind the shield. He leans the shield into the blocker. On the command, the blocker fires his hands and punches up through the shield. He fully locks out his arms as he punches up through the shield. What we are looking for is the reverse C in the blocker back. That means he shot his hips and lifted in his punch.

Diagram #1. Frame Drill

In the next part of the drill, the shield holders move backward after the punch from the blocker. What I am looking for in this part of the drill is the bend in the knee exploding. As he straightens his legs, his quad and glute muscles will explode, causing the blocker to end up on his stomach. He has uncoiled his power angles in his hips, knees, and ankles.

We call the next drill a knee jump. This reinforces the explosion from the ground. The player gets into a position on his knees. This is not a difficult thing to do as long as you have some flexibility in your hips and power in your legs. He jumps from his knees to his feet. What I look at is the position of the feet. If the lineman cannot lay his

feet flat in a kneeing position, he is not very flexible in his ankles. When I say flat, I am talking about space showing between the toe and the floor. The area from the toes to the shin should be on the floor with no space showing.

To make the drill harder, we add a small medicine ball. The player holds the ball in front of him and does the knee jump. Obviously, we want him to have his balance as he jumps to his feet. You can also add a weight bar across the shoulders.

In the two-point drill, we work with partners (Diagram #2). The blocker gets into a two-point stance and a fitted position on the shield holder. The blocker has a good fundamental football position with all the power angles cocked. He reaches out and gets his hands on the dummy. The face is into the dummy. On the command, the blocker does the same thing he did in the frame drill. He explodes through the dummy and locks out his arms. We look for the reverse C in the blocker's back. In this drill, the blocker drives the dummy holder back five yards using his duck demeanor steps.

Diagram #2. Two-Point Drill

The emphasis of this drill is to keep the power angles intact and use them to block. As we walk the dummy back, we keep the power angles in place.

The angle drive drill teaches the lineman to take the defender down the middle and drive (Diagram #3). In this drill, we work against the shields except we come out of the stance instead of the fitted position. What I am trying to teach in this drill is to

Diagram #3. Angle Drive Drill

push the defender straight down the field. If the blocker tries to push the defender outside, the defender spins back to the inside. If you try to push them inside, they spin to the outside. If you push them down the middle, they will go where you want them to go.

I was taught to fire off the ball and gain ground. I am not that concerned about gaining ground as I am getting movement.

We use the same techniques to teach second-level blocking. When the blocker comes off the ball, he uses the power-walking techniques, and he goes up to the linebacker. As he gets to his block, he has to reset his helmet angle to get into position. After he gets to the linebacker, he goes back to the previous drills. He uses his power angles and punches to block the linebacker.

I am going to start with the right tackle and talk about the inside zone play (Diagram #4). It starts with the right tackle and the base drive block. We want to make this block from the inside going to the outside. The defender is aligned to the tackle's outside. The tackle takes a drop step with his outside foot so he can take the defender going inside-out. We do not want the 5-technique defender to cross the face of the offensive tackle. If the tackle thinks the 5 technique is going to spike inside, he makes a "treo" call. I will tell you what that is in a minute.

Diagram #4. Base Drive 5 Technique

The next block is a combination block on the 1 technique. I call this a Rico block (Diagram #5). The right guard wants to buy some time for the center to catch up with the block. He uses the jab pop technique. He uses his inside hand to stymie the 1 technique until the center can take over the block. When he uses the technique, his inside foot and hand have to strike at the same time. The foot must be in the ground, and the hand has to hit the defender simultaneously. When he feels the center take over the block, he moves to the second level

for the Mike linebacker. He uses the technique I talked about in the second-level drill.

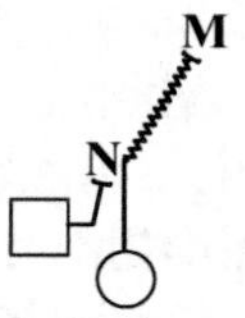

Diagram #5. Rico

If the foot and hand do not hit at the same time, there is no power. If his hand extends out and hits the defender before the foot gets on the ground, there is no power. The same thing occurs if the foot strikes the ground before the hand gets on the defender. It has to be in sync for all parts to work. If the guard comes off the ball late, that is a better situation than him getting off early.

If the center has a shade defender on his right shoulder and we are running the inside zone to the left, the backside guard is the takeover blocker (Diagram #6). The shade nose is coached to turn his butt to the backside guard and grab the center so he cannot get into the playside gap. The center cannot let that happen. The playside guard has a call he can make to the center. If he has a loose 3 technique aligned on him, he makes a "loose" call. That means we are staying with the inside zone play. The playside guard blocks the loose 3 technique outside, and the backside guard and center combo on the shade nose, with the center coming off for the Mike linebacker.

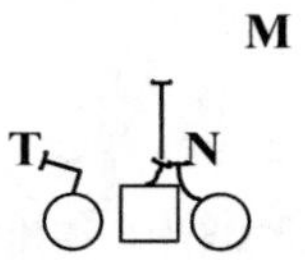

Diagram #6. Loose

The center uses the jab pop technique on the shade nose. The backside guard uses a drop step to get behind the centers inside foot and comes up inside him for the takeover of the block. The center keeps his eyes on the Mike linebacker and holds off the shade nose with his backside hand. He cannot let the nose grab him as he goes across. The backside guard is angle drive blocking, looking to get square on the shade nose.

If you run the spread offense, you must have a backside tackle who can cut off defenders. We teach the shuffle takeover on the backside of the zone (Diagram #7). When I saw this technique for the first time, I thought there was no way it would work. The tackle shuffles laterally down inside and up the field. He shuffles inside and rips through the 3-technique defender. He bucket-steps off the line with his inside foot and shuffles inside the 3 technique. He does not cross over with the outside foot. He stays square as he comes down the line.

Diagram #7. Shuffle Takeover

When we teach the backside combo block, the backside left guard can use the shuffle takeover steps to get up on the shade noseguard (Diagram #8). This works for us. The guard shuffles behind the center and gets his right hand on the center's shoulder. He pushes the center off the block on the nose to let the center know he has the block. He gets his left hand on the nose and works for a square position. He never tries to put the right hand back on the nose. If he does that, he has to turn his shoulders.

Diagram #8. Shuffle Takeover Combo

If the linebacker cheats out of the A gap with a 3-technique defender, we use a fake hand. We call that "Speedo." As the tackle goes through the 3 technique, he wants to jolt the outside shoulder. He is not waiting for the overtake block. The 3 technique, when facing a combination block, is thinking about flattening out on the line of scrimmage. That makes it easier for the guard to use the shuffle takeover and releases the tackle to the linebacker earlier.

I want to go back to the "treo" call (Diagram #9). Treo is a three-way call. If the offensive tackle thinks the 5 technique is going to slant inside, he calls "treo." The guard knows he is working with the tackle and not the center. The guard reads the inside hip and foot of the 5-technique defender. If the 5 technique slants inside, the guard uses the angle drive block to seal him. The tackle puts his inside hand on the slanting tackle and holds him off until the linebacker threatens the line of scrimmage. When the linebacker threatens the line, the offensive tackle comes off for the linebacker.

Diagram #9. Treo

Even though his gap responsibility went inside, he wants to help the guard. He hand-shivers the 5 technique to make sure the guard can get on the block. We call that taking the edge off the block. The 5 technique is moving inside on a slant. The little shove on the shoulder by the offensive tackle makes it easier for the guard. The shove knocks the 5 technique off balance and changes his angle slightly.

We can run the treo call against a three-man game (Diagram #10). If the guard and tackle are both covered, the center will be uncovered. If we have a three-man surface over the guard and tackle, we could get the treo call that way. The center overtakes, the 2 technique, the guard overtakes the 4 technique, and the tackle comes off for the linebacker.

Diagram #10. Treo vs. Three-Man Game

The GAT is the call for the guard and tackle (Diagram #11). This is a double-team on a 3-technique defender with one of the linemen coming off on the linebacker. The guard and tackle come hip-to-hip and foot-to-foot on the 3-technique defender. If the linebacker comes under the double-team block, the guard comes off and blocks him. The tackle stays on the 3 technique and blocks him. If the linebacker comes over the top of the double-team, the tackle shoves the 3 technique onto the block of the guard and comes off on the linebacker.

Diagram #11. GAT

On the zone play, you must cut off to the backside. This is hard for a big tackle to cut off an inside defender because they have to get so low. It is hard for a big man to open his hips. When we cut off, we take a full bucket step to the inside and a crossover step with the back foot. His bucket step should hit in the middle of the defender, and the cross should bring him to the defender's inside foot. From that point, the lineman wants to rip through the hip of the defender and get upfield. He is not blocking the defender. He is ripping through the inside and making the defender go behind him.

You have to work with your center extra hard with all the footwork. He has an added responsibility of snapping the ball and working all the blocking schemes. The first thing we want the center to do is extend the ball as far as he feels comfortable. He has to snap the ball in the shotgun. We do not tell him how far to put the ball. We tell him to make the snap, but he knows what we want him to do. If he can get the ball out in front of him, it puts us farther off the line of scrimmage, which is what we are trying to do. We are getting off the ball as far as we legally can.

I want to talk a little about the pass set before I get to the team plays. We like to run the ball, but we do throw it some. When we get into a pass set, there is one coaching point I want to cover at the beginning. If your feet are going one way, the helmet has to be going the other. That is called counterbalance. If the blocker is sliding to the right, and the defender goes to the left, that presents a problem. If the blocker's helmet is going the way of

his outside knee, he cannot recover to the inside, and we have a sack. When we set, we keep the head opposite the outside knee. That means if we pass-set to the right, our helmet is leaning to the left side. That keeps us balanced if the defender goes either way. We counterbalance the weight in our pass sets.

We work on our pass sets from all different alignment of the defenders. If the defender is head-up on the lineman, he wants to set to the inside. The lineman moves his inside foot to take away the inside move of the defender. If the defender moves inside, we are already there. If the defender is on our outside shoulder, we kick out with the outside foot, but the aiming point is the inside shoulder. If the defender aligns on our inside, we have to accelerate the inside foot and gain inside position on the inside technique.

The wide pass rusher is a particular problem for the tackles. I tell them they need a camera in their butts. He has to know where he has to get to. The rusher picks a spot to rush through to get to the quarterback. The offensive blocker has to beat the rusher to that spot. He kick-slides to the outside and gets depth as the rusher comes. He wants to be under control as he retreats.

If you get an extremely wide rusher coming from a walk-away position, there is no way your tackle can block him using conventional techniques. The rusher comes too fast, and the tackle's technique is too slow. We use a technique called a swap set. In this technique, the tackle does not kick-slide on his first step. He takes his inside foot and steps to the position of his outside foot. He swaps his feet. He moves both feet, but he moves at an angle and replaces his outside foot with his inside foot. With that done, he uses his kick-slide to gain the extra width and depth. It is as if he aligned farther outside.

We do all kinds of footwork drills. We do a wave drill with the lineman. I get them a cadence; they break their stance and move according to the directions I give them. I move them side-to-side and up-to-back. They get in their pass-set position and move in the direction I give them. On each shift of weight, they counter the helmet to the other side. The head constantly moves to the opposite side as they change directions.

We do the shield drills in our pass-protection drills. We incorporate the pass-set skills with the punch drills in the running game. We use the frame drill as a passing drill also.

We use a shuffle punch drill. The offensive lineman shuffles down a line with a shield holder. His helmet lean is opposite the movement of his body. If he is moving to his right, his head position is to the left side. As they move in the shuffle drill, I want the punch whenever the right foot hits the ground. We do the same drill holding a weight plate. We shuffle down the line. Each time the dominant foot hits the ground, we punch out with the weight plate.

I get them in a stance and stand out to their right side with a shield. On the snap to the ball, I swing the shield at the lineman's head. The lineman gets his hands up and punches the dummy. Sometimes, I fake a swing. If they punch at something they do not see, they end up off-balanced. They cannot punch unless there is something to punch. They have to use their eyes in this drill to maintain their balance.

We do a zigzag drill to work on their footwork (Diagram #12). I set up three lines of cones. The blocker gets in a pass set at the first cone. On the command, he pounds laterally to the second cone. He reaches that cone and kick-slides to the third cone on the second line. At the third cone, he pounds laterally to the fourth cone. He repeats the same drill through the last two cones.

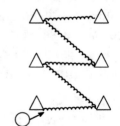

Diagram #12. Zigzag Drill

I also use the duck demeanor drill in the pass drop. We do the same type of drill except we use it going backward.

The eyes of the offensive lineman are tremendously important to his success. He has to understand what the defense can do from certain positions. When he is at the line of scrimmage, he has to look at the alignments and at his assignment. He cannot give his assignment away by his eyes, but in some cases that is all right—particularly in a pass-rush scheme. He can finesse a defender to charge upfield on a draw by looking at him. In some case, we want the lineman to look at the rusher. Everyone knows it is going to be a pass, so he may as well take a good look at him.

I am going to show you the inside zone play (Diagram #13). We align in a shotgun set most of the time with a tight end and a flanker. In this set, we have a split end and tight slot left opposite the tight end and flanker. The defense is a normal 4-3 defense with a 6 technique on the tight end. The center and right guard are scheming the 3 technique with the right tackle angle-blocking out with the tight end on the 6 technique. The left guard, tackle, and slotback are cutting off the backside. The quarterback zone-reads the backside defensive end.

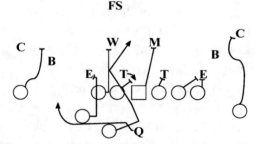

Diagram #13. Zone Read Right vs. 4-3

The backside guard can drive the 1 technique to the strongside, and the back can cut up behinds his block. The center has a free release to the second level; however, he cannot be in a hurry to get there. He has to release through the frontside A gap before he can get up on the linebacker.

The next formation is a trips set to the left with a tight end to the right side (Diagram #14). The defense is a 4-3 defense with a linebacker stacked over the tight end. At the last minute, the defensive stemmed the line to the fieldside. The backside guard and tackle have a combo-block on the 3 technique. However, the guard makes a "Speedo" call and goes straight to the backside linebacker. The playside guard and center combo-block on the 1 technique with the guard coming off for the Mike linebacker. The tackle and tight end angle-block on the two outside defenders.

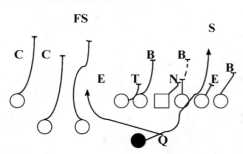

Diagram #14. Zone vs. Field 4-3

The playside guard holds off the shade until the linebacker starts to press the line of scrimmage. To the backside, we have a number of options. We can combo the 3 technique with the guard and tackle. We can use the Speedo call. The other option is for the guard to call off the zone scheme and go to a man scheme (Diagram #15). With that scheme, the guard blocks out on the 3 technique, and the tackle folds around for the linebacker.

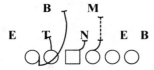

Diagram #15. Backside Fold

We had an extremely good quarterback. He ran the ball well. We aligned in a trips set to the tight-end side. The defense is a normal 4-3 defense (Diagram #16). We blocked the zone scheme by combination blocking on the 3 technique with the

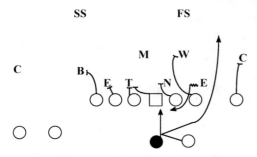

Diagram #16. Zone Read Quarterback Keep

guard and center. The tackle angle blocks to the outside. On the backside, we shuffle cut off the backside defender. If backside defense end closes, the quarterback keeps the ball.

I have told you about the treo call. That is a three-man game. If I want the entire line involved, I can make a gap call. That means the entire line block their playside gap. We can change the tempo and catch the defense in a transition, trying to substitute. We do not wait on the defense to get set. If they are having trouble or late substituting, we snap the ball and go. By using the gap scheme, the linemen may not have anyone in their gap. We line up and go. If the defensive end away from the zone play shows the quarterback his shoulder, we want the quarterback to keep the ball. When I call the gap scheme, I am trying to tell the linemen to forget the zone scheme.

If the defense runs an exchange on the backside, the end closes on the zone back, and the linebacker scraps to the outside for the quarterback (Diagram #17). The quarterback reads the end closing and pulls the ball. He has made a mistake. The defense ran an exchange and sent the linebacker outside for the quarterback. When that happens, the quarterback comes as tight to the butt of the closing end as he can and turns the ball up. Hopefully, the linebacker will overrun the quarterback.

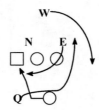

Diagram #17. Exchange Call

We had a situation in a game with the nose holding the center. He kept him from flowing on the combination blocks (Diagram #18). I told the center to tackle the nose. That took the backside guard off the combination on the nose. He pulls around the nose and comes up on the linebacker on the other side of the ball.

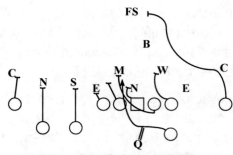

Diagram #18. Zone Guard Pull

Being a zone-read team, you must have a speed option as part of your scheme (Diagram #19). On this play, we are reaching all the way. The tight end and tackle try to work a combination on the Sam linebacker over the tight end. We run a combination block with the center and backside guard.

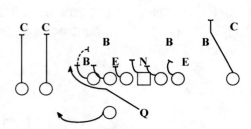

Diagram #19. Speed Option

Fellows, that is all the time I have. Thank you for your kind attention. I appreciate it.

WHY AND HOW TO RUN THE TRIPLE OPTION

United States Naval Academy

It is an honor for me to be here. I have lived on the East Coast for 15 years, but I am an Island guy. Before I get into the lecture, I want to share a few things with you. I sometimes wonder if I am using certain terms to impress the players, or someone else. Many times, simpler terms exist that carry more meaning with the players. Coaching is not about how much you know. It is about how much you can communicate to your players. They have to know what you are saying.

I went to a clinic and listened to a coach. He is a great offensive mind, but I found myself wondering what he was talking about. He made a simple explanation of an out cut that made me think I should go back to engineering school. This is a great game, but it is not very complicated.

This is something I learned at the United States Naval Academy. I have been coaching for 20 years, all of them at the college level. The thing that separates the Naval Academy from the other schools I have coached at is *leadership*. Football is the most unselfish sport there is. In what other sport do you have so many individual skills? Everyone's individual skills are unique to themselves. When the ball is snapped, everyone must do his job for you to have a successful play. Everyone must worry about his individual skill as it fits into the total play. They are not concerned with what someone else is trying to do. When players do that, they excel as a team.

I coached at the University of Nevada, Las Vegas before I came to the Naval Academy. We had four players at UNLV who were considered draft choices for the NFL. We were more talented there than we were at the Naval Academy. We were spending countless hours at UNLV on the offense, but we were barely scoring 18 points a game. When I came to the Naval Academy, the players were not as strong or as fast, but the offense was better because the players did their jobs. We had less material, but we were so much more efficient with our offense. We have averaged close to 30 points a game since I have been there.

We had a player come back from Iraq and talk to our team about leadership. He talked about two things. He talked about *leading* and *teaching*. He said that when you lead men, you have to love those that you lead. That fits in with a coaching staff. You have to love the guys you lead.

The second thing is to lead by *example*. If you are the coach and you want your players to play with high energy, you have to show high energy. If the coach has his hands in his pockets and is yelling at his players to show some energy, they look at him. What kind of example is that coach showing?

When you lead, you have to *lead from ahead*. Everywhere that player went in Iraq, he was in front of the troops. The players have to see that their coaches are just like them. Regardless of your title, you're not trying to be something better than they are.

The last thing is *devotion to your men*. If you use the words *love, example, ahead,* and *devotion* as an acronym, you get the word lead. I have learned these things at the Academy. We have players and coaches who are not as strong as the people we play, but the leadership in our group is tremendous.

We have early morning workouts. We start at 5:30 in the morning. We call the workout the *fourth quarter*. We are doing football drills, but we are working on mental toughness. We do eight different drills that are football related. We used to use monkey-roll drills, but we do not do that anymore. You do not need to teach players to get on the ground. We want our drills to be football related, but what we are looking for is *perfection*. We want to make sure everyone does everything right.

It is important in a football organization to have *staff unity*. We want the coaches to be "all in" when it comes to the team. When the coaches walk through the door, we are a coaching staff that is on the same page and reacts as *one*. Players watch what is going on with a staff. If there is some friction in the staff, they sense and know what is going on. We want all the arrows pointing in the same direction.

The scheme we use at Navy gives our players a chance to play. We have been using this scheme for some time. When we practice the offense, we have a team option drill. In this drill, we have two huddles. I noticed in the national championship game that the University of Texas' second quarterback did not look like he had taken too many reps in practice. That is the reason we run two huddles in this period. We prepare our depth, and we get up to 40 plus reps in a 20-minute period. If you run the triple option, you must rep the offense.

The secret to this offense is to *keep it simple*. When you have a simple plan, you can play fast. Add that to the repetitions you get, and you have a chance to be good. We want to be sound in the offense. Running the option attack at Navy is like Karl Malone and John Stockton running the pick-and-roll in basketball. Everyone in the NBA knew they were going to run it, but no one could not stop them because they adapted to every scheme the defense presented.

We do the same thing. Everyone knows we are going to run the option. We have to get good at our scheme and adapt to what the defense is trying to do. We do not care what the defense does. We try to get good at what we do and run it.

Be Demanding: Don't Make Excuses

- Toughness
- Great effort
- Ball security
- Flawless technique

When you run a football program like the one we have at Navy, you have to be very demanding. We do not make any excuses for players. One good thing about players at the Naval Academy is that they are all mentally tough. We try to build off that trait. We want to emphasize the intangibles in football. The *toughness* and *effort* are the things that we must excel in. You do not have to be talented to have great effort or toughness.

When you run the option attack, you have to coach *ball security*. We do not think of the offense as a high-risk offense, but we do not want the ball on the ground. We coach the four points of pressure on the ball, and we want the players to know it is important.

When we run our offense, we will align and see how the defense is going to play us. We have been running this offense for a long time. There are reasons we run the offense.

Why Play Option Football?

- Help in recruiting
- Do not have to block everyone
- Three days to prepare for the option is not enough

Personnelwise, we do not have to block everyone in this scheme. It may be their best player that you do not have to block. The offense itself is a unique offense, and it is hard to prepare to defense the scheme. To play an option team, the defense must play *assignment football*. When you force the defense to play assignment defense, you slow them down. You stop their blitzing game by running the option. It becomes very high risk for the defense to blitz linebackers. Someone must play the dive, quarterback, and pitch.

To play in the option offense, the players have to be unselfish. If you are a player who wants to run the ball 20 times a game, it will not happen in this offense. We were in a recruiting battle for a running back. The other service academy told the player he could play in the I bone and run the ball at least 20 times a game. He asked how many times he would run the ball with us, and I told him I did not know. I do not want to mention any names, but the other service team had a *lightening bolt* on their helmet. Players who come into our program are not worried about how many times someone carries the ball. They are focused and do not care if they run the ball 20 times or if they block 20 times a game. That helps us compete with the teams on our schedule. We do not have the physical talent that most of our opponents have.

The statistic that favors a team like Navy is *time of possession*. We run the football, which is something we led the nation in four out of the last five years. We do not turn the ball over, and we do not commit too many penalties. If we do those things, we have a chance to beat anyone.

The top three rushing defenses in the country are the University of Alabama, Texas, and Texas Christian University In today's football with all the spreads and the bubble screens, there is something to be said about running the football and stopping people from running the football. If you can stop teams from running the football, you force them to be one-dimensional.

We have to coach the intangibles and we talk about that daily to our players. We stress the *brotherhood within the team*, and they feel accountable to their teammates for how they play. The players believe in each other, and those are some of the things they take with them as they go to serve our country. They are very proud to be American and will do whatever it takes to serve their country.

I want to cover the triple option and go over the rules of how we run the offense (Diagram #1). We try to run this play 20 times a game if we can. The playside wide receiver is assigned to the deep defender. If the coverage is cover 3, the wide receiver blocks the corner. If it is a two-high safety look, he blocks the high safety to his side. The playside slotback is called the *A-back*. His rule is to block the run support. If the strong safety inverts

out of the secondary to support the run, the A-back uses an arc release and blocks him. If the cover-2 corner rolls down as the support player, the A-back kicks him out. The wideout and slotback are responsible for perimeter blocking.

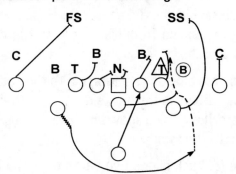

Diagram #1. Triple Option

The playside tackle has the playside linebacker. To block the linebacker, he takes the best release available to him. The definition of the *playside linebacker* is any linebacker from the tackle's outside shoulder to the inside. It does not matter whether it is a linebacker. It is a defender on the second level of the defense aligned over or inside the offensive tackle. It could be a nickel back. He has a simple rule for his release. If the guard is covered, he takes an inside release. If the guard is uncovered and can prevent a B-gap run-through, he takes an outside release. Those are two simple rules.

The playside guard has a base rule. If a down lineman covers him, he blocks him. If he has a 2i-technique defender, he steps with his inside foot. If he has a 3-technique defender, he steps with his outside foot. If he is uncovered, his assignment is the playside linebacker. That puts the playside guard and tackle on the playside linebacker. The playside guard and tackle, in that situation, are responsible for the playside linebacker and backside safety. If the linebacker scrapes outside, the tackle blocks him and the guard goes up on the backside safety. If the linebacker hangs or blitzes, the guard blocks him and the tackle takes the backside safety.

The center and backside linemen have a *scoop rule*. If the center is covered, he is responsible for the playside A gap and scoops half of the nose. If the nose stays frontside, he drives on him. If the nose stays backside, the backside guard has the other half of the nose and tries to take over the block. That allows the center to climb to the second level. We define the backside guard's responsibility as from his crotch to the crotch of the center. The backside tackle has the same rule. He scoops inside and is responsible from his crotch to the backside guard's crotch.

They are blocking an area rule to the backside. If anything shows in the backside A gap, it belongs to the guard. If anything shows in the backside B gap, it belongs to the tackle.

The fullback aligns five yards from the football depending on his speed. If he is faster, he can get more depth. If he is slower, he may move closer to the line. The backside A-back aligns on the tackle's outside foot.

The split of the offensive linemen is three feet across the board. The guard aligns with his hand on the toes of the center. The tackles take their alignments on the guards. We used to align with our hands on the heels of the guard, but we got too many penalties for not being on the line of scrimmage. The line is uniform across the board with three-foot splits and their hands on the toes of the center.

If the defenders will split wider than three feet, the linemen will attempt to split them up to five feet. The farther the defender will go, the more natural running lanes we will have. Most defenders will not let you split them that wide.

When the lineman comes off the ball, we try to play with a flat back. In their stance, we are heavy weighted forward in the stance. We have 60 percent of the weight forward. We have an elongated stance and their hips are higher. We are not like a zone team and have narrower bases in our stance. All we are doing is coming off the ball. We have a blocking scheme where we double-team the 3 technique and combo for the playside linebacker.

The backside A-back is the pitchman on the option. When he comes in motion, his aiming point is at the butt of the fullback. He is on a dead sprint for the butt of the fullback. After he gets to that depth, he mirrors the quarterback. Ideally, we would like to have the A-back take three flat steps and turn up. On this play, we are trying to get north and south. We are not trying to attack outside. If the quarterback turns up, the A-back has to keep up with him.

We want the pitch relationship between the quarterback and the A-back to be a 4x1-yard relationship. We want to pitch the ball parallel to the line of scrimmage. We do not want to pitch the ball perpendicular or behind. We want the ball parallel to the line on an outside pitch.

The quarterback's read is the first down lineman. His pitch read is the next threat going to the outside. We have tried to read the head, numbers, or whatever. We coach the quarterback on the read with a simple rule. The rule we give the quarterback is: Can the defender tackle the fullback? If he can, keep the ball. If he cannot, give the ball. Our quarterbacks are so smart and we do so many reps that they know the difference. We try to make it as easy as possible.

I am not trying to hide anything from you. That is what we tell our quarterback. The secret to the read is *repetition*. The second step the quarterback takes is different from most people. We do not have a ride step. We try to get the second step of the quarterback on the ground as quickly as we can. He wants to extend the ball back as far as he can and keep his eyes on the read.

Sometimes the feet end up in a stagger. That is a personal preference with me if that happens. If he ends up with his feet parallel, it makes it harder to extend the ball back. By the time the ball reaches the quarterback's front hip, he has made his decision to pull or leave the ball with the fullback. The staggered feet allow the quarterback to make some last-second decisions.

If the reach key and pitch key are both on the line of scrimmage, we tell the quarterback to look through the first defender to the second one (Diagram #2). The defender that will tell the quarterback everything is the second defender. If the second defender closes inside, he gives the ball to the fullback. Too many times, the quarterback is concentrating on the first read and gets hit in the lips by the crashing second defender. He has to *see* the read defender, but he must *feel* the pitch key.

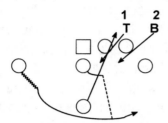

Diagram #2. Pitch Key

If the second defender is coming hard, the quarterback disengages from the fullback but does not attack the second defender. He wants to keep space between himself and the defender. He wants to see what the defender is doing. We want to know if he is attacking the quarterback or going to the pitch.

The disengagement from the fullback gives the quarterback a split second longer to see what the defender is doing. If the defender comes to the quarterback, he loses a bit of ground toward the pitch and delivers the pitch outside. Obviously, if he attacks the pitch, the quarterback keeps the ball.

The blocking technique for the center is the playside number of the nose. He wants to get his second step on the ground and keep his shoulder square to the line of scrimmage. He wants to rip through the playside armpit and keep a vertical line up to the backside linebacker. If the center is uncovered, he works through the A gap and climbs for the two linebackers. If the playside linebacker blitzes through the A gap, that is his block. If the playside linebacker flows, the center climbs for the backside linebacker.

The backside blocks are more of a banana step. We are not trying to run flat down the line of scrimmage. The first step is a 45-degree angle, and the second step is a 90-degree angle. We want to cut off and get upfield.

We want the playside tackle to stay tight on our outside releases to the playside (Diagram #3).

The first step is at the armpit of the linebacker, and the second step is to the crotch. If the defense runs a C stunt with the 5-technique tackle and the 30-technique linebacker, the tackle does not want to miss the scrape of the linebacker. The quarterback does not look at the inside linebacker. He concentrates on his outside keys. If we miss the block on the scraping linebacker, the quarterback gets earholed by the linebacker. That is when you get a fumble. We want the tackle to stay tight on his release and get vertical.

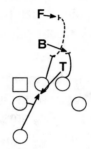

Diagram #3. C Stunt

The fullback aims at the outside hip of the guard and reads the first down lineman inside of the read key (Diagram #4). If the center is covered by a nose or has a shade defender to the playside gap, his rule is to reach playside. If the nose works hard to the playside, the center may be able to block him past the handoff gap. That tells the fullback whether to stay on track through the B gap or bend behind the block of the center.

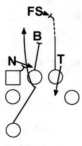

Diagram #4. Fullback Read

Anytime we have a double-team at the point of attack, the fullback looks to stay on track (Diagram #5). If the scheme is to double-team the 3 technique, the fullback stays on track and does not cut back. If the center and playside guard double on the nose and the tackle veer releases inside, the fullback stays on track.

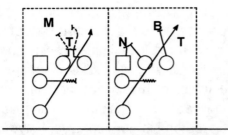

Diagram #5. Double-Team Track

We give the offensive tackle some options on his releases depending on how the defender tries to handle him. If the defender tries to cancel any inside move by the tackle, he can take the outside release. That is contrary to our rules, but we are flexible in that area.

This is a simple scheme. I learned it at the University of Hawaii, and you have to keep it simple for us Island guys. Anytime the defense has two stacks, the quarterback reads the area. If the linebacker blitzes for the fullback and the defensive end steps outside for the quarterback, we can read that. We work on that in practice daily. All they have done is swap responsibilities and we can handle that.

If the center has an A-gap responsibility to the Mike linebacker and he fast flows to the strongside, the center climbs to the backside safety. During the course of a game, the linemen move their splits in and out to find out what the defender will do. We flex the A-back and move the splits of the wide receivers to see what adjustment the defense will make.

This offense is simple and sound. It is all about getting numbers in the right places. We also take advantage of the angle we have on the defenders.

On the midline option, the fullbacks aiming point is the playside cheek of the center. The read for the quarterback does not change. He reads the first down lineman. There are different things we can do with the play after the read. The quarterback can carry the ball, or he can run the option and get it out of his hands.

Against the 3-4 look, the playside tackle turns out on the 9-technique defender (Diagram #6). The quarterback reads the 5-technique defender. The playside guard climbs to the 30-technique linebacker aligned on him. The center blocks the nose. The backside guard wants to run through the heels of the nose and get vertical to the backside linebacker. We can motion the A-back toward the fullback and turn him into the B gap for the playside linebacker. They work a combination scheme. The backside A-back comes around for the pitch as window dressing for the play. The quarterback gives the ball to the fullback or keeps it in the B gap. If he keeps it in the B gap, he follows the block of the A-back.

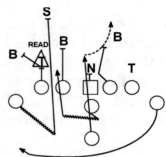

Diagram #6. Midline Option

One thing we do when teaching ball security is to have the backs get up with the ball. They get off the ground each time and give the ball to the officials. We do not want to leave it on the ground. If we do not secure the ball, we cannot beat anyone.

The thing the midline does is to soften the 3- and 4-technique defenders. When we have to base block them, it is an easier block. If we want to give another look to the play, we bring the A-back in motion behind the fullback and lead him up to the other side of the play (Diagram #7). Instead of being the pitchman, he becomes the isolation blocker for

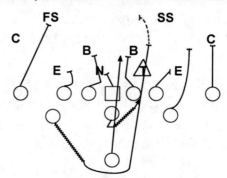

Diagram #7. Midline/Cross Motion

the quarterback. The good thing for us this year was that the quarterback was a strong runner. By the time the defense found him, he had gained four yards.

When the playside tackle turns out on the defender, he wants to stall the inside shoulder and get separation. We run the counter option (Diagram #8). If the defense is in a 3-4 look, it is a simple play and most of the playside rules are the same. On this play, the fullback runs opposite the playside. The fullback and backside tackle are responsible for the two defenders to the backside. The center and playside guard are blocking back. In this case, the center is covered and combos with the playside guard for the nose and backside linebacker.

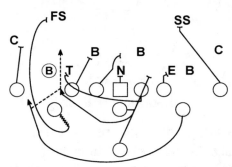

Diagram #8. Counter Option

The playside tackle and backside guard are responsible for the first down lineman and the playside linebacker, whoever that may be. If the 5 technique closes across the playside tackle's face, he locks onto him and drives him down the line. The backside guard pulls around the offensive tackle and blocks the playside linebacker. If the 5-technique tackle plays to the outside, the playside tackle goes inside for the linebacker and the pulling guard logs the defensive tackle.

The A-back comes in step motion toward the fullback and turns back to block the support player. The split end to that side has the deep defender. The backside A-back is the pitchback on this play.

The quarterback steps toward the fullback and counter runs to the playside. He options off the #2 defender to that side. In his pre-snap read, he has to locate the #2 defender to the playside. If he is on the line of scrimmage, as the quarterback steps for

the fake, he has to peek over his outside shoulder on his second step to see if he is on a hard charge inside. If he closes on the quarterback, he pitches the ball to the A-back.

The quarterback steps with his foot to the fullback on his first step. His second step should be perpendicular to the line of scrimmage. He pivots away from the line of scrimmage on his outside foot. I learned this offense from Coach Paul Johnson when we ran it in Hawaii back in 1989.

The A-back tried to confuse the defender who was keying on him with his release. We found if we arc released with the A-back, the defender read that release as a run block. We released the A-back straight at them. They did not know if it was a play-action pass or a run, and it froze them. From time to time during a game, we change up the techniques of the A-backs.

When we go into a game, we do not have a call sheet. We have assistant coaches watching positions to see how the defense is playing the option. We have coaches watching the secondary, the defensive ends, and the linebackers.

Against the 4-4 front with 1- and 3-technique defenders, we want to run the play to the 1-technique side (Diagram #9). The fullback cuts off the backside, blocking the 3-technique defender. The backside tackle turns back on the defensive end. The playside guard and center run a combination block for the 1 technique and the backside linebacker. The playside tackle areas the stack over him. He releases inside and blocks the B-gap defender. The pulling guard blocks whichever defender is playing the C gap. The A-back comes in

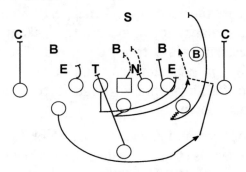

Diagram #9. Counter vs. 4-4

step motion and turns back on the safety. The split end to that side blocks the corner. The quarterback options the outside linebacker to that side.

Defensive ends like to chase the triple from behind and try to run the quarterback down. When we see that, we run a reverse.

We run the triple, midline, and counter. We also run the zone play to take advantage of aggressive running linebackers (Diagram #10). On this play, we base block at the line of scrimmage. The fullback, on the zone play, still reads the first lineman to the backside. The fullback reads the zone play like any other zone play. If the A gap is open, he runs it in the A gap. If the Mike linebacker plugs the A gap, he looks to bend the ball behind the backside down lineman.

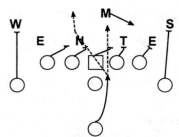

Diagram #10. Inside Zone

We use this play when we find the Mike linebacker cheating into the wide field. If he is running to the alley, it is hard to block him. This play slows him down and makes him play more honestly. This becomes a cat-and-mouse game with the Mike linebacker.

I want to finish up with our play-action passes. When we run the play-action game, we try to get crossing patterns going against the action of the triple. When teams defense the triple option, they have to use their secondary to support on the run so they can balance the defenders to blockers. When the backside safety tries to run the alley to the triple option opposite him, that is what we are looking for. We throw the ball to slow the secondary down.

In our protection scheme, we block big on big. The fullback is responsible for the linebacker to his side (Diagram #11). The backside A-back comes in motion and becomes the pressure release blocker

to the frontside of the protection. The backside split end takes the top off the coverage and clears the deep third. The playside A-back runs a six- to eight-yard drag pattern against the grain of the play. He is running high or low off the linebackers. The split end to the playside runs a climbing inside route. He is looking to create space for the drag pattern. He occupies the safety and keeps him from falling down on the drag route. We do not talk too much to the receiver about route running—we ask them to get open.

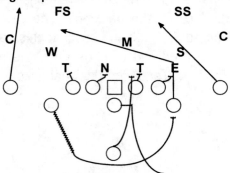

Diagram #11. Drag

We run a post wheel pattern from the triple option fake (Diagram #12). The wide receiver runs a three-step pattern to the post. The A-back runs the wheel route behind the post cut. The wide receiver tries to keep the post skinny and stay away from the backside safety. He tries to split the corner and safety. We keep the pattern on the same side of the hash marks and high-low the corner. We are trying to get the patterns at two levels so we can stretch the corner.

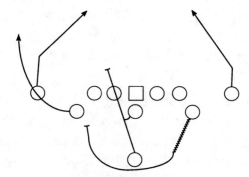

Diagram #12. Post Wheel

I like to throw the ball, but the only time we can do it is in definite running situations. The offensive line cannot protect unless it is that situation. We spend our time on the option and not the passing game. We do not spend enough time on it to be very good at it. We have to pick our poison. We do not have our players long enough to teach a multiple-faceted scheme. It is a preference for us. We spend all our time on the running game.

We have a pattern that we try to run by the safeties (Diagram #13). We run a vertical pattern with the A-back and split end to that side. This pattern takes advantage of the safety trying to get to the alley to stop the option. Oftentimes, the defense will try to replace the safety with the linebacker away from the play-action. They roll the safety down into run support and try to invert the backer into the middle.

If they read the pattern, we stop the receivers at 12 yards. The offensive linemen have to come off the ball and run block to sell the play. If they try to

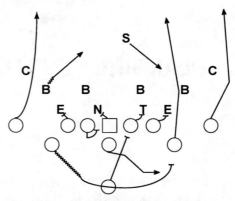

Diagram #13. Two Verticals

pass set, all they do is back up. The quarterback we had this year could definitely throw the ball. He is the best play-action quarterback we have ever had.

I do not have any secrets. Everyone knows what we do. We accomplish what we do because of the repetition we put into the attack. Thank you.

PLANNING YOUR FIRST 10 PLAYS: HOW AND WHY

Ball State University

I want to give you a history of how this talk came about. I think you will like the lecture. It has some philosophy included, and it has some guts to it. It is real football. They are the things I believe in.

I want to talk to you about my background. I started out as a high school coach in 1969 in the Youngstown, Ohio area. I spent six of the greatest years of my life coaching and teaching. I was an assistant coach for three years, and I was a head coach for three years. I taught six classes. I coached freshman basketball, and I coached track. In those six years, I never went straight home after school one day. My starting salary, including coaching, was six thousand dollars. Every two weeks I would get that $142.72 check, which I still have a stub. I keep it to remind me of where I am today. My attitude was, *I can't believe they are paying me to do this.*

My impulses got in my way as we continued to win. I was no different than a lot of young coaches; I thought it was us and not the players. We are the reason we are winning. I ventured into college coaching. I went to Purdue University as a graduate assistant coach. Then, I went to Wabash College in Indiana. I was there 10 months. We played for the national championship in Division III, and I got the head coaching job. I got to be the head coach there for five years. I had been a head coach for eight years and I was only 32 years of age. From there, I went back to Purdue as the quarterbacks coach.

My next stop was at Marshall University. I was the first head coach to have a winning season there since the airplane crash of the Marshall football team in 1970. I did not stay long enough at Marshall University. I moved to Kansas State University as the head coach, and they fired me in two-and-a-half years. We won two games in three seasons.

What I had been telling my players about getting up off the deck when they were knocked down, I then had to apply to my own situation after that experience at Kansas State. I had to start my career all over again. I got the opportunity to go to Rutgers where I coached for six years. I had several opportunities to leave Rutgers during that six-year span; but the head coach there at the time was Doug Graber, and he gave me a shot. He took me off the unemployment line. My dad, who coached for many years, never let me forget that situation. When I would talk with him about taking another job for more money, he would tell me that was for all the wrong reasons.

We had played Penn State at Rutgers and we had played them well. Soon after playing Penn State, I got the break of my coaching career. Lloyd Carr of the University of Michigan was looking for a quarterbacks coach. He liked what we did at Rutgers. I flew into Ann Arbor on a Friday night and the interview lasted for a long, long time. I did not have a change of clothes. He asked me to stay over and continue the next day. I told him I would stay over if the clothes I had on looked ok to him. We interviewed part of the next day, and he hired me before I left Ann Arbor.

I got to spend six years in Ann Arbor with Lloyd Carr. Part of those six years was in 1997 where I got to coach on a national championship team. We had two quarterbacks there. We had Brian Griese and Tom Brady. I got to see the best of the best. Again, a coach may stop and ask the question: Were they that good, or was it the coach that made them good?

Next, I had an opportunity to coach in the NFL. I coached for Jon Gruden with the Tampa Bay Buccaneers. In our first year, we won the Super

Bowl. I had joined a team that won a national championship in Division III in college, another college team that won a national championship in Division I, and a Super Bowl championship team in the NFL. It just does not get much better than that.

Two years later, I was looking for a job. As it happens so often in coaching, an old friend called me about a job. It was a coach by the name of Brady Hoke who I had worked with at Michigan. I had roomed with him on the away games. Brady Hoke called and said, "I need you to come to Ball State University to work with us." I was thinking, *From Michigan to Ball State. Brady, I am not sure.*

A few days later sitting at the kitchen table drinking coffee, like most unemployed coaches do, my wife said to me, "Stan, you need to get back to work. Go to Ball State." So I called Brady and I took a job with him at Ball State. I did not know what I was going to get paid, and I really did not care about that aspect. I had a three-and-a-half hour drive from Ann Arbor to Muncie, Indiana. I made a critical decision in my coaching career that I want to share with a lot of you younger coaches.

I said, "This is the back part of my career, and for the very first time, it is going to be all about the players and not about me. It is not going to be about where my next job is going to be or how much money I am going to make."

It was an honor, as an assistant coach from Ball State, to be selected in 2008 to go to Little Rock, Arkansas as one of the nominees for the Frank Broyles Award. I kept thinking, *Who would have "thunk" it, coming from Ball State?* I have coached at a lot of places, but I never thought this would happen with me coaching at Ball State. I will never forget the day Coach Broyles called. I was shocked. I was not concerned about those kinds of things or any award. I was concerned with us winning the next game. I was interested in how we were going to make a first down.

The thing I am telling you is that it took me 35 years of my life in coaching to get it. If you think on those terms, you can be all that you can be. My message is this: I have been there. I have learned a lot of things along the way. I have always been the head coach, the quarterbacks coach, or I have run the offense my entire coaching career.

When I started putting the offense together at Ball State, I asked myself this question: What can I do better here that I did not do in Michigan? I really have to give credit to what we are going to do and to my talk tonight to my experience in the NFL. I got to work for a very unique individual in Jon Gruden. Jon had worked for Bill Walsh and Mike Holmgren. He had worked for the best of the best. He made a video of everything he was ever involved with in football. That is why he came in at 3:47 each morning. Those are not fairy tales. Do you know why he came in at 3:47 a.m.? Because he knew we would be there about 4:30 a.m. At 6 p.m., I knew why I was tired. That was a long day.

The way Jon Gruden presented the football to the players was very interesting. I decided at Ball State when I took the job as offensive coordinator, that I was going to introduce the football to the players at Ball State the way Jon had done with the Bucs. I said, "If I am ever going to coach again, I am going to do it the same way as Jon."

What this does is to open up a lot of other avenues. I am going to show you pictures of us playing, and I am going to show you photos of what we do, but, first, I want to talk to you about what it does to your staff and to the players around you. The term I use is *inclusion*. The more inclusion you have on your coaching staff, the stronger team you have. The stronger character you have on your team. Think of the situations where you did not feel you had inclusion on your team. You were always looking for another job, weren't you? On the other hand, you wanted to do things *your* way. I think inclusion is such a big part of what we're going to do.

We present to the players 10, 11, or 12 plays that we are going to open the game up with, except when we are backed up deep or we are in a short-yardage situation. In a timely fashion, we present to our players the 12 plays we are going to open the game with. I want you to think about how you will present these plays to your team and how you will proceed to include them in the selection of these plays during the week.

I want to show you how we decide what we are going to do and how we present it to the players. Also, I will cover how we sell it to the players and how we polish it up, and then I'll show you how it works in a game. The great part of this program is that it gives us some good openers for the second half. I learned this as we were going along.

I am an offensive coach. When the weather is good, we want to receive if we win the opening toss. I want to score a touchdown. I want to set the tempo. I want to set the tempo before the defense gets the information. It is important what you do with that information in the middle of the game. How many games have you lost where you said, "Man, we just did not come out in the second half?" Another thing teams do is to play grab ass in calling plays the second half. Therefore, we have second-half openers that we go over. We have been able to learn a great deal on calling plays the second half.

We all know if you have a plan, you can succeed. If you have no plan, you have to be lucky to succeed, and more times than not, you will not be successful.

We recruit all of our players within a driving distance of four-and-a-half hours of our campus. We do not recruit Florida and Georgia. We go after players that are within that four-and-a-half-hour radius from our campus. We signed two high school players from Kentucky this past week. We signed 21 players including two from Kentucky. I hope that we will sign more in the future.

Let me talk about our *openers*. What are they? They are the plays we are going run to start the game. They are our first 10 plays. We have a hard time getting 10 plays anymore. Our coaches get excited when we work on the openers. We work on them on Thursday morning. We have a hard time arriving at 10 plays. As you will find out, having 12 or 13 plays selected is great to me. I do not mind if I have a few plays left for the defense. It is like the 440-yard dash in track. The man with a little left at the end wins the race. We try to win the race.

Let me talk about some reasons why we may stray from our openers. I may come in at halftime, and the assistant coaches may tell me to get back on the openers. They may tell me to get back to what we are doing. They may tell me that I am all over the place with our play calling.

The reason I may have gone away from our openers was because on our first play, we went 65 yards and went down to the 18-yard line. I went away from the openers and went to the red zone script. If you can score against teams easily, you really do not need a script. However, I am talking about games when we need to help the team win.

Down-and-distance is one reason we get off the openers. If we run the first play and gain eight yards on that play, we end up with second down and two to go. If the second play on the list is a dropback pass and we do not like that play, then we get off of the script. That is why we have a short-yardage script.

Field position is a second reason why we get off the openers. If our kick returner makes a mistake, comes out of the end zone, and is downed on our one-yard line, which we call the *black zone*, we are not going to run the first play in our openers. I was with Bo Schembechler and Lloyd Carr long enough to know to put in two tight ends and bang the ball up the middle to give the kicker some room to punt the ball out of the end zone.

We use our openers to get a fast start, and we want to score first. We want to establish the tempo of the game. From the time we put the plays in on Thursday night, all we talk about is *scoring*. Jon Gruden was the greatest salesman I have ever seen. By the time he got through the openers, the assistant coaches were agreeing with him on the play selection.

You must have some dynamics. You must put some excitement into the introduction of the plays to the players. You must be enthused about each play. If you are not dynamic in the presentation of the plays selected and they go to sleep, you go from play to play. Not all coaches have a lot of dynamics in their presentation of the openers.

We try to teach our guys a lesson. For four years, we had a tackle who looked down at the ground his whole life, if you know what I mean. He was a shy kid, and he was not a very good student. We all have one of those players on our team. He was a good player, but he lacked self-confidence. He did not want to get up in front of the room to talk with the team. He just did not want to do that. He always sat over by the lights in the meeting room. Before we presented our openers, I would always say, "Andre, hit the light for me." One night, by accident, I said, "Do you like them or love them, Andre?" He said, "I like them." I asked him again, and he said, "I like them." The players got on him a little and I think he learned a lesson.

Later in his senior year, we were playing in the GMAC Bowl. We were in a hotel room, and we asked him the same question. "Do you like them or love them, Andre?" He stood up and started doing a dance. He was a 325-pound tackle. He shouted out, "I *love* them, Coach P." The room erupted. Do you see what I am talking about when I talk about inclusion with a player? This all happened by accident, and that is why I am telling you. Get a player to let the team know they love the selection of the openers. The greatest coaches are copiers.

This is the part I like the best. How do we select the plays? How many of you are head coaches or offensive coordinators that do what you want to do all of the time without any input from the staff? Put your hands up. Keep them up. Ok. You suffer from what I suffer from. I speak to you as a friend. As coaches, we are not entitled to do *anything*. As coaches, we are privileged to do what we do. It is just a mind-set.

The best thing about doing the play openers is that it goes back to the word *inclusion*. It makes everyone think a little more. It gets everyone involved. Even the offensive linemen get involved. They look forward to giving their plays to the line coach to be considered for the openers. Even the defensive linemen and the defensive coaches get involved. This is how we do it.

We pick the coach who is the neatest writer to print out everything across the top of the sheet (Chart #1). Each coach is listed on the chart down the page. They will come to see me the night before the selection process and ask me where they are in the order of selecting the plays for the next day. I may tell that coach that he is going to bat cleanup for us.

My first coach up may be my offensive line coach. That would be Coach Burnett. I ask him to give me his favorite play. He may call out, "Dark, right, 32 split." That is an inside zone split play. I tell the coach who is taking notes to write it up on the chalkboard. Next, I will ask if anyone else on the staff has selected that same play in the first line of their openers. If we have several coaches with that same play on their list, I will tell the writer to move the play down. That means we are selecting that play to use in our openers. By moving the play down, it means we are writing it down to use.

Coach	Play 1	Play 2	Play 3	Play 4	Play 5	Play 6	Play 7	Play 8	Play 9	Play 10
Parrish										
Faulkner										
Lynch										
Mattix										
Eck										
Henry										

Chart #1. Play Selection Order of Selection by Coaches

I go to the next coach. Each coach selects his favorite play, and then we take a vote. The first couple of weeks you do this, the line coach may not know all the plays that some of the receivers coaches or running backs coaches suggest.

After we have about three plays selected and we all agree on them, then I start pushing some buttons. The head coach is entitled to push buttons. You are the boss, for gosh sakes. By pushing buttons, I mean saying something like, "There are two plays that I thought everyone would have up on the board." Now, the staff is starting to think, *what does that guy want?* I will remind them they cannot use the red zone plays. We are grinding along.

We are trying to accomplish one thing here. We want to gather as much information as possible. How does an offensive team draw information? We gather information through the study of *films, communication, formations, motion, movement,* and *shifts.* We are looking at all of these things. At this point, my offensive line coach calls a play to add to the list, "Roger, rifle, 32 split." He gave me the same play, but he gets us in a formation and then he moved us around with some motion. I will tell the staff that I like that better on the inside zone split because I can get a lot of info from that move rather than just to line up and run the play.

We do not want to give the defensive coaches too much credit. That is always one of my favorite speeches to our offensive players—don't overrate the defensive coaches. They do not have a bunch of rocket scientists sitting over on their side of the ball. What they want to do is to get a bead on you. They want to get a bead on your formations and they want to find out what you are doing.

We train the offensive staff on play selection for the list of opening plays. The running backs coach and the line coach are the two coaches that are hard to get involved in the selection process. They live in their own world. We want to get them involved with the formations. We want to make sure they understand how we can use the play selection to our benefit.

The first time you do this procedure, you will say, "The coach from Ball State is crazy." Just remember, Rome was not built in a day. Even if you run the spread offense with the no-huddle concept, you can still run the openers. You do the same thing, but you are going to do it faster. The coach on the sideline is calling the plays or the quarterback is running the plays in the openers.

That is how we select the plays for our openers. We get down to the last one or two plays, and I will tell the staff, "No one got the two plays I had selected." My plays are like my children—I love them. I want to include them in everything. Occasionally, I exercise my privileges and insert my two plays. I tell the coach, "I think we should add this play or that play." I loved it a couple of years ago when our offensive line coach said, "Coach, we need to throw a double-move play." I asked him if he was talking about our *stutter-and-go play.* He agreed it was the play he was referring to and wanted to use it in our openers.

I want to show you our openers from our game against the United States Naval Academy two years ago (Chart #2). They were a good football team. We beat Navy in our first game of the year. I am going to show you the plays we ran as our openers. Then, I have the halftime adjustments and the plays we ran after that.

1. (12) (Trade) Rt Wing 32

2. (12) Dark Lt Pistol 73 Hold Wave & Go

3. (12K) Cluster Lt 29 Dummy

4. (Bub) Bubble Rt

5. (10) Doubles 73 "4"

6. (12L) Roger Love 28 Extra

7. (11D) Trips Lt Yac 73 Y Wheel

8. (12) Roger Rac 38 Man

9. (Hur) Hurricane Lt 39 Jet

10. (12) Louie Rifle 33

Chart #2. Navy Openers

I was an assistant coach who was up in the press box most of my career. I believe in being able to see what is going on. In my next life, even as a head coach, I may go up in the press box. I think it is important to see what is going on during the game. If it is not the head coach up in the press box, then it has to be the next best offensive man up there. It should be a coach that shares your vision and a coach that looks through the same glass that you look through.

What are the things we look for when we are looking for future plays? Let me assure you, "What you see is what you get." You must know what you get so you can make the adjustments when you get to the locker room. To me, the most important thing is coverages. To me, the most important thing I want to know relates to *coverages*. Today, the defensive coaches do a good job of disguising the coverages on defense. Back in the day, way back, we knew we would see a free safety in the middle of the field, two corners, and some dude in the flat. Football was played that way for a long time. Today, you cannot tell the quarterback to read the strong safety. That is not easy to do with the defenses we face today. The defense runs out on their sets and they disguise the defenses so well.

Let me talk about *formations*. We have some unique formations where we feel the quote I used earlier applies. "What you see is what you get." You should not have an offense with a formation where you only have one play from that formation. If you are going to put in plays, you should sequence plays so you have a few different opportunities.

Next, I want to talk about *motion, shifts*, and *movements*. I once coached with an old coach who later coached in the NFL. I wanted to use motion, shifts, and go through a lot of movements. He was the offensive line coach. He complained about us moving around so much; the offensive line did not know whom they were blocking. When you are a zone team, as we are today, he would be right.

You must make the motion, shifts, and movements meaningful. Boise State is a team I am trying to figure out. I have been watching them on film for about five years now. Boise State University

uses motion, shifts, or some type of movement, or else they line up in some type of unbalanced look every play of the game. They are not going to let the defense rest. Their feeling is this: Sometimes it hurts us, but most of the time, it does not hurt us. When it comes to gathering the information needed to run the offense, they are the best.

We broke down some of their pass offense because we looked at a few of their plays. I had a couple of young coaches assigned to looking at five Boise State games, and then I asked them to tell me what they saw out of Boise State. They told me Boise State was shifting or moving or doing something unusual on every snap. Then I looked at the film, and, yes, that is what they do each play. They have a few concepts and a lot of window dressing. That is what the West Coast offense is all about when you study it closely. When I coached with Gruden, we really got to the roots of the West Coast offense. We only had six or seven concepts, but we had a hundred ways to do them.

It is about getting the right players in the right places. How many of you have a player that you think is a superior player? How many times have you said, "We just could not get the ball in his hands enough?" We feel we must create touches or we must get him the ball more.

Now I want to go to the running game. The number one thing we do with our openers is this: Any running play in our openers must have a play-action pass off that running play. That is the single most important thing we do on our openers. Our wide receivers coach watches nothing but the back end of the running plays. So we check for the play-action pass plays.

We know we must be able to run the football. This past year, we could not run the ball two feet. As a result, our play-action game took a big hit. Even with all of our coaching concepts, our running game did not have a chance. We wanted off the hook.

We have a couple of plays where we count the number of defenders in the box. When the quarterback gets through counting, he is wrong as much as he is right. We have some two-for-two plays, but, again, with all of the jumping around in the secondary, the quarterback has a hard time making the correct call.

Next, we get down the field to the *red zone*. I have been coaching for 40 years, and I can assure you that the defense does less in the red zone than they do in any other area of the field. Number one, they are afraid to give up a touchdown. They do not give you the free play. What they do is what they do. You can predict, the closer you get to the goal line, the more defenders you will have to block and the more the defense will blitz you. That only makes sense because they have a smaller area to defend.

You must train the coaches in the box to get their eyes on the right thing. Our young coaches make the mistake of watching the game and not watching for *information*. You cannot watch the game. You must get the information assigned to you to watch for. You must get ready and you must talk to the right people.

Are you the type of coach that thinks, *I have Joe up in the press box because I do not know where else to put him?* I know that everyone wants to be a rock star. When it comes to games on TV and games with the press on the sideline, everyone wants a piece of that pie. I understand that point. An assistant coach must make some decisions and go listen for the information that will help the team. If you put him up in the press box, you must include him in the decision making as the game progresses. This is critically important. I did such a bad job of that for so long; I am ashamed of what I did to some coaches. I thought it was me, and it is not me. If you put him up in the box, you must include him.

You cannot have a man up in the box and have the offensive line coach talk the entire game and never talk with your man in the box once. We all have the fancy phones now. We can click them and talk if we want to communicate with the coaches in the press box.

Here is our presentation (Chart #3). This is where the fun starts. We list the openers down the left-hand side of the sheet. We have numbers in parentheses to indicate our personnel groups. Next, we list the plays. We put the plays on acetate, or, more accurately, they are on the PowerPoint now. We go over the plays one at a time. We cover the bottom plays up and look at the plays one at a time. Then, we uncover the next play and talk about it. We go all the way down the list. We give all 10 of the openers to the kids. This is when I asked Andre how he liked the plays. He did not answer with the enthusiasm I expected, and the other players got a big kick out of this. The thing I like about this is the fact that we have the kids' attention on the procedure.

The coaches have picked these 10 openers. How are we going to get the players to buy into these plays and to take ownership of the plays? We do a thing called *move the field*. If we play on Saturday, we do it on Thursday. You would have to back it up to fit your schedule.

Looking at the chart, you can see the first play is on our two-yard line. Do we run the openers in this situation? No. That is an extenuating circumstance, and that is a black zone play. By running the openers, I am also getting to fudge a little and work on our number one play in the black zone.

If you look at the number two play we run, it is the second play on the chart that we run as well. It is a double-move play. We make a decision that we are going to run that play on a first-down play where we have a second-and-one situation. If it is third-and-one, we are still going to run the play. What if it is fourth-and-one? If we are on the plus side of the field, ok. We have made the decision in the coaching office in our planning session. I have learned the decisions we make in the locker room are a lot better than the ones we make on the field. In the locker room, you are calm and you have your emotions under control. If I could take back some of the decisions I have made when my emotions have gotten the best of me, I might not have screwed up the plays. The decisions you make ahead of time will be the best calls most of the time.

In the outside column where we have comments, we have a 1 or a 2. We feel it is important to let the second-team players get into the game in

#	H	D/D	P	Formation/ Play	Defense	Com
1	L	-2	12	(Trade) Rt Wing 32		1
2	R	-12	12	Dark Lt Pistol 73 Hold Wave & Go		1
3	R	-12	12	Roger - 28		2
4	L	-18	12K	Cluster Lt 29 Dummy		1
5	L	-18	10	Dbl Rt Gun - 20 Kill		2
6	R	-22	12C	Bubble Rt Home - 38 Man Kill		1
7	R	-30	BU	Bubble Rt		1
8	L	-30	10	Doubles 73 "4"		1
9	R	-35	12L	Roger Love 28 Extra		1
				Halftime / Flip		
10	R	40	11	Trips Lt Yac 73 Y Wheel		1
11	L	40	12	Lou Rifle - 33 Nkd Smash		1
12	L	40	12	Louie Rac 39 Man		1
13	R	35	13O	Hurricane Lt 39 Jet		1
14	L	25	11	Trips Rt Gun - 33		2
15	R	15	12J	Lou Sq - 72 Dbl Post / Reno		1
16	L	8	12	Louie Rifle 33		1
17	R	7	13H	Dk Lt Flex - 73 Hold Seattle		1

Chart #3. Move the Field Script—Implement Plays/Do Not Omit Regular Plays—#1 Scout

a few of those situations. You always have some 2s that are 1s. We want to let everyone be included. Those plays were decided on when we were off the field. The coaches are running in subs just as they do in the latter part of the game. I cannot tell you how many times we have screwed up the substitutions and I really got upset, and we started over. I let them know they made a mistake. Is that mean? Would you rather have your rear end chewed out on Wednesday or Thursday night instead of game day? I know which day I would prefer.

This is a full-speed drill. It is just like a game. I may throw the best player we have out of the game. I may say, "I do not like your body language."

They ask me what I am talking about. I tell them, "You know what I am talking about." Now, if you throw your best player out, you better have a way to get him back in the game.

After play number nine, we take a halftime. All the players can go off the field and get a drink. I think this is a great idea. The players get together on the sideline and talk about what is going on later on that night or the next day. I like this because there is some confusion going on over on that sideline. After a few minutes, I will blow the whistle and we will move the ball down the field.

If you will look at play 14, we are on the 25-yard line. How many of you start your red zone offense on the 25-yard line? We start on the 25 instead of the 20-yard line. We want to score touchdowns. We feel we have more room starting from the 25-yard line than we have from the 20-yard line. The closer you get to the goal line, the harder it is to throw the ball for a touchdown. For years, we used the 20-yard line, but now it is the 25-yard line for our red zone.

I think the toughest play to call is third-and-five yards to go on the five-yard line. That is tough. We decide what that play is going to be before we get into the situation. We do it by running it in practice and having our play selected so everyone knows what we are doing. That can promote a great discussion. When we get through discussing the openers on Thursday morning, then we have a staff meeting at 8 a.m., and we are in the offensive room by 8:10. We put the offensive script on the board. We get this done in about one hour. They have to get all of the info ready to be printed and set up with the new technology.

Some coaches may not have time to get everyone together during school. I have talked to some coaches that stay after practice the night before and work on the plays. One coach sent out for dinner for all of the coaches so they could stay and work on the openers. Another coach had food ordered for the families of all the coaching staff and they ate outside when the weather was good. They got the planning done, and they had their families around them while they worked. I knew that coach had it. The one way to bribe coaches is to feed them.

We run the plays against the defense in the openers. We are running full speed, but we are not tackling. We are in shoulder pads and shorts.

When we go to the hotel the night before the game, we put on the film of the openers we ran the day before. We select plays and we show them plays. We will compliment them if they make a good block. On the other hand, we try to brainwash them. I will tell them that we look so quick. I have seen us run a Thursday script where we completed very few passes. Everything was a short dump pass here and another one on the other side. I did not put the incomplete passes in the film. If we have a nice screen pass, I will include that in the film. We try to make this a very upbeat, positive session. We try to reinforce what we are going to do and stress to them that we are going to do it even better in the game.

We list the openers again. We let them know the process: We presented them, we practiced them, and now we are reviewing them. They let us know they have the plays down the way we have covered them.

If we run a formation that is not one that we have used a great deal of the time, we will show them how the defense will align against that set two or three times in the film. We give them a synopsis of what we are going to do so we are ready to go.

You must fine-tune the special plays. I am a big believer in *trick plays*. We have won four games in five years with a trick play that busted the game open for us. They are plays we practice every night. They are plays the kids have fun with in running them. We usually show them a trick play the night before a game when we scored on a trick play that scored a touchdown. It is not part of the openers, but we want to be all-inclusive with what we have. You have your checklist, and you make sure everything is ready to go, and you go win.

In almost everything we show the kids, we have something superimposed with us ahead on the scoreboard. With the technology today, you can do that. We may show a star player with the ball in his hands or something successfully oriented. The players can visualize along with us.

My favorite saying about football is this: "It is not that hard." When you win a game, it is not that hard. The offense is not that hard and the defense is not that hard. It is a matter of getting the players to understand what you are doing and getting them to do it fast.

Now is the fun part. We are going to look at our openers against Navy from two years ago. We beat Navy two years in a row, and they were good teams that won two bowl games. We beat them 31-30 and 35–28. When you give the ball up to them, you are not getting it back. The first game we punted twice, and the second game we punted once. We put a lot of quality preparation in for this game, perhaps more so than we put in others. We knew they had a good offense and we were not going to get the ball back if we punted the ball to them.

I want to thank you very much for your attention. You are welcome to come visit us anytime. If we can help you in any way, let us know. Thank you very much.

TEAM CONCEPTS AND PATTERN-MATCH COVERAGES

University of Alabama

I certainly appreciate being back in Pittsburgh because this is about 100 miles from where I grew up. A big day for me was to go see the Pittsburgh Pirates one time a year. I can give you the entire lineup of the 1960 World Champions. It is great to come back home. It is interesting to hear people talk about winning two national championships at two different schools. I am sure there are a lot of coaches in this room who have won championships and a lot of coaches who have had some tough times.

Believe me, we have had our share of tough times. The first year at Alabama, we lost to The University of Louisiana at Monroe in Bryant-Denny Stadium. I thought I was going to be run out of town. There are high expectations at Alabama, and it is tough to live in the shadow of Bear Bryant. I have been on both sides of the winning and losing.

I have a tremendous amount of respect for what you do. There is no one except my parents that had a greater influence on me than my high school coach did. Sometimes, coaches get caught up in the clutter and criticism from the parents, community, and the press. You are having an impact on guys that you are committed to helping. The influence you have on them is more than you know or realize. You are teachers, and there is nothing more important than what you do as coaches.

The kids are different. They grow up wanting a lot of immediately self-gratification. They do not have too much commitment to anything, and they do not have perseverance to stick with anything. We teach those things as coaches. We teach commitment and perseverance. It is very important in terms of consistency and performance that goes into being successful.

I appreciate what you do. You engage with them and take an interest in what they are doing. You inspire them. You have to make it about them sometimes. Everybody is self-absorbed. What is that? It is the idea of "How does it affect me?" The players that you coach think the same way. When you get a player who gets upset when you move him from one team to the other or from one position to another, remember he is no different than you are. That is the way we all are. Sometimes, we have to make it about them, and give them a good reason why, and tell them how it is going to benefit them. That is what inspires them.

Everyone is an individual, but you do not want his or her selfishness to upset what you are trying to accomplish with your team. I think it is important for us to inspire players to do the right things. They do it because of the example you set and the principles and values you define in your organization. You can impact what somebody does in the leadership you provide and leadership you have within your organization to the values and principles. That is important to having a team, and it is important to being successful.

I worked for Bill Belichick in Cleveland. He put up a sign, which was the only one in the entire building. It reads: "Do Your Job." That went for everyone in the organization. He defined what everyone's job was and a standard of excellent that everyone should do in completing the job. He defined the quality control of how to evaluate whether the job was done on not.

He was talking about accountability. You have to define it, and people have to know what to expect and what you expect from them. That is important to get what you want. It is important to have a successful program because of what we do for our community and our state. Over 31 million people watched our SEC championship game and 51 million people watched the national championship game. How our team represents that says a lot about the state of Alabama, the University, their families, and everyone else involved.

When I was at LSU, Jesse Jackson talked to our team. If we played on Saturday night at LSU stadium, you could stand at the 50-yard line and smell the bourbon. He told me that our stadium was closer to God than his church. What he said was the rules are clearly defined, everyone has a common goal, and everybody is together trying to accomplish that goal. Blacks with whites, rich with poor, and it did not matter whether they were on the field or in the stands. Everyone in the stadium was together with a common goal. He said he did not get that in his church. He said there may be nothing in your community that can get it better than your team.

I am telling you this so you will understand how much I respect what we do and how much I respect what you do. It is so important to our communities to bring people together. If you do it the right way, it can have a tremendously positive impact.

I am going to tell you the reason we are going to be successful. I know people think we are successful because we had two number-one recruiting classes in a row. The first year we recruited at Alabama, we only had two players who were good because we did not get started recruiting until January 10. The second year, we had a number-one class, and there were some good players in that class. Last year, we had the number-one class, and those players were freshmen. Out of that bunch, only one of them played a significant role, and six more freshmen played on the kickoff teams.

The reason we got better at Alabama was because of the players. The players who were there got better because of how we developed them and what they did. They got better as people, students, and football players. It all matters and counts because "who you are, is more important than what you do." The individuals on your team make the team what it is. The team does not make them. They make the team because of their character and attitude.

The human condition is to survive. A lot of us as coaches think the human condition is to be the best you can be. How many people will make an A on a midterm test, take two weeks off, and do nothing constructive? They take the next test, make a C, and are happy they have a B average. I know a lot of them. Most people I know are like that. It is not natural to win a championship. It is not natural to be the best you can be. That is because the human condition is to survive.

As coaches, how do we change all that negativism? The first thing you have to do is define what you want. It is as Bill Belichick asked, "What kind of team do you want?" I tell our players all the time that we want a team that nobody wants to play. They do not want to play us because of the effort we play with, the toughness, and the discipline that we have. None of those things takes any ability. It takes no ability to give effort. Toughness is not God-given; it is a choice. The discipline to execute is a habit.

To do those things, you have to be in great physical condition. We loaf when we get tired. We make mental errors when we get tired and we will not be able to execute. The great Vince Lombardi said, "Fatigue makes cowards of us all." When you are tired, you do not play with the same kind of toughness. We must be a well-conditioned team. Our team knows how we are going to play, and we will be relentless in the way we play. We are going to dominate the competition in everything we do.

When you dominate someone, you cannot dominate them in the first round. You cannot start to dominate the fight until the 13th or 14th round. It takes a relentless competitive attitude to play like that. You have to play every play of the game as if it has a history or life of its own. Whatever happens on the play before, you forget about it, and line up again to play the next play.

Relentless is like Freddy Krueger. All those horror guys have one thing in common: you cannot kill them. That is how you want your players to compete. In the movies, you think you have Freddy, and his hand comes through the wall and chokes you to death. That is the way we want our team to play. That is the way we want the opponent to feel. Whether we win or lose the down, we are coming back to play with the same kind of effort, toughness, and discipline. The teams we played this year could not match our intensity for 60 minutes.

Everybody talks about how there is no "I" in team, but there is in win. You must have tremendous intensity and a sense of urgency to it right now. You have to play with intelligence and be smart in what you do. That takes a lot of discipline.

We did not have better players than Texas or Florida. Our team had a relentless attitude about what they wanted to accomplish. That is so important to being successful. Sugar Ray Leonard said it the best. The first time he fought Marvin Hagler for the title, he knew the opponent, he worked hard, and he studied and prepared to fight the best fight of his life. He lost the fight. The next time he fought for the championship, he did all the same things. There was a difference. He had a feeling in his heart that he would not be defeated in his effort to do what he wanted to accomplish.

You must have passion to accomplish what you want to do. Part of being a coach is inspiring people. It is important to tie everything within your organization together so you can do it. How many of you in here have a mission statement? We have one at Alabama.

UNIVERSITY OF ALABAMA MISSION STATEMENT

We are going to create an atmosphere and an environment where we can help our players be successful. First as people, second as students, and third to graduate from school and develop a career off the field. We want them to succeed as football players, have an outstanding college career, *be the best they can be, and see if they can develop a football career at the next level. We want to use the resources that we have personally and as an institution to launch their career when they leave the program.*

Everyone in our organization is working toward some part of that statement. We have a pyramid of success that has nothing to do with winning a game. I have a tape I can show you of players, talking about their goals for this season. Not one time did they talk about winning a game. They talked about all the things you have to do to win a game. The word winning is not mentioned. Dominating is mentioned a lot.

We have to get away from all the external, result-oriented types of things because that is the world we live in. That is what creates expectations and sometimes leads to performances in a negative way with the players. You have to get that out of your program.

We never talk about the other team. The other team is technical for us. We talk about their plays, defense, and coverages they play. We do not talk about the other team at all. We do not control what the other team does. We can only control what we do.

Until you play together, you will never win together. The first thing we have on the pyramid is to be a team. Together, everyone will accomplish more. We break that down to respect and trust. If you have two players fighting on the field, they are fighting because they do not respect each other. They do not respect each other as people and as someone trying to do their job. They do not trust in the principles and values of the organization, and they do not buy into them. Buying into those things is the only way you can have trust on the team.

We are self-absorbed people. They are not going to put you before the success of the team. We had six All-American players on our team. That is the most in the history of the NCAA for a first-team selection. I told them if we have team success, the individual recognition will come. We also had the Heisman Trophy winner along with the Butkus

Award winner. None of those players would have won those awards if we had not won 14 games. Every one of them said he "accepted the award on behalf of all my teammates that made it possible for me."

If you continue to do the same thing you have always done, you will continue to get the same results. That is guaranteed. That works both ways. If you do the right things, you will get good results. If you do the wrong things, you are not getting good results, and you should change some of the thing you do. We do everything the same at Alabama that we did at LSU. We got the same results, too.

You must have a positive energy in your organization relative to how people feel about what they are doing. Your organization must be happy doing what they are doing. You have to know what you and the organization are selling and who is buying. When our players have a bad practice, I ask them what they are selling today. I want to know if they are affecting a teammate in a positive way. You cannot be a great player if you do not affect your team in a positive way.

I tell our coaches all the time, if they are not coaching it, they are letting it happen. We have a rule on our team that we do not wear earrings at a team function. If I walked by three players with earrings in, and no coach said anything to them, what should I think about that coach? You are supposed to take your hats off when you come into the office because it is a place of business. If they do not do that, whose fault is it? If they do not coach it, they are letting it happen.

If a player does not run through the cones, you have to address that. However, you do not have to say it in a negative way. There are all kinds of ways to address the problem. You could say, "You are better than that," or "We do not do it that way," or "You have to finish being a good player." There are a lot of positive corrections you can use.

The best way to be successful is know what you want to do, put all your positive energy toward that, and do not worry about any external problems. A coach has to be focused on how to get his players to play the best they can for 60 minutes. He cannot be focused on the criticism he gets in the media.

Every play has a history and life of its own. If they play like that, I can live with the results. You cannot listen to the bad things or the good things because they do not know you. You have to focus on the process to have consistency in your organization. Positive energy and attitude is a big part of that.

You must take responsibility for your own determination. That is accountability. People cannot be accountable for what they do not know. The sign that Belichick put up has to be defined. When you define the talent you are looking for, you know what to look for. If you go to recruit a player and do not define what you want, what are you going to get? If you do not define for your players what is important and what you want, what should you expect to get? You have to do it with the coaches, players, and everyone involved with the organization. If you do not do that, then how can people be accountable for what they do not know?

They also know they will be confronted if it is not done right. If you are going to be a leader, you need to be doing that. If you are a leader, you cannot care what everyone else thinks. You have to be fair, honest, treat people with respect and dignity, and you do not have to do anything in a negative way.

The hardest part of the plan is to dominate the competition. They are trying to dominate you. The way you dominate starts with knowing what you want to do and having the passion to do it. Passion to me is Ray Charles singing "America the Beautiful." He is blind and cannot see what he is singing about, but he has great passion for the music and the song.

You must have passion for what you do, and people will see it. What you do will rub off on others. It is a commitment to a standard of excellence. What the Marine said was exactly right, and he said it better than I could. The commitment has to be defined and established so people know what to expect. If you do not make the players run through the line, they will not do it.

When we run sprints, I tell the players to run as fast as they can. Some of them, when they get ahead, look over at the player next to them. They even slow down as they beat him. Who is determining how good they can be, themselves or the how fast the player next to them is? I do not care if he wins the race or not. I want him to run as fast as he can run.

When I went to Alabama, I told the team to line up on the line, and we were going to run ten 10-yard sprints. They had to line up with their hand on the line and finish through the 10 yards. We had to run 29 sprints to get 10 perfect 10s. The entire team ran. You have to do it that way. If you get a penalty in a game, the entire team gets penalized. They do not assess the penalty against one player. Little things are important, and the team is the important item, not the player.

You cannot have a good program if you do not work. You have to earn it. You reap what you sow, and you get out of it what you put into it. We are a "hard work" program. The reason I got here when I did was because I was not leaving until we were done with our fourth-quarter program. That is our off-season program.

Everything in our program is branded. The fourth quarter stands for discipline, commitment, effort, toughness, and pride. They want to be best they can be and finish everything they can do every time they do it. The indoor program is where it all starts for us. It is hard to do. This is Buck Nystrom's program. We started using his program in 1983. We still run it. He won a national championship doing it. We have won a couple doing it.

The conditioning we are doing now will not have anything to do with the game next season. But it is important to do because we are establishing intangibles that are important to our organization.

You must have perseverance. You have to have bad things happen in your program. We had five players, who had started at one time or another during their career at Alabama, who are no longer on the team. They could have started in the Bowl championship game, but they were no longer on the team. I had to put them off the team. Those players did not do what they were supposed to do. It was not a football issue. It was something outside the program. It was about other rules in the organization. Some of it was academic, but it all counts. We lost those five players and still won the national championship.

Not everything bad that happens is bad. It is an opportunity for everyone else to learn something that can benefit your team and makes it grow. It is the same thing when you do not have success in the game. You do not dwell on it. You learn and teach from it, and you get better because of it. Everybody understands the responsibility of what their job is, and you show them. That is how you should grade the film. How many still grade films and give your players grades?

When I was at Michigan State, we played Illinois and got the hell beat out of us. We did not simply lose the game; we got our butts kicked so bad there were no seam left in our pants. The next day, we graded the film, and the linebacker coach had two of the three linebackers with a winning percentage. We gave up 40 points. How could anybody on that defense have a winning performance? I said from that moment forward, no more grades. We grade the defense, and every down-and-distance is a win or loss. Everything is defined as to what the individual's job is.

If the situation is first-and-10, and we gave up four yards, somebody screwed up. I look at the film and list the individual performance of who did what. I write it down in a column: "#5 got lost contain, #58 got hooked." That is why the play was not successful. The next day, we show the players that sheet. We tell them they do not have to make every play, but you have to do your job. It takes a lot of perseverance. You cannot be frustrated and get upset when things go bad.

There is a book out there called *The Road Less Traveled*. A priest gave it to me when I was defensive coordinator at Michigan State. He told me it was a spiritual-development and positive-attitude book. He told me to read it, and it would help me a lot. I got the book, and the first statement in the book is a negative statement. It said, "Life is difficult." The book was about so much more. If you think things are going to be difficult and you are going to have to overcome adversity, it is a part of building character and being successful.

You have to fail to have success. That is how you learn and grow. When the recruits come in, they want to know if they are going to play as a freshman. I told them that we played four freshmen last year and that was more than anyone in the country was. However, four out of 25 is not very good odds. We only played one last year. I ask them if they were a better player as a freshman than they were as a senior. They started to laugh as if it was a dumb question. I followed that up with, "What makes you think you will be better as a freshman than as a senior in college?"

They think because they are a five- or four-star player they can make an impact on an established program. That is not fair to the player because the expectation level is so high. That sets the player up for frustration.

The first question I asked quarterbacks in the NFL draft was, "What is the hardest thing you had ever had to overcome in your life." If the player could not tell me, we were not going to consider him as a draft choice. How can a player play the quarterback position, distribute the ball every play in a game, and not know how to overcome any kind of adversity or the negativism he has to deal with? When you play quarterback, you get more praise than you do deserve, but you also get more criticism.

I am constantly talking to our team about pride and performance. I want them to be as good as they can be and not worry about winning. If you can get players to do that, you will be successful. I tell my coaches all the time, if a player does something right, tell him. That gives him confidence. Everyone has self-imposed limitations. The self-imposed limitations are "I cannot."

I am going to talk some football to you now. You can play coverages three ways. You can play zone, man, or pattern-match man. Pattern-match man is a coverage that plays the pattern after the pattern distribution. That means you pick up in man coverage after the receivers make their initial breaks and cut. We number receivers from the outside going inside. If the #1 receiver crosses with the #2 receiver, we do not pick up the man coverage until they define where they are going.

If you play a three-deep zone, this helps you play against spread offenses. In high school, the hash marks are 17 yards from the sidelines. The numbers are nine yards to the top of the number from the sideline. The bottom of the number is seven yards from the sidelines. We need to know those measurements so we can talk about divider in the outside third. The dividers are the relative distance the corners are from the middle-of-the-field safety.

If the receiver aligns outside the divider, we want the corner to align on the inside of the divider. If the receiver aligns inside the divider, the corner aligns outside the divider. The divider is one yard on top of the numbers (Diagram #1). If the ball is in the middle of the field and the receiver aligns outside the divider, the corner aligns inside the divider.

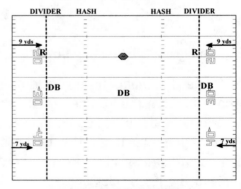

Diagram #1. Divider Middle

If the ball is on the hash mark, the defender playing the boundary divider is eight yards from the sidelines or the middle of the numbers on the field (Diagram #2). The divider to the wideside of the field moves midway between the numbers and the hash mark. That puts the divider four yards outside the hash mark.

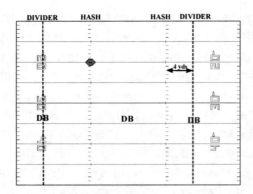

Diagram #2. Dividers Hash

We play country cover 3 (Diagram #3). Offenses attack cover 3 with four-verticals, double post, deep-sail routes, and four streaks. In this defense, we have two hook defenders, two curl/flat defenders, and a safety in the middle of the field. The corners play a press-bail technique. They align in press coverage, and bail out at the last minute. That means we have four down linemen, with four underneath defenders, and a three-deep secondary.

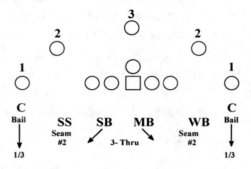

Diagram #3. Country Cover 3

We define the seams on the field as the high school hash marks. If the #2 receiver runs the seam, the curl/flat defender drops down the seam. If the #2 receiver goes vertical, the defender man-matches his pattern and plays like it is cover 1. The corner plays off his divider and squeezes the #1 receiver inside from a bail position or an off-the-ball position. The hook players have to know one thing: they play the hook, but they have to play the #3 receiver wherever he runs through. When the offense runs four verticals, the running back comes through the line and becomes a checkdown receiver. The hook players are zoning that pattern.

If the offense runs a combination pattern, we have different reads (Diagram #4). The formation in

the diagram is a 2x2 tight-end set. The split receiver to the right runs an out pattern. The slot receiver runs a seam. The tight end runs a crossing pattern, and the flanker runs an in route. The seam defender and the hook defender have the #2 receiver bracketed on short routes. If he runs an outside a pattern, the seam defender has him. If he runs inside, the hook defender plays him. The seam defender gives an "under" call to the hook defender if he runs inside. If he runs vertical, the slot defender plays him man-to-man.

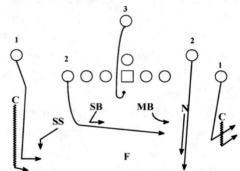

Diagram #4. Country Under Coverage

Since the #2 receiver goes vertical, the hook defender looks for the #3 receiver. He is playing a zone, looking for #3. The tight end is the #2 receiver. The tight end runs a crossing pattern to the inside. The seam defender, who is covering the tight end, gives an "under" call to the hook linebacker and drops into his curl zone under the #1 receiver. The hook defenders play zone on the tight end and pass him from one zone to the other zone. The corners are man-to-man on the #1 receivers, but there is a deep safety in the middle of the field. In this defense, we have better run force because we can bring the safeties down wherever we want them. In addition, we can match all the patterns from this coverage.

Against the trips set, the assignments are the same (Diagram #5). The corner takes the outside receiver, and the seam defender aligns on the #2 receiver. The #3 receiver to that side is the tight end. The hook defender has the #3 receiver on the run-through. To the single-receiver side, the corner has the #1 receiver man-to-man with a middle-of-the-field safety. The backside hook and seam defenders are in zone coverage. The safety in the middle favors the trips side of the formation. We can play pattern match out of this set or skate the coverage.

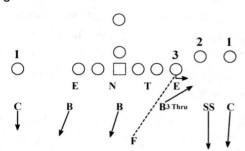

Diagram #5. Country to Trips

Everything on this coverage relates to the speed of the #3 receiver to the flat. If the linebacker matches up with the #3 to the flat, we pattern match and play the defense. If the offense floods the zone, we can soften the flat coverage and play under coverage with the safety taking the flat. That depends on the release of the #2 receiver. This is a much better way to play three-deep zone and just as easy to teach.

The next question is how to pressure from this type of coverage scheme. We play this coverage with our fire-zone scheme. We have three under defenders instead of four in our fire-zone blitzes. The hook defender only has a "3-through" rule if the back releases. I will show you America's fire-zone blitz (Diagram #6). That brings the outside and inside linebackers off the edge. The defensive end and tackle to that side slants inside. The nose on the opposite side slants around the outside for contain.

the middle or play the flat. The linebacker who is not blitzing has the #3 receiver through. The corner is man-to-man on the #1 receiver. If we get a "man" call, the strong safety rolls down and takes the #2 receiver man-to-man. The backside linebacker plays the #3 receiver through, and the drop end is a wall/flat player. In the man call, we can bump the receivers to the next defender. That means if the receiver releases on an inside route, the defender calls "under" and turns him over to the next defender. That rule includes the corner on this defense.

If the #2 receiver goes inside, the strong safety calls "under" and turns him over to the linebacker. The linebacker takes him. If he continues to run across the field, the linebacker gives the "under" call and turns him over to the drop end. We run a zone principle with the linebackers and drop end. We end up in a three-under, three-deep with the corner playing man-to-man.

There is a situation when we play a zone scheme to the strongside. If the offense has two backs in the backfield, we make the "zone" call (Diagram #7). The inside linebacker has "3-through." If the #2 receiver on the back of the I formation goes strong, we have a problem. We makes a "Saints" call, which is the zone call. It is like making an "under" call before it happens. The safety becomes the flat zone defender in the strong flat zone. That releases the tight end to the inside linebacker if he makes an inside move.

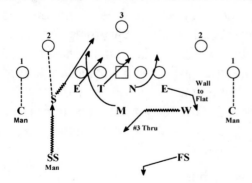

Diagram #6. Fire-Zone Blitz

On the fire zones, the seam defenders are "wall/flat" players. They wall the receivers out of

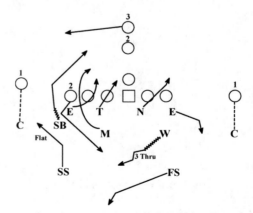

Diagram #7. Zone Call

The other call we make is for a single receiver to the backside of the formation to align in a reduced split. This generally happens on the backside of a triple set. If that happens, the corner gives a "2" call to the "#3 to hook" defender (Diagram #8). In this coverage, if split receiver goes inside, the corner calls "under" and becomes "the #3 to hook" defender. The linebacker picks up the under route by the split receiver. It does not affect the wall/flat player.

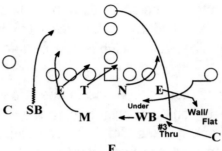

Diagram #8. 2 Adjustment

Texas ran a 2x2 formation for most of the game. The quarterback was in the shotgun with the back aligned to one side or the other (Diagram #9). At some times, the #2 receiver was a tight end. We played a 3 technique to the side of the back and a 2i technique away from him. The corner to the side of the back played an outside alignment on the wideout. To the other side, we played an inside alignment. The reason we did that was to take away the now routes or the bubble pass. Now routes are hitches and one-step patterns. We played split safeties in the secondary. The outside linebackers played outside the box in walk-away positions on the slot receivers. We played a five-man box.

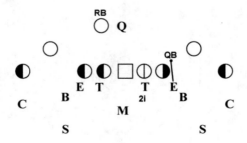

Diagram #9. Texas Defense

The defensive end aligned on the outside shoulders of the tackles. The backside end played the quarterback on the zone read. The end to the side of the back played normal. If they ran the zone play, the center tried to reach the 2 technique. When that happened, the 2i defender became a two-gap defender by pushing the offensive guard into the B gap. We played the Mike linebacker behind the center. We played a five-man box the entire night, and the only play that hurt us was the jet sweep. That happened because we had our split safeties on the receivers.

We can play any type of combination we want, but against them we put the corner to the side of the back in an outside bracket position on the #1 receiver. In that coverage, the backer is the force player on the run. If we double bracket, the corner is outside force on the run. We have an adjustment we play called "cut the corner" (Diagram #10). In that coverage, the corner and safety play the defense like cover 2, but we are man-matching in the coverage. If the #1 receiver goes up the field, it is man coverage. If he goes to the flat, it becomes a zone.

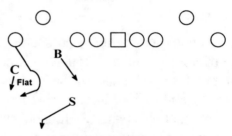

Diagram #10. Cut the Corner

Do you have any other questions? This is late for me. Everybody thinks I work all night like Belichick. I leave the office every night at 10:00. I go to bed at 11:00, and I am up at 6:00. I am an obsessive personality. I try to do everything the same all the time. Every day, I work on the same thing from Monday through Friday of a game week. I work on it at the same time and in the same order. I do not get distracted, and no one bothers me in that time frame. I have a set time when I meet the press and other people.

I will be honest with you. I would rather be the secondary coach than the head coach. I love coaching the secondary. That is what I always coached, but it does not pay as well. Therefore, I took the other job and still coach the secondary. I appreciate your attention. Thank you.

THE PRO STYLE RUNNING GAME

University of Washington

There are a lot of philosophical things I could get into tonight. I love football. I hope that you guys do, too, and that is why you are here. I am a firm believer that the more things you do well, the harder you are to defend. You have to identify what you do well to keep from reaching for straws. Let me tell you something that will lead us into what I am going to talk about tonight.

I was born and raised in a pro-style offense. I played it in high school, junior college, and in the Canadian Football League. I played for the only team in the league that aligned the quarterback under the center. I got a chance to call my own plays at quarterback. It was like old-school football with Sammy Baugh. I went through Brigham Young in a pro-style offense. Every coaching position I had, we ran a pro-style offense.

When I talk pro-style offense, every play starts with two backs in the backfield. The formation was an I formation with near backs, far backs, and split backs with the quarterback under the center. We ran the football and used the play-action pass.

After seven years at USC and a great run with Pete Carroll, I took the job at the University of Washington. I took over a football team that had been a spread-oriented football team for the past six years. They were in the shotgun set with a zone-read scheme, running the option. That is who they were and what they were about.

I believe part of my job is to get our players ready for the next level of football. I want to train and teach the athletes I have so they have a shot at playing pro football.

UNIVERSITY OF WASHINGTON QUARTERBACK PHILOSOPHY

Personality
- Be a leader on and off the field
- Compete
  - ✓ Never settle for second place.
  - ✓ Compete in everything you do (drills, conditioning etc.).
- Be prepared
  - ✓ Be early and alert.
  - ✓ Know your assignment.
  - ✓ Spend the extra time it takes to be a champion.
- Have a good attitude
  - ✓ Embrace new ideas and concepts.
  - ✓ Be coachable.
  - ✓ Respect yourself and your teammates.
- Be tough
  - ✓ Mental: Be the rock. Handle success and adversity.
  - ✓ Physical: Always be there.
- Be a football junkie (the great ones are)
  - ✓ Study film: We can always do more.
  - ✓ Strive for a good work ethic and consistency: Is that you?
- Have confidence and energy
  - ✓ Give others something to believe in.
  - ✓ Be excited about the opportunity to play. It's contagious.
  - ✓ Enjoy what you do.

The quarterback has to be a leader both on and off the field. You do not develop leadership; it is innate. Some players have it, and some do not. They have to be the best competitors on the football team. We want them to compete in every drill and every conditioning drill. The player's will to win is higher than anyone else's is.

We want them to be early and alert. This may sound funny, but no quarterback will show up in our building until he has showered. I want the quarterback clean-shaven, alert, and ready to begin work. When they get to that point, they will know their assignment. Their willingness to spend the extra time to be a champion will increase.

When we talk about attitude check, it has to do with their ability to embrace new ideas and concepts. I believe that all of us at some point have ADD (Attention-Deficient Disorder). I test our kids for it because I need to know their threshold and when they lose it. I am continually looking for fresh ideas and new concepts for our players. I want it fresh for them.

Toughness is an important trait for any quarterback. He has to be mentally tough as well as physically tough. You have to know if your quarterback is mentally tough enough to play the position. You have to coach your quarterback hard. I think everyone feels the quarterback is taken care of and babied. That does not happen on our field. The quarterback is getting coached and coached hard. That is how I find out if he can handle 85,000 screaming idiots when we go on the road. If he cannot handle me at practice, he will not be able to handle a third-and-four at Autzen Stadium in Oregon.

We want to know if he is physically tough enough. I want a quarterback who will refuse to come out of the game unless I take him out. He will not come out of the game regardless of the amount of physical abuse he is taking. I do not care if he has a broken leg; he has to make me take him out. Our quarterback has to show energy and our team feeds off it.

Game Management

- Take care of the football.
  - ✓ Ball security: Exchange, handoffs, "dawg claw"
  - ✓ Passing game: Decision-making. It's okay to throw the ball away.
- Master the situations of the game.
  - ✓ Understand down-and-distance.
  - ✓ Master the two-minute and four-minute drills.
  - ✓ Red zone: Touchdown or checkdown mentality
  - ✓ Understand the objective of backed up, short yardage, and goal line.
  - ✓ Always know the clock.
- Control the huddle.
  - ✓ How you present the play determines the success of the play.
  - ✓ Tempo: Get in, and get out; maximize our opportunities.
  - ✓ You are the coach on the field.
- Understand defense.
  - ✓ Must be able to identify fronts and coverages.
  - ✓ Where are the weaknesses, and how do we exploit them?
  - ✓ Dog/Blitz: What are the keys? Where are the soft spots?

From a game-management standpoint, the quarterback has to know how to take care of the ball. The quarterback must have the "dawg claw." If he is hit from behind on a blitz, he has to hang on to the ball. Ball security is tremendously important to the success of any team.

In the passing game, the hardest thing a coach has to do is get the young quarterback to throw the ball away. It is okay to throw the ball away. The competitive players do not ever want to give up. They always want to make a play. That is not a bad trait to have, but there is a fine line in forcing the ball and throwing it away. It is the hardest thing for a quarterback to learn.

The game to coaches is made up of special situations. It is not just running plays. We never practice random plays. Everything we practice is focused on a situation in the game. We cannot get the point across to everyone on the field. The quarterback controls the huddle, and he has to master the game situations to make the scheme work. The quarterbacks are the coaches on the field. They know all the buzzwords for the special situations. They know the tips and reminders for the offensive line when we get to a goal-line situation. They have to know it all. It is not about throwing curl routes. It is about embracing and embodying the position.

When you run the offense, you have to understand fronts and the pressures that come out of them. You have to know coverages and their strengths and weaknesses. You have to know the keys and where the soft spots are in the coverage. Between every series on game day, there is a lot of dialog on the sidelines. It is not a dictatorship at the University of Washington. There is constant dialog so we are on the same page as to what we are trying to accomplish.

Run Game

- This is not a playoff.
- Get us out of a bad play and into a good play
- Get your block. Carry out fakes, and set up play-action pass.
- Work off of the clock be disciplined with your feet.
- Work to get the ball to the back with depth and vision.

We do not have time to waste plays. The NCAA keeps making it harder with the clock rules in a game. They want to squeeze the game down so you cannot waste time. We have to get out of bad plays and into good ones. We give the quarterback the ability to do that.

Running the type of offense we run, we depend on the play-action pass. The quarterback has to get his block. That means he has to carry out his fakes and set up the play-action pass. We have to

establish the running game so we can use the play-action pass. The quarterback starts setting that up early in the game with his ball handling and faking.

Passing Game

- Incompletions are okay. Avoid interceptions and sacks.
- Understand the objective of the play: efficient or explosive.
- Know where all hot receivers are. We must handle pressure.
- Get good pre- and post-snap reads.
  - ✓ Front to secondary scan
  - ✓ Read key
  - ✓ Film study (What did you learn to help you in the game?)
- Trust your eyes. You must believe what you see.
- Be efficient with reads and progressions.
  - ✓ Get off primary to secondary targets.
  - ✓ Know where all checkdowns are.
  - ✓ Know all alerts, and take advantage of big-play opportunities.

In the passing game, incompletions are good. If the ball is incomplete, it is not intercepted or there is not a sack. In my opinion, every sack in this day and age is the quarterback's fault. The ball should always be thrown away. There should never be a sack. They have to understand the objective of the play. Is the play an efficient, move-the-chains type of play, or are we trying to score? He has to know the objective of the play. He has to know the difference. He has to know where his hot receivers are on all patterns.

Preparation will set you free. The quarterback has to trust his eyes. He cannot guess what is happening. If he cannot see it, nothing good can come from it if he throws it. He has to believe what he sees. I am okay with the first couple of times if the quarterback tells me he did not see it. If the quarterback is good, prepares himself, and understands the play, anticipation will kick in, and he will get to the point of knowing what he sees. If the window is there, he knows it, and he knows if it is not there. When it is not there, he resets his feet and goes to the next progression.

Being efficient with the reads and progression is a huge point for me. That is coaching. If the quarterback becomes a robotic player and is not efficient in his reading ability, he is in trouble. The defense recognizes the pattern and knows where he is going with the ball. They are breaking as the quarterback releases his throws and are knocking them down or intercepting them. He is good in the classroom setting and understands the progression and what we are trying to across. However, he is not efficient on the field. It is your job to keep pushing at them and coaching them to be efficient in their throws.

You have to know where your alerts are and be ready to take advantage of your big play opportunities. If we call a post cut and get zero coverage, we have to throw the ball to the post cut and try to score. We may not hit all of them, but I want the opposing defensive coordinator to know that my quarterback knows what he is doing and that we are going after him.

The difference between a good quarterback and a great quarterback is the ability to check the ball down. If you want to be good you will complete 58 percent of your pass. If you want to be great, you get to 68- to 70-percent completion. The 10 percent comes from the quarterback's ability to find secondary reads and get off the primaries. He has to be willing to check the ball down and maintain drives. That is how you get the first downs to keep the ball moving. By doing the checkdown passes, you keep the defense off the field. That is how the great quarterbacks play. In the Super Bowl, the two quarterbacks who play have the ability to check the ball down. That is why their passing percentage is so high. It is clear to me that is one of the key elements of a quarterback who wants to get the job done. He wants to get the job done so we can be an effective offensive football team.

I run a pro-style offense. That may not be for everybody, but I do believe in the quarterback's ability to lead, manage, and control what we are trying to get done. We are a big tempo-efficiency offense. We want to get in and out of the huddle, and use a lot of personnel groups. If the quarterback cannot handle that, our team is not going to handle it. The quarterback has to understand the entire game and embrace everything for us to be an effective football team.

That was the biggest challenge we faced coming from USC to Washington. I grew up with this offense since the sixth grade. This is California football.

Everything I do has a fullback in the offense. We are a two-back team. The fullback has to be a versatile football player. He has to do three things for the offense. He has to block. I do not need a killer. I need a player who will put his face on the defender, get his hands inside, and work his feet. This player has to be smart enough to align all over the field, shift, go in motion, and do different things in the formation. The third thing I want him to have is hands and some athleticism. He does not have to be the best player on the team, but I would like him to be a high school basketball player. He is 5'11" to 6'0", weighs around 235 pounds, and can move.

Our primary play is a weakside isolation play. We call it "13/12 BOB." I know this is not reinventing the wheel. It is not new but this play is about attitude. We are a weakside isolation team and a strongside power team. I want to give you some coaching points for the play. When we get the over front, we like to oversplit the tackle to the backside bubble (Diagram #1). The objective is to make a bigger B gap. We use an A-block combo with the center and playside guard up to the Mike linebacker. The playside tackle man-blocks the defensive end. The backside guard and tackle run a deuce combo block on the 3-technique tackle up to the Sam linebacker. The tight end blocks the defensive end in a 6-technique position on his nose.

The fullback leads on the Will linebacker. The fullback attacks the outside shoulder of the Will linebacker. By attacking the outside shoulder, we want to widen him. If he is a box player and spilling the ball to the Mike linebacker, I want to create as much room in the B gap as I can.

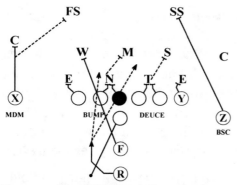

Diagram #1. 13 BOB vs. Over 4-3

The fullback has to be aware of the free safety rolling down to the box. We need to know if the Will linebacker is spilling the ball to the free safety. I will talk more about this is a minute.

The running back uses inside zone footwork to run this play. We do that to simplify our teaching. The running back takes an open step, crosses over, and rolls, aiming at the outside leg of the playside guard. He attacks the B gap and presses the heels of the offensive linemen. He is aware of the Mike linebacker. If the Mike linebacker is a fast-flow player coming over the top of the playside combo block, the running back takes the ball into the backside A gap.

That is why the backside deuce block is so important. We want the backside guard to stay on the double-team and not be too quick to come off for the Sam linebacker. We want to take care of the down lineman first. The 3-technique defender is usually the most physical defender on the line. We want to get physical and knock the defenders off the ball. This is an attitude football play, which illustrates our resolve to play hard-nosed football.

The split end to the outside has to block the secondary force player. He reads the coverage and blocks the corner or the free safety. He has an important block because the play can break to him if it gets past the second level. He blocks the MDM (most dangerous man).

We cannot line up in a 21 personnel group and let teams play seven-man-front football against us. We have to make the defense put one of the safeties into the box to stop us.

If we run the play against the under 4-3, there is little change in the blocking scheme. We have a different set of combos (Diagram #2). The center and backside guard use the ace combo on the nose to the Mike linebacker. The playside guard and tackle are covered by 3- and 5-technique defenders. They have to be alert in this alignment because of the possible pirate spike from the defensive end and tackle. The backside tackle and tight end run a mango block for the 5-technique tackle and Sam linebacker. That is a name for a man scheme. The fullback leads on the Will linebacker, and the tailback takes the same steps into the hole.

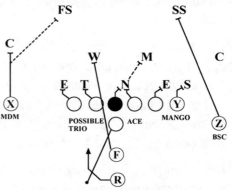

Diagram #2. 13 BOB vs. Under 4-3

We have a possible treo block to the outside. People try to spike the 3 technique into the A gap and try to pick off the center so he cannot get to the Mike linebacker (Diagram #3). When we give the "treo" call, the ace combo of the backside guard and center is called off. The backside guard handles the nose by himself. The center becomes the A-gap blocker and takes the 3 technique on the spike inside. The playside guard reaches the 5 technique as he spikes into the B gap. The tackle steps up and seals the linebacker coming over the top. On the

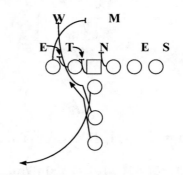

Diagram #3. Treo Scheme

backside, the tight end and tackle have to be alert when the Sam linebacker softens up and gets off the line. In that case, they run a zone scheme for that stunt.

The fullback has to be aware when there is a 3 technique aligned on the guard. He reads the 3 technique for his path to the linebacker. The quarterback has to be aware of the 3 technique because the fullback's track may change and get tighter to the quarterback. The last thing the quarterback wants is a collision with the fullback with the ball extended. The quarterback has to clear the fullback before he extends the ball to the running back.

The reason we run this play is what it says about us. It is a downhill, smash-mouth football play. It establishes an attitude about our football team. I hope that we can continue to get better at these plays at the University of Washington. There are some variations of it I want to show you.

Off the BOB play, we have a draw (Diagram #4). Nothing changes with the blocking assignments. The only difference is we pass-set in the offensive line. When we run this play, we like to open the formation up. In Diagram #4, we play with three wide receivers and no tight end. The coverage we see in the secondary is some kind of quarter coverage. The strong and free safeties are generally at eight yards reading the tackles. They want to get down in the box on any runs or double up on the outside receivers in the pass game.

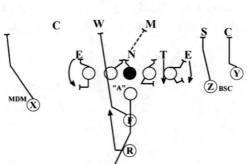

Diagram #4. 13 BOB Draw vs. Under

The tackles set outside and invite the defensive end up the field on the pass rush. The backside guard

sets inside on the 3-technique defender and takes him to the outside. The ability of the nose guard will determine how we will block him. Normally if he is more to the guard than the center, we step the center into the backside A-gap and up on the Mike linebacker. This is an easier way to block the line of scrimmage. If your offensive line is not quite as good as the defensive line, this gives them a better chance.

The quarterback does not ball hold the ball up and he leaves the center. As soon as his second step hits the ground, he is looking for the back and handing the ball off. That allows him enough time to clear the fullback and find the back.

We are firm believers in the outside stretch play with the lead fullback. That is why we look for fullbacks who are the athletic type, who have some feel, and have some savvy to them. I do not want a 250-pound lughead. I want a fullback who can understand what the tailback is looking at.

The play is 16 force (Diagram #5). The tight end and playside tackle run a triple scheme. The tackle's aiming point is the outside number of the defensive end. If there is a 3 technique on the guard, the tackle drop-steps and blocks any 6, 7, or 9 technique to his outside. He works for outside leverage on that defender. The tight end wants to get in a position on the defensive end so that he is a half man inside of the tight end. He is blocking the outside half of the defensive end. That allows the offensive tackle to get his outside leverage. He wants to knock the defensive end's shoulder up so the offensive tackle can overtake that block.

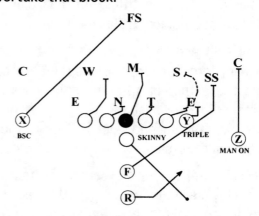

Diagram #5. 16 Force vs. Over

The defensive end can fight hard to the outside. If he does, we use the term "distort the read." That means the tackle knows he cannot get to the outside number. He punches the defensive out on top of the tight end. The tailback read for us is the first down lineman to the outside. If the tackle cannot reach that man, he launches him onto the tight end and the back will turn up inside the defensive end.

This is a huge coaching point you want to remember. Do not get caught saying the ball has to go outside. It does not have to go outside. That is where we want the play to go, but we can take it inside. The fullback and tailback read the same keys. On the third step, they make their decision of where to run the ball.

The next critical coaching point is not included in the diagram. The fullback on the diagram goes to block the strong safety. If the defensive end fights out, the fullback is not going to run up the butt of his tackle to get to the strong safety. He is going to cut inside and go to work. The playside guard is reaching the 3 technique. That is probably the best player on the defensive line. If the fullback comes inside and sees the 3 technique, he chip-blocks on him. He does not want to stay on the 3 technique, but he bangs him to help the offensive guard.

When the fullback turns up, if the 3-technique defender is reached, we have a play to the frontside. The center takes what we call a "skinny" charge through the A gap up to the Mike linebacker. If the Mike linebacker is a fast-flow player and the center cannot get to him, the fullback blocks him. We do not want to get caught up with telling the fullback he has to block the strong safety. He runs the play as if he were carrying the ball and blocks the first color he sees.

The backside guard is cutting the nose. If we get the nose cut, the ball can break behind the 3-technique defender. The tailback runs the ball in the C gap. It may look like he is running behind the 3 technique. However, when the ball cuts up, the 3 technique has moved his position to where the tight end was aligned to start the play.

If we reach the end, the ball goes outside. If we cannot reach the end but reach the 3 technique, the ball goes outside the 3 technique. If we cannot reach the end or the 3 technique, the ball bends behind the 3 technique. If the backside guard has cut the nose, we have a play. The thing to remember is the fullback is making all the same reads. He can end up behind the 3-technique defender, blocking the backside linebacker or free safety.

Against the under front, there are some key coaching points (Diagram #6). The tight end reaches for the outside number of the Sam linebacker. Normally, the Sam linebacker is a box player and will fight to stay outside. That creates a natural crease in the C gap. We run a double scheme with the playside guard and tackle. They are going to combo on the defensive end to the Mike linebacker. The tackle does what the tight end did on the over front. He tries to get a half man outside the defensive tackle. The same thing we told the tackle in the over, we tell the guard in the under. His aiming point is the outside number of the defensive end.

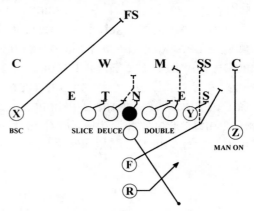

Diagram #6. 16 Force vs. Under

The guard does the same thing the tackle did on the over front. If he cannot take over the block on the 5-technique end, he launches him onto the block of the tackle to distort the edge and elevates up the field for the Mike linebacker. On the backside, the center has to reach the nose. He works for the outside number of the nose.

The backside guard and tackle have a deuce block on the 3 technique and Will linebacker. We will run a deuce slice on the 3 technique. The guard comes inside the 3 technique and climbs up to the Will linebacker. He cannot put his hands on the 3 technique because the tackle is going to cut him. That is because of the chop-block rule. If one player puts his hands on a defender and another player cuts him, that is a 15-yard penalty.

The fullback has the same blocking rule. He is to block the strong safety. However, he reads his keys as he goes to determine his path. If we cannot reach the 5-technique end, we turn the ball up. The fullback as he turns up could end up blocking the Will linebacker off the backside.

Defenses today, especially those with good coaches, disguise everything they do. You never know where the #4 strong defender is going to be. They can bring the safety down to the weakside, which allows the Mike and Will linebackers to fast-flow. If that happens, the backside guard cannot cut off the Will linebacker, but your fullback can.

To the weakside, we call the play 16/17 Bronco (Diagram #7). The play does not change from frontside to weakside. The playside guard and tackle use the double scheme, working for the 5-technique defender. The guard is working for the 5 technique but has the Mike linebacker in mind because he is the B-gap play on this type of flow. They are not working for the Will linebacker. If the defensive end spikes inside, the guard takes him, and the tackle works for the Mike linebacker.

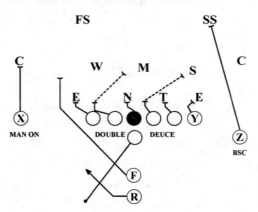

Diagram #7. 17 Bronco vs. Over

If the Will linebacker walked up in the B gap, the guard would take him, and we would sort out the rest of the play as it worked outside. The Will

linebacker on this scheme is not in the offensive line scheme. On flow to the weakside, we block the fits of the linebackers. The Mike linebacker is a B-gap fit on this play. To the backside, we use the deuce slice with the backside guard and tackle for the tackle and Sam linebacker. The center reaches the nose, and the tight end cuts off the backside defensive end.

The fullback searches for the Will linebacker. He reads as he did on the tight-end play. The ball can go outside, up, or bend.

With this play, life gets a little hairy with the under front. We have a 3 technique to the playside. We tell the guard and the fullback to draw a line, running through the 3-technique position or outside shoulder of the guard. The center has a single block and will never block any defender aligned outside that imaginary line. The fullback blocks the first thing outside the imaginary line. That keeps everyone on the same page, and no one is confused about who blocks whom.

On 17 Bronco against the under defensive front, the playside tackle reaches the man aligned on him (Diagram #8) The playside guard reaches the 3 technique aligned on him. The center blocks through the A gap and climbs. The backside guard and tackle will use a slice deuce call on the nose to the Mike linebacker. The tight end cuts off the defensive end.

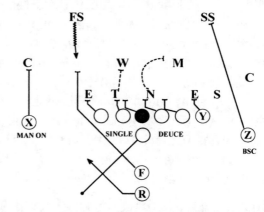

Diagram #8. 17 Bronco vs. Under 4-3

On this play the playside tackle, guard, and center may have to run a treo scheme, if we get spiking inside by the 5 and 3 techniques (Diagram #9). If we use the treo, the center, guard, and tackle take the slanting defender, with the tackle coming up for the Will linebacker. If we get the treo call, the fullback leads up on the free safety.

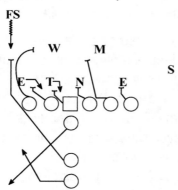

Diagram #9. Treo 17 Bronco vs. Under

I am going to show the power now, but I feel like I am in God's country for the power. I watched the Pitt Panthers run the power 56 times in one game. I was in shock they ran it that much. I want to make one point about the power: I do not know if the power is the best-designed play in the world. I do know there is a belief in the play if you coach it. The players have to believe in the play.

The play will not be pretty some of the times. You will gain short yardage on some occasions, but it is a play we believe in. If you go to the COOL (coaches Of offensive linemen) clinic in Cincinnati, you will find out it is God's play. We run it, and we believe in it for a lot of reasons.

When we run the power, all we are trying to do is get more blockers to the point of attack than the defense has defenders. There are a lot of theories about the power, but if we can get more blockers or as many blockers as they have defenders, it is a winning formula. In our thinking, the power is an A-gap run. The aiming point for the running back is the outside hip of the guard. The ball starts in the A gap and bounces to the outside. We have found the big runs come when the linebacker start to get nosy coming over the top.

The play is 24 power versus the under front (Diagram #10). This is our two-back power play with the fullback blocking the Sam linebacker and the backside guard pulling for the Mike linebacker. The quarterback reverses out and brings the ball back to the mesh point with the running back. He brings the ball as deep as possible and carries out his fake. The playside guard blocks down on the nose versus the under front. On the power play, the playside tackle blocks with the tight end on the 7-technique defender. They use the combo to come off for the backside linebacker. The center blocks back for the pulling guard on the under defense.

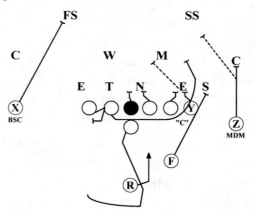

Diagram #10. 24 Power vs. Under 4-3

The Z-receiver on this play is blocking the MDM, whether it is the corner or strong safety.

The backside tackle uses an alley hinge technique on the B gap. He steps into the B gap with his inside foot and hinges back to the outside to cut off the backside. The backside guard pulls for the Mike linebacker. He sets his eyes to the target immediately. He wants to meet the linebacker on his side of the ball. He does not pass a color below the A gap in the defense. The running back takes a drop step and meshes with the quarterback, going downhill. The aiming point is the outside hip of the playside guard. He maintains proper relationship behind the pulling guard.

I want to talk about two things that I think are important from an offensive play-caller's standpoint. The first thing is you need to know what you believe in. The second thing is you must know the answer when the defense takes away what you believe in. You have to know without hesitation, and it has to be from the player's point of view.

If we are a two-back running football team and defense goes to an eight-man front football to stop our running game, how do we attack their three-deep coverage? Are we going to use flood routes or seam routes? We have to take advantage of coverage to get the most out of our offense. We want the running game to be so effective that the defense has to commit another defender to the box to stop the run. When the defense does that, we can take advantage of the three-deep coverage by using play-action passing and vertical routes.

In all the running schemes you run, the big plays come because the wide receivers are blocking downfield. If they can block the secondary support players or the rolled down players, we have a chance to make something big happen. Wide receivers do not play in our offense unless they block.

If the defense goes to an eight-man front scheme, we are going to attack them by giving unbalanced formations and maximum protection schemes. We are going to run 2-on-2 patterns in the secondary and beat the defense. We will run double post or double comeback and flood the coverage from the backfield.

This is our two-back pass play with slide protection. We generally slide to the weakside away from the tight end (Diagram #11). The front is working the four down linemen to the Sam linebacker. The fullback has the Will linebacker. The running back has the Mike linebacker and scans the defense, if he does not blitz. The backside tackle blocks the defensive end. In this protection, we slide the protection to the Sam linebacker. The frontside tackle is locked on the defensive end to his outside. The frontside guard slides to the Sam linebacker. The center, backside guard, and tackle are sliding to the Sam linebacker.

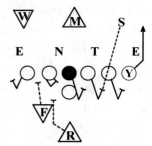

Diagram #11. Slide Protection

The front four are responsible for the four down linemen and the Sam linebacker in their protection

scheme. The fullback and running back have the two remaining linebackers. The fullback has the Will, and the running back has the Mike linebacker.

An example of a play we would run against a three-deep secondary is Z spear (Diagram #12). These passes come out of the 13 BOB play-action. This is a three-receiver flood to the left. The quarterback reads the patterns long to short. The X-receiver runs a 15-yard break to the post. The Z-receiver in the slot runs a deep cross route, working to 18 to 22 yards at the sidelines. The fullback has an arrow route to the flat. The quarterback looks post, cross, and flat as his progression read. He reads the near safety. If the safety jumps the spear route, he throws over the top to the post.

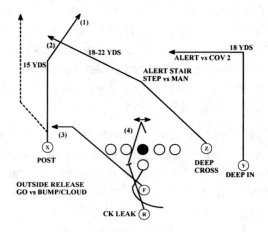

Diagram #12. Z Spear

If there is no blitz by the Mike linebacker, the running back runs a checkdown route over the ball at four yards.

I want to show you two more examples before I stop. This pattern is a flood pattern with the slot receiver running a corner route behind a post route by the X-receiver (Diagram #13). We are working on the outside corner with these patterns. The quarterback looks to the corner as his first read, the post second, and the fullback as the third choice.

The last pattern, Z hooker, is a similar pattern (Diagram #14). The slot receiver runs the post into the middle to hold the safety. The Z-receiver comes in motion and trails the X-receiver off the line. As the X-receiver breaks to the post, the Z-receiver breaks to the corner and hook. He has to sell the corner route to the defender. The fullback runs the arrow to the flat. The quarterback looks high to low in his read. He looks for the corner and then the flat pattern.

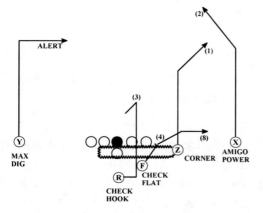

Diagram #13. Corner/Post

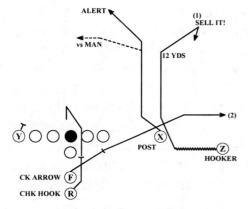

Diagram #14. Z Hooker

When we attack three-deep coverage, we throw a lot of flood routes and double-post routes. You can create many yards in chunks by using a play-action pass out of a two-back offense. It is the quarterback's best friend. It allows him to play pass without a concerted rush. He can step up in the pocket, see the field, and get yards in chunks. Our patterns are more effective from the play-action pass because of the tighter splits of the receivers.

This concept of a two-back offense with an active fullback and play-action pass scheme puts a strain on a defense in a certain way. It makes the coverage for the defensive backs harder than a quarterback playing in a conventional offense does. If makes them responsible for something other than the pass. This offense allows you to do what you believe in, but you must have the answers for the zone blitzes and stacked boxes. It is our job as coaches to give the players the tools to be successful. We have to devise the plans to make them successful. We have to do that in formations, motions, shifts, and personnel groupings. That keeps the defense from identifying what we are going to do.

I appreciate your attention. Thank you.

DEFENSIVE PRINCIPLES AND SECONDARY DRILLS

University of Alabama

I appreciate you being here today. I appreciate everything you do for the profession. Coaches are overworked and underpaid. I know that because my dad was a coach in Georgia for 30 years. I know the time and effort you spend in coaching. I appreciate that very much.

Before I start, I want to tell you that you will not hear anything that is revolutionary or anything we have invented. We win because we can run the ball and stop the run. It is that simple. People say that is old-school mentality. It is, and we practice that way. Everything else we do comes off that premise. Historically, the teams that can run the ball and stop the run win more games.

The offenses today want to throw the ball. The players like it, and it is fun. At the University of Alabama, we are not about *fun*. We are about *toughness, being physical,* and *winning ball games*. The players have fun by winning games and championships. We do things that way, and our players buy into that idea and play hard for us.

Today, I am going to go through some defensive drills we use. I will tell you why we do the drills. At the end of the lecture, I want to talk about some man-coverage concepts and ideas. There is nothing special about the drills. When we start the drill session, we start everything with *A, B,* and *C*. We want some kind of *agility in the drill*.

We want to see *block protection* on defense. These are drills for every group on the defense. We do drills for the linebackers, defensive line, and defensive backs. We do cut-block drills, stalk drills, and drills of that nature. We are no different from anyone else. We are working drills in which we use our hands. You cannot play defense without using your hands. We want to play with the hands, lock out, and control blockers.

We want to see contact in our drills. The *C* in our drills stands for *contact*. You cannot play football without contact. We may not take players to the ground; however, we are physical in these drills. In our practices, we do not take players to the ground except in two or three scrimmages each year.

We do not teach the drills on the field. We want to prepare the players for what we are going to do in a position meeting. When we go to the practice field, we do not want to spend time explaining the drills. We do not want to explain what we want to accomplish. We want to repeat the drills and not have to teach daily. Drill work is important, but the time we have to work on individual skills is limited. When we get to the practice field, we want to get as many repetitions as we possibly can.

Our managers set up the drills and have them ready to go when we get to the field. This is all part of organization so you can be more efficient with your practice time. With the restrictions the NCAA places on colleges, it is imperative that we do these things. We have to utilize every second we have with our individual groups.

We do the same drills daily. These are defensive back drills. The first drill we do is a *down-the-line drill*. This is a simple backpedal drill. We work from the sideline to the hash marks. In this drill, we are looking for *proper technique*. In the stance, we want the feet close together. We want their feet somewhere between four to six inches apart. We want the feet no wider than a toe-to-instep stagger.

We want the feet barely clipping the grass as they backpedal. We watch the posture and footwork of the backs. We do not want any false steps as they push off. We push with the back foot, and then we push with the front foot. When we coach in an individual period, we do not want to stop the drill to correct what someone is doing. You do not want people standing and watching while you are talking to one player. We run the drill and make the corrections on the fly.

We do not waste time doing different drills or creating new drills. We want the repetitions for the individuals, and we want to make the most of the time we have.

The second drill we work on is the *weave drill.* When we teach this drill, we want the defenders to stay square. When they do the weave drill, we are working on a backpedal. The coach stands in front of the players and starts them on a backpedal. He gives directions left and right to weave off and on the lines. When they weave, they do not turn their hips in that direction. They keep their shoulders square to the line and weave from side to side. We do the weave drill to control leverage on a receiver. If we have outside leverage and the receiver stems outside, we want to weave outside and keep the leverage position without turning the shoulder to do it.

The next drill we incorporate with the weave drill is a *flip turn.* We start out in the weave. On the coach's signal, the defensive back executes a flip turn and runs. We add a turn to one side and the run. After that, we add a turn going both ways. We use these drills with our corners and safeties.

The next drill is a *plant-and-burst drill.* When we break back on the ball, we want to have the foot on the ground. Freshmen come in as toe planters. They want to plant with the toe and not the entire foot. The toe planters may only have two cleats in the ground when they attempt to break. We want the sole of the foot on the ground with the foot to the breakside turned at a 45-degree angle to the direction of the break. When we drive on a pattern, we feel we have more ground traction if you have all the cleats of the shoe in the ground as the defender bursts to the ball.

When you work these drills, you must work off both feet. We break them to the right and then to the left. In these drills, it is easy to get false steps in the backpedal and burst drills. Every false step the defensive back takes is lost time, which means a completion.

The next drill is the *two-line drill.* We never do all these drills on the same day. We may use a two-line drill on Monday and a one-line drill on Tuesday. However, the defensive backs know the drills, and we do not spend time teaching the drills. We go into the drills and work on the techniques. We do not have to teach the actual mechanics of the drill to get started.

In the two-line drill, we want the defensive back to shuffle. We are incorporating our cover-2 scheme in the drill. We teach the corner on a cover-2 technique that when the receiver breaks off the line of scrimmage, the corner does not sink or drop off the receiver; he jams the receiver and shuffles for two steps. After the corner does his shuffle steps, the coach gives him a direction. He rolls the ball out as a fumble or throws the ball up in the air for the back to react to the ball and high point it for an interception.

If the coach rolls the ball, the defensive back reacts and works on his scoop-and-score drill. If the coach throws the ball, he reacts to it and works on his ball skills. The defensive back has to catch the ball.

We incorporate in the drill the drive on the out cut (Diagram #1). The defensive back does the same thing he did in the shuffle drill except we are going to defend a receiver. We teach two different techniques. We teach the burst drop as a man-coverage technique and a 45-degree angle drop as a zone technique. In that technique, he opens his hips and drives to a spot.

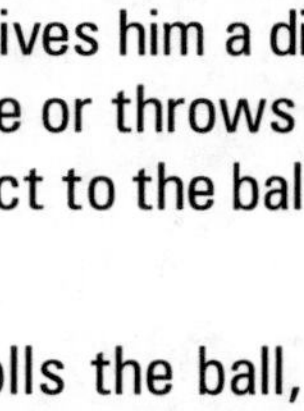

Diagram #1. Out Burst

When you do these drills, you should be able to find live-action shots of them in game films. Everything we teach in the drills, we should see in the games. If you can show the players the drill in a game film, they will work harder to perfect the skill you are trying to teach. If they know they are getting better by using the drill work, they will work harder in the drill. You have to let them know why you are teaching the drill.

The next drill is a *speed turn on the out pattern*. We teach a zone turn on the out first drill. In the zone turn, the defensive back opens his hips to the quarterback. He reacts back to the receiver at a 45-degree angle. On the speed turn, the defender runs the pattern with the receiver. He does not open his hips to the quarterback. He flips his head and shoulder to the outside away from the quarterback. We use this drill as an out-and-up drill to work on the deep ball.

I have been with Coach Saban since 2006 when I coached with him at the Miami Dolphins. I have learned a lot from him. We came to Alabama in 2007. I think Coach Saban is the best defensive backs coach I have ever heard speak or watched coach. He does a great job of teaching the players. He does not go into the film room and criticize the players. He tells them what they did wrong, but he reinforces that with positive comments. That is the best thing I have learned from him. I learned to *teach* and not to *criticize*.

When we recruit a player, we want to know *if he can play man-to-man defense*. You cannot play college football at our level if you never play man-to-man defense.

The second thing we want to know about a recruit is *if he can tackle*. You cannot play defense unless you can tackle. In a defensive back, it is harder because he has to tackle in space most of the time. A missed tackle in the secondary is double trouble. A five-yard hitch pattern and a missed tackle can amount to a 60-yard touchdown.

The third thing we want to know is *if he can play the ball in the deep parts of the field*. Defensive corners end up in bad situations too many times.

They are isolated and have to make plays on deep balls. If they cannot do that, they cannot play in our scheme.

We do the *out-and-up drill* to improve our ability to play the ball in the deep part of the field. There are two factors at work in the deep field. The back has to be able to adjust to the deep ball and he has to catch it.

When we do a speed cut, we do not want to stop and start again. When you stop, you have to start from zero. We want to roll off the inside foot and keep our momentum going. We want to keep our speed when we play any kind of double move. If the defender loses his momentum when the receiver turns the move deep, it is difficult to recover and catch up.

We work all kinds of ball drills. We have a *high-ball drill* and a *low-ball drill* to teach catching and concentration on the ball.

The next part of our drill work is the *B*, which is *block protection*. The corner has to play the blocks of the wide receivers primarily. One of my favorite drills to do is a *middle-butt drill*. We even do this drill in our off-season program because we feel it is that important. It is a simple punch drill. The defensive backs punch with the hands into the breastplate of a defender. We want the hands inside and the thumbs up on the chest. Putting the thumbs in that position will bring the elbows in tight to the body.

We want them to pretend they are sitting on a barstool. We want the weight back and the head up. We want to punch and lock out the arms. Playing corner as a defensive back is similar to playing tackle against a rushing defensive end. We use the kick-slide technique when we play corner. The difference is we are not trying to lunge and do an explosion drill. We want to sit back and use our hands. When the receiver approaches, the defensive back can use his hands and knock the crap out of him. If the defensive back keeps his elbow in tight, he has an extra foot or more to lock out on the defender.

In the drill, we want to work outside and we work side to side. We do not want the receiver to turn the defensive back one way or the other. We always make sure the heels of the receiver are apart. We do not want the feet together. We want to use a step movement with his feet as if he were an offensive tackle. We never want him hopping. We always want one foot on the ground.

The next drill is an extension of the butt drill. We call it *shuffle-run-cut* (Diagram #2). We start out the drill the same way. We punch and lock out the blocker. The blocker moves to the outside. The defensive back shuffles, separates from the blocker, and runs to the outside. The second blocker comes out of the backfield and tries to cut him. The defensive back has to play the cut with his hands and feet. The key thing to playing the cut block is to keep the outside leg free and to the outside. The defensive back has to get the outside leg past the hat of the blocker. The defender gets cut if the blocker gets to his outside leg.

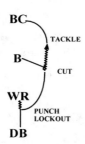

Diagram #2. Shuffle-Run-Cut

We are going to do some form of tackling every day. This is the block protection drill with a tackle on the end. We do the shuffle-run-cut drill and have a tackle on the end. I stack two blockers and a ballcarrier in a line five yards apart. The defensive back punches and locks out on the first blocker. The last six inches of a bench press is what we teach in the lock-out movement. That is where the explosion comes from and what we are teaching in this movement. He shuffles and runs to the second blocker. The second blocker tries to cut him. He plays the cut and comes off the block.

When we teach tackling, we teach *near leg* and *near shoulder.* I see players squat all the time when they tackle. We do not teach that at all. In basketball, with a jump-ball situation, the players

jump for the tip with their inside leg and their inside hand. That is how we teach tackling. The tackler hits with his nearest leg to the ballcarrier and rolls his hips up and through the ballcarrier.

We do the same thing on an *angle tackle*. If we hit with the near shoulder, the next step is *through* the ballcarrier not to the ballcarrier.

We teach a *stick tackling drill* (Diagram #3). The defensive back gets into a backpedal. He sticks his foot in the ground and drives up for the tackle. When he gets to the tackle position, he executes the near shoulder/near leg technique and makes the tackle.

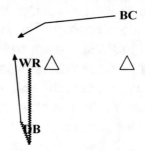

Diagram #3. Stick Tackle

The next drill is a simple *angle tackle drill.* The coaching point in this drill is to make sure they use the near leg and same shoulder. Coming on an angle, they can get the opposite leg forward and the near shoulder. Make sure their feet are in proper position as they run through the ballcarrier. You have more power with the near leg and shoulder as long as the feet are pointed north and south.

In the open *field tackling drill,* we put the ballcarrier and defender 15 yards apart. The defensive back wants to close the distance as quickly as he can. When he makes a tackle in the open field, he has to open his hips to the ballcarrier. If the defensive back cannot open his hips, he will struggle in the open field. When we open the hips, we have to flat step to the ballcarrier.

If it comes to an angle tackle, he has to open his hips and flat step to the ballcarrier. We want him coming downhill on his flat step. He does not want to turn his shoulder and run on an angle. Some defensive backs cannot run straight ahead and flat step because they are too tight in the hips. In the open field, we do not want to turn the shoulders.

You want to close the distance, open the hips, flat step with the shoulders square, and strike with the near leg and shoulder.

On a sideline tackle, we do not want to give the ballcarrier a two-way go. We do not want him to cut back with the ball or get down the sideline. We want to attack straight ahead and close the running lane.

This next drill teaches *pursuit tackling* (Diagram #4). It works with our cover-2 roll. The corner and safety work in the drill together. In the drill, we set a dummy holder in the area of a toss sweep. The corner has to play off a receiver and force the ball from an outside-in position. The safety fills inside the corner. In this drill, we are trying to simulate a missed tackle. We teach swarming defense. There are good running backs in the SEC. You do not knock them down on the first contact. We have one of those good running backs.

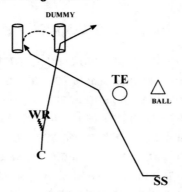

Diagram #4. Pursuit Tackle

The dummy holder has to be firm with the dummy. The cornerback closes on the dummy and delivers a hit on the dummy. After the hit, the dummy holder moves the bag to another position. The safety is flying to the ball inside the corner. When the dummy moves, he has to adjust his angle and hit the dummy.

The next thing we do with the defensive back is to work on *releases*. When our defensive backs press, we want to play quick with our hands and feet. The worse thing that can happen to a defensive back is to lunge at a receiver. When the defensive back steps forward, he spreads his feet. After he spreads his feet, he cannot move his feet

unless he steps back inside himself. He has taken three steps, and he did not move from his original position.

We want the weight on the big toe of the up foot. From that position, he cannot spread his feet. When they snap the ball, we want to stay square and force the receivers to release around us. We use our step-step footwork to channel their paths. We say that playing corner is like being a pitcher in baseball. You cannot throw the fastball all the time. Eventually, the hitter will catch up to the fastball. He has to have a change-up to keep the batters off balance.

We have to do the same thing at defensive back. We cannot defend the receiver with the same coverage scheme or technique every time. We have to change up what we do. We can play cover 2, or we can play what we call a *tough jam*. That is a hard jam with the inside hand. When we do this, we do not lunge at the receiver or jump across the line of scrimmage to get to the receiver. The problem with the tough jam is there is too much risk if the defensive back misses the jam. If that happens, it is probably a touchdown. It is a risky play.

We run drills with the receiver and the corner working on out-and-in breaks by the receivers. We also have to work on the breaks of the safeties in a cover-2 shell. They have to break downhill on a secondary break and back for the deep break. On one day, we work breaking *down*, and the next day we work breaking *deep*.

On cover 2, the corner is the primary run support. On a cover-2 concept, we make the safeties drive out for the first three steps because he is the half defender. We make them read the receivers. They want to know if the receiver blocked the corner or released. We do not read run or pass with a half-field safety on a lineman. We check the receivers. It could be a toss sweep pass or a flea-flicker. If he reads run from the receiver, he flat steps and comes out of the half-field back into run support.

We play our corners a little different on cover 2. We coach the corner on his support path. If he sees air inside the receiver and can beat him in there, he takes it. Instead of taking on the receiver, he beats him inside and boxes the run. However, the safety has to make him right by getting over the top and playing secondary contain.

We do not play much off coverage on the wide receiver. However, the first day of fall camp, we play good on good in a pass drill. We play off coverage because most corners do not understand leverage. The secondary plays cover 3 (Diagram #5). The quarterback has three options: He can run a toss sweep, a three-step quick slant pass, or a five-step comeback pattern. The defenders do not have any linebackers underneath coverage, so all the cuts have to be out patterns by the receivers.

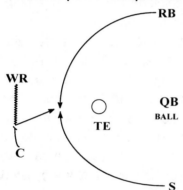

Diagram #5. Leverage and Fit

We have to read run or pass and play run or pass. We do not expect the corner to make the play on the running play. However, we are asking him to play block protection techniques on the receiver and get up to force the play inside. The worst thing the corner can do is to run outside the block of the wide receiver. We tell the corner to two-gap the receiver and play two-thirds outside and one-third inside on the receiver.

The safety is coming inside the corner for run support. If the corner picks a side of the receiver, he has made the receiver's job easy. We are teaching the corner and safety their fits on a running play. That makes the safety and corner tougher players. If we read pass, it is going to be some kind of outside breaking pattern.

Some days we play cover 3 in the drill, and other days we play cover 2. We do not want the corner penned inside on a running play when we are playing cover 2 (Diagram #6). The safety can make him right, but we do not want it to happen. If he decides to run through on the receiver, he has to get there. We use this type of play if we have a large tight end playing the split receiver. In a stalk situation, that is a mismatch for the corner. The corner can read the tight end and align on the wide receiver. When he sees the tight end release inside, he is a rolled-up cover-2 corner.

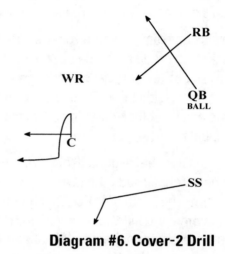

Diagram #6. Cover-2 Drill

We play the slot receiver differently than most people. Most people press the wide receiver and play off the slot receiver. We play that way because we need run support from the man over the slot. If the slot blocks, we have run support from the strong safety. If the slot releases, we are man-to-man with the strong safety. We leverage the slotback based on where the help is. If we do have help inside, the defender leverages him outside.

Today in college football, the huddle occurs at the line of scrimmage. The offense aligns on the ball and the coaches call the plays from the sideline according to how the defense aligns. If you change your defense, they call the automatics from the sideline. You can do two things in that situation. You can set in the defense you are in or change the defense. We are not going to allow the offense to do that to us. We do not show our defense when the quarterback gets under center or uses the hard count to get us to move. We do not show what we are in when the quarterback drops his hand in the shotgun to get the snap.

We are going to put a *kill call* into our defensive calls. When we use a kill call, it is the same as a defensive automatic. We kill pressure to pressure, pressure to coverage, and coverage to pressure. If the offense reads cover 2 and decides to check to a draw, we kill our call from coverage to pressure. The offense checks to a play to run against cover 2. We kill the cover-2 coverage scheme and go to a blitz scheme. We tie our blitz to another coverage scheme. We go from a cover-2 call to a zone blitz and a quarters or man scheme in the secondary.

We can also go from pressure to pressure. If the offense thinks they read an inside blitz scheme and automatic to an option play, we can change from an inside blitz to an outside blitz. They think they have an advantage and can block down on all inside gaps. We bring the blitz off the perimeter.

The last kill we have goes from pressure to coverage. The offense reads the pre-snap as a blitz scheme. When they automatic to change the protection scheme, we kill the blitz and go to some kind of max-coverage scheme. We can play a match-man concept or go to some other coverage scheme. We want to make sure we stop any type of now pass. The offense ties it into a blitz-prevention plan.

We are not going to sit back and let the offense do what they want. We do not have to use a kill call. We can use bluff tactics to make them think we are coming when we are not. The kill call we use most is the coverage to pressure call. We package these calls as part of the game plan. We will match a fire zone blitz with the country cover 2.

At times, we get hurt with the kill calls, but we are not going to let the offense match their play to our defense without giving them some problems. When the offense does not get the coverage or blitz scheme they thought they saw, it builds doubt into their heads.

The key to what we do is the game plan. In our film study, we match our coverages to their formations and tendencies. It is not like we are grab bagging coverages. The offense is going to game plan to what they see also. We are not any smarter than the other coaches are. However, we are not going to sit back and let them pick up with the play they want to run.

Offensive coaches use dummy calls to make the defense think they are changing the play when actually they are not. It becomes a big crapshoot sometimes. However, we think we are better off using that system.

The obvious problem when you start to check from one blitz to another or change from coverage to coverage is the communication of that call. You must have people on your defense who will take charge of those things and make sure the defense is on the same page. The automatic calls have to be simple so that you do not end up with two different coverages in the secondary. If we make a mistake in a blitz call, it will not hurt us as much as a blow in the secondary. That kind of mistake can lead to a big play. When we check our coverage, we want to go from zone coverage to some sort of man scheme.

We can play pattern-match coverage or a man-free scheme. When we check from a particular coverage to another, we do not want the automatic every time we think the quarterback is changing the play. If you do that, the offense will figure out what you are doing and take advantage of it. You cannot always do anything about it. If you always check cover 2 to a particular coverage, the offense will figure that out. We want the offense to guess when we are checking off. It all comes back to *disguise*. If we can mask what we are doing, we will win most of those situations.

My time is up. I will be around if you have questions. Thank you.

THE PUNT: "THE GREATEST PLAY IN FOOTBALL"

West Virginia University

Thank you, it is nice to be here today. I was the special teams coordinator last year, but I am giving that up this year. I knew the special teams were not going to be great, so I took the job and did it myself. I am going to delegate a lot of that responsibility this year, but I am never going to give up the punt team.

I am going to talk fast because we had to de-ice the plane to get out of town, and I do not know how we will get back into town. When I left, we had two feet of snow and 12 more inches coming. I will spend as much time with you as I can.

WEST VIRGINIA UNIVERSITY KICKING GAME PHILOSOPHY

I think the punt is the most important play in football.

Outwork Them

- WVU gives great effort
- Attention to detail
- Practice results we want

Outsmart Them

- WVU will not beat WVU
- Fundamentally sound
- Attack opponent's weakness

Intimidate Them

- Win the physical fight
- Play with confidence
- Outblock, outtackle, outhit, outhustle opponent

We want to be aggressive. I want to be like the New Orleans Saints in the Super Bowl game. I love what they did. The onside kick was outstanding.

That is the way we want to coach our special teams. I talked to Steve Ortmayer, who coaches at the University of Kentucky, about kickoff and kickoff return. I took his kickoff and we tried to run it in our game against The University of Louisville. Trent Guy is the best in the BIG EAST, and he scared the fire out of me.

Our punter was second in the country last year in net punting. He also did some rugby punting. In our punt formation, I want a two-yard minimum split between our center, guards, and tackles (Diagram #1). I want a three-yard minimum between the tackles and ends. It can be wider depending on what we want to do. We could have as much as a five-foot split between our tackles and ends. The shields or outside protectors in the back wall must be at seven-and-a-half yards from the line of scrimmage, and I want it exact. I want them aligned in the guard/center gaps to their side.

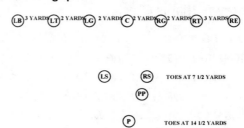

Diagram #1. Punt Alignment

The personal protector is the quarterback of the team, and he barks out the signals. He stands to the side and calls the signal, then he steps into the gap between the shields after the ball passes.

I want to put two defenders into the center/guard gaps. I put one defender in the rest of the gaps. We number the defenders starting on the outside and moving to the inside (Diagram #2). The defender aligned outside the right end is numbered R1.

We continue to number the defenders until we reach the center. There are five defenders to each side. We number them R1 through R5 and L1 through L5. The way we number does not change. We number from the outside to the inside on the right and then on the left. We do not stop counting until we get to 5. Both of the number 5s can be on the same side of the center. If they were to put 11 defenders on the line, I tell the punter to catch and kick.

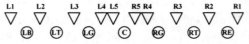

Diagram #2. Numbering System

On this punt team, we have seven bullets. When I was the special teams coordinator under Rich Rodriguez, they tried to get me to do this for two years. I did not know this scheme. If I do not know a scheme, I do not want to teach it. I fought him for two years. Finally, against Boston College in a game at Morgantown, they returned two punts against us for touchdowns. On both of them, we were backed up and had to punt against the wind. In Morgantown, that is a task.

After the game, we sat down and Rich told me that the game was passing us by and we had to change. I told him it was time to go to the spread punt game. We went out on a fact-finding mission and this is what we came up with. We got this from Wofford College, Texas A&M University, and Bowling Green State University. We went to three schools and came up with this plan.

If we kick the ball to the right, we call *red* or *Roger* to designate the direction we are kicking. It could be any other R word. If we kick the ball to the left, we call *blue* or *Louie*. This is how we number our blocking scheme. If we call red, the right guard, tackle, and end, block the R3, R4, and R5 defenders (Diagram #3). The right shield blocks R4, and the personal protector blocks R5. The left shield blocks L5. The left guard, tackle, and end block the L4, L3,

and L2 defenders. The L1 is the widest defender away from the punter and we release him. The punter is stepping to the right.

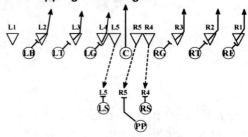

Diagram #3. Red

If we call a blue punt, the blocking is the exact opposite (Diagram #4). The left guard, tackle, and end block L3, L2, and L1. The left shield blocks the L4 defender, and the personal protector blocks L5. The right shield blocks the R5 defender, and the right guard, tackle, and end block R4, R3, and R2. As in the case before, the R1 is the widest defender and we release him.

On their blocking assignments, the guards, tackles, and ends attack *through* their assignments and destroy the defender's charge. We shed the defender fast and cover. The shields and personal protector stand their ground. They do not initiate contact until the attacker is within six inches of them. They put their hairline on the defender's chin and destroy his charge. If his assignment gets blocked by someone else, gets picked, or does not rush, he picks up the next man through. He corrects the mistakes of others because he has time and distance on his side. The bullets release through their blocking assignments and covers. The center has a hot release off the ball. He snaps the ball and covers. He does not have a blocking assignment.

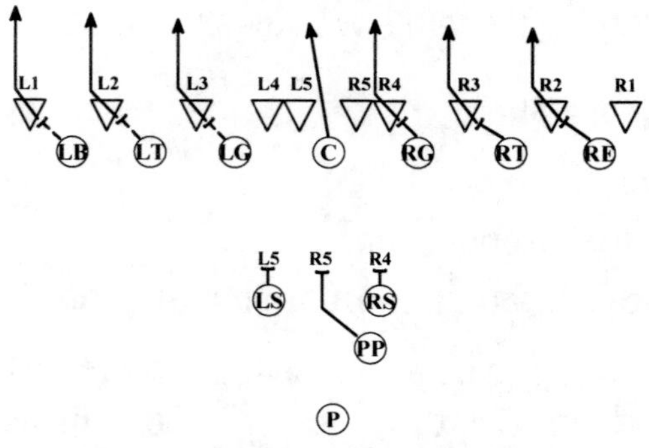

Diagram #4. Blue

That is our base protection for red and blue punts. You must have a base coverage that your players understand. This is the first thing they do in camp. Instead of running them in conditioning sprint drills, we do our running while working on punting the football and our protection schemes. I have defensive starters on this team. This is the most important special team.

I want to go back to the gaps and talk about the movement of defenders on the line. If the defense moves a defender into the B gap on the right with the intent of picking him off the right guard and freeing up his blocking assignment, we handle that situation. They are trying to cause confusion between the right guard and right shield. Our adjustment goes back to what I told you about the shields having their toes at seven-and-a-half yards. He is also aligned in the middle of the center/guard gap. Whichever player the right guard blocks, the shield picks up the other defender and keeps the protection solid.

We want to get into a base protection and react to what the defense shows us. We are going to break the huddle and come out fast. We are going to use motion and shifts to confuse the defender to the point that they call a *punt safe call*. Punt safe means they are playing defense against your punt team instead of rushing the punter or setting up a return. They think you might run or throw the ball from that set. We run reverses and fakes from our punt formation. This is the base we use, and we are not going to change what we do.

Every high school that plays football has a kid in their school who can punt. You have to get out in the halls and find him. It could be the point guard on the basketball team, a soccer player, or the second baseman on the baseball team, but every school has someone who can do this. He needs quick hands, eyes, and feet. I do not care if he punts the ball 40 plus yards.

I admire you men who work in the high school ranks. The reason I admire you is because of the people you have to deal with. You have to put up with the board of education, the parents, the principal, and the board members. I do not have to put up with that and we are lucky. If a parent complains about his kid's playing time, we bring them in and show them the films. That generally stops the complaining.

You have to find the kid in your school who has good hands and quick feet. All we want him to do is kick the ball. I do not care if it goes end over end with no hang time. All I am looking for is 40 yards—that does not have to be in the air. It can be 40 yards counting the roll. I am covering with seven bullets, and there will not be much of a return.

Last year, we were second in the nation with Pat McAfee as our punter. He rolled to the right or left to kick the ball all the time. He averaged 44.71 yards per punt. For his career, he averaged 43.0 yards per punt. The player we had this year could not roll punt as well, but he was the best punter I had. We let him take a couple of steps and punt the ball. We were seventh in the nation this year with a 40.5 average. The point is this system works with a roll punter and a nonroll punter. That is the beauty of the system.

The *roll* is the rugby punt to the right (Diagram #5). All the blocking assignments in roll are the same as red; therefore roll equals red. You can actually roll to the right facing the sideline and kick the ball down the field. The blocking linemen, instead of destroying the charge and shedding fast, destroy the charge and hold the block for one full second. After they hold for one second, they shed and cover.

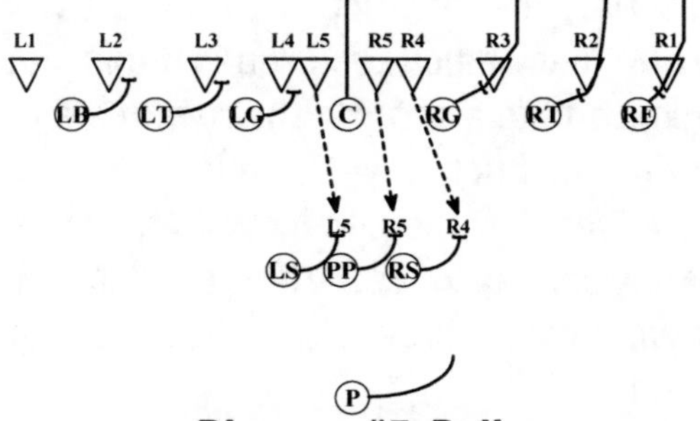

Diagram #5. Roll

The blocking shields aim for the outside armpit of their assignments. If they lose their blocks, they have to make sure they lose them to the inside behind the punter. The punter's technique is a rugby-style kick. It will be no higher than 10 feet off the ground because that will give the ball a good roll. If we give a read call to the punter, he reads the EMOL (end man on line). If that defender rushes, the punter punts the ball. If he backs off, the punter runs the ball.

If you can get creative, you can get into some good schemes. If you have a kid who can roll to the right and cross kick, it opens up some avenues for you. We get into a trips left formation. The trips left formation splits the left guard, tackle, and end away from the punt formation. Your blocking assignments do not change. The defense will send three defenders with the guard, tackle, and end, which means the guard, tackle, and end have a hot release to the ball. The defenders aligned on them are no threat to the punt. They escape the best way they can and cover. The shields and personal protectors block their normal roll protection. The punter rolls right and cross kicks the ball to the left into the three bullets.

I have talked about the spacing and blocking, and now I want to tell you about the next important thing. The spacing and depth is critical and most important in this scheme. The blocking is ABC simple and this is the third thing. I was a center in high school because no one wanted to do it. I ended up snapping the ball and got a scholarship doing it because no one else wanted to snap the ball. The next important thing is the *coverage*.

When we cover the ball, the ends go directly to the ball. They are covering with reckless abandon. We do not coach much technique on this player. We want him to take a shot on the return man. We are not trying to hurt anyone, but we want them *reckless*. We want them to blow up the punt-return man if they can. I do not care if he hits him or not. We do not want him to break down. We want him to go make a hit.

The three most important players on our punt team are the punter, middle shield or personal protector, and the center. The punter's importance to the punt team is obvious. The middle shield makes all the overload calls and adjustments based on what the defenders do. He calls the fakes also. He has to be a sharp football player. That position is usually our Mike linebacker. The center has to snap the ball. I want a strong safety type snapping the ball. I want a player with a linebacker mentality. I want someone who can run down the field and make a tackle.

The center is generally a hot player with no blocking assignment. The center we had this year was not fast enough to get to the ballcarrier. I wanted him to break down five yards from the ball. The reason I did that was to show the colors in the middle. I wanted the return man to see gold or blue in the middle—those are the colors of our jerseys. He was not good enough or fast enough to get all the way to the return man. The outside bullets were taking the shots at the return man.

I wanted the center to show up in the middle so the return man could not take the ball up the middle. It is like a quarterback who cannot step up in the pocket. He feels he has nowhere to go. When he starts to dance, we have him. It is like a pack of wild dogs. If the bullets do not get him, the pack will. If you have a linebacker or free safety who can snap the ball and run, you can use him as your third bullet with the two outside runners.

Our linemen on our punt team are defensive backs, strong safeties, and linebackers. If you have a tough wide receiver, you can put him on this team. The left and right ends are hot to the ball (Diagram #6). They want to force the returner to run north/south. If they cannot make the tackle, they make him jump or disrupt his running lane. They attack from the outside to the inside and try to attack the returner's outside hip. The left and right tackles run in lanes 10 yards outside the returner. They attack the runner's near armpit. The right and left guards run in the lane five yards outside the returner. They attack the near number on the returner's jersey.

The guards on the punt team are generally bigger and have more girth than the tackles and ends. They are the ones who have to bang on the

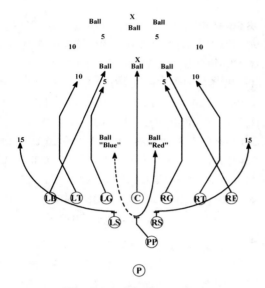

Diagram #6. Coverage

defensive tackles coming off the line of scrimmage. The center is hot to the ball. He snaps the ball and goes to disrupt the return. The left and right shields run in lanes 15 yards outside the returner. They hustle downfield and attack from outside in. The personal protector is a delayed bullet to the ball. He releases right of the center on red and left of the center on blue. The punter is the safety and mirrors the returner.

In practice, we do not go live. We catch the punts and move with it right and left. If he goes to the right, the bullets are there first. The guards cover five yards outside the returner. In practice, the guards come down and touch the return man on the butt. He moves forward down the field, and the tackles are 10 yards outside the return man and they touch the returner on the butt. He continues on down the field, and the shields are 15 yards outside the returner and are next in line to touch the returner.

If the ball is kicked with a chance to get into the end zone, the center and ends go to the goal line and try to catch the ball in the air. The guards, tackles, and shields, go to the returner. The returners try to draw the coverage to them when they are trying to let the ball get into the end zone by faking a catch away from the ball. We send the bullets to the goal line, and everyone else goes to the returner. We do this as drill work, and that is how I condition them.

We can change our punt formation and get creative. If the call is trips right formation, the right guard, tackle, and end split to the right side (Diagram #7). The personal protector has to count the box. If it is a 10-man box, three of the defenders will have to cover the spread trips set. That leaves six blockers for seven defenders. With two defenders gapped to each side of the center, there has to be a *gap call* made to the left side of the line. The gap call tells the left guard, tackle, and end to block down a man. This leaves the L1 unblocked. Because of his distance from the block point, he will not be able to block the punt.

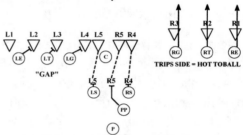

Diagram #7. Trips Set vs. 10-Man Box

We do not call a trips formation with the ball in the middle of the field. I call it from the hash marks.

To have a 10-man box, there can be only one return man deep. If there are two men deep to receive the punt, we can block everyone at the line of scrimmage with our base protection scheme. This allows the left guard, tackle, and end to block outside on the defenders.

If I make a *doubles call*, I split only the tackle and end to that side (Diagram #8). If I call *doubles right*, the right end and tackle split into a twin set. Both of them must be on the line of scrimmage.

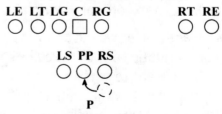

Diagram #8. Doubles

If I want to call doubles and use a motion call, I call *double up* (Diagram #9). That takes one of our shield players and moves him into the offensive line. He replaces the guard, and the guard moves out to the tackle position. I can back either one of the split players off the line and use him as a motion man. It serves a double purpose; I can motion him to free him in his coverage or create doubt in the defense. They have to think fake with a motion call. That is particularly true if we motion him from one side of the set to the other.

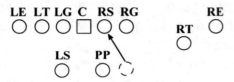

Diagram #9. Double Up

If I want to motion the back from one side of the formation to the other, I call *double-up fly*. Also, by putting a shield into the line, I put a bigger body against a defensive defender. It is tough for the shield when the defensive tackles get a seven-and-a-half yard run at them. This lets the shield hit the defensive tackle in the mouth and help out the deep line.

We can also use the *up call* with our trips set. We move one of the shield players into the guard position and take one of the wide players off the line as an eligible receiver.

As soon as I see someone press our trips players, we get an automatic *switch call*. The defender will get into a position as a defensive back playing press coverage. They are trying to force the bullets to the outside and wall them out of the middle. When we see that, we make a switch call and begin to cross our coverage lanes. We push the defender back to six yards and switch the coverage.

If we want to improve the coverage, we can use the up call and motion one of the bullets to free him to cover. If we want to run him on a reverse, that is the best way to get him into the play. This is also a good way to get into a jailbreak screen on the outside. When the defense sees all the motion, more times than not, they will check out of what they had called and play punt safe. When that happens, we go to our seven-bullets game.

This scheme gives you a chance to be creative in what you do in the punting game. The thing you have to watch is the position of the ball on the field. If Bill Stewart calls a trip formation in the middle of the field, I have hung my punter out to dry. The problem is the defender aligned on the split guard in the trips set. He has a short distance to come to the punter. The shield has to block the #4 defender coming from the inside. The #3 defender from that side can sneak inside off the guard and rush. He is coming unblocked from a position where he can get to the ball.

If that happens, the punter has to cover up for the mistake. We drill that in practice. As soon as he sees that situation, he gets the ball off. I do not care what type of kick it is as long as it is not blocked. It is a catch and kick for the punter.

I want to show you a situation which occurred in our game against the University of North Carolina (Diagram #10). The score was 31-30, and it was a critical time in the game. We had to get the punt off. They had a one-man returner, which meant they were going to have a 10-man box. We kicked from a trips right formation. North Carolina overloaded to our trips side. If you are thinking about using this kind of game, you must pay attention to this point. When we numbered the rushers, both #5 rushers were to the trips set side of the ball. That meant both shields were going to block to the right. We had to get a gap call to the left side. We turned the L1 to the backside loose and punted the ball.

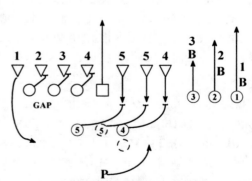

Diagram #10. Overload

In the game against Syracuse University this year, we used a double formation (Diagram #11). We were backed up and had to punt the ball. They aligned with eight men in the box and two on the doubles split with one returner. At the last second, they brought one of the defenders from the split coverage back into the rush. The right guard blocked the R4 rusher, which left the right shield to block the wide R3 rusher. The personal protector blocked the R5, and the left shield blocked L5. The backside ran a gap scheme and released the L1 rusher from the outside. The rusher coming off the double set belongs to the punter to catch and punt the ball.

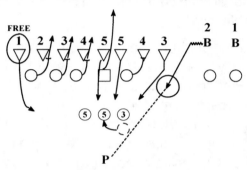

Diagram #11. Catch and Punt

When we run the double up, we want to make the defense defend the field. If they make a mistake and do not cover someone, we will take advantage and fake the punt. All it takes is the right situation and the guts to run something like that with the game on the line. When you start to use the double and trip sets or anything with motion, you need to tighten your splits.

I am not trying to sell you anything, but this is what we do in a backed-up situation. We have a tight punt formation. However, I want coverage from this formation. We call *tight over right, roll* (Diagram #12). That gives me one bullet. I want to be able to cover the punt and keep the defense from getting a return into a short field. If you put the entire punt team into the formation, the defense can pen you in.

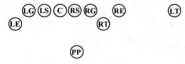

P
Diagram #12. Tight Over Right, Roll

I move the left and right shield into the line in the left and right guard positions. I told you earlier that the guards in the base formation were players with more girth. They are linebackers and tight end types. They now become the tackles on the tight punt formation. The interior five linemen are the biggest players on the punt formation team. I do not put linemen into the game.

The left end aligns in a tight wing set outside the left tackle. On the right side, I align the right tackle in a tight slot position between the right guard and right end. When I talk about the right guard, I am talking about the right guard who is now in a tackle position in this formation. The left tackle position is the split bullet to the outside. The personal protector is still the personal protector for the punter.

In a tight situation, we do not use a count for our blocking assignments. I do not like any kind of numbers game when you are backed up. Those things are confusing and are built-in excuses for mistakes. We use an *iron cross technique* in the gaps. As the lineman stomps, he brings up his arms into an extended position to form a cross with his arms and body. The lineman to his outside will be doing the same technique. Their arms will overlap into the gaps and help seal the gaps.

The right shield aligns on the heels of the center with a six-inch split. On the snap of the ball, he stomps with his inside foot to close that six-inch split and forms the iron cross. He wants to be heavy in the A gap and seal it. The right guard has the same alignment and performs the same technique and gets heavy in the B gap sealing it.

The left shield and guard do the same thing to the left side. The wing is tight off the left guard's butt. He is heavy in the C gap and makes any defender run the hump if he goes around him.

The ends and tackles in the spread punt formation are ends, defensive backs, and receivers. The guards are bigger with more girth. They are Sam linebackers and players of that type. The personal protector is the middle linebacker. He is a tough and sharp football player. Reed Williams, our All-American linebacker, played that position this year. He was tough and dependable.

The right tackle sits in the slot in a tight wing position on the outside hip of the right guard. He is the C-gap player. He uses the same technique as the left wing on the left side. He iron crosses the inside gap and makes everyone run the hump to get around him. The right end is aligned in a tight position with a slight split between him and the right tackle. On the snap of the ball, he takes a drop-step with his outside foot and hits the widest rusher with an inside flipper under his chin. We want him to play that technique so he does not get collapsed to the inside by an outside rusher.

When you use a scheme like this, you have to change up what you do. I will go trips to the left side and roll right. If you use the rugby punt, you must remember if the punter runs with the ball before he kicks it, the trajectory will be low. You have to be careful not to let a defender get in front of the kick. A defender running from the line of scrimmage at the punter can block the ball because it comes out so low. If you are going to try to rugby punt, do not let the punter run too far with the ball. A short two to three steps is all I would recommend.

I am no name-dropper, but I learned something important from Coach Belichick. I am not talking about Bill. I am talking about his father, Steve. He told me that when a punter catches the ball from the center, he has to keep the ball away from his body. He has to catch the ball with the arms extended. The first step is with the foot with which he punts. If you are a right-footed punter, your rhythm is right-left-punt.

A three-step punter cannot punt for West Virginia. They may be able to kick it 50 yards, but they cannot kick in our scheme. I cannot take them and I will not take them. I am a two-step coach. When you are practicing with the punter, always punt into the wind. Never let your punter kick with the wind. I want the punter to catch the ball, get it fully extended, and punt with a nice spiral.

When defenses use stacks at the line of scrimmage in their punt-rush schemes, you have to count the defenders in the stack with two numbers. If the defender is off the ball, do not count him

because he cannot get to the ball to block it. If you will roll your punter right or left, you will not have to worry about blocking every single defender.

The right shield has time and distance on his side. He splits the A gap, and his toes have to be at seven-and-a-half yards. On the backside every time, the left guard calls the number of returners. If there are two returners, we are in base blocking. That allows the splits to get wider for the ends. The defender aligned on the end will split because he is an eligible receiver.

I hope I did not bounce around too much. I absolutely love special teams. At West Virginia, we take pride in our special teams. I watch every special teams film, and I have been the special teams coach for the last two years. I am going to give that up this next year to two good people. However, I am going to coach the punt. I want the team to know that I think the most important play in football is the punt. The hardest thing I had to get across to the quarterbacks was that the punt was a good play. It is good to punt the ball. It is not a beautiful play, but it is a good play. If you can punt the ball, you can control the field position.

Put your best football players on the punt team and punt the ball. Our starters are on our punt team, and I spend a lot of time with it. It is what you do more than anything. The second most important phase, in which we have stunk at for the last two years, is the kickoff. It is a tragedy and embarrassment, and it has to get better.

You need to think about the importance of the punt. You have to be creative and let your young people have some fun. The punt team comes with me, and we work on their conditioning in a coverage drill. The rest of the team works on their conditioning, and we work in a team punt drill. I do that for a reason because I want to sell to the team the importance of the punt.

You had two West Virginia country boys talk today. You heard Larry Slade first and then me. Larry is a good friend of mine and a great football coach. Thank you very much, and God bless you. Come see us in Morgantown.

OFFENSIVE LINE ZONE BLOCKING CONCEPTS

University of Kentucky

It is good to be home. I left here in January of 1981, and 30 years later, I get to come back and be a part of the program for the University of Kentucky. They say timing is everything in coaching. At my age and time, the timing is right for me. I was very fortunate when I received the call from Joker Phillips. The reason I am coaching at Kentucky is because of Coach Phillips. His excitement about the program really pumps me up.

It has been an interesting ride for me the last several years. Early in my career, my wife and I talked a long time about the level of coaching I was interested in pursuing. We set two criteria for the level and type of coaching job I could be happy in and I would be able to enjoy working with young people. The first criterion was this: we would never take a job based on the amount of money we would be paid. We felt what we were doing was born out of passion for the game of football, born out of commitment and a love for working with kids. How much a job paid did not hold a value for us. The second criterion on taking a coaching job was this: we did not care where the job took us or where the opportunity to coach led us. We would be willing to say, "Let's go do that." Our motto was: "This is going to be the best place we have ever been."

I have tried to stay like a sponge as much as I could in terms of information and ideas. A long time ago, when I first came to this clinic back in 1980, it was the first thing I got to do as a college football coach. I was so excited running up and down these hallways. I was shaking hands with coaches and greeting people. I had that feeling of "I am a football coach. I am excited about coaching."

I attended all of the lectures I could. I wrote down every word the speakers said. It was a tremendous experience. That year, Woody Hayes was the guest speaker. After listing to his lecture, I knew exactly what I wanted to do with my career. I wanted to be a football coach. I wanted to lead and teach young people.

Some of you have heard me lecture before at clinics. The thing I always start my clinic talks with this point: to me, the most important part of coaching is the relationship that you have with your players. More than any devout coaching scheme, pass protection, zone reads, or anything else that you could give your players to help them out is the relationship and respect they have for you. It is the most meaningful part of this whole process. How you can develop that relationship and lead the group of players you work with is special. It is important to get your group to feel special and to feel they are the best and most important part of the football team.

I have taken my group to go bowling, fishing, and frog gigging, to play basketball, and to do a lot of other activities. A lot of the times, I have the upper hand. At other times, they come out on top. That is the fun of it for them.

I really feel fortunate to be working with the offensive line. That group of players is a team within the team. They need to feel they are a team within the team. When our offensive line leaves the locker room, I want the other players to know they have left the room. I want a special feeling when they come on the field. I want the offensive line to be special when they come onto the field. I want that presence when they come onto the field. When they get that feeling as a group, then you are starting to develop an offensive line. I feel the offensive line relies on that feeling of unity and togetherness more so than any other group. I think you short-change the coaching aspects if that is not at the forefront of working with the group. Make it a point to make your group feel special, and make them feel their coach is a part of the group.

All of the lectures I do center on technique and development. I do this because coaches run different systems, and we all believe different things. There is no right or wrong way to do it. If everyone that gave a clinic lecture said, "This is the way you do it," someone would be teaching it wrong. You teach the players a certain way because you feel this is the best way to teach them. As a result, I do not spend a lot of time about running one play or another play. Most of my lecture centers on technical development.

The one thing I feel I am responsible for is to design drills and teach the drills to the group so we are getting reps while we are doing the drills. We are not just teaching one player when we run our drills. We do not want a drill where we are working with only one player while a dozen or more are just standing around watching.

While I am out on the road visiting high school practices, it is to my advantage to try to visit four or five schools during the day. It is interesting to compare the styles of the practice schedules. It is amazing to watch the practices to see how coaches get their ideas communicated. The coach who can teach with repetition and purpose, and can cover everything with the group, can get a lot more done in practice. He gets more done than the coach who puts his arms around Johnny and tells him repeatedly that he did the drill wrong, while the rest of the group stands and waits for the coach to come back to the group. You need to let the group know that the time spent on each drill is valuable to them, and that it is going to mean something to them later in games.

I want to get into the way I teach blocking techniques. I do not have the absolute way of teaching blocking, but this is how I do it. I am going to start with the way I teach base blocking. I had players tell me after they had attended a combine session that the pro coaches asked them to explain how they learned to base block. Most of them made a simple statement to the fact they came off the ball and just blocked the man. That frustrated me that they did not have the terminology to explain how we taught them to base block. I came up with a system where the players could communicate the fundamentals of what they had to do in blocking.

In our fundamentals of run blocking, the first thing I want to do is to talk to you about what you need to do when we snap the football.

Fundamentals of Run Blocking

- Aiming point: Feet
  - ✓ J-step
  - ✓ Y-step
  - ✓ L-step
- Landmark: Eyes
  - ✓ Playside number
  - ✓ Playside armpit
  - ✓ Outside shoulder
  - ✓ Outside hip
- Contact: Hands
- Finish: Heart

The first thing I want to talk about is the aiming point. The aiming point has to do with the feet. When we snap the ball, the foot has to go somewhere. We teach three steps: J-step, Y-step, and L-step. These letters came to me when I looked down at my feet when I was demonstrating the three different steps.

First is the J-step. It is an over-and-up lead step. Any time we are trying to knock someone off the ball, we teach the J-step. If you took a marker and stuck it down through your foot, you would draw a "J" in a line on the ground. The step would be over-and-up. When that step comes up, what happens to the shoulders? My shoulders stay square. Any time I am trying to create a vertical push, I am going to use the J-step when I come off the ball.

The next step is the Y-step. We use this for a gap block. If I am the left tackle and I am blocking down in the gap toward the B gap, I want to turn my inside toe toward the target. When I point the inside toes, my shoulders turn inside, and I gap-block with the Y-step.

The last step we teach is the L-step. We completely open up the hips. The position of your feet is in direct proportion to your shoulders. If your feet are not in the right spot, your shoulders are not in the right spot. Certainly, that is a critical aspect of what we are trying to do.

The next coaching point has to do with the landmark. This is our teaching progression. Landmarks have to do with your eyes. I teach full landmarks. I do not teach down-the-middle, head-up landmarks. The reason why we do not teach the middle head-up landmark is because you do not have a place for the head to go when you stick someone in the sternum. I am not saying this does not happen, but it is not what we teach.

I teach a playside number landmark. That is the tightest landmark we would teach a player to block. A blocker can come off the line and stick his eyes on that playside number, drive his head, and get some vertical push, and then squeeze his head up under the armpit. That is the tightest landmark we use for a vertical push.

The outside armpit would mean we are going to widen the landmark, and take less of the defender. We use this landmark for a wider hitting play or a combo block run play, where you are trying to get the shoulders turned.

The outside shoulder block would be a reach block wide. We do not use this block a huge amount of the time. The other point is the outside hip landmark. Those are the only four places where we want our eyes looking. I am trying to be very specific about what is right and what is wrong.

The next point is contact and use of the hands. When you listen to line coaches, you hear them talking about the use of the hands. I spend more time on the hands than anything else that I do. We have more hand violations than anything else that comes up in terms of mistakes made with the guys that we block.

I tell our players this: If they block with the hands outside of the shoulder, and come off the ball and make contact with the defender, and the hands are outside, it is because they are scared. They are afraid that they do not have the ability to move my feet far enough to hang on to the defender. They do not have the confidence they can bring their hands inside and stay engaged with the defender. As a result, they put the hands outside and try to block the defender.

We all know you cannot block with your hands outside. Nevertheless, every coach has players that do it. They do not have the confidence to move their hands inside and keep their thumbs up, shoot their elbows, and be able to press with their hands inside.

If you are 300 pounds, and I am 300 pounds, and we line up a foot apart, and we go "Set, hut," we are going to fit together and push on each other, and we are most likely going to end up in a stalemate. If it is a stalemate, the defense is going to win. We have to create movement to win on offense. The way we are going to do that is to generate momentum with our hands. We are going to load our elbows when we come off the ball on our first step. We load the elbows tight with our hands by our hips.

On the second step, where the contact is going to be made, we are going to cover our split with our first step, load our elbows, and strike with our second step. Now, when we strike, we are going to be able to generate momentum with the hips. I get the same momentum with a power clean. I can get that hip-snap movement so my 300 pounds has a pop to it. It gives a chance for movement. I can take a 300-pound defensive man and move him. We can create movement and create an edge and push. The hands become very important.

The last point is to finish. That has a lot to do with your heart. How much of a killer instinct do you have? How willing you are to pay the price to win the battle?

I had some players at Arkansas last year to whom I was teaching these principles who I felt did not have the concept of finish. They felt if they were on the backside of an outside zone play, and they engaged their defender, as the play developed, if their man got off his block and made the tackle 15 yards down the field, they felt they had done a good job on their block. They did not feel they needed to be concerned with the backside of a play. I made sure to let them know that was not good enough.

I had a large board put up on the wall in our meeting room. We called it our "Defender Elimination Board." I gave them a plus or minus on every play of the game, based on whether the man they were to engaged on a play was in, on, or at the pile at the end of each play. I could be an 80-yard run, and the backside defensive end ran all the way down the field and tackled our back at the two-yard line. If our backside tackle's assignment was to cut the defensive end off, and the end got off and made the tackle, our blocker received a minus on the Defender Elimination Board.

That grade to those players in the room became as important to them as the grade for their assignment grade. The players who scored 90 percent and above demonstrated to me the players with the most heart in the group. It told me which players cared about the finish on each play.

When a player misses a block when we are on a 12-play drive, and he is trying to base reach a 3 technique, and he misses his landmark and hits him on the backside, the defender will turn me up the field and make the tackle for a two-yard loss.

Going back to the huddle, the player is 25 to 30 yards away from me on the sidelines. I am not going to run out on the field in that 12-play drive and tell him he missed his landmark. "The landmark is on the other side of the man. Get your head on the outside numbers." I am not going out on the field, during that drive, and tell him he missed his landmark. But he still has plays in this 12-play drive that he still has to go execute his assignments.

I want that player going back to the huddle thinking, "Gosh, I can't believe I missed that landmark. I hit the players on the wrong side of his numbers. I have to get my eyes outside on the playside number." I want the player to know this. I

want him to fix the problem. I want him to understand that he has four landmarks to choose from. On this play, his landmark is on the playside numbers. If he does not do that, he is going to give up a two-yard loss. I want him to be able to fix the block.

I ask you to tell me the four things that are important in run blocking. Again, they are the following:

- Aiming point: Feet
- Landmark: Eyes
- Contact: Hands
- Finish: Heart

They are things that have to do with feet, eyes, hands, and heart. Can you fix those things? Certainly, I can fix them. We ask the player what is the problem. They will respond, "It is my landmark, but I will get it fixed." Now, we have teaching going on. Now, we have players who know what is expected of them. Now, they can perform and do the things that are expected of them.

Blocking Linebackers

Blocking linebackers can be a different animal. I want to go over a few points in dealing with linebackers. The first thing we have to do is to measure the distance the blocker and the linebacker. A space element here was not present when we were blocking down linemen or line-of-scrimmage players.

- *Measure the distance:* We are going to cover that distance full speed. However, when we come within one yard of the linebacker, we must come to balance. Running backs do this all of the time in that they come to balance before they make a cut.
- *Preparation for contact (pad level):* We must be able to come to balance, collect ourselves, and put our hips, hands, and knees in a position to strike.
- *Strike on the rise:* We must get low enough in that last yard to get into position to hit on the rise and drive the feet where we can accelerate.

We want to take our momentum and go from low to high on his pads and continue to drive him back.

- *Finish with a base:* We must continue to drive the defender back by keeping a good base under our shoulders and hips.

Here is our cut rule. If the defender forces, we are going to cut him. If he fades, we stay up. This is how we know when to cut and when not to cut block.

I want to cover some zone-blocking ideas. As I went from one hospitality room to another, most of the questions I received concerned how to teach zone blocking. They wanted to know if I thought they could use zone blocking in high schools. I am not sure what offensive line coaches talk about at clinics other than zone blocking. That is going to be my next topic. It is the subject most covered in clinic talks in all of football. This is how I teach zone blocking.

In zone blocking, there are two concepts. There is a man concept and a zone concept. Based on the defensive front used, determines if we are in a man or zone concept. This is what determines how the individual blocker must read the defense. As I teach this to the players, they must understand we must have the following elements.

We must have two elements to zone block: a base protector (an offensive lineman who is covered) and a tail protector (an offensive lineman who is uncovered). The players must understand that we must have these two things. This is not difficult. If I am covered, I am a base protector. If I am a base protector, I use in a man scheme. Again, you don't have a tail protector, you are in a man scheme, not zone.

If covered after I come to the line of scrimmage, I am a base protector. If I am a base protector, I am in a man scheme. We want to base reach the defender on his outside numbers. From this point, we will confine the talk to the inside zone. In the power zones, emphasis is on movement of the defensive lineman. In the speed zones, emphasis is on eliminating the linebacker.

If the offensive lineman comes to the line of scrimmage and is uncovered, he is "Tail Protector." The tail protectors are the linemen that make all of the combination calls. The communication system is important for all linemen. I am sure everyone has their own way of how they communicate upfront. This system needs to be thoughtful and elaborate. They do not have much time to talk. They need to have everyone on the same page.

If the base protector is covered when he gets to the line of scrimmage, he is in a Man Scheme. He is going to base reach the outside number of the defender. This is true unless he gets a combination call that tells me I have a tail protector. It can be a combination between the tight end and tackle, which we called "EAT." If it is between the guard and tackle, it is called "TAG." If I am a guard, I come to the line of scrimmage, and I am uncovered, I make the "TAG" call so it would let my tackle know he is going to combination block with the guard. He comes off his man scheme, and goes to the zone scheme. Why? Because he knows he has a tail protector.

If I am the tight end, and the defense is playing in an under defense, it means they have a 9 technique on me, and I am covered. The tackle has a 5 technique on him, and he is covered. The tackle does not make a call because he is a base protector. The end must block the 9 technique. That tackle cannot make a call. The end knows he is in a man scheme. The tackle must base reach the 5 technique.

If the guard calls "TAG 58," we call 58 the Linebacker. Now, the tackle must work through the 5 technique to the linebacker. Using his hands, he is going to power zone to the linebacker. The calls tell all of our linemen how they are to block. Using this system, we can block any defense we would ever see, and it would not matter if they are covered or uncovered.

As we come to the line of scrimmage, the center will identify the front to the quarterback. He will call out either "four down," or "three down." This is all we need to know at this point. The quarterback comes to the line and calls out, "Four down. Four down." Next, he identifies the point linebacker. The point linebacker is the direction we are going to start from to let the line know who the center has. In the 4-3 defense, it would be the Mike linebacker. For us on the inside zone, the point linebacker is the zero linebacker strong.

The center comes to the line of scrimmage and is uncovered, so he knows he is a tail protector and that he has to make a call. He tells his right guard, "RAY to 50." The 50 is the middle linebacker. That starts the communication. The right guard just received a call for a combination block. He is in a power zone blocking area for the linebacker.

The tackle is uncovered in a 4-3 defense. The tight end is covered. They have an opportunity for a zone block. The tackle calls out "EAT 45." Now, they know they are going to be working on a combination block. That is how we put our combination blocks together.

If the defense stems to an under look, what do we do? Now, the guard becomes a tail protector. We call, "TAG 52," and we pick them up. If the defense stems back to the regular 4-3 defense, we call, "RAY 45".

The defense can move anywhere they want, and we will always be in the right combination because we are either covered or uncovered. That is how we communicate with our line.

This is a steadfast rule. If you do not have a tail protector, then you are in a man scheme. You can't zone if that is the situation. How do you know if you have a tail protector or not? The tail protector is going to tell you by his combination call. If the lineman is uncovered, he is going to make a call. It becomes easy for everyone to listen for the call of the uncovered lineman.

As the scheme develops, if I am the backside tackle in any type of zone scheme, I am considered uncovered. He is a tail protector, and he is always working with the backside guard. Let me stress one point: the combination between the center and right guard the call is RAY. The call for the center and left guard is our LOU. The other calls are the same on the right and the left. They are the same if they are the run or pass combinations.

There are two types of zone blocks: power zone and speed zone. The question that always comes up on this subject is this: "How long do I stay on the down lineman until I get to the linebacker?" There must be some emphasis on what we are trying to do. If we are running an inside zone play, we want to use a power zone blocking scheme. We want emphasis on moving the down lineman. We want to push the down linemen.

As the center and guard are blocking a 1 technique, how do we know when to get off the down lineman to go get the linebacker? We are going to fit together and push the down lineman. As we create movement on the down lineman, and the linebacker separates, then the guard and center separates. If the linebacker stays stacked on the inside tackle, then we are going to stay on the vertical push on the 1 technique. Therefore, we have to know the type of zone block we are going to use.

Power Zone

The technique for the power zone is this. If I am a base protector in the power zone, my landmark is a spot on the playside number. I am going to take a six-inch J-step to the playside number. I am going to load my elbows, and put my eyes on that landmark.

If I am the tail protector on the power zone, I am taking a six-inch J-step, and I put my eyes on the landmark on the inside numbers. The push is going to go vertical. The J-step controls your shoulders for the vertical push.

Speed Zone

The speed zone is what we use on an outside zone play. Now, we are going to try to cut off the down linemen. The emphasis is on climbing to the second level to get to linebackers. The landmark changes now. If I am a base protector in the speed zone, my landmark is the outside armpit. The tail protector is trying to drive his eyes to the far number so he can push the base protector off.

It is easier for me to cover that with the team inside in a classroom and then go to the field and say, "Okay, here is the defense. If you are a tail protector, make a call." We expect them to be able to make the calls. We can show them several different defenses and have them make the calls for each defensive set. It is like a math equation. There is a definition for everything you must do. Because of that, we know exactly where we have to be.

There are three different categories to teaching zone blocking. First is an outside shade on the base protector. Second is head-up on the base protector. Third is an inside base on the base protector. These are the only things you have to teach when you go out to teach zone blocking.

Now, I want to show you the three zone blocks. First is the power zone block technique to the right. Second is the head-up Technique. Third is the outside shade technique.

It is very easy to set the drills up. I put the down linemen in their position first. We need to understand how to fit the down linemen. As an outside shade on a base protector, on inside zone, I take a six-inch J-step, roll my elbows, put my eyes on the outside number, fire my hands, and drive for movement (Diagram #1).

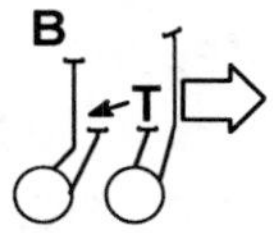

Diagram #1. Outside Shade

If I get width, then I am going to power on my inside arm, and drive for movement toward the pylon. That is his technique.

If he is a head-up man on the protector, we take the six-inch J-step, and it may not go very far because the defender is head-up on me (Diagram #2). I know if the man is head-up, he is not going to stay head-up. He is head-up for a reason. He is head-up or leaning going inside or outside. I take the J-step to cover his movement to the outside. My eyes are going to that landmark.

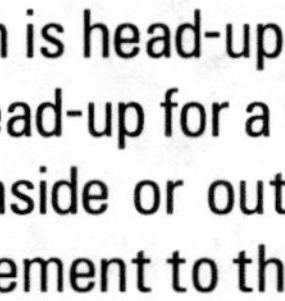

Diagram #2. Heads-Up Technique

When I am on a defender, and I am trying to load my arms and block, and he disappears inside, I go from two hands to one hand and make sure he is secured to my tail protector (Diagram #3). As I work vertical to the linebacker, that is against an outside shade and a head-up defender.

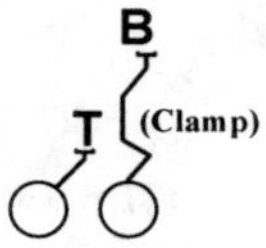

Diagram #3. Inside Technique

The technique changes for the inside shade on the base protector. The guard zone steps with the playside foot. Everyone is going to step to the playside first. No one is stepping with the backside foot. The second step is going to go vertical, and then drive back into the 3 technique. I am trying to clamp the defender. We want to clamp the 3 technique at that point. This gives the center a chance to get to the zone fit and cover the split.

The guard takes a six-inch J-step, and then the guard takes the clamp step, drives vertical, and then does a splash up on the linebacker. We work vertical, and then we splash on the angle of departure to the linebacker.

That technique is a little different because of the clasp aspect. That allows the tail protector to cover his split, and still get vertical push as he comes in on the block. This includes the three looks you should work against as a base protector. It is easy to set the drill up.

The ultimate rule in zone blocking is that the blocker is a gap protector. If at any time, one of the linebackers came up into the gap, and became a gap player, now it became a man scheme instead of a gap scheme. The term to communicate that for us is "base." If the linebacker is at regular depth, and then all of a sudden he walked up into the gap, now the zone blocks are off. We call it out: "Base, base." Then, we went to our base blocks from that combination.

Three-man zones are the next area we need to cover. We know if we are going to run zone schemes, to be effective, we know we are going to need to run them against zone pressure. I think it is the best thing you can do. To me, zone blocking helps your offensive line. We have a tail protector. I can come off the ball. I do not have to worry about a player moving, slanting, or angling outside.

There are two schools of thought in talking about zone blocking in terms of footwork. Jim McNally was a great coach who made his career off zone blocking. He teaches a bucket step and then drive-off-the-ball type of footwork. That is how he teaches it. He teaches the bucket step and then the duck walk to cover the defenders. They shield the defenders so they cannot see the running backs so they can find a hole and take off. I am not that type coach. I am not a bucket-step, duck-walk coach.

Alex Gibbs is a zone guru, if you will. He does the second school of thought on executing the zone-blocking techniques. He teaches a lead step, come off the ball, and capture the neutral zone. My option background will not allow me to take a bucket step, to block anyone in the running game. I can't visualize it, or approve the bucket step. To me, it allows penetration. You listen to Coach David Turner, our defensive line coach, and he will tell you they want to penetrate. They want to make the offense make the shallow cuts.

We want to capture the neutral zone. That is why we teach the J-step. That is why we teach coming off the ball. That is why we use the five-man sled. I do not believe you can teach the bucket step and still create a push on the defensive line. I do not believe the duck walk will allow you to get the push you need. That is my own personal feeling.

Let me get to the three-man zones versus pressure. This requires some identification by the offensive line. Three-man zones all have words that allow us to communicate on who is working together. We identify them based on the two covered base protectors. In this diagram, we are getting a zone blitz from the tight-end side (Diagram #4). The way the offense identifies the defense is the fact that they have two head-up players over the tight end and tackle on the strongside. Something must clue them that we are getting that

type of line movement. Normally, we would expect the end on the tight-end side to be in a 5 technique, and the Sam backer in a 9 technique. You can see they have moved down to even techniques. The Sam Linebacker is in a staggered stance. The nose tackle is tight on the nose of the center. The Mike linebacker loosens up. We studied this defense all week long. We know we must make some adjustments.

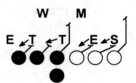

Diagram #4. Three-Man Zones

Now the tight end calls, "Full, full." The tight end knows when we call "full," we are in a three-man zone mode. He is not blocking the Sam linebacker. He is going upfield to seal the Mike linebacker. The tackle takes the Sam backer, the guard takes the defensive end, and the center comes out on the Will linebacker. Now, we have a big play outside against the zone pressure.

If we face a 6-1 pinching defense, we do the same thing. The center normally would call out "4–4," but the center sees the Will linebacker has stemmed to the outside to form the 6-1. The Sam linebacker is on the outside on the tight-end side (Diagram #5). The center calls out "6-1, 6-1." Now, we call out, "Triple, triple." Now, we have the center and backside guard and tackle working together. The onside guard, tackle, and tight end work together.

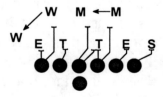

Diagram #5. From No Linebacker to Zone and to = "Base-Base," and Stem to a 6-1 Front

If the defense moves the down line to a different zone scheme and plays the Mike linebacker in the middle over the center, we block a little differently. If we cannot call the number of the linebacker on the TAG, then I do not want to run through the hole and block air. If the defense stems the front and moves the linebackers inside to give us a 6-1 look, we want the backside guard to block down on the tackle, and our up fullback would be responsible to block.

When the defense starts changing their alignment, the offense knows what to do because they have seen it before. They know they can block any defense with these principles.

I have included two schemes that most everyone runs today. First is the inside zone schemes with a "lock" call on the backside. If we ran this without the lock call, the tackle would zone through for the Will backer. The fullback would be on the end. We have been more successful by putting the fullback on the Will backer and the tackle turning out on the end. We zone everyone through on the play. The cutback has been more effective by running the fullback on the Will backer (Diagram #6).

Another thing we want to do on the zone offense is to distort the defensive line. They want to stay gap sound. Our offense wants to create running lanes. We have a better running lane with the fullback coming outside on the Will linebacker on the lock scheme.

The last zone scheme is the force scheme on the outside zone (Diagram #7). We can let the running back make the cut in the B gap, C gap, and the ball is never going to get to the strong safety.

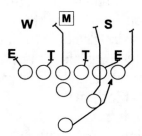

Diagram #7. Zone Schemes: Force

I can see my time is up. Thank you for your attention.

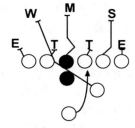

Diagram #6. Zone Schemes: Lock

COACHING THE COMPLETE WIDE RECEIVERS

Clemson University

I appreciate you all hanging around to hear my lecture. We have some real ball coaches in here tonight. If you do not hear anything else tonight, make sure you hear this: this is the greatest profession there is. I do not know if any of you have worked at something else. I have. If you have a passion for teaching and changing young men's lives, there is no other job like it. I heard Billy Graham say something that has always stuck with me. He said that a coach influences more lives in a year than most do in a lifetime. That is an awesome responsibility.

I am here by the grace of God and my coaches I have had along the way. I am from a dysfunctional background, but I had coaches from middle school to high school and into college who impacted me. They kept me headed in the right direction. If you ever wonder what kind of impact you are making on one person's life, you have to look no farther than Clemson. That is why I am there. I could have strayed many different times, but my coaches were always there to help me along.

Thanks for having me here, and thanks to Clemson for giving me the opportunity to represent Clemson. I hope you coaches have had a good clinic. It is a new clinic, and I hope it grows. We grow that way as coaches. We get together, exchange ideas, and talk ball. You learn from each other's mistakes. You experiment and do different things, and you learn from doing.

You also are establishing some relationships. That is what this business is. It is about whom you know. If a coach is going to hire someone, he wants to pick someone he can trust. If you are a young coach, I encourage you to branch out and get to know people. Clinics are the way to go. Coaching is about knowledge and learning your craft and expertise of the position you coach. You have to know the people you are coaching against as well. That is how you continue to grow.

We have come a long way at Clemson. I am proud of our team and what we accomplished this past year. There were many questions a year ago when I was hired. People did not know why I was hired or why I hired the offensive coordinator I did. We lost the bulk of our defensive line, and no one knew who our quarterback was going to be. Whoever it was, he was going to be a first-year player. We lost two receivers and two safeties to the NFL. We lost our long snapper and punter. With all those parts to the puzzle, that team only won seven games.

We won nine games last year. There were 20 new staffs in the country last year, and Oregon was the only team that won more games than we did. They won ten games. We won our division in the ACC for the first time. We had the best record at Clemson since 1991, and we won the bowl game for the first time since 2005. We had two first-team All-Americans, and we were among the leaders in the country in fewest penalties. We had eight all-conference players and had the biggest win on the road by beating a top-10 team. The thing I am most proud of is the fact we had seven academic all-conference players.

Tonight, we are here to talk about offense. I believe the key to offense is balance. There are many different ways to go about doing that, but you have to commit to what you choose. We had the most balanced offense in Clemson history, and we scored the most points in school history. C.J. Spiller was the player of the year in the conference, and we had all-conference performers at lineman, receiver, tight end, running back, and a freshman quarterback. C.J. Spiller broke a 31-year record for all-purpose yards at 191 yards a game.

We had tremendous improvement from the 2008 season to last year. We had good balance in our offense. I have always had a passion for and will be committed to having a good passing game. To excel in the passing game, you must have receivers that can get open. They have to catch the ball and run with it after they catch it. This is my 16th year of coaching, and my background is in coaching receivers and tight ends. I have coached at two places. I played at Alabama for five years and coached there for eight. I have had some success coaching wide receivers.

The secret to coaching is not developing the ready-made All-Americans. Anyone can coach those types of talented players. The secret to coaching is developing talent that is not so good. Aaron Kelly was 6'5" and 163 pounds. Tyler Grisham had no offers coming out of high school. He is playing for the Pittsburgh Steelers right now and playing well. He will probably take Hines Ward's place. Aaron Kelly needs three touchdown receptions to break the 57-year Clemson record. Those receivers developed into great ones. However, you must have the right characteristics and tools.

That is what we are going to talk about tonight. Developing the complete wide receiver starts with the fundamentals of the position. We start with stance and start, and go to route running, break points, releases, yards after the catch, ball security, and blocking. I am going to roll through this lecture and try to cover a lot of things.

The thing I am biggest on is fundamentals and technique at every position. If you have a player with average ability, but who is a great technician and fundamentally sound, he can help you. That is what I was. I had to maximize everything with my technique, fundamentals, and knowledge. If you have a player with talent who will buy into technique and fundamentals, you will get Jerry Rice.

Jerry Rice was the greatest wide receiver of all time. Not because he was talented—other players were more talented. What set him apart from the others is he was a true technician and devoted to fundamentals. He outworked everybody. When you have that type of talent and work ethic, you get a superstar.

There are three basic criteria you need to be a great wide receiver. This has nothing to do with ability. These things are non-negotiable. It all starts with great effort. We want effort in everything we do. It does not matter whether it is in a meeting room, on the practice field, or in a game, you must have great effort. If you have a receiver that will give you great effort, he will be consistent and will have confidence. Those are important attributes for a wideout.

The next thing is intensity. You must have focus and concentration. I cannot stand lackadaisical players. When it is time to go to work, they start. If a player is lackadaisical, mistakes will happen because he is not focused. When the player steps between the lines, he needs some intensity in his demeanor. He has to focus on doing it right.

When you play football, you must be physical at any position you play. They have to be aggressive in everything they do. They cannot all *be* great players, but they can *want to be* great players. Consistency, concentration, confidence, and toughness equal playing time for the players.

The physical talents of a player are important, but those critical areas I talked about are non-negotiable. Those things develop the culture of your football team. The individual player must have them to have a chance to be a complete football player.

The first thing we talk about at all positions is fundamentals and technique. It does not matter if you are the center or quarterback; that is the starting point of all teaching. The place we start is with the stance.

The first thing we talk about is the legs and feet. In our stance, we teach the inside foot to the ball as the forward foot in the stance. We want the feet a little wider than shoulder-width with a stagger in the feet. The size of the stagger is different for all receivers. The receiver needs enough stagger so that he does not drop-step as the ball turns over.

Bend both knees and shoulder in a comfortable position. If the back leg locks, the receiver has to break it before he can move. We want to concentrate the weight on the ball of the front foot. The receiver needs as much weight as it takes to keep him from picking up the front foot at the snap of the ball. If the balance is not right, the receiver will pick up the front foot. If he does not have enough stagger, he drop-steps.

The back is straight as he bends from the waist. He leans forward with his head up so he can study the defense. He looks in at the ball because wideouts move on sight, not sound. In your receiver drills, if you are calling cadence, you are wasting time. In every drill we do, we move a ball or snap one. That is relevant to the position. Every drill you do should be relevant to the game.

The shoulders should be square to the line of scrimmage with the arms in a comfortable position. If the receiver can get his knee over his toe and the chest over the knee, it helps him get his weight where it needs to be. We want the receiver to move without any false steps in his release. If you want to make that point, time your players in the 40-yard dash. They will understand that the clock starts when they move regardless of which direction. If they take a drop-step or pick up the front foot and put it down, their time will reflect that.

It does not matter the time they run. If they are 4.8 in the 40, that is the time I want them to run in the game. I do not want them playing at 5.1 speed because they false-step. When I watch the film, I want to slow it down in super-slow motion to find out if the defensive end is beating the wideout off the ball. I want to hold the wide receiver accountable because we are after efficiency in our stance.

I do not want the receiver up on his toe. I want the weight on the ball of the foot as if I were in a chute. The big receivers will cock the foot in their stance. When the ball snaps, the first thing they have to do is uncock the ankle to get the foot on the ground. They have moved and not gained an inch downfield. We want to drive off the back foot and roll off the front foot.

We align with our inside foot up. If you watch the NFL, half of the receivers have their inside foot up and the other half have their outside foot up. We put the inside foot forward in our stance for a number of reasons. If the receiver aligns with his inside foot back, he has a tendency to turn his shoulder inside as he looks in to the ball. That means he has to square the shoulders before moving downfield. That is a natural movement. If you put the inside foot forward in the stance, it is unnatural to turn the shoulder and to look inside.

The release of the receiver is all about speed. It is maximizing the 1.2 seconds of time. The receiver must have an internal clock in his head. The quarterback is in a bind. He has defender coming off the ball, trying to get to him in 2.9 to 3.0 seconds. Every tenth and hundredth of a second matters in whether we have a completion or a sack. How many times have you seen it happen? The quarterback gets sacked, and everyone blames the offensive tackle, when the real problem was the efficiency of the wide receiver.

When you watch the film, you find the wideout takes false steps all over the place and wastes time. All those problems start with the stance of the receiver.

We start practice tomorrow, and this is what the wideouts will do. They will start with stance and start. When you teach them, make sure you teach it right. You must teach the "drive and roll." It is like the sprinter coming out of the blocks in a race. We drive off the back foot and roll over the front foot.

I apologize if I get a little fired up. I am passionate about this game, and it takes me back to my roots. The next skill the receiver must master is the release. We spend more time on releases than anything we do. If the receiver cannot get off the line of scrimmage, it will be a long day at the office. If the defense can put one defender on your receiver and eliminate him, you are in trouble. If the defense has a good defensive end, they will get to the quarterback if he has enough time. It does not matter who you have blocking him; he will get there. If the defensive back can disrupt your receiver and buy time for the defensive line, that is their objective.

The internal clock in the receiver's head tells him when he has to present the target for the quarterback. We spend more time on releases than anything we do. We do it daily. The release has to become one motion. It has to be natural and a reaction for them. The hands, eyes, and feet have to work together. When the eyes see the release, the hands and feet execute it. It has to be quick, and they cannot think about it. When you walk down the halls in school, you are not conscious about running into someone. You move around them without thinking. That is the way it is on the football field. You are not consciously thinking about making the move, it just happens. When the defensive back presses the receiver, he has the confidence to beat him because he has worked the release so many times that it is second nature. He is confident in his ability and technique because he has done it so many times, he can take it to the game field. We spend the majority of our time in practice getting off press coverage.

We are trying to do a couple of things to the defender. We want to freeze him and get his weight on his heels. After we do that, we want to "get long and lean" up the field. That is the terminology we use to describe the route coming off the ball. We do not want an arc or humps in the route. We want the receiver to knock a hole in the defender's shoulder.

If the defensive back takes an inside leverage position on the receiver, we have an edge. The receiver never wants to turn his shoulders to the sidelines. The receiver comes off the ball, knocks a hole in the defender's shoulder, and holds his ground in the pattern. He cannot let the defender force him to the sidelines. On our practice field, we have an orange line painted five yards from the sidelines. That is no-man's land.

When we attack zone coverage, the release is in a straight line. We attack an area of the field rather than a man. The receiver releases in a straight line to get the proper depth on his pattern. If the receiver is bumped out of his pattern, he works to get back on the pattern. He must preserve the spacing and stretch on the zone we need to have.

I am going to spend most of my time talking about man-to-man coverage. Against press coverage, the release is more difficult.

- A clean release requires concentration at the line of scrimmage.
- You must have quick, concise moves with the hands and feet.
- The hands, eyes, and feet must work together.
- He wants a long center of gravity, and he should play behind the pads.

There are all kinds of pressure coverage. If the defender is off, but is still in press coverage, we handle that differently than a defender in heavy press coverage. All the moves we are going to talk about, the receivers must be able to do at the line of scrimmage as well as on the move in space.

If the defender is playing off in his coverage, but he is playing press man, the receiver drives, rolls off the line, and goes after the defender. However, if the defender is in the grillwork of the receiver, it becomes a different deal. The first thing the receiver wants to do is narrow his base somewhat. He does not want as much stagger in his stance. He has to get his feet up under his body quicker to execute the move he is using.

He wants to get his hands up behind his pads. By narrowing the base, he can get his feet under his shoulders quicker. He wants to have a low center of gravity and play behind his pads. He never wants to expose himself. For every action, there is a reaction. We do drills to execute our releases. The important thing about a drill is that it must help them perfect the skill you are trying to teach.

When we talk about releases, it becomes a game within a game. The receiver cannot use one release and expect to escape the defender. They have to understand the different types of releases and use them. The receiver has to change up the way he releases off the ball.

The first release is a speed release. That technique is what it is. The receiver blows off the ball and tries to rip or swim through the defender. He wants to go as fast as he can when coming off the ball. This may be a running play, but the release is the same for the receiver. We do not want to tip off—by our demeanor, stance, or our intensity coming off the ball—the play we are running.

Too many times, our receivers do not understand that the defender is coached as well. They study tape of the receivers and pick up on his habits. They notice if the receiver adjusts his gloves every time it is a pass play. If he does not come off the ball at the same speed, they know he is not involved in the play or it is a backside play. They study the splits of receivers, and how they align on certain plays. That is what coaches do. They study tendencies and techniques and use them to give their players an advantage. The coach has to get his receiver to understand the "game within the game."

The next release is a single move. That move is what it says. We make one move and go the other way. If the receiver is going to the inside, he fakes to the outside and explodes to the inside. He uses a pressure step and attacks the inside of the defender. We turn the shoulders and rip through the inside of the defender. We cannot let him keep us on the line of scrimmage. We have to get vertical up the field and not flatten down the line. When we start to teach the single move, we start with the receiver's hands behind his back. We want to stay tight to the defender and get by him by using a swim or rip move.

The double move is the best move in football. If you have a player who can master the double move, he can kill the defensive back. It does not matter who the defensive back is. If he can master the double move, he will get open. The defensive back will catch him, but he will get open. To do the double move, the receiver fakes in the direction he wants to go. The move is not two distinctive steps. The receiver does not have time to do that. He fakes to the outside, shifts his weight to the inside, and explodes back to the outside. He does not step inside. It is a subtle weight shift to the inside.

On the weight shift, the defensive back gets frozen. He is like a deer in the headlights. That is the way the defensive back is coached. They coach them to sit on the first move. On the first move, the defensive back gets heavy on that hip. When the receiver shifts the weight and breaks back outside, the defensive back will be grabbing air.

We use the read release against the defensive back who is "playing the game within the game." He is changing up how he plays. He gives the receiver an illusion that he is in press coverage. However, he bails or repositions inside or outside on the snap of the ball. When we do film study and see what the defensive backs are doing, we work our read and release drills during practice that week.

In a perfect world, the receiver would prefer to release to the side of his cut. If he has to run a curl, he wants an inside release. That is not going to happen, but in the end, the receiver will own the defender with route-running techniques. When the defender is jockeying around for position, we use the read release. We release and figure out what the defender is doing on the move. After we know what he is doing, we will win with route running, break point, and influence techniques. On the read release, if the defender jumps inside, the receiver takes what he gives him and runs his pattern.

The squirt release is a great release. We use this release on our slant plays. If the defensive back presses the receiver with an inside technique, I can use the squirt release. If he has a three-step slant, he still runs the pattern. The receiver challenges the defender's technique. He fires off the ball, and on the third step, he explodes through the inside shoulder of the defender and turns him. When he gets the defender turned, the receiver has up to four yards to win on the route. He has to stick his outside foot in the ground, get his hip turned, and gain ground with the inside foot. You can use the squirt release and run a fade pattern. If the defender sits on the squirt, the receiver is gone on the fade route.

We can use a shuffle release. We get this type of release in practice more than in the games. In practice, there is no scoreboard or fans in the stands. The defensive backs are not as conscious about getting beat deep and are bolder in their techniques. They will start from an off position, roll down, and jam the receiver. They try to be extremely physical with the receiver. When we recognize that technique, we shuffle off the line and go past them. The receiver uses the shuffle and then one of the other releases we have talked about.

The receiver has to realize where the weight of the defender is. It could be heavy forward, or his feet could be staggered. The defensive back is reluctant to work this technique from this position. He ends up lunging at the receiver or drop-stepping. They prefer the press position. We come off the ball, shuffle, and single release. You can perform any kind of release, but the trick is to go fast.

The space release is used after you get off the line of scrimmage. All the technique we have talked about must be used in space against the defender. If the defender plays off, you have to do all the techniques on the move. We make the single and double releases on the move. The defender presses from an off position. The receiver does not know what the defender will do and has to react to what he does.

The moves that help a defensive lineman escape the block of the offensive lineman is the same moves we use to escape an aggressive defensive back. When the defender plays press coverage on the receiver, he has to escape because it is almost like hand fighting. We use the swim and rip as movement to escape the hands of a defender. They want to swim and rip over the hands of the defender. The only difference is we cannot grab as much as the defensive line. They are both effective move to get away from a defender.

We use a "slam dunk" against the hard-press defender. We use this move sometimes. During the course of the game, when the defender walks up on you, you want to come off and hit him in the chin as part of your release. I mean hit him hard right in the chin. That will give his something else to think about. Once the receiver gets an edge, he has to knock a hole in the defender.

We do all kinds of drill work on releases. The important thing to remember is when we start to do them, to go slow until they learn what to do. When we do the drills, we start from a standing position. We start with the single move. I make the receivers put their hands behind their back and work with the feet. You have to go slow to begin with. You have to learn the technique before you can do the move. When we work the single and double moves, we work against someone holding a bag and punching at them. It helps to keep their balance and use their hands.

Every drill you do should help your players. The drills must be game-specific. They must be situations they will face in the games. That applies to any position and not just the receivers.

When we teach the squirt release, we do it with two bags. The first bag is four yards off the line. That is the point the receiver wants to fire through the inside shoulder of the defender. The second bag is at the point the receiver wants to get his foot in the ground and force himself vertically by the defender. The receiver gets his inside foot in the ground and fights upfield.

We use a redirect release against zone defenders. We do not want to take a straight release off the ball so that all he has to do is react to what we do. I want to come off and squeeze the defender inside. I want to pressure him in my release and force him to redirect where he is going. We call that moving the defender. We push him somewhere he does not want to go and break away from him.

Keys to Route Running
- Speed
- Leverage
- Influence

- Body control
- Defense

Those are five keys to route running. That is the way I teach them. You need speed off the ball. You need speed in the cuts. You need speed out of the cuts. The most important part about speed is to run as fast as you can. If you are a 5.0 time in the 40, run that every time you run a pattern. That is hard for receiver to understand.

Your players must understand leverage. If we have a slant pattern to run, and the defender is outside, the receiver has the leverage. He comes off the ball, attacks the inside shoulder of the defender to keep his leverage, and breaks to the inside. If the defender is inside, he has the leverage on the receiver. We do not want to run straight up the field. He has to stem his path coming off the ball and attack the inside shoulder of the defender so when the receiver does break, he is between the defender and the ball.

Sometimes, the receiver cannot get the leverage. If he cannot get leverage, he has to influence the defender away from where you want to go. The receiver has the advantage because he knows where he is going. He wants to use the hips to influence the defender. He turns the hips away from where he wants to go. If a wideout runs up the field with his eyes down looking at the ground, he does not pose a threat. If he is running downfield and he raises up and his arm fly out, he has lost all his momentum. The greatest weapon the wideout has is the threat of going deep.

The defender does not know where the receiver is going to cut, but he does know he is not going to let him get deep on him. The receiver has to threaten the defender with the deep route until he gets to the break point. That is when he can separate from the defender and run his pattern. Route running gets you open, but influence gets you touchdowns.

It is essential that the receiver keeps his body under control. Having body control means the receiver can accelerate into a break and accelerate out of it. You do not want to slow down. The eyes of the receiver have to look through the defender. He does not look at the defender; he looks *through* him. The player has to see all that is going on in the defense. Before the ball is in the air, the player has big eyes.

The last key is defense. The wideout has to understand defense in order to know when to adjust his route. You have to teach the wideout defensive schemes and coverages.

When you talk about route running, you have to talk about break point.

Objectives of Break Point

- Gain advantage on the defense
- Increase distance on defense
- Gain desired position versus zone
- Decrease angle

The objective of the break point is to gain an advantage on the defense. We want to increase the distance between the defender and the receiver. The receiver may have great technique up to the break point, and then everything goes in the toilet. The receiver has to understand what he is trying to do and create an illusion. You have to create an illusion that you are going somewhere other than where you are. You have maintain speed so that when you stop, the receiver keeps running for another step. If you accelerate out of the break point, you get distance and separation from the defender.

When you reach the break point, you need a low center of gravity. We must have the arms bent and the elbows in. The feet need to be spread when you make the cut. The difference between a good receiver and an average receiver is the acceleration going into and out of the cuts. You have to do cutting drill to improve the break-point technique.

We do a simple cut drill where the receiver cuts through cones (Diagram #1). The receiver starts at the bottom of the drill, breaks outside the cone, and angles down to the second cone. Then, he plants, cuts past the third cone, and finishes the drill.

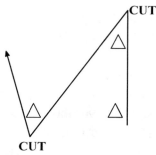

Diagram #1. Zag Drill

Your receivers have to work in and out of cuts (Diagram #2). Wes Welker of the Patriots is amazing getting in and out of cuts. We do a simple in-and-out drill, cutting with the outside foot each time.

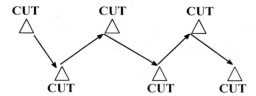

Diagram #2. In and Out

We do these drills daily. The wide receiver lines up on the line of scrimmage and jogs straight off the line (Diagram #3). The coach is standing at an unspecified position somewhere around 10 yards from the receiver. When the receiver gets around the five-yard area, the coach holds up a number. The receiver calls out the number and makes the cut for the pattern. We are training the eye and reacting to the pattern.

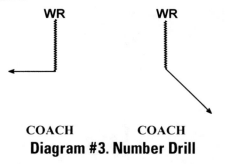

Diagram #3. Number Drill

We do a drill called "feel it" (Diagram #4). The receiver starts at the line of scrimmage with a bag holder over him. On the snap, he executes a release off the bag. He comes down the field, touches the yard marker, and run a hitch route. Hitch patterns are three-step patterns. That takes the receiver between five and seven yards.

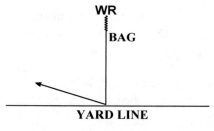

Diagram #4. Feel It

In the cone drill, we set up four cones in a square (Diagram #5). The receiver starts with a release on a bag. He runs in and out cuts until he reaches the second cone. He sprints across the top of the square and runs ins and outs until he reaches the fourth cone. When he reaches the fourth cone, he cuts through the diagonal of the square, and the coach throws him a ball.

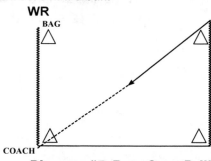

Diagram #5. Four-Cone Drill

The most important thing to the receiver is catching the football. I am on the quarterback's side. If the receiver can touch it, he should catch it. Catching the football is repetition. The ball has to be caught in the hands. We have all kinds of fingertip drills we use. We use the JUGS® machine for repetitions for the receiver. You have to work countless hours so the ball is second nature to the receiver. The eyes are the most important factor to catching the ball. The last 15 inches of the ball's flight is the most important part of catching the ball. If the receiver turns his eyes off the ball at that point, he cannot catch it.

We have a statement we use with the receivers. We say, "See it, freeze it, and squeeze it." We use tennis balls instead of footballs to focus the sight of the eye on small targets.

I am running out of time, so I will give you some of the drills we do. We use an over-the-shoulder drill. We run the fade route and catch the ball over the shoulder with one hand. Make sure you go both ways so they use both hands.

A receiver must high-point the ball when it comes to him. He cannot wait for the ball to come to him. He wants to come back and catch the ball at the highest point in the arc. That may be an advantage.

We work the wrong-shoulder drill. We throw the ball over the wrong shoulder, and the receiver has to make the adjustment to catch the ball. We use a number of ways he can correct the problem. He can speed turn and catch the ball, or the can adjust his body to the flight of the ball.

We use a drill we call the blaster as a distraction drill. The receiver runs his pattern, and the coach blasts him with a dummy as the ball arrives. We fire through the blaster and catch the ball on the other side. We use a distraction drill, where the quarterback passes the ball through defenders, waving their hands and arms to block the view of the receiver. The receiver must concentrate on the ball, ignore the distractions, and look the ball into his hands.

We work a sideline drill. We align five yards from the sidelines. We pass the ball as the receiver moves toward the sideline. He has to catch the ball and tap the feet to stay in bounds. This takes focus and concentration. The receiver has to focus on catching the ball, but get his feet down as well.

Fellows, I am out of time. I hope you got something out of this. I appreciate your attention.

PRINCIPLES OF COACHING: THE GOOD, THE BAD, AND THE UGLY

Villanova University

I looked at a lot of the topics coaches go to clinics for, and I have been to a lot of clinics in my coaching experience. What I want to do is to talk about how I can make what we do as coaches better. We can do this through using better technology and by having people work with coaches and with players. We need to develop a chemistry that I feel is very important.

My topic is this—"The Principles of Coaching: the Good, the Bad, and the Ugly." I will cover some thoughts on what I went through and how I almost derailed my career by the mistakes I made. I hope you will not make these same mistakes. I will be very factual with you. When you get older and get into the position I am in, it is not that you do not care, but I am what I am, and this is what I do. This is the way I feel today in my career.

If you want to get to the same position I am in today, you will have to go through a process where you go through some changes and go through a political process. I will give you some examples that have happened to me in my career. I will cover 12 coaching principles and comment on each.

Hitch Yourself to a Star

If you are thinking of going into the coaching profession, it is time to hitch yourself to a star. If you want to move up in the coaching profession in high school or college, you want to be in a program where the head coach is going to be moving up. This is something you need to look at. You have to look at the balance between a coach who is going to move up but may be a crazy man, and a coach who has a balance between coaching, family, and other considerations. The bottom line is this: If you want to move up, you must hitch yourself to a star.

In my case, I was a high school coach for a couple of years. Then, I moved to Springfield College as a GA. At that time, my wife was working as a teacher. I got a job offer to Middlebury College in Vermont. My wife was not very pleased that I would consider going to the "end of the world" for a college football job. I had a hard time convincing her that this was my chance to be a college football coach. I told her I was going to take the job and if she wanted to come that would be fine, and if not, I was still going to take the job.

That was stupid on my part when you think about it. I went to Middlebury College and, lucky for me, she joined me about three weeks later. You think about the situation, and you can see that was not a very balanced decision I made that would affect me the rest of my life. It was not a sane thing to do at that point in my life.

The coach I worked for at Middlebury was John Anderson. He is dead now. Nevertheless, John was the star I had selected to go with. He had coached with Bob Blackman back in his day. John came in at Middlebury and got the program rolling, and in four years, he had the program on top of the league and we had an 8-0 record. John got the head coaching job at Brown University in 1973, and I went with him to Brown. At age 26, I was the offensive backfield coach at Brown University. Just think about this. Four years earlier, I was ready to leave my wife to coach in Vermont.

That was important for me to get my coaching career going. I spent six years at Brown University starting in 1973. We were fortunate to win at Brown. In the years prior to 1973, Brown had not had a winning season for several years. In 1976, we won the Ivy League championship at Brown.

I got my first head coaching job at St. Lawrence University in New York. I spent five years there before coming to Villanova University in 1984. At the time, Villanova did not have a football team. I had to start the program up again. I was fortunate to get the job at Villanova because I was able to settle down as a football coach.

I hitched to my star, John Anderson, and learned a great deal of football from him. He was a grinder type of coach. It was not unusual for him to call a staff meeting on Christmas day. It was not unusual for him to have the staff work all weekend in the off-season.

I was deep into the work ethic that I learned in my early years of coaching. However, as time passed, I have changed somewhat. It is tough for an old guy to change. I am 56 years old. In the last several years, I have tried to become better at what I do, and I hope I will continue to improve as I continue coaching.

My version of success would be doing something over a long period of time in a successful fashion. When I look at my career, I have been doing several things the same way for over 25 years. However, it is the consistency of what I do that is critical to our success. It is having the same staff, the same chemistry, the same types of kids, and changing those kids, that are all a part of trying to be there at the end to win a national championship. It took us 25 years to win the championship. Truth be known, we probably could have won four national championships over the years. For whatever reason, we did not win them.

You can find excuses if you look long enough: Your quarterback breaks his hand toward the end of the season or your school does not bid high enough to get the Division II playoff game at your home field. It does not matter if you are seeded higher than the team you are playing against if they bid more money for the playoff game. Again, you can find reasons for not winning if you look long enough.

I see coaches today who are moving every year. I think it is important to pick the coaches you want to work with. If you want to follow them from school to school, you need to make sure it is in your best interest. It is important to take a long look at your situation. You can find a good coach and stay with that coach. You need to hitch to a star.

How Important Is Family, Time, and Money?

You need to think about these points in your lifestyle. How important is your family, time, and money in what you are looking for in your life? There is no question about it, there are some of you guys in this room who could be just as successful as some of the big-name coaches out there today if you would be willing to sacrifice and give up certain things. You have to decide in your life what you are willing to sacrifice. How important is your family? How important is your time? How important is your money?

It is obvious that family was not important to me when I was young as a coach because I was willing to leave my wife. I ask you today, where are you now with your wife and kids? Are you willing to leave your wife to take the coaching job of your dreams?

How much is time important to you? Do you have children? Are you like me in wanting to have a family life with a 35-year-old son and a 25-year-old daughter? As a young coach, I did not have much of a family life coming up with them. Now I know it was not as important for me to do some of the things I did then when I could have spent more time with my kids when they were growing up. How many school plays have you missed? How many dance recitals have you missed? How many hockey games? How many baseball games have you missed because you were coaching?

I am now a father who is trying to get to know my two kids again. I am trying to be a better father today than I was when they were growing up. In the last 10 years, I have tried to change my views on my family and have enjoyed the additional amount of time I spend with them. I dug myself a hole when they were young and I was very much involved in football. Are you willing to say family time is important? I know it is tough sometimes because if you lose too many games you are in trouble at most schools. You must figure out what is best for you.

The next phase is the money aspect of the game. You are looking at a profession where you are working for a lousy amount of money. Most Catholic schools are not going to spend a lot of money on coaching salaries. That is not the way Catholic schools work. However, I put a premium on the fact that did not bother me. Villanova likes to win, but I do not have to win a number of games to stay there. It is close to my home. I am from the area. I have a nice campus with nice kids and nice professors. It provides a good coaching atmosphere for me and my staff. It is all good.

I gave up money for the type of coaching situation I am involved in at Villanova. You need to think about where you are in your job? As coaches, we all hear that so and so is making so much money, and this coach makes this much money. In most cases, that coach does not make as much as what we hear he makes. Therefore, what you have to do is to ask these questions about your situation: Am I comfortable here? Is my comfort zone good? Do the people treat me well?

In most surveys today, the most important thing to working people is their work environment. It is not necessarily how much they are paid. If you have a good work environment and you like the people or the person you work for or with, you need to think about that aspect of coaching. I do not think you can put a dollar amount on that aspect of life.

Is your wife mobile? My wife was not interested in moving, but I was. You do not ever want to do that. Are you going to move your kids every two or three years? Are you willing to work for a grinder type of coach? If the head coach is a grinder, it is something you need to consider. I worked for a grinder for nine years. It was tough on me all of those years.

Then I took a Division III job. I had to coach the offense, defense, and the special teams. I had to do the recruiting as well. I did not have any full-time coaches on the staff. The staff consisted of coaches who were head coaches of other sports in the college. I added five years of my life where I actually worked harder than I did when I was at Brown University.

When I started the program back at Villanova, we had no coaches, no players, no schedule, and no nothing. We had to start from scratch. We had to decide what type of program we were going to have at Villanova. We had to decide if we were going to get into a league or conference. We had to decide what level we were going to compete on and how we would work in with the NCAA programs.

You have to think about the person you are working for. If that person is going to call a staff meeting on Easter Sunday, you will have to be ready to go to work on that day. It is all in what you want and how you think when you commit to work for someone.

Don't Burn Bridges

If you only take one thing from this lecture, make sure it is this statement: *Don't burn bridges!* I will say it again, *don't burn bridges!* If there is anything you can do to avoid it, take the high road. You have to work for and with good guys.

Soon after I took the job as head coach at St. Lawrence, I started hearing rumors about the job I did as a recruiter at Brown University. Stories started to surface that I did not do a good job of coaching the backfield at Brown University. I was at Brown for six years, and we won the Ivy League conference my last year there. Nevertheless, the stories were getting back to me that I had not been a good coach at Brown. I could not stand it anymore, so I went back to see the head coach at Brown and I let him have it with both barrels. I told him I did not want to hear any more bad stories about my coaching ability while I was at Brown. I had helped them win a championship and now I was hearing criticism about the job I had done at Brown. I felt the rumors were coming out because I had left Brown and took another job. I made sure I had the last word with the coach and left.

A year later, I got a call from an Ivy League school wanting to come to visit with me to see if I would be interested in becoming their head coach.

They came up to St. Lawrence to see me to make sure I would take the job. They had me come down for an interview, but they wanted to know if they offered me the job that I would take the job. I agreed and went to visit them.

I went for the interview, and they told me they were going to hold a press conference at 3 p.m. and announce me as the new head coach. I told them I would take the job. I called my wife and told her we had hit a home run, because they were going to name me the new head coach.

In the meantime, the head coach at Brown University called the athletic director of the Ivy League school. They were friends and the Brown coach wanted to tell his side of the story about me. They were going to name me as the new head coach in a few hours when he called. The athletic director changed his mind, and I did not get the job.

I went back to St. Lawrence where it is 30 below zero for six months of the year. I had three more years to serve at St. Lawrence. I figured out, based on what coach took the job and what he earned later in his career that I had lost about four million dollars by not getting that Ivy school job. The same people that I had worked with for six years knocked me out of the job. It was all because I had to have the last word with them. I had to burn the bridge with them. In the end, instead of being way ahead of the game, I was back as a Division III head coach with three more years to serve at St. Lawrence.

I decided that I would not get another chance to get a better job if that happened again. What do you do next? Now it was damage control time. I started calling the people up that had cost me the job. I told them what I was making as a coach at St. Lawrence. I let them know I was getting a lawyer to assist me with a defamation of character suit. I wanted them to know I had gotten my butt kicked by what they had done to keep me from getting that Ivy League job. I told them the next time it happened, I did not want them to say anything and I would not have to sue them for defamation of character.

Later, I was a finalist for two more jobs but did not get either one of them. I thought I was going to be at St. Lawrence the rest of my life. In reality, it would not have been a bad deal. Nevertheless, I had to burn bridges that prevented me from getting a head coaching job at an Ivy League school.

As it worked out, I had a chance to go back to my hometown to coach when we started up the program at Villanova. I got a chance to live my life the way I wanted to live it and to coach at a great school. Twenty-five years later, we win a national championship. It turned out to be a good story.

I do not care if you are a college coach, a high school coach, or a youth league assistant coach, you are going to run into politics. You are going to meet people that you do not like. My suggestion is not to burn any bridges. Take the high road with everyone. We have enough enemies as it is, and we do not need more enemies. We have 11 teams on our schedule that want to beat the crap out of us. Why would we want another person out there that is our enemy?

If you get involved in a situation where it is something that will reflect on your career and you can walk away from it without a stink, you should do it. I know it can be costly and it will hurt your career. Again, if you get anything out of this talk, this is it: *Don't burn bridges!*

Put All of Your Eggs in One Basket and Watch That Basket

This is something I have always believed in. The big word today is *multitasking*. We all do it. We work that BlackBerry® and everyone is on the computer today. You are talking to one person but doing something else at the same time.

We look at the coaching situation, and we find a lot of coaches at the college and high school levels who have one foot in the basket and one foot out of the basket. They are coaching at one school, but they are interested in moving to another school to coach.

As a head coach, we want to be able to help our staff move up in the coaching world. As a head coach, we need to know when our assistant coaches are looking for another job, and we need to know where we stand with each coach. I am the type of person who wants to help my assistants move up in due time. I start with my coaches each year, and I want to know if they are going to be with me or if they are going to have one foot in the basket and one foot out of the basket.

I have a saying that I like to use in dealing with people: *It is nice to be important, but it is more important to be nice*. It does not cost me a penny to be nice. I want to be a nice guy. However, at some point in time, I am going to stand up and be counted because enough is enough. If we are getting ready for the season to start, I need every coach to give us their full attention.

What I have done in every job I have had is put all of my eggs in one basket and watched that basket. It does not matter what college, high school, or other level I am coaching at, that school is where my eggs are going to be.

In college coaching, there are so many rumors about coaches leaving and going from one school to another school. It is unreal. It is rumor control 101. Some of those coaches are only interested in where the next job is or what is going on at another school. It is OK to be thinking about your career. At some point in time, you are going to need to settle down, put your eggs in one basket, and become good at what you do. Whatever you do, be good at it.

I am not real good at X's and O's anymore. I have an offensive coordinator who is better than I am at that subject today. I have a defensive coordinator who is better than I am at this time. I am the best recruiter on our staff. I am the best politician on our staff. I am the best "get-along guy" on our staff. On our staff, we reduce things to the lowest common denominator. I am the best at doing this on our staff.

If we sit down as a staff and I ask them what they think, I get 10 different answers. Some of the answers make sense, but some of the things I get are way out in space. I may not be good at teaching the zone defense, and I am not good at teaching the quarterback how to throw the ball. I do not spend my time doing those things. I am a good fundraiser. I just spent four weeks trying to figure out what type of championship ring we were going to have.

What do you do? What are you good at doing? As a head coach, I tried to figure out what I was good at, and that is what I work at doing. I hire the other guys and they must be good at what they do.

There are certain coaches who want their hands on everything. They do this for a simple reason—they are insecure. In some ways, we are all insecure. At some point in time, we have to step up and make a decision. We like to use this expression about our work situation at Villanova: *Love where you work, and work where you work*. That is important.

Build Your Cell Phone/Email List

Get an iPhone® or a BlackBerry and learn how to use it. Stay in touch with coaches and administrators that can help you. This is networking 101 and you need to stay in touch with people. Work camps and go to clinics. If you want to move up, your contacts are going to be important.

I talked to a career agent who used to be a head coach in college. He is the man the colleges and universities call on now to get a list of coaching prospects when a job opens. They'll say, "Give us 10 coaches that you think could be our head football coach." Then, he goes out and interviews the prospects for the schools. After he interviews the prospects, he calls the colleges and gives them a list of 10 coaches they should look at in selecting a new coach.

In the old days, you put your application in for a job and you called up the AD and had a conversation with him. Then, you got four or five other coaches to call the AD to put in a good word for you. That does not happen today. Today, you have to go through the human resources department to apply for a job.

I can tell you now, if you want a football job in college, high school, or youth league, you need to know someone at the school who will speak up for you in a positive way. They need to be able to get you in front of someone who can make the decision to hire you. Very rarely today can anyone get you the job—very rarely. However, they can get you in front of the man who is going to make the decision to hire the new coach.

This is why it is important to build your phone list and to build your email list. At an early age, go to camps and get to meet people. Build a solid relationship with people along the way. This will help you in a big way.

Coaches need to be able to communicate today. I have a BlackBerry, and I know how to use it. Some of the coaches that are 40 years old and older tell me they do not know how to use those gadgets, and they do not want to know. I tell them if I can learn how to use one, they can too. You need to learn how to text and use all of the gadgets that are out there today that can help you stay in contact with your friends and people who can help you. You have to learn how to network.

Some players we are recruiting do not open their emails for three or four days. We text everyone to make sure they get the message that day. It is an easy way to stay in touch.

You Can Never Have Enough Friends

You can never have enough friends. Be a good guy, and be willing to help anyone and everyone. I think most coaches are this way. We think it is important to make friends with the people you play against.

When your field goal kicker misses a kick or misses a PAT, are you on his case when he comes off the field? When our kicker comes off the field, I put my arm around him and I tell him, "I am the best coach you will ever have. I am going to give you two coaching points that will help you the next time. Keep your head down, and follow through."

What else do I know about kicking? Nothing! No one really knows much about kicking on our staff. However, I do know one thing. That kicker is going to like me, and he is going to know I am his friend at the

key point in his life and in a game. This is all part of who I am.

Why would anyone want to have an enemy? Do you guys remember Tubby Raymond from the University of Delaware? We had a great rivalry for several years. People in Delaware hate us, and our people hate the people in Delaware. However, over time, Tubby and I became friends. I got a picture of Tubby and I together before a game. I was with him and I asked him to sign the picture so I could put it in my office. At the bottom of the picture he wrote this note: *Often in combat, always friends.* What a great thing for him to say. Isn't this what it is all about?

I do not know who your big rivalry is or what team you play that is special on your schedule. Would it not be great for the two coaches to have that philosophy that Tubby and I had? *Often in combat, always friends.* I will meet you at the 50-yard line and we will play our tails off, and you play your tails off. Whatever happens happens. After that, it is over, and we are friends. I love that attitude.

We have 20 teams in our league. We have some great coaches in the league. I work with all of the coaches on some special projects. The other head coaches are very cooperative. One area, off the field, which we have organized with the other schools in our league is with the National Bone Marrow Foundation. With this group, we work to have potential bone marrow donors entered in a national bone marrow registry, increasing the odds of a needy patient being able to find a match for their bone marrow. Since November 1, 1993, we have been responsible for over 11,500 people being tested with the National Marrow Donor Program. This past year, we started the "Get In the Game and Save a Life" national bone marrow registration campaign. We have enlisted 30 college football programs from all levels to take a part in this campaign. The group combined to test 8,022 potential donors. Our football players go out in the Villanova community and ask people to come in and take part in the bone marrow screening program. The other teams in the league have joined in with us on this project.

Think About the Decisions You Are Going to Make

I do not like to keep things on the table for very long. I want to make a decision and move on. Sometimes, you do need to think before you act. That is critical to the decisions you are going to make, especially when it is critical for a player, for the team, and for your coaching career. It is important to sit down and think before you make a decision.

At times, coaches get excited about moving away to other coaching jobs across the country. Coaches can make rash decisions, and it can cause all kinds of problems for the coach and his family. You have to sit down and weigh each situation and make sure it is the best decision for you and your family to make a move in coaching. You have to come to reality in making a decision to change jobs and move across the country.

Do you have a confidant you can talk about your situations with? I am sure most of you have someone you can turn to with your problems and a person you can go to for advice. Go to that person and ask him what he thinks you should do.

Things Are Not Always What They Seem

Let me give you a couple of examples. Philadelphia cream cheese is not made in Philadelphia. It is made in Chicago. I bet most of you did not know that. The Canary Islands are not named after birds. Things are not always what they seem. This is something that concerns me all of the time.

When you are looking for a job, you must do your research and find out what you can about the situation before you take the job. Ask yourself this question about the job: Why would *you* be able to win when the previous coach could not win?

Always Try to Please Your Assistants

This has changed from the time when I first started coaching. Head coaches today must understand family situations. We want to orchestrate the best working conditions for our staff. My philosophy is to *delegate* and not to *abdicate*. I want to let them know what my job is and what their job is. We want a good chemistry at all costs. Karma is the key. We want an atmosphere that is conducive to all staff members doing their best work.

What Is Your Comfort Zone?

A coach needs to know his limits and understand what is best for him and set the table according to his mind-set and his vision. In the end, it is about you, your coaches, and your players.

Put It in Writing

I am talking about the coach's contract. If we put it in writing, we all know what is expected. Today, we need to make sure everything in the contract is clear and that we do not have questions about what is in the contract.

Can You Enjoy the Journey?

Are you having fun? Are you staying healthy? Are you making a difference? You must ask these questions each year before you start another season. Are you making a difference in the lives of the staff and the players you meet on a daily basis? Following are some quick points used in motivation, planning, organization, and teamwork at Villanova.

Leadership

Leaders are so hard to find. When you get one, nurture and hold onto him.

I Am a Benevolent Dictator

- Nice guy most of the time
- Make the hard decisions when necessary
- Delegate and not micromanage
- Subscribe to the 80/20 principle (80 percent of your success is created by 20 percent of your people)

A great manager, coach, or leader does the following things:

- Has a knack for making players believe they are better than they think they are

- Forces you to have a good opinion of yourself
- Lets you know he believes in you
- Makes sure you get more out of yourself
- Reinforces the idea that once you learn how good you really are, you never settle for playing with anything less than your very best

Fear as a Motivator

- Has been a motivator of man's actions since time began
- Used in the home, in society, and in institutions and government
- Used in business and industry: layoffs, loss of status and dismissals
- Is negative in nature
- Can be destructive and results in limiting the growth of an individual because the very basis is restrictive

Attitude Motivation

- The philosophy is based on a true understanding of human nature
- One believes that all people are basically good
- One accepts responsibility because it provides an opportunity for growth, for developing creativity, and for helping his fellow man reach personal goals
- Is the most powerful and lasting force one can use on himself and others
- When a man changes his attitudes toward his family, his friends, and his work, and, most importantly, toward himself and his life, he alters the basic structure of his personality
- In motivating people, it is important to communicate so there are no misunderstandings

Adversity

- We are going to have it, so be ready to handle it. It is not so much what happens to you, but how you respond to what happens.

Resilience

- Resilience is what allows us to struggle long and hard with tragedy, loss, misfortune, or change and still manage to dig deep and find our second wind.
- You will have lived life to the fullest, never giving up or accepting bad breaks and moving on.
- Each blow we are dealt no longer shatters us like a hammer hitting a brick—it makes us stronger.
- Keep tapping the rock.

Commitment to Excellence

- Teams and companies make this claim all the time.
- Little things are important.
- Teams and companies must exhibit class.
- Everyone is comfortable with the person who has class because that person is comfortable with himself.
- If you have class, you have it made.
- If you don't have class, it doesn't make any difference.

Class

- Never runs scared; is sure-footed and confident
- Has a sense of humor; knows that a good laugh is the best lubricant for oiling the machinery of human relations
- Never makes excuses; it takes its lumps and learns from past mistakes
- Knows that good manners are nothing more than a series of small, inconsequential sacrifices
- Bespeaks an aristocracy that has nothing to do with ancestors or money; some wealthy blue bloods have no class, while some individuals who are struggling to make ends meet are loaded with it
- Never accept mediocrity as excellence. When you commit to excellence, you start by defining class and seeking excellence in all that you do.

Personal Philosophy

- Never lose your capacity for enthusiasm.
- Never lose your capacity for anger aroused by something unjust.
- Never judge people too quickly.
- In a pinch, always assume first that a person is good and that, at worst, he is in the gray area between good and bad.
- If you can't be generous when it is hard, you won't be when it is easy.
- The greatest builder of confidence is the ability to do almost anything well.
- When the confidence comes, then strive for humanity.
- The way to become truly useful is to seek the best that other brains have to offer. Use them to supplement your own, and give credit to them when they have helped.
- The greatest tragedies in the world and in personal events stem from misunderstandings. Answer = Communicate.

Let's all have a winning season in 2010.

DEFENSIVE SECONDARY DRILLS AND SKILLS

Auburn University

The way I am going to speak today is the way I coach. I do not lecture my players; I hate that. I was one of those guys who sat in the back of the room, and if the teacher kept talking long enough, I fell asleep. If you have questions as I talk, you can stop me at any time and ask them. We can go as fast as you want, or we can slow it down if you do not understand. If I double-talk, point it out, and if I say something you do not believe, call me out on it.

At Auburn University, we are a 4-4-3 defense. Our base defense this year was probably more two high safeties than anything else was. We graduated to some other things as we got into the season, but, for the most part, we were a cover-2 shell. If you can align right in football, you can be 85 percent successful. If you get your alignment right and the keys right, you have a chance to win.

When we start to teach the defense, we start with two-back reads. After we teach the two-back reads, we work in the one-back reads. We play our defense against two-back sets with a 6 technique aligned over the tight end (Diagram #1). We play with a 3-technique defender to the tight end and a center shade away from the tight end. The backside end aligns in a 5 technique on the outside shoulder of the offensive tackle. The linebackers in our defense have to be in the position they are coached to play in practice. The Sam linebacker aligns in a +40 technique. He is head-up the offensive tackle to the tight end side five yards off the football. The Mike linebacker is aligned in a +10 technique. That means he is aligned on the inside shoulder of the offensive guard to the tight end side. The Will linebacker is what we call a support linebacker. He is head-up the offensive tackle to the openside of the formation in a -40 technique.

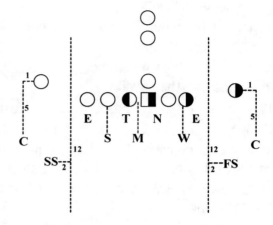

Diagram #1. Base Alignment

The corners are at one yard outside and five yards deep off the #1 receiver to their side. The safeties will align two yards outside the hash marks and 12 yards deep.

When the linebackers align in their positions, three sets of eyes go to the tailback in the formation. That is their primary key. If the tailback steps to the strongside of the set, the Mike linebacker's responsibility is to carry the #2 receiver on a vertical route and his eyes fall on the tight end.

Teams have begun to get away from the isolation play in football. That play used to be a staple run in high school as well as college. In our conference, not many teams run a two-back offense. The University of Alabama runs it. The University of Mississippi and Louisiana State University tinker with it some. The teams that run the two-back offense the most are the University of Tennessee, the University of Georgia, and Alabama. At the end of the season, Alabama was running the one-back offense with some Wildcat plays stuck in.

As I continue to talk about this, it will all tie in together. When it does, it will make an easy read for the linebackers. On the tailback's first step, the linebackers are going to know who is vertical with the #2 receiver. In a pro set, the #2 receiver is the tight end.

We called this technique the *Urlacher technique* after the linebacker for the Chicago Bears. When the tailback stepped to the strongside, the Mike linebackers would drop to the middle of the field between the two safeties. That was the Tampa-2 adjustment to four vertical routes. What was happening was the tight end was running 10 yards and sitting down. That was a 10-yard completion anytime the offense wanted to run it. Urlacher opened his hips to the run then put himself in position on the tight end so he could play him if he sat down on a pattern.

If the Mike linebacker hauls his butt into the middle of the field, he gets too high on the tight end. Urlacher's technique was to shuffle outside. If the tight end tried to outrun the linebacker, he ran with him.

If the offense runs an isolation play, the Mike linebacker checks the tight end first (Diagram #2). If the tight end is engaged with the 6-technique defender, the linebacker falls back on the run. He is a spill player on the fullback in the A gap. He fills the A gap and takes the fullback on with his outside shoulder. The Sam linebacker fits outside the fullback. The Will linebacker on the backside becomes a B-gap player to the backside. The 6-technique defender has the C gap, and the 3-technique defender fills the B gap. The Sam and Mike linebackers fill the A gap on the fullback and

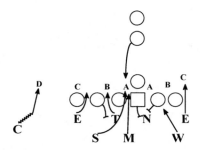

Diagram #2. Isolation Strong

tailback. The noseguard to the backside takes the A gap, and the Will linebacker fills the cutback lane in the B gap. The 5-technique end plays the C gap to the openside. We spill everything to the sideline.

The hardest play on the isolation play is the play run to the weakside away from the tight end (Diagram #3). The reason for that is the alignment of the Mike linebacker is a cover-2 defense. His alignment is a +10 technique. If the offense runs the weakside isolation play, the guard has the angle on the Mike linebacker; he can cut him off. The Will linebacker has to spill the fullback's block and force the play out. That gives the Mike linebacker a chance to play over the top of the guard's block and fill outside.

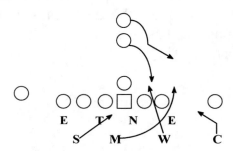

Diagram #3. Isolation Weak

In cover 2, we are not going to get support from the safeties. The Mike linebacker cannot get penned to the backside of the play. When we play cover 2, we want to disguise the coverage to look like a free shell. We want to discourage the weakside run. To do that, we align the Mike linebacker in a stack position behind the nose tackle in the shade technique. He does not end up in that position. He walks back and forth from the +10 alignment to the -10 alignment. We do not want the quarterback to be able to read the coverage off the alignment of the Mike linebacker.

We play enough quarter coverage so the alignment of the Mike linebacker in the +10 technique does not give away the secondary coverage. When we play cover 2, the Mike linebacker has to be in the +10 position. However, he does not have to align in that position until the ball is snapped. We want to discourage the offense from running the ball when we play a cover-2 defense.

The safeties in cover 2 are two yards outside the hash marks and 12 yards deep. They cannot be anything but secondary support on any play. They are out of the run fits. We must have corner support on outside runs.

The play we see at our level repeatedly is the *split-belly play* (Diagram #4). The Mike linebacker is aligned in the +10 position, and the Will linebacker is the -40 position. They are keying the tailback. The offensive line uses a zone blocking scheme on this play. On the split belly, the Mike linebacker has to fit into the weakside B gap. That takes good footwork to get back to that gap. As the tailback steps strong, the first thing the Mike linebacker sees is the tight end. If he is engaged with the 6-technique end, he falls back to the run. As the Mike linebacker falls back, he has to fall back inside the openside offensive tackle.

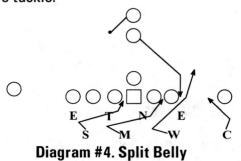

Diagram #4. Split Belly

He cannot get penned by the center. The 5-technique end fits under the fullback, and the Will linebacker fills outside. We want to spill everything outside to the corner. The Sam linebacker falls back into the strongside A gap. The corners play a *slam technique*. We start them off at eight yards and bring them down to five yards. They play with their inside foot up in their stance. They read the quarterback for three steps. If he sees a hard run key, he has to support quickly. The safeties are 2x12 on the hash mark and are going to be late on the run fits.

We learn how to play these plays, and each of our players can draw the plays. We want them to do that because it leads to understanding the play. We make them draw the five or six running plays we will face. If you let them do that, they will enjoy that more than sitting there listening to you lecture

them. Let them get on the board in your meetings, and let them show what they know.

We see *power plays* in our league. When we prepare our scouting report, we want to know where the power play is going to hit. If you play Alabama, the power play hits inside the guard. If you play against Ole Miss, #22 will run the power more like a stretch play into the boundary. If #44 is in the game, he runs it on the inside. Every week is different as to the point of attack on the power play.

When you play a particular team and a particular back, you have to know where the target of the play is and where they want to hit it. We played both Ole Miss and Alabama this year, and that was the play we stopped. We used a safety to fill the gap on the power O. He knew exactly where the back wanted to run the ball, and he beat him to that gap.

If you played Alabama with Mark Ingram, he hit the ball inside the playside guard. People tried to play over the top or slant their line to the outside, and he never ran the ball out there. He came inside the guard.

For us, we were going to target the power O on all our coverages (Diagram #5). The Sam linebacker was going to fit under the fullback. The Mike linebacker was going over the top, and the Will linebacker was going to run through the strongside A gap. Running the Will linebacker through the A gap is another Urlacher deal. If we tried to fill the A gap with the Mike linebacker, he will overrun the gap.

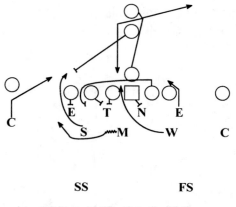

Diagram #5. Power O

The play looks like it is going wide and hits tight. The Mike linebacker is aligned in the A gap, but due to the look of the play, he is going outside. The guard and tackle are running a combo scheme on the 3-technique defender. They are thinking the Mike linebacker as their slip block. They do not look at the backside linebacker, and he comes unblocked most of the time to that gap.

The only thing the offense can do is bring the guard off the double-team on the 3 technique to block him. If they do that, they have effectively turned your 3 technique loose. The technique of the Will linebacker looks like a blitz.

The next play is the *stretch play*. In the SEC, if the defense plays a 6 technique over the tight end, you will see a stretch play. When offenses see the 6 technique, they see space. They feel that all the inside gaps are gone. Most tight ends in this league cannot block—they run the stretch play instead. At Auburn, we play a 6 technique on obvious running situations. If we have a long-yardage play, we may move him out to a 9 technique.

The offensive tackle blocks down on the 3-technique defender (Diagram #6). The tight end bases on the 6 technique. They pull the guard and center to the outside. The Sam linebacker fits inside the fullback's block. The Mike linebacker fits inside the pulling guard, and the corner turns in the play. The backside tackle cannot cut off the Will linebacker. The Will linebacker for us was a runner. No tackle in the league could cut him off. The safety plays pass first then becomes a support player.

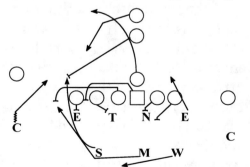

Diagram #6. Stretch

The reason we played the 6 technique instead of the 7 technique was because of the tight ends in the league. If we went inside the tight end, we gave them an angle on the defensive end and leverage. When we put him head-up on the tight end, we felt like he could not block us. If the 6-technique defender could knock the tight end back off the line of scrimmage, it made the pulling linemen bubble to get to the outside. It caused the linemen to run in what we called a *profile run*. They were running sideways instead of downhill.

We told our linebackers that if the linemen were in a profile run, they could attack them and they could push them back into the ballcarrier because they had no power. They simply run through their outside pads and give a box look. We coach the same way on the running backs. There are two views to the defenders, a *profile look* or a *frontal look*. If the running back was running sideways, the linebacker or safety running downhill had a green light to take a shot on the back. However, when he turned up and got square to the line, that was a frontal shot. If we have a profile view, we take the shot. If you have a frontal view, you better get your big-boy pants on.

Any time we played cover 2 in the secondary, the defense was going to spill the first threat in the running game.

Those are the four runs I wanted to cover. You need to teach your players those plays every day. Once they get the scheme down and they can draw the plays up, it becomes simple.

People are getting out of cover 2 because they are afraid of the four-vertical pattern. People say the Mike linebacker cannot run down the middle pipe and stop things in there. It is not the Mike linebacker. I had a Mike linebacker at the University of North Carolina who ran a 5.1 40, and no one ever got behind him. It is not the middle linebacker; it is the guys who play around the scheme that have to help.

In cover 2, the Sam and Will linebackers have to control the hash marks. We do not want a reroute in cover 2. We are going to body the receivers off the hash marks. In a reroute, the defenders start to turn their hips and move receivers. Once we turn to try to get a reroute, we are going to get an opposite high/low or corner high/low pattern. We do not want that in cover 2.

If the defender turns to get a reroute, his eyes leave the quarterback. In cover 2, there is a progression of reads. We read the tailback first and then the quarterback. In passing situations, we read the quarterback only. We read him and mirror his actions somewhat. If the quarterback takes three steps and stops, the linebacker wants to stop. If he continues to drop, the linebackers continue to drop.

If we have two linebackers dropping into their zones, they look at the quarterback. The offense will always have a checkdown back in their patterns. He normally sits down between the inside linebacker drops. The quarterback goes through a progression of reads. He reads one, two, and checkdown. If the quarterback looks at one of the linebackers, the other linebacker breaks on the checkdown pattern by the running back. They watched the quarterback's eyes. If he was focused to the outside, he was reading his primary routes. When he looked back inside, he was trying to locate the linebacker closest to the checkdown pattern. When he looked at one of the linebackers, the other backer broke on the checkdown. The linebacker the quarterback looked at knew the receiver was on one side or the other. He peeked to see where he was going to break.

In the four-vertical pattern, we wanted to funnel the receivers together. We wanted five yards of space between the #1 and #2 receivers. If we could do that, we felt we were in good shape. When we played a team that ran the four-vertical attack, we wanted to find out where they threw the ball. We used film study to tell us that. We wanted to know if they were going to throw away from the Mike linebacker, to the wide field, or off the Mike linebacker's back hip. That was the key for us to playing the pattern.

Back in the day, everyone wanted to bend the ball back into the middle of the field (Diagram #7). They would run one inside receiver outside the hash marks, and the other inside receiver would bend into

the middle. It was very similar to the way you want to attack three-deep coverage. Teams were attacking the Mike linebacker. If the Mike linebacker opened to his right, they threw the ball behind him to the left.

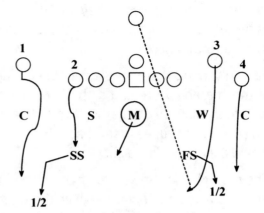

Diagram #7. Four Verticals vs. Mike

The way we countered that strategy was with the play of our safeties. They were reading the #1 receiver as he broke off the line of scrimmage. They were not automatically running over the top of the #1 receiver. They stayed over the top of the #2 receiver and played zone with their eyes on the quarterback. We stayed in the zone as long as we could. If the quarterback looked to the strongside, the safety had to get off the hash mark, but he was not hauling his butt over the top of the #1 receiver. The corner will protect the safety on the #1 receiver up to 22 yards. All comeback patterns are run at a depth of 18 to 22 yards. If the quarterback turns and launches the ball, the safety has to go, but he has time and space to make the play.

When the quarterback looks to the strongside, the safety has to come off the hash into that side of the field. The Mike linebacker favors that side of the pattern also. We know they will try to throw the ball off the Mike linebacker's drop and play the backside safety in a position to make a play on the inside vertical route. He leans and favors the inside receiver. The safeties will never get inside the hash marks. He cannot get to the middle of the field because of the threat of the #1 receiver to his side. All the linebackers and defensive backs are on a string to the quarterback's head. If he looks one way, they favor that direction.

If the quarterback looks down the middle of the field, the safeties have to get some width. Normally, when the quarterback looks down the middle, he is trying to look the Mike linebacker off one of his receivers. The Sam and Will linebacker will not control the hash marks. All they are going to do is put a body on the #2 receivers and make them get outside the hash marks so the safeties can play.

That is the same thing you would do if you were playing three deep. If the offense runs four verticals, the corner is playing a divider between the #1 and #2 receivers to his side. If the quarterback looks away, the corner leans toward the #2 receiver. The technique is the same in cover 2. The only difference is the corner and the safety have switched positions. The safety plays the divider between the #1 and #2 receivers. The Mike linebacker is the free safety and the corners are flat players.

We teach the two coverages together. We show them cover 3 first with all the lane markers and dividers. After they learn that, we show them the Tampa-2 coverage. The key to the coverage is the Sam and Will linebackers bodying the #2 receivers and the safeties cheating their coverage on the #2 receivers to their side.

If the offense goes to a 3x1 formation to the field, they will attack you the same way they did in the 2x2 (Diagram #8). The #1 and #2 receivers run outside the hash marks and on the sideline as they did on the 2x2 set. The difference is the #3 receiver has to get to the opposite hash mark.

If the tight end runs down the middle of the football field, the Mike linebacker takes him all the way. Teams are running the #3 receiver to the opposite hash mark and down the field. We play that the same as we did with the balanced set. In the old days, we used to control the #2 receiver with the Will linebacker. When offenses started to run the four-vertical route from trips, the Will linebacker could not cover to that side of the formation.

The Mike linebacker has to stay on top of the #2 receiver as long as he is vertical. If the Mike linebacker has two threats on the outside, he has to stay on both receivers. If the #2 receiver sits down in his route, the Mike linebacker sits down too. He does not know what is happening on the backside of the pattern.

If we go to three-deep coverage, our alignments change (Diagram #9). In this coverage, the Mike linebacker aligns in a -10 alignment. The Will linebacker moves wider into a -50 alignment and becomes a slot player. The Sam linebacker tightens to the ball and aligns in a +30 alignment. We show the two high safeties and roll into three deep with the free safety down in coverage and the strong safety in the middle. We start out in a 2x12-yard alignment and roll down into 2x5-yards outside the tight end.

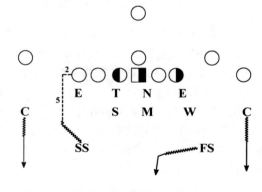

Diagram #9. Cover 3

The strong safety and Will linebacker are the outside box players. We align the linebacker to stop the weakside isolation play. The run fits for the linebacker change from this alignment. The Will linebacker fits outside the fullback, the Mike

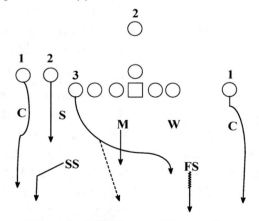

Diagram #8. Trips vs. Tampa 2

linebacker fits inside the fullback, and the Sam linebacker fits into the A gap to the strongside.

This also means your noseguard becomes a more active player on this alignment (Diagram #10). When the Mike linebacker was in the +10 alignment, the weakside guard got a running start on the nose. He jammed him onto the center's block and moved to the second level to block the Mike linebacker. With the Mike linebacker in the -10 alignment, the offensive guard cannot come down on the nose. He has to combination with the center, but he cannot come down aggressively on the nose. If he blocks down on the nose, the Mike linebacker is gone before he can come off. The nose will become a player in this alignment and make some plays. If the guard does not block the nose and comes directly to the Mike linebacker, the nose will play inside the fullback's block. There is no way the center can cut off the nose or reach the nose by himself.

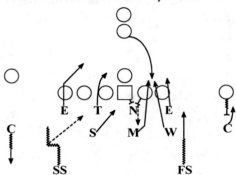

Diagram #10. Cover 3 vs. Weak Iso

In two-deep coverage, the read is the tailback. In three-deep coverage, the read is the fullback. When the offense uses a two-back scheme, it creates the eighth gap we have to cover. With one back in the backfield, there are only seven gaps. The fullback creates the eighth gap because he is a blocker. Wherever he goes, that is the eighth gap and our defenders have to follow him.

If the fullback goes to the flat on the openside, the Will linebacker has him. If he goes to the flat to the tight end, the strong safety has him. On the run outside, the Sam linebacker fits inside the fullback and the strong safety fits outside the fullback. On the inside and outside plays, the Sam linebacker spills to the strong safety and the Mike linebacker spills to the Will linebacker.

Our run fits are better to the weakside on the split belly from a cover 3 (Diagram #11). The 5-technique end fits inside the fullback. The Will linebacker fits outside, and the Mike linebacker fits inside the offensive tackle. There is no chance for the center to cut off the Mike linebacker like in the cover-2 run fits. The Sam linebacker fits into the strongside A gap.

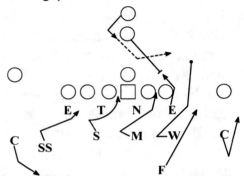

Diagram #11. Cover 3 vs. Split Belly

This is good run support for us because we have eight defenders in the box. If the guard blocks down on the nose and the center blocks the Mike linebacker, the Sam linebacker is turned loose to the ball unblocked. You cannot run the ball when we play cover 3. As long as your defenders are reading the fullback and following him to his gap, it is a great defense. They only have seven blockers, and we have eight in the box.

The Will linebacker has to be a runner. He cannot get cut off by the weakside tackle. That happened in the University of Kentucky game, and they scored a touchdown on it. The Will linebacker must have his inside foot on the outside foot of the offensive tackle and not get cut off to the outside. He has to read the tackle and push to get vertical. If he does not, there is a small crease on the outside.

On the power-0 play, the strong safety is fitting outside the fullback block (Diagram #12). The Sam linebacker fits inside the fullback. The Mike linebacker aligns to the weakside in a -10 technique. He becomes the A-gap player on the power 0. The strong safety comes down to give us the eighth defender in the box. When the guard and tackle double-team the 3 technique, the Mike linebacker blows the strongside A gap. If they try to hold the guard back for the Mike linebacker, the 3 technique will be penetration and the Sam linebacker becomes a free hitter.

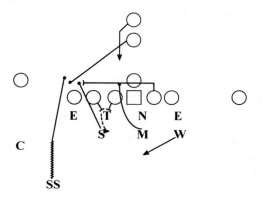

Diagram #12. Cover 3 vs. Power O

If the Mike linebacker's alignment is a plus alignment, he cannot blow the A gap. When we went into the under front, teams knew we ran a zone blitz scheme from that front. They thought if we ran the under front and the Mike linebacker played to the weakside, we were in cover 3, cover 4, and cover 6. In those coverages, the Mike linebacker aligned in the minus alignments.

Cover 4 is our quarter coverage, and cover 6 is quarter-quarter-half coverage. We aligned the Mike linebacker in the nose stack and played cover 2. Offenses thought we were in cover 3 and went to the three-step game. We baited them into throwing into a rolled-up corner. In our defense, the Will linebacker and the strong safety will be our best hitters. Everything is spilled to those two players.

You have to control the four-vertical pattern from the cover-3 scheme (Diagram #13). We played the Will and Mike linebackers as inside-half players. They dropped one yard inside the hash marks. Their drop was determined by the remaining back. The Sam linebacker and the strong safety were going to control the verticals. If the #2 receiver and tight end both pushed vertical, the linebackers took them man-to-man. In this coverage, you end up with a free safety in the middle of the formation.

If the offense is a threat to throw the corner route to the inside receiver, the Sam linebacker and strong safety play outside leverage on the receiver to force them into the free safety. If they cannot throw the seven cut (corner), we get inside

leverage and force the receiver wider, and the corner can help out on a deep ball that way. The alignment of the Sam and strong safety is a scouting report type of thing.

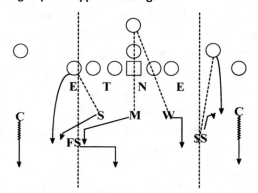

Diagram #13. Cover 3 vs. Four Verticals

If the #2 receiver goes inside immediately, the defender spot drops to the #1 receiver. He uses his burst to get to the outside under the #1 receiver. If the #2 receiver goes to the outside, the defender pushes to the curl and down to the flat. On any type of short route by the #2 receivers, the coverage becomes cover 3. If the #2 receivers run a vertical route, the coverage becomes man-to-man.

The problem occurs when the #3 receiver gets involved with the pattern or there is only one vertical by the #2 receiver. If the #2 receiver on the right goes vertical and the #2 receiver on the left runs across the field, we have some problems. We can cover it on paper, but doing it on the field may be a problem.

It matches our Mike linebacker with a slot receiver crossing short in the middle of the field. When the Sam linebacker reads #2's release to the inside, he spot drops outside. On the other side, the strong safety has #2 running vertical. If #3 flares, the Will linebacker has him, and the Mike linebacker is man-to-man taking the cross. That is a disadvantage to the defense. In both situations, the match-ups favor the offense. Having a running back on a linebacker or a slot receiver on a linebacker is not an ideal situation.

If we get a four-wide receiver look, we go to cover 4, which is a progression read. Teams in the NFL will tell you they do not try to mix two of these types of coverages together. Cover 3 is a spot drop.

Cover 2 is a backpedal. Cover 4 is a progression-read coverage. In a progression read, you must take your eyes off the quarterback and watch the receivers. That takes a lot of time to play that much coverage. Your players will have to get up early in the morning to meet if you try to master three coverages. If they can master two of them, that is enough. I would never try to master three coverages because each one of them has a different read. Cover 2 reads the tailback, cover 3 reads the fullback, and cover 4 is a progression. Each one of the coverages has a run-read difference and each one has a pass-read difference. For us, it is all about time and how many reps we can get of each coverage. There is no sense of running multiple coverages if you do not get enough reps to run them.

When we play cover 2, it is a change-up for us. Cover 3 and cover 4 are our staple coverages that we play all the time. Cover 4 and cover 3 have the same run fits. The only difference in the run fits is when the eight-man box becomes a nine-man box.

In cover 4, the strong safety reads like he does on cover 3. We play with a 6-technique end most of the time. That means the strong safety is the D-gap player. Everything bounces to him. That alignment is a tight alignment for him. However, if the defensive end aligns in a 9 technique, that becomes a wide alignment (Diagram #14). That means the safety is now the C-gap player. It almost makes him a linebacker. His alignment becomes tighter to the inside because he keys the tackle to the fullback. If the tackle blocks down on the 3-technique defender, the Sam linebacker takes on the fullback. He will spill the ball to the strong safety. That means the strong safety has to fill in the C gap right now.

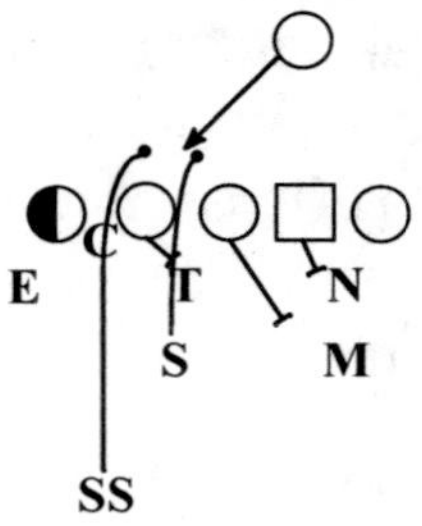

Diagram #14. Nine-Technique End

Not only does he have to fill the C gap, but the ball is also coming downhill hard into that gap. If the safety hears wide, he has to attack. If he hears tight, he comes outside.

The safety to the backside is looking at the same thing the linebacker sees. He looks at the guard to the fullback. If he gets a run key from the guard, he attacks right now. Each one of these coverages requires a tremendous amount of eye transfer. That means the defensive backs are looking at different things in each one of the coverages.

In a cover 2, the eyes focus on the quarterback. In the cover 3, the box players look at the fullback. In cover 4, the free safety reads the guard to the fullback in his progression read. That is a lot of reps you have to get to your players. The best way to get the reps and knowledge is to test them. This season, for the first five games, the coverage was the same. The last seven games, things began to change as we got the reps to change up what we were doing. You have to teach the coverages. You need to draw plays for every situation you will see.

Once the players learn the four or five runs and four or five pass concepts, you can expand your teaching. You can add what you want to add. Once they get the route concept, the coverages become easy for them.

They will accept the challenge. If you tell the strong safety to fill the C gap hard on the wide call, it will only take one time for him to know why you want him to do it. When he gets run over, he will know he has to fill in a hurry. They will know why they are at five yards rather than eight yards.

The split belly is a hard play for the safety. There is no linebacker to his side. The Mike and Will are on the other side of the ball, and the Sam linebacker fills the A gap. The strong safety has to fill the C gap with no help.

When we get into our cover 4, we are going to stop the run (Diagram #15). We play the nine-man box from cover 4, and the corners are on an island. The front is the same. The safeties align at 12 yards and walk down to eight yards. The free safety is reading the guard to the fullback. The strong safety is reading the tight end to the fullback on a tight call and the tackle to the fullback on a wide call. We want to get both safeties into the run support.

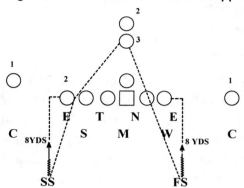

Diagram #15. Cover 4

To get good at anything, you have to put in the reps. At Auburn, we talk about the three Ts. That is *tackles, turnovers,* and *third down.* When we practice tackling, we practice two types of tackles. We practice *profile tackling* and *frontal tackling.* When we use a profile tackle, we run through the tackle. If we tackle in a frontal position, we try to break the kneecaps. The frontal tackle is when the back turns up and runs downhill. We put the helmet on the kneecap. If we miss, the back will fall over the body of the defensive back.

To get turnovers, you must practice stripping the ball. You will get what you emphasize. If you practice it and emphasize it, you will get it. We do every drill imaginable. If the defensive backs could catch the interceptions that are thrown to them, they would lead the conference in interceptions. If you want interceptions, your players must be able to catch. Work on ball drills and catching drills in practice.

We practiced the third-down pass plays repeatedly. Get the step-up by knowing what is coming. That is how you break up passes. You work on them in practice until you know the pattern by the second step.

Any other questions? I want to thank you for your attention and time.

THE RED ZONE OFFENSE

The Ohio State University

I want to thank you for having the Marines as part of this clinic. Sometimes, you get busy doing what you are doing with all the recruiting we do. On occasion, you start to feel sorry for yourself and want to go home. From Christmas Eve night to last night, I have slept in my own bed four times. After 35 days, I am anxious to get home. When I finish here today, I am going straight home.

When you follow a group on the dais that is undefeated, it is humbling. The Marines are undefeated in regards to our country. We should remind ourselves there will be more students that go to the military than go on to play college football. Each year, 1 million kids play high school football. Of that total, 47,000 go on to play college football. From that pool, about 150 players go on to play in the NFL.

I am a 57-year-old guy who did not go to Vietnam. My draft lottery number was 252, and I have always had a bit of a vacuum in my soul because I did not serve. I have always had a tremendous appreciation for the men and women who serve in our military. I have tried to teach my teams about the appreciation we should show and feel for the people in the military.

I had a chance to go overseas with our troops this summer and visit some of the places where we have military stationed. We went to Germany, Turkey, Iraq, Kuwait, and Spain. We saw thousands and thousands of our young men and women who are serving our country. It was incredible to see the men and women who are protecting the world. We were told 75 percent of the people serving were under 25 years old. The average age was between 20 and 25 years old.

We met so many kids who were excited that college football coaches were coming to visit them because they played high school football. They love football. The highlight of their weekend comes at 3:00 in the morning. They work all day, and at three in the morning, they watch college football. After being in harm's way all week long, this is their highlight. It reminds them of home and explains the reason they are there.

You must remember this military is the most talented and brightest in the history of our country. The officers will tell you these troops are the best we have ever had. You coaches in here today are going to coach thousands of kids who will go into the military to make sure we stay free. That trip was a humbling experience for me.

What you coaches do is incredible. You are working with these young people and making a difference in their lives. The players we recruit will not end up serving the country in the military. Some of the players you coach will end up making a difference in this world. It is a big deal at our place. We constantly have military people come in to address our team. We have a director of military appreciation who does nothing but connect with Ohio National Guard so we can do something for returning service personnel. It is a big deal to us to make sure our team knows how blessed we are.

I have a slide of our 2009 championship ring. The reason I put that at the front of the presentation is what I tell my players. Every year, if we win the conference championship, our seniors get to design the championship ring. They put on it whatever they want to put on it. As they designed our ring, they wanted to point out we had won the Rose Bowl, were Big Ten champions, that they had won five straight championships, and that we had beat our rival. It was typical in what they wanted on the ring.

However, they wanted to remember for the rest of their lives a four-letter reminder we had talk to them about for four years. The "G H C R" that appears on the right side of their ring stands for something special.

The "G" stands for "gratitude." The 2008 team graduated 28 seniors and had three leave early for the NFL. We lost 31 players, and we had a young team coming back for the 2009 season. We thought we were going to have talent, but we were going to be immature and young. We felt that the young players needed to be grateful.

Before you have a chance to progress as a human being, and in particular as a young person, you have to be grateful for your blessings. If our players could learn to carry an attitude of gratitude, we were going to have a chance to have a good team. We had capable players.

The "H" stands for "humility." Most of our players were hot shots. They are four- and five-star athletes who have been catered to since they were seven years old. Everyone has told them they are wonderful. How would they think anything else? They are too young to understand that those things are just smoke. All the hype is temporary. We felt this group was talented, but they needed to understand what humility was. There is a verse in Proverbs that says it best: "Humility comes before honor." Before you can be worthy of honor, you will first have to be humble.

We needed to talk about, personify, and help them understand humility. That was particularly true with our team. We thought that was critical.

The last initials were "C R," which meant "combat ready." Our players know the difference between real combat and what we do. We make sure they know what we are talking about. We want our team to be as combat ready for football as the American soldier is ready for the real battle. That is the way we like to train and emulate what the military goes through in their training. We do things that are very difficult because we want to be combat ready.

Those four letters were everywhere as we entered our season. The college coach's new year is February. Recruiting is over, and you know who will be on your team for next season. It is time to start training for the upcoming season. Right now, we are trying to define what next year's team is going to be about. I thought the fact that they put that on their ring was cool, and we did what we set out to do.

When my son was getting ready to go to college, he visited Ohio State. I was the head coach at Youngstown State at the time. He visited as a student, not as a player. John Cooper was the coach at Ohio State, and he did not recruit my son. Woody Hayes did not recruit me. We were not good enough to play for them. My son was there at an honors program, and an engineering professor was talking and he put this quote up on the overhead:

Concern for man and his fate must always form the chief interest of all technical endeavors. Never forget this in the midst of your diagrams and equations.
—Albert Einstein

I was sitting in the audience as a father, not a football coach. I saw that quote, and I thought, "That speaks to us." I did not know where Albert Einstein coached, but that quote speaks to us as coaches. That is what we do as teachers and coaches. We should make sure the concerns are for the players, and their future and must always be the chief interest of our technical endeavors. That was a profound moment for me.

I took this back to my staff, and we approached the importance of the game. I know we have to win games, because that is a reality. But what is truly important? Does anyone remember who won the 1976 national championship? The answer is, "No." We all remember watching our kids grow up and remember letters that they wrote us. The concern is for man, and the chief interest should be his fate.

Never forget this in the midst of our diagrams and equations. Do not get all caught up in the X's and O's. My coaches get a little crazy because we do not spend as much time on that part of the game as they would like. That is especially true when someone new comes on our staff. I have not had a staff change on my nine full-time coaches in about four or five years. We believe we have to take care of our young people and help them grow as men.

My father told me a long time ago that the players "do not care how much you know until they know how much you care." The do not care about your X's and O's or the workouts. They do not hear you until they know you care about them. When they believe you care, they will hang on every word you say.

You cannot fool them. If you do not genuinely care, they know that, too. If they think we are trying to use them and trying to play them, they know that. If they know how much you care, they will do everything, and it might not be the right thing. We might prescribe a terrible weight-lifting program, but if they think we care about them, they will do it. They believe in their coaches, and they will do it.

Football is a game of pressure. We need to be the ones applying the pressure. If the offense is applying pressure to the defense, the defense feels like it is off balance. The defense feels as if they are a step behind. If the defense is applying the pressure, the offense is off balance. They are the ones in control. When you get into the red zone, the problem amplifies. When you play against a good defense, the closer the offense gets to scoring, the better the defense plays. That is the mentality of a good defense.

The good defenses we play against will get better the closer we come to scoring on them. If defenses are not any good, we will beat them anyway. Everything we study and work on is built on the premise that the opponent is as good as, or better, than we are. We must have a plan to beat them. We have to make sure we are the ones applying pressure.

Pressure the Defense in the Red Zone

- Tempo change
- Personnel change
- Formations and motion
- Passing and running balance
- I play fastest when...

Two things in college football today can apply pressure to the defense. The first one is tempo change. If the offense hustles up to the line, they force the defense to make their decisions quicker. Offenses are using fast counts and doing different things that affect the tempo of the game. You do not have to be a spread team to use fast tempo, but those types of teams were some of the first to use that scheme.

When the NCAA changed the clock rules, offenses in college football started to play with more urgency so they could get more plays off. Fast tempo took some of the disguise out of the defense, and they had to show their hand sooner. That made it a popular idea among some coaches. We have faced some good tempo teams.

Tempo applies pressure to the defense particularly if they struggle to line up. If fast tempo hinders the defense's ability to disguise, it becomes an issue. If the defense can disguise their alignment, that presents a problem for the offense. When you cannot disguise what you are doing on defense, that becomes a problem.

What we did to get ready for Oregon was to line up two offenses. The first offense ran a play. The second the play was over and the ball was put in play, the second offense sprinted to the ball and ran a play. The plays were pre-called. There was no huddle time. As soon as the ball was placed down, the next offense sprinted to ball and ran their play. We did that repeatedly in the drill. The defense's tongues were dragging. We did that so Oregon would not be the team applying the pressure.

We feel we can pressure the defense in the red zone by using multiple formations and motions from the same personnel group. Our defense is all caught up with which personnel group is in the game. At least one time during the game, I will hear one of my staff say, "They have never run that from that personnel group!" The offense puts pressure on your defense when you do not prepare for something they do. When you do something from the personnel group that you have not done before, it makes the defense vulnerable.

The red zone is high anxiety. You do not want to overthink what you want to do in that area. We have to find a way to do enough different things to affect the defense without fouling up your offense. We think that is important.

Having a run and pass balance in the offense is the toughest thing on a defensive lineman. They do not know whether it is a run or pass. If the situation is third-and-10, the offense probably will pass, and if they do not, we will be all right. However, if it is first or second and you do not know what they are going to do, that puts pressure on the defense. If the offense is 50/50 in those situations, the defense feels the pressure.

We want to have the ability to align in any formation we have with the people we have on the field. Our regular grouping is 21. That means two backs, one tight end, and two wide receivers. The silver grouping is 12. Our red personnel grouping is 10 personnel. That is one back, no tight ends, and four wide receivers. If the grouping has five wide receivers, it is white. If the formation is gray, it has one back, one tight end, and three wide receivers. In all those personnel groupings, we want to have the ability to do the same thing.

If the defense has scouted us so well that they can match the plays with the personnel grouping, we are in trouble. If they can do that, we have not put any pressure on them. When we have a silver personnel group on the field, we want to be able to align in gray alignment.

I have a question that I ask my position coach to have their players response to. It is like a fill-in-the-blank question. The question is, "I play fastest when _____." I want the players to fill in the rest of the sentence. You can apply pressure when you are playing fast. The end of the sentence is "when I know what I am doing." I play fastest when I know what I am doing. There is a certain amount of pressure applied when we are playing as fast as we can. When there is indecision, we do not play as fast.

If we are playing with fast tempo, from different personnel groupings, using formations, and keeping the run to pass ratio balanced, we are building some indecision in the defense. When they have indecision, they do not play as fast. That lets the offensive team apply the pressure.

There is one thing you cannot forget about applying pressure in the game of football. It is the ultimate way to apply pressure. This is a statement from Evander Holyfield: "Everybody has a plan until they are hit." The greatest way in this game to apply pressure is physically. When you get your head knocked off or you are smacked around, you are the one having the pressure applied. We can never lose sight of the fact that the physical team wins. That is the game of football. That applies the most pressure on any team. If you get outhit, you will probably lose.

In the red zone, the player who decides how well we do is the player with his hands on the ball. It does not matter what level you play. If the quarterback does not handle the situation, you will not score. In the red zone, the quarterback becomes more of an impact in those pressure situations. He becomes the extra ballcarrier, the movement player, or the run-pass threat.

What to Ask of the Quarterback and How to Get It Done

- Decision-making
  - ✓ Total understanding: Down-and-distance
  - ✓ Situation learning
  - ✓ Repetition under fire
  - ✓ Film and mental gymnastics
  - ✓ Experience
- Big play
  - ✓ Recruiting
  - ✓ Confidence
  - ✓ Complete knowledge of down-and-distance
  - ✓ Experience

- Elimination of turnovers
  - ✓ Belief
  - ✓ Numbers or lower
  - ✓ Don't force it"
  - ✓ Pressure in practice
  - ✓ Experience

We have three things we ask of our quarterback. We ask him to make great decisions. When we are in the red zone, the thing we cannot do to emotionally change the game is to error. The decisions the quarterback makes in the red zone have a huge impact on our football team. What I like about decision-making is you do not need any talent at quarterback to be a good decision-maker. Terrelle Pryor is 6'6" and runs 4.3, but his ability to make decisions is what is going to affect us, not his freakish athletic ability. It does not matter whether your quarterback is my size or Terrelle's size; he is the person who can make the decisions.

We are going to help him learn how to do it. First and foremost, he has to totally understand us and totally understand them. That does not take size or speed. It takes work. In this day and age, with all the video technology, there is no excuse not to make the teaching material for your quarterback to be successful. If you do that, you will win a heck of a lot of ball games.

We have to put our quarterback in the entire situations he will face in the game. He has to practice in the red zone and know the defense is going to blitz. He has to know the defensive backs are not going to back up. There is nowhere for them to go. We have to put him in those situations and pressure him. The worst thing you can do to a quarterback is make everything easy in practice and make everything work. You have to put the heat on him in practice and make sure it is as hard as it can be.

You have to put him in tough situations and give him repetitions under fire. Film, video, and mental gymnastics can make him a better decision-maker. It is up to us to see that the quarterback is prepared to take his team into the red zone.

If you look at the teams that have won the national championships, they have had experience at the quarterback position. You have to give those players as much experience as they can get.

The second thing we ask our quarterback to do is make big plays. Our quarterback has to make plays. We can recruit a quarterback. You have to find someone in your school who can make the big play. He could be on your basketball team. He is there somewhere; you have to find him. He may be in your youth-league program right now. You need the player who has the football every play to make plays.

You must have confidence in your quarterback. He has to have confidence that he is the pressure-putter. He does not feel when he gets in the red zone that the pressure in on him. The pressure is on the defense.

To make big plays, he has to have complete knowledge of the offense and down-and-distance. Good decisions can lead to big plays. The more experienced the quarterback, the more likely he is to make a big play.

The third thing we ask the quarterback to do is maybe the most important point. We ask our quarterback on the field, and especially in the red zone, to eliminate turnovers. I watched the Super Bowl this year. It was an interesting game, and both teams were not making any big plays. Both teams were playing good defense. Then, the turnover happened, and the game changed.

Our quarterback came to Ohio State with glowing statistics and a national reputation. In his freshman year, everyone was talking about how good he was going to be. He took us to a BCS Bowl, and we won the conference in his freshman year. Five games into his sophomore year, they are saying he is no good and we should move him to wide receiver. The critics went from one extreme to the other.

He was either humble or humbled. Either all the criticism made him humble, or it humbled him. I do not know which one it was. Nevertheless, he believed from that moment on that this was the most important job he had. His job was to make sure we did not have any turnovers. He had to learn that.

We use a phrase all the time that says, "If the receiver is in front of the defender, the ball has to be delivered at the numbers or lower." If the ball is thrown high, and the receiver does not make a clean catch and tips it, we have an interception. The tipped or batted ball in the secondary is the easiest interception to make. All the velocity is taken off the ball, and it is a dead duck. If it hits the numbers, the ball is going to the ground.

The quarterback has two options when he is trapped. He can try to make the throw or throw the ball away. The mature quarterback throws the ball away. Never force the ball. Do not think you can make the throw. The maturity has to override the ego.

I've said this before. One of the worst things we can do as coaches is making it fluffy for the quarterback in practice. In the game when the heat is on, he will force the ball because you let it happen in practice. Has he seen a full-speed drill where the defensive backs are going hard? Did we put a color shirt on him and tell everyone not to touch him because he is the only one we have? We have to put pressure on the quarterback in practice. When the quarterback gains experience, the better he will be at eliminating turnovers.

Everything with the red-zone offense is about applying pressure to the defense. You have to do it in a variety of ways. There are many great ideas, but the only ones that work are the ones we can do. I am sure some of you in here today have different amounts of practice time. You have an offensive day and a defensive day. Our offensive players practice all day.

You have to be careful when you see something on an NFL film that you like. They have their players from eight in the morning to six at night for 23 games, counting the exhibition games. We have to be smart and not try to do something that we cannot execute.

Here are some of the things we like to do in the red zone. We want to be sure our quarterback can be added as a dimension in the critical times. Our quarterback is a great runner. The worse thing we can do for him is design too many runs for him because he is also our passer. You do not want to jeopardize his worth to the team by running him too much.

We design some runs for him, but his best runs are the spontaneous runs. He flushes out of the pocket with an open field in front of him. If he has four designed runs and five or six spontaneous runs a game, that is enough.

Paul Brown was a great coach in Ohio. He was head coach of the Browns and Bengals. He said when you are making decisions about personnel and discipline you need to be careful. When he had to discipline someone for breaking team rules or not doing what he was suppose to do, he had a rule of thumb to follow. Discipline is in direct proportion to how good the back-up at the position is. It is the same thing about hitting the quarterback. That is in direct proportion to how good his back-up is.

In the red zone, we want to align in a formation so the quarterback is a possibility as part of the run. If we run an option, we want to design the play so the quarterback will pitch the ball to a running back. We use the running backs to run. We use the quarterback to run and pass. You cannot over do it with regard to running the quarterback.

These are examples of plays we would run as part of the red zone offense. They are game film plays, which are suited for this type of situation.

The first play I want to show you is a zone option (Diagram #1). We believe that running an option in the red zone is critical. People like to blitz in the red zone to make something happen fast. They also play man coverage in the red zone. If we can block the linebacker, and the defensive backs are in man coverage, they have no one to play the responsibilities of an option play. The formation is a trips set to the wideside of the field with the quarterback in the shotgun. The running back is set into the trips side. This is an obvious passing set, and the quarterback is in a position where he could throw the ball. Beside the option, we have a zone-read threat and a quarterback-run threat.

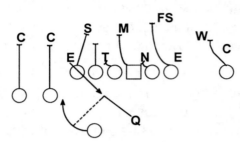

Diagram #1. Zone Option

The next play is the same formation with the exception of the running back is set to the single-receiver side. We are going to run the inside zone play (Diagram #2). The defense brought the backside end down hard and took the running back. The quarterback pulled the ball and outran the linebacker to the end zone. If we can get to the point of the quarterback or the running back having to beat one defender, we like those odds. The quarterback sees the backside end taking the dive, and he thinks he can outrun the linebacker, which he can. The man who was faced with the job of taking the quarterback was the inside linebacker, coming from the inside-out. That is a tall order in that match-up.

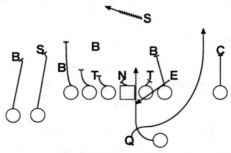

Diagram #2. Zone Play

The next play is a power formation. We have two tight ends and two backs in the I formation (Diagram #3). We align in the I formation about 30 percent of the time. On this particular play, we run the inside isolation fake to the tailback, and the quarterback pulls the ball and runs outside the end. We bring the flanker back inside to crack on the defensive end and pull the backside guard. We know

the goal-line defenses will commit additional hats to the box. The defensive backs are close to the line of scrimmage, and the anxiety is high. When we get the ball into the red zone, all bets are off on the quarterback running the ball. He can run it as many times as he wants in the red zone. We want to give the look of the base power and run it wide with the quarterback.

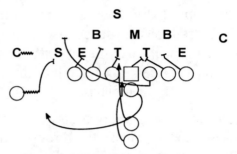

Diagram #3. Power Boot

We like to run the ball out of the twin set. Our centers make all our calls. They have a better handle on things when there are two wide receivers to the field. They read the coverages better from that set instead of a double-wide set. Our most productive run in the last five to six years is when we run out of twins and get to the right seam. On this play, we run the power option to the tight end (Diagram #4). The backside guard pulls, and the frontside blocks down. The fullback kicks out on the defensive end.

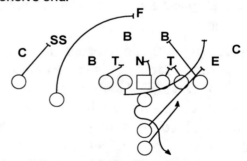

Diagram #4. Power Option

When we get inside the five-yard line, we want the quarterback under the center. That fits our passing game better. With all the blitz schemes in that area, we want him to get the ball quickly so he can throw quickly if he has to. When we are outside the five-yard line, we like him in the shotgun set. He has more freedom in the set, and it presents a better scramble scenario for him.

When we throw the ball in the red zone, we want simple gap protection, and we throw the quick game. The defensive backs have nowhere to backpedal, so everything must be thrown quickly. We throw fades and fade comebacks along with the quick outs and slants.

Another thing we like to do in the red zone is to put the formation into the boundary. We like to align the trips set into the boundary and the single receiver to the wideside of the field. We think we can get a good read off how the secondary is playing and if they are man coverage or not.

The quarterback reads the number of safeties in the middle. If there are one or two high safeties, we know there could be a blitz. However, if he read no high safeties, he knows they are coming, and he has to get rid of the ball quickly.

There are two reasons we like to have everything in our arsenal. We want the opponent to have to make the adjustment to play us, but we also want to show all kinds of formations to our defense. When they have to practice against all the formations we use, they are better equipped to handle the opponent. I want my defense to face empty sets, power sets, trips sets, and one-back and two-back formations. I want to do everything so my defense is prepared well and we have flexibility in the red zone.

I want to thank you once again for your attendance and attention. I appreciate everything you coaches do for the young men you are coaching. I want you to know football is the greatest business you could ever hope to be associated with. Our doors are always open at Ohio State, and if we can ever help, you do not hesitate to call on us.

FOOTBALL KEYS AND KICKING GAME TIPS

University of Pittsburgh

Thank you. I appreciate everyone being here. Any time you get a chance to spend time with fellow coaches, it is a positive thing. It is good for me because it makes me think and reflect back a bit.

The first clinic I was involved with was in Pittsburgh after I got out of college. After the clinic, I felt like I might want to get into coaching. My coaches in high school had inspired me and made a difference in my life.

In between graduating and trying to make a professional roster, I was doing some student teaching. My high school coach asked me what I was going to do. I told him I definitely wanted to coach and I had a teacher's certificate from the University of Pittsburgh. He told me there was a clinic going on that weekend and it would be a great induction to coaching. I had just gotten married. He told me to tell my wife I was going to be with his staff and we were going to a football clinic over the weekend.

I packed my bag and met them at the hotel where the clinic was going to be held. When I walked into the lobby, I met two of the assistant coaches. They told me to drop my gear and come with them. They had 15 cases of beer in the car and needed to get them up to the room. We carried them up to the rooms and iced them down in the bathtubs.

After we finished with that, I came back down and was ready to learn some football. They told me we had to go pick up the food and chips. We finally got up to the room. There were all kinds of guys in there playing cards, smoking cigars, and drinking beer. Six hours later, it was time for bed. I did not have time to get my bag out of the car, and I bedded down on the floor with a couple of other guys.

I was lying on the floor looking at the ceiling and thinking to myself, *Man, this is what coaching is all about?* I was one of the first guys to make sure I had the dates for the clinic the next year.

I try to do things with my coaches because this is such a people business. I was on the staff that went from Miami University to the Dallas Cowboys. It was a difficult situation because Tom Landry, the legendary coach, had been let go and replaced by a bunch of coaches that had not coached in pro ball before. They were after us before we even lined up. We went 1-15 the first year, and that made it worse.

At one point in the season, we were 0-7. We were supposed to have a meeting, but Jimmy Johnson said, "Let's go for a walk." At lunchtime, Norv Turner, Tony Wise, Jimmy, and I left and went for a walk. There was nothing we could draw up on the chalkboard that was going to make a difference in beating the Giants. It was a long walk. We decided we were going to get fired if we did not figure a way to get some players. We walked for an hour and a half. We figured we had two players that anyone would want. There was Troy Aikman and Herschel Walker. However, Troy had a no-trade contract. By 4:00 that afternoon, Jimmy had made the decision to trade Herschel Walker. That trade had the biggest impact on a professional franchise than any other in history.

The point I am trying to make is this did not happen in a highly intense coaches meeting. It happened when we were together walking and talking. Those kinds of atmospheres are good for me. That is why it is so good for me to come down here and share with you guys. Sometimes, when we get away as a staff, we get a lot more work done.

I want to try to make some key points before I get into the X's and O's. There are many different ways to win. Football is a very trendy thing. When someone wins the Super Bowl, the other NFL coaches want to try to copy what they did to achieve that success. If you look back on the history of successful high school, college, and pro programs, there are many ways to win.

When I was at Dallas, I watched the Kansas City Chiefs and I was impressed with the defense they were playing. They were playing an under defense that was a form of the 3-4 defense. We had always been a 4-3 defense. That was all we played at Oklahoma State University and in Miami, and it was what we brought to the Cowboys. We could not stop anyone, and I made the suggestion to Jimmy that we should look at the 3-4 scheme.

He told me that we had been successful with the 4-3 defense. We knew it better than anything else we did. He said if we started changing, we would take a step backward. To change defenses would require a complete change in philosophy. If you have a solid foundation, you should be able to adjust and tweak the defense to keep an edge on the opponent. That is better than undergoing a complete change in philosophy and scheme.

Here at Pittsburgh, we are a dinosaur of college football. Last year, in 12 games, we had 55 two-back running plays against our defense. We ran the ball 47 times out of the I formation against the University of Cincinnati. We run the two-back offense because we believe in it. If I were to ask one of your players what your offense was all about and they had trouble coming up with an answer, I would call that an uncertainty. Where there is uncertainty, there is not going to be the conviction, and the team is not going to be that good.

If you ask any of our players what we do on the defense, they know. We are going to turn the down front four loose and bang on the receiver with the defensive backs. We are going to get in their faces and make plays. Whether it works or not, that is what we do. On offense, we are going to run the power play and the power pass. We are going to do it repeatedly.

That goes back to the head coach's philosophy. You must make sure the assistant coaches are sold on it. Are they 100 percent sure it is best for us? When I coached the Dolphins, I was playing golf with Wayne Huizenga, who owned the Dolphins, and Jack Welch, the CEO of General Electric. Jack Welch said, "You cannot talk in those big meetings and get anything done. You have to keep the operation simple and almost brainwash people to get things done."

When I took the Pittsburgh job, I put in every room in our facility the words *trust, accountability,* and *desire.* I put them in the meeting rooms, weight room, training room, coaches' offices, and anywhere our players might be. Those three words were going to be what we built our program on.

When we talk about a player, we want to know if he is the kind of person you can trust. Is he going to be accountable to his teammates? Does he have the desire every day to be as good as he can be? Keeping the foundation simple from a philosophical standpoint gives you a chance with the players. You do not have that much time with them. They are here for four years, if they stay until the eligibility is gone. You must keep the message simple so they have time to buy into what you believe in.

We keep it simple and are very clear as to what we stand for. When you have a position meeting, keep the message simple and precise; let them know exactly what you expect and how you are going to do it. I worked for Don Shula for about two months before we went to the Cowboys. He told me, "In coaching, every year you are going to lose a game or two and have a slump. The key is to get the team turned back upward as fast as you can. When you are riding high, you have to keep pushing and capitalize on the momentum."

The quickest way to turn things for the better is to go back to the foundational things. You do not have time to change philosophies and schemes when you are playing against other good coaches and players. That reminds me of the story of the man who had a crack in his living room wall. He tried to fix it, but it showed up again about a month later. He had the neighborhood handyman try to fix it and the same thing happened. Finally, he called in an expert. The expert came into the house and walked right past the crack in the living room. When the man questioned him about where he was going, the expert told him the crack was not in the living room. He said that the crack was in the foundation in the basement.

Whenever we hit adversity, I remember that story. When you have problems in coaching or with the scheme, go back to the basics. My daughter went to Indiana University. I got to know Bobby Knight. I used to go down and watch his practices. He had a sign hanging up in his coaches room. I have the same sign in my office. It says, "I do not teach a player plays. I teach a player how to play." That is just another statement that says to teach the fundamentals.

Last year, the games we did not win were probably our fault. It was not what the opponent did but what we did. Last week, we were going through all the big plays we gave up on defense. In all the plays we saw, there were 10 plays where someone ran a good scheme on us and got a big play. The other plays were fundamental mistakes by our players. We did not key and got beat by the play-action. We missed a tackle or took the wrong angle. Those types of plays go back to breakdowns in fundamentals.

The coach has to think about the things he can control. He can always say he does not have much talent and does not have the players the opponent does. He needs to think about the things he has and can control as a coach. A coach can control the *conditioning* of his team. It does not take talent to condition. There is no reason why your team cannot be the best-conditioned team.

Last year, we were one of the national leaders in least-penalized teams. We did not make critical turnovers in games. I take all that back to our off-season program and our conditioning. We tie the off-season program and conditioning into the *discipline* in the program. In our weight room, everyone is dressed alike, and there is no jewelry allowed in the weight room. When we line up,

everyone has their hand on the line. We work on the discipline in the off-season and it carries over to the season. When players get tired and are not disciplined, that is when they get silly penalties and lose concentration.

Coach Bill Parcells told me if I had a receiver or running back that fumbled the ball, I needed to get rid of him. He said, "He will get you fired." I asked him about all the fumble drills that we run as a way to improve on that situation. He said that for whatever reason, there are players who simply will not protect the ball regardless of the drills you do.

The coach can control the *effort* of his team. I just hired a new linebackers coach. My linebackers coach went to Central Michigan University as the defensive coordinator. I hired a coach who played for me at the University of Miami. When you are having success, it is easy to compromise on some things. You win a big game and you have a tendency to overlook some of the things you should correct. That is just human nature.

The new linebackers coach was watching our defensive cut-ups from the previous season and pointed out a particular player whom was not giving great effort on a pass rush. I told him the player led the nation in sacks. He said that he still should have made the sack, and he was right. You can control the effort, but sometimes, as coaches, we accept some things that we know are not right because we are winning.

Two years ago, I lost my special teams coach, Charlie Partridge. I lost five coaches off my staff at that time. I was trying to figure out who was going to coach what and trying to hire coaches at the same time. I would rather do anything than have to deal with all the staff problems.

I made a decision that I would coach the special teams. I run every special teams meeting. I watch all the tape and prepare all the game plans. I have a bunch of young guys who help me. That did two things for me. It gave me an opportunity to spend more time with the down-the-line players. They are the players who play the special teams but may not figure too heavily into the offense or defense. This gave me an opportunity to bring those players along at a faster pace.

Last season, we led the nation in blocked kicks. That included punts and field goals. The second thing that came out of my taking over the special teams was my attitude about kick blocks. Since I am the head coach, I make the decision on when to try to block the kick. I developed a confidence in what we were doing.

When I went out to watch high school players, the thing that frustrated me the most was watching the ball hit the ground on punts. I said to myself, *When I am coaching, I never want to let the ball hit the ground.*

The offense was giving up yards of field position every time they let the ball hit the ground on a punt. We have just finished our season breakdowns, and we let the ball hit the ground on punts one third of the time. That is terrible. If we have to go to three-deep on the punt formation next year, we will because we are going to catch the ball.

I want to show you a couple of drills that I think are important. You do not need pads to run this one drill, and it is a defensive drill not just a special teams drill. This drill is a *come-to-balance drill* (Diagram #1). Most of the tackles missed in a game are open field tackles. We use this drill for the coverage teams on punts and kickoffs.

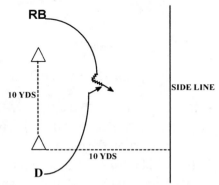

Diagram #1. Open Field Tackling

In this drill, the defender aligns on the end of a lined-off box, which is 10 yards deep by 10 yards wide. We start the running back at the other end of the box. He enters the box and can cut inside or outside the tackler. The defender has to run into the

box and come to balance. He never wants to stop his feet moving. He targets the running back and gets his head across the body. He wants to strike with the shoulder, although it is a head-on drill.

In our conference, we were at the top of every defensive category. We played good defense this year. In this next drill, we try to emphasize a good breakdown position. Three years ago, we were getting ready to play West Virginia University. That was a season when they ranked high in the national rankings. Halfway through practice, we were working on offense and defense when I noticed our special teams coach on the other field doing this drill.

I walked over and asked why he was working on this drill instead of something else. He told me we were ready to play on offense and defense. He said the game was going to come down to being able to tackle. In that game, we had three missed tackles. That was when they had Steve Slaton and Pat White.

In this drill, we want to wrap up the running. We teach all the fundamentals of tackling. We get the head across, sink the hips, grab cloth, and run through the tackle by driving the legs. Every position does this drill even though it does not relate specifically to them.

There are two things important in making a tackle. The *aiming point* and the *wrap-up* are the two important items. This is something the secondary should work on. The big, open field runs are not the ones that run down the sideline. Most big runs occur when the back or receiver breaks across the middle of the field. We tackle in space, and what I am going to say is more clinic talk than anything.

The final part of the tackle is wrapping up and grabbing cloth. You do not see that much in a football game. The key to the secondary defender is the aiming point. The defensive back wants to aim for the *V* of the neck. If the running back goes down the sideline, the tackler approaches with the aiming point of the *V* of the neck. If the runner continues down the sideline, the tackler hits him in the *V* of the neck and drives him out of bounds.

The thing we are trying to defend is the cutback run. If the runner cuts back, he cannot cut across the face of the tackler, and we keep him out of the middle of the field. That is a small point, but it is huge in importance to the safeties and corners. If you can get this skill taught, it will save you one or two big plays a game.

Jimmy Johnson was a great defensive coach. He told me if there was one drill he could spend 15 minutes on, it would be this drill. It is a *string-out drill* (Diagram #2). If you were to put on your films from last year, you would find the sprint-out drill in almost every play. There are three segments to the drill. In the drill, you need two offensive blockers and a ballcarrier. The blockers and the ballcarrier are in a line five yards apart. The first segment is the initial block at the line of scrimmage. The defender is in a stance over an offensive blocker. On sound or movement, the offensive blocker tries to reach block the defender. The defender has to defeat the block and escape. The defender uses whatever techniques you teach to defeat block. He can use the rip, swim, or whatever you teach.

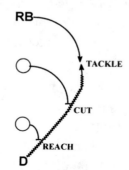

Diagram #2. String-Out Drill

As soon as the defender beats the first block, the second blocker attacks the defender and tries to cut him down. You adapt the drill to fit the opponent. If we have to play Navy, this part of the drill is a cut block. The second blocker comes on the defender and tries to cut out his outside leg. If you do not want the blocker to cut, let him stay up and try to run through the outside shoulder of the defender.

When I was at the University of Miami, it seemed like we played Oklahoma every year for the national championship. Everyone coaches the hands

in defeating the cut block. The hands are important and the eyes are important, but the thing that keeps you from being cut down is the *feet*. I can have great hand placement, but if the blocker gets to my outside foot, he can cut me down. The emphasis in playing the cut block is to make sure the outside leg stays free. Beating the cut block is all about getting the outside leg outside the blocker.

The second the defender gets off the second block, the ballcarrier starts. The finish of the drill is the first drill I showed you. We come to balance and make an open field tackle on the ballcarrier. We want to get our head across the ballcarrier, wrap him up, and drive him back for five yards. We do this drill with all positions. The linebacker starts out in his linebacker stance, and the secondary defenders start in their stances. This drill occurs in almost every play in a game. This is as good a drill as there is for defensive football and coverage teams.

We work the drill going to the right and left. We can do the drill without pads, but the intensity level is controlled. The drills that you work in practice, you should see in the game film. Every drill we do should have a relative use to the game. This is a drill to get the motor running and is a fundamental drill.

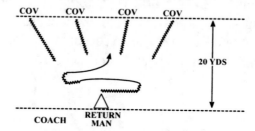

Diagram #3. Gather Drill

The second practice this spring we will do this drill. It is a *gather drill* (Diagram #3). This is where you find your coverage defenders. We put everyone through this drill—that means the receivers and running backs. By doing this drill, I can locate the players I want to work with on my coverage teams. In the drill, we try to simulate a punt or kickoff. We line up four coverage players with a return man. The coverage defenders sprint down the field toward the return man. I am looking for players that can break down and keep their shoulder square as they cover.

The defenders, as they come down, have to keep leverage on the ball. They want to keep the ball on their inside shoulders. The return man makes three moves before he gets vertical. He can start one way and reverse his field going upfield. The coverage defenders keep their shoulders square until the ballcarrier goes vertical up the field. Once that happens, the defenders turn and pursue to the ball. The first defender down the field stops the ball.

When we cover kickoffs or punts, everyone on the coverage teams contains the ball. They all keep the ball on their inside shoulders. When you cover kicks, you try to contain the ball even when you make a tackle. If we miss the tackle, the ball should have to break back inside. We miss the tackle going to the outside of the return man. He always keeps his outside arm free and the ball on the inside shoulder.

We control the drill by blowing a whistle to start the drill. I have one coach control the kick returner. When the coverage people get inside 10 yards to the return man, the coach releases him. He does not run straight up the field. He probes and fakes before he goes upfield. If the coverage people turn their shoulder before the ball breaks up the field, he will lose leverage.

The biggest problem that you have on your coverage teams is *discipline*. We have good coverage teams, and we back that up with stats. The first thing to good kickoff coverage is to kick the ball outside. We want it between the numbers and the sideline. Never kick the ball down the middle of the field. Against the University of Notre Dame, the punt they returned, we had kicked down the middle of the field. I told our punter that I would rather he kick the ball 10 yards down the field out of bounds than 45 yards in the middle of the field. In our punting, we want to directional punt.

Let me tell you something that will reinforce that thought. If Mike Tomlin was up here talking about special teams, he would tell you that on the 45-man roster, there are only four or five players who want to cover a kickoff. None of the starters cover kickoffs because they do not want anything to do with special teams. In their minds, they do not get paid to cover kickoffs.

Eighty percent of the NFL kickoff coverage is the kicker. He gets hang time and places the ball to the inside of the numbers. You put the four or five players who want to cover the kick to the side you kick the ball and cover it.

We have a special teams board we keep in our locker room. We have every special teams player listed on the board from the snapper to the holder, and all the other special teams players are on the board. At the bottom of the board, we have a scoring system for positive and negative points. From that board, comes our top special teams player. They amass points by making tackles and blocks among other things. A player could make three tackles and three mental mistakes and end up with zero points. We keep the board current for each week. The board is the first thing they want to see. It is a motivational tool for the younger players, and it reinforces the importance of the special teams.

When we kick the ball off, we want to kick to the corners. Hang time is more important than distance. If you have a kicker that cannot reach the end zone, get him to hang it for four seconds and you will be able to cover it. If he can kick the ball to the 15-yard line with close to a four-second hang time, that is better than the kicker who line drives the ball to the five-yard line. Obviously, hang time is the most important thing in punt coverage.

The next drill is an *over-the-top drill* (Diagram #4). We use this drill for our kickoff and punt coverage teams. The most important thing is to keep the eyes on the target. The target is the ballcarrier. We work on this drill, and we are disciplined on this skill. Most players who cover kicks get caught up with the player blocking them. That is where all the creases in the coverage come from. It is critical that the coverage team keeps their eyes on the return man. As the coverage comes down the field, they want to get over the top of the blocker to the side of the ballcarrier.

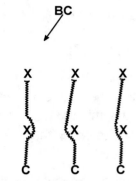
Diagram #4. Over the Top

If the defender covers a kick, as he approaches a blocker, he wants to play over the top of that blocker to the side of the ballcarrier. If the ball is to the defender's inside, he wants to avoid or play over the top of the blocker to the inside. If the ball is to his outside, he wants to go the other way. It does not matter how the defender gets past the blocker. He can swim, rip, or jump over the blocker, but he must end up on the side where the ball is.

When we set the drill up, we have two rows of three bag holders 10 yards apart. The bag holders are five to seven yards apart. We have three coverage players coming down the field. There is a ballcarrier behind the second row of dummies. The ballcarrier moves to give direction to the coverage players. The coverage defenders rip through the first group of bag holders making sure they attack the bag to the side of the ball. If one of the coverage players goes to the right of a bag and the other player goes to the left, there is a crease in the coverage.

On the punt or the kickoff, when the coverage player gets in close proximity to the ballcarrier, he wants to square up on the blocker and not give the return man an avenue. He gets his hands on the blocker and wants to be able to play either way off the block.

Kickoff Coverage Principles

- Get off the ball
- Eyes on target
- Over the top; avoid to ball side
- Feet gaining ground
- Hands on blocker

- Feet still gaining ground
- Make the play

When our kickoff coverage team runs up to the ball, we want them inside or at one yard from the line when the ball is kicked. If they are deeper than a yard from the line, they are late. I do not care how far they run up or where they align, but I want them within one yard of the line of scrimmage when it is kicked.

As soon as the ball is kicked, the coverage team has to find the ball and get their eyes on the target. The next thing is to get over the top of the blocker. If the defender can avoid the blocker, he does it, but he must do it to the correct side of the ball. We do not want him to run behind the block. All the coverage players come over the top to the same side. That way, there are no creases or defenders running into one another.

Once the defender gets over the top, he continues to gain ground. That means he is staying in his lane as he covers down the field. When the defender gets to the ballcarrier, he has to get his hands on the blocker until the ballcarrier decides which way he is going.

Every kicker is different with their approach to the ball. You must make sure the coverage team is in sync with the kicker. If the takeoff point is timed with the kicker's run up, the cover defender does not need to look in to the ball.

When a player is double-teamed on the kickoff coverage, he cannot run around it. If it is on the outside or a wedge block, he has to split the double-team. If he tries to run around the double-team, it creates a huge crease in the coverage. We drill the double-team with bag holders. The defender has to learn how to split the block.

Punt Return Middle

- Ten-man holdup at the line
- Gain ground on the holdup
- Make the blocker think you want to block the punt

We have two kickoff returns and one punt return. The walled sideline returns on punts are good, but you need a perfect kick to try it. You can work your butt off all week and never get to use it because the kicker is kicking into the wind or he kicks the ball too short. We avoid that by working a middle return every time. We run a middle return on the punt. We hold up the coverage people at the line of scrimmage. We align head-up, punch them under the chin, and drive them back. If we can drive them 10 yards deep, that is what we do.

If the blocker thinks we are coming to block the punt, he will stay in and block. The minute he thinks you are not coming, he will release and cover. When the ball is kicked or they decide to cover, we run with them and try to hold them up. The fliers on the outside are double-teamed or single-pressed and played like a defensive back in pass coverage. We want to keep them out of the middle of the field.

When we work on the punt blocks, the time we shoot for is 2.2 seconds to the ball. The key to blocking a punt is to take the ball off the punter's foot. The all-time NFL pass deflector was a guy named "Too Tall" Jones. He played for the Dallas Cowboys, and I had the privilege of coaching him the last year he played. He was successful because he got in front of the quarterback and had the ability to get his hands up at the right time. That is no different from blocking punts.

We tell our players when they block punts they have to go down to block them. You go high to block a field goal and down to block a punt. If a defender breaks free on the punter and goes high to block the punt, the punter will punt the ball right underneath him. You have to go to the foot and take the ball off the foot.

The most effective way we have blocked kicks is to run a pick for one blocker and run someone up the field behind the pick. The secret is that he cannot lose ground as he comes around the pick. If you try to get everyone involved with the block, you will not be successful. We have one or two blockers that will get all the kicks. We run the game for those people who have the knack for blocking the kick.

Each week we scout the punter and give the block team the block point. Some punters are one-, two-, and three-step kickers. We want to block the kick and not rough the punter. They know where he will kick the ball, and that is the point they attack. We mark the spot and work to that point in practice. When we film the block drills, we film them from the rear of the punter. You can see the player's faces as they come in to block the ball. Some of them are not comfortable with blocking the ball. They close their eyes and flinch. Some players have a knack for blocking the kick and they are the players you send to block the kick. When we practice the blocks in practice, we use volleyballs.

On the field-goal block, you have to understand the path of the ball for the kick to be good. If the ball is on the hash mark, the block defenders have to align in the middle of the goalpost. For the kicker to make the kick, he will have to kick over those defenders. If we can get three steps of penetration, the blockers only have to get 10 feet in the air to block the kick. The defenders get the penetration, and the jumper tries to get the ball. We should develop a rhythm with the jump. They are stepping and jumping. The rhythm is 1-2-3 jump and hands up.

These things will win games for you. We are not twisting or pulling people. We are pushing for three steps of penetration and trying to get our hands up. We spend time with this and it is important to us. Our players know it, and they perform because there are more games won by one point than there are by 20 points. Extra points and field goals are a big part of the game of football. Blocked kicks are one of the best momentum turners in any football game. Big plays in the kicking game can turn the game from a loss to a win.

Coming to a clinic is not necessarily about drawing plays. It is not about the plays—it is about teaching the plays to the players. I hope that some of the fundamentals I talked about will help you and give you an edge. I appreciate your attention.

USING THE TIGHT END IN THE SPREAD OFFENSE

University of Florida

I am fired up to be here. I am a New England guy from Massachusetts. My father was a high school coach. I grew up in coaching and it is in my blood. My brother coaches for the Minnesota Vikings. This is the greatest profession there is. Every convention I attend, I try to get one idea that can make me a better coach. If I get one idea, it will be a successful clinic.

I coached with Coach Barry Alvarez for 11 years. I coached with Lou Holtz for two years as a graduate assistant. They always talked about ways to become a better coach and teacher. They talked about communicating efficiently with your players. The buzzword we used was to create *unconscious confidence*. That means you have trained the players so well that they are performing and not thinking.

Coach Holtz used to say all the time that it was burned in his brain. What is coaching? Coaching is the *constant conditioning of correct behavior*. To do that, you must have a framework of drills that you believe in. Do not drill just to be drilling. Coach Alvarez always told us that the drill work had to transfer to the game field. Do not make up drills that are going to do anything but take up your individual time. Your drills have to apply to real-life situations.

You should be able to see your drill work on the game films. When you see them, you point them out to your players. That way they can understand why they are doing the drills.

Unfortunately, a lot of coaches do not know what correct behavior is. You have to find out what correct behavior is and the correct fundamental that teaches it to the position you are training. After that, you have to demand repeatedly of your players. You have to condition them repeatedly so they can go out and perform with unconscious confidence.

I am going to talk to you about using the tight end in the spread offense. If you watched the University of Florida play, you saw Aaron Hernandez used very effectively. He won the John Mackey Award this year for the best tight end in America. To his credit, he deserved it. We were thin at that position. We only had two tight ends on our roster. He is probably the smartest football player I have ever coached. He was so versatile and could handle everything. We used him as an attached tight end. We used him as an unattached tight end. We used him as a slot receiver and a back. He was a dynamic athlete that allowed us to be multiple in many ways.

It is rare to get someone as talented as Aaron. We used him to create problems in match-ups. Football is a game I call *violent chess*. On offense, it is 10 offensive players versus 11 defenders. The reason for that is the quarterback never blocks. The defense is always plus one on the offense. If the quarterback hands the ball to the tailback, the defense is plus two. You have to find ways to manipulate defenders. You have to know how to create the 1-on-1 mismatches. You can do that with an athletic tight end.

We were very creative on offense. Aaron could beat a corner. We felt it was a mismatch if we could get Aaron isolated outside on a cornerback. It was a mismatch if we got him isolated on a linebacker in the slot. The advantage we had was Aaron was a blocking tight end. You do not get many high school tight ends that want to block.

I am a believer in fundamentals. Schemes do not win games. Fundamentals win games. If you have good coaches and players and can play with correct behavior, you will play winning football. If you have the talent and the schemes that present problems to defenses, you can be very good.

At Florida, we do an outstanding job of focusing on the ball positioning of the runner. The catchphrase for correct ball positioning is *high and tight*. When you think of Tiki Barber, you think of a great running back. However, he is usually associated with fumbling the football. The New York Giants coaches demanded that he carry the ball high and tight and trained him in that fundamental. When they ingrained that fundamental into him, he stopped fumbling.

The game of football is entirely about the ball. It is not very heavy. On offense, you try to protect the ball and score with it. On defense, you try to contain it and take it away. It is that simple. I tell the players that high and tight is the apex of the curl exercise they worked on in the weight room. That is where we want the football carried. We always try to condition body position for strength. This is one of those positions and it is critical. The tip of the football must be pointed up toward the football gods. You want the tip of the ball pointed at the sky and the elbow clamped. Fumbles occur when the tip of the ball comes down and the ball comes away from the body.

If you are not coaching ball security on every snap in your offensive practice, you are hurting your players because you are not conditioning them. There needs to be some form of reinforcement either positive or negative on every play. If the ballcarrier has it up, tell him that was a good job. If he did not have it up, remind him to get the tip up. One way or the other, emphasize it every play.

When you coach the receivers, tell them, "Eyes to the tuck." That means to watch the ball all the way into the tuck position, which is high and tight. If you are not coaching it on every snap, you will have turnovers. I can be proud in my 24 years of college coaching of that one thing. Wherever I was, we were good at protecting the football. That includes Syracuse University when we were not very good. We did not win many games, but we were good at securing the football. That comes from constant conditioning and coaching the ball position all the time.

One of the things a tight end must do is block on and off the line of scrimmage. He has to block with his hand on the ground and off the ground. He has to run routes and be a match-up problem for the linebackers. He has to play multiple positions in the passing game.

We have to evaluate the tight end as a run blocker. We have to know if he can be an effective blocker on a combo block with the offensive tackle. He has to block gap schemes. He has to block the zone play on the front and backside of the offense. He may have to be the point of attack in a man blocking scheme. The Indianapolis Colts ran the outside zone as a true man scheme. The outside zone is a great football play, but you must handle the C gap for it to be successful. If you cannot handle the C gap on the zone play, do not run the play. There are a million plays.

You have to evaluate whatever the tight end can handle in his blocking assignments. This is a diagram of the tight zone play (Diagram #1). There is nothing magical about the play. The tight end works a combination block with the tackle if the tackle is uncovered. They work the combo for the defensive end and Sam linebacker. The tight end is on the playside, but he is not at the point of attack.

Everything the tight end does goes back to fundamentals and starts with the stance. The feet in the stance have to be in the ground. We want the back flat and balanced in the stance. He has to have perfect weight distribution so he can move out of his stance. However, to move from that stance he has to load the weight to the opposite foot he plans to move. If he plans to move his right foot, he has to load the weight to his left foot. That is what we call a loaded stance. A loaded stance is feeling the burn when you are in your stance. The burn is the feeling you get when you exhaust a muscle.

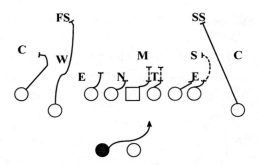

Diagram #1. Inside Zone

When you put 70 percent of your weight on the left side, that is telling your body you have to step with the right foot. That allows you to take a short, quick step when you are an on the line of scrimmage player. When we get in the stance, we want both feet on the ground with the toes pointed forward.

You have to teach your players how to watch films. When we teach the tight ends, we talk about *triangles of defenders*. The thing that drives me crazy is players who play in a tunnel. They do not have panoramic vision and do not play with their eyes. Aaron Hernandez had predator and panoramic eyes. His eyes were alive so that he could see and communicate the information he saw. The triangle is the man aligned on the tight end, the outside linebacker, and the near safety. In the diagram, he keys the defensive end, Sam linebacker, and strong safety. He has to know how the secondary is rotating.

On this play, what he sees is the linebacker dropped down to the line of scrimmage. That tells him there is going to be some type of zone blitz with the strong safety dropping down. That means we will have to account for the safety in the run scheme.

When we run our tight zone, it is a backside A-gap play and it can break to the backside B gap. It is a tight dive play. The aiming point for the back is the backside hip of the center. The tight end on this play knows the play will hit to the backside and blocks the most dangerous man to the play. He wants to get his body between the ballcarrier and the strong safety. The running back is not looking at frontside defenders. He is reading the down linemen and free safety on the backside. We do not want

him hit from the side by someone he is not looking at. His rule on this play is playside gap and defender #3. The third defender to that side is generally the Sam linebacker or rolled-down safety.

We can run the same play with the tight end in an unattached position. He aligns in a hip position on the offensive tackle (Diagram #2). Nothing has changed in his assignment. He blocks the Sam linebacker. Not every block for the tight end has to be a pancake block. He needs to do his job and cover up defenders. Most tight ends in America are not road-grader, smash-you-in-the-mouth types.

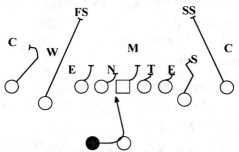

Diagram #2. Hip Position

Tight ends are covering people up and keeping position on the defenders. They are not running over linebackers. By being smart, they can play tight end.

I want to stop right here and make a comment about the running back in the zone play. This will help offensive line coaches as well as running back coaches. When the running back makes a cut, he needs to evaluate where he is making the cut. Football is a game of space, and defense is always trying to position defenders. The running back has to close the space on defenders to create space in the open field.

If the back makes his fake three yards from the defender, he may move the defender in the direction but the defender can redirect on his cut. The move was made too far from the defender, which allows him to commit and then correct to the back's cut. The running back wants to close the space, so when he makes his move, the defender has no time to redirect. Football is a game of angles. If the defender can recover and make the play, the back made a mistake. The running back closes the distance to the defender, fakes to the outside, and busts through the inside shoulder. That is how you break long runs. He eliminates the space between himself and the defender and creates space behind him.

A receiver cannot make cuts in space. We constantly coach him to close the cushion on the defender. We do that so he can eliminate space to create space. If he does not close the cushion, he will not get open. It is not complicated, but it has to be conditioned into to the athletes. You do that through drill work.

In the stretch zone play, the blocking assignments stay the same but the targets change. When we talk about targets, we refer to *hat, hands*, and *feet* targets. On the tight zone, the hat target is the breastplate of the defender. The outside foot target splits the crotch of the defender. The tight end wants to be inside out on the defender because the ball is going inside. On the stretch zone, the hat target changes to the armpit of the defender. We want to stretch the defender. The footwork is an outside bucket step so we can shade the outside number of the defender. The foot target on the stretch is the inside foot splitting the crotch of the defender. You can evaluate those things.

The play I want to show you is the *stretch play from the I formation with a man blocking scheme* (Diagram #3). The Colts run this play. They run the play with the tailback at seven yards deep, and they hand the ball off instead of using the shotgun. The tight end has a man blocking assignment on the defensive end. He is at the point of attack and must win for the play to be successful. On the man scheme, his foot target is foot to foot with the defender. We want him mirrored up. He has tight inside footwork so he does not get beat inside. We want tight hands and elbows on the block to establish leverage.

We look for the tight end to hit on the rise and get the reverse C in his back. We want the power angles in his ankles, knees, and hips to explode, and he wants to climb up the defender. You climb the defender with the hands and finish the block with the feet.

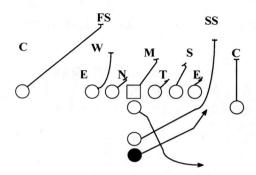

Diagram #3. Stretch Zone Man

One of the things I learned from Urban was to *run the number*. This keeps us from getting holding penalties. If the blocker feels he is losing the block, he runs the inside number of the defender. He takes his inside hand and pushes on the inside number as he runs upfield. That makes the defender play behind the blocker's hip.

That is a great coaching point. It is a good technique for receivers that are stalk blocking. The technique is universal, and we use this as a coaching point for all our positions. If they are about to lose the block, they run the numbers. If they will run the number with their inside shoulder and pad, they will never be called for holding.

You have to be able to evaluate the ability of the linemen to get their second foot in the ground when they attack an "on-the-line-of-scrimmage defender." The linemen cannot be caught using big steps before contact. The good linemen can get the second foot down quickly so they can make contact on the third step. If they take long steps, the defender will jack his butt up and defeat him every time. This is critical in the zone game. How quickly the linemen can get their second foot on the ground and hit the target is paramount in the zone game.

If they can do that, it puts them in a body position of strength. When we run the stretch play with zone blocking, the assignments are the same. On that play, the tight end will end up blocking the Sam linebacker. On any running play, you will not get everyone blocked. We tell the running backs if they want to make it at the next level, they make those people miss. The running back in the open field has to make defenders miss. If we can get the line of scrimmage blocked, he has to make the second level defender miss.

In our offense, everything comes off the tight zone look. We run the tight zone, stretch, zone read, split zone, and isolation from the same look.

Every week, we talk about window dressing our run game with the tight end. That gives us the ability to have a running game with multiple alignments by the tight end. We want to maintain a basic run game with the multiple formations and run the power game using the same techniques. Every week, we are trying to window dress what we are doing but we are not trying to create new plays.

Our run plays do not change. We have six running plays that will be in every game plan. We do not deviate from that, and we know they will be in the game plan. What we have to do as coaches is figure out how to run them. We have to decide what sort of window dressing we are going to provide in formations and motion so we can run the same plays. We want to do this without causing confusion among the players.

We can align the tight end in the backfield in a power formation. We can align him outside and motion him into that position. We are trying to force communication on the defense. When you start to move people in motion, the defense has to communicate. They have to realign and adjust. The more communication you force on the defense, the better chance for miscommunication. That leads to busted assignments. If it occurs in the secondary, you get a big play.

We run the power play from the power position (Diagram #4). The most effective way to run it is with motion. On this play, the tight end motions across the set and kicks out the C-gap defender. He blocks the defender that defends the C gap regardless of who it is. We pull the backside guard and lead up on the linebacker. We can run it with different backfield action and different backs carrying the ball. It is a standard power play with the offensive line blocking down and the tight end or fullback kicking out at the point of attack. The backside guard pulls and turns up on the playside linebacker.

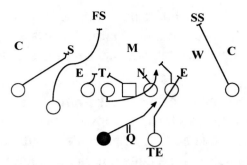

Diagram #4. Power

If the playside tackle reads an outside blitz with the 5-technique defender spiking inside, he gives a *rifle call* (Diagram #5). That tells the tight end there is a blitz coming from the outside. The offensive tackle slows down and takes the 5-technique defender on the stunt, and the tight end kicks out the linebacker. Everything else remains the same.

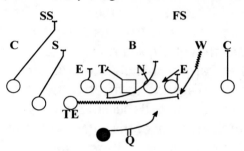

Diagram #5. Rifle

There is nothing magical about this play. You all have seen it before. When the tight end kicks out, he has to watch his hand position on the block. We teach hand position every day in a simple drill. We take two players and put them in a lockup position. One player has an inside hand position, and the other player has his hands outside. The blocker duck walks the defender back five yards. When they reach the five-yard line, the defender captures the inside hand position and walks the other player back five yards. They continue to repeat the drill recapturing their inside hand position each time they walk five yards.

We also have a completion leverage drill. We do this drill when a blocker misses his target. This teaches him how to regain leverage. I learned this drill from Joe Moore, the legendary line coach from the University of Notre Dame. The blocker in this drill has one hand inside and one hand outside. He has to get both hands inside on the breastplate. He does it two different ways. He can chop down with the outside hands and regain the position. On the other hand, he can dip and rip the hand underneath the arm of the defender. If he does that, he uses a circling motion to get under the arm and hand of the defender.

This is a competitive drill. Both players start with one hand in and one hand out in the middle of the five-yard area. The first player that can regain hand position pushes the other player back to the five-yard line. It is a combative drill with both players trying to gain inside position and push the other player back. In training camp, we do this drill every other day.

I would recommend you incorporate these drills as part of your teaching techniques. We have used them for a long time and they work.

We can run the power play blocking and use counter action in the backfield (Diagram #6). This play is an inside run, which starts in the A gap and works its way to the outside. In the diagram, this is a quarterback run with the tailback faking across the play and cutting off the backside of the play. We use power play blocking for the offensive line. Nothing changes for them or the tight end.

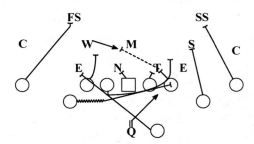

Diagram #6. Counter

We can run the counter and pull two linemen off the backside (Diagram #7). The playside tackle blocks the 5-technique defender instead of blocking the B gap to the backside linebacker. This is a man scheme for us. This gives us a change-up for the counter. It is particularly good against teams that have the 5-technique squeeze and cause a train wreck on the pullers. The backside guard pulls for the first linebacker, and the tackle pulls for the second linebacker.

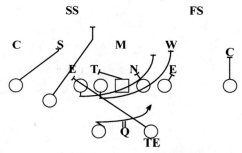

Diagram #7. Counter—Man Blocking

We have a play we run off the read play that we call *book* (Diagram #8). Book is the strongside read play. The tight end influences the 5-technique defender with a hard down block influence move. After he makes the move, he arcs up and sits between the two linebackers. His block on the linebacker is not important. The influence on the 5-technique defender freezes the defender, and he does not squeeze down on the running back. If the tight end simply runs out of the play, the 5-technique defender squeezes down and makes the play. This does not look like much of a play but it is effective.

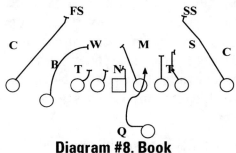

Diagram #8. Book

I want to talk about some of the screens and shovel plays we run. The shovel play is a form of triple option (Diagram #9). The quarterback does not attack the defensive end but stays on a parallel course to the line of scrimmage. If the end comes up the field for the quarterback, he shovels the ball inside to the tight end coming behind the line. If the defender closes on the tight end, the quarterback runs the option outside and pitches off the pitch key. If the quarterback shovels the ball to the inside and we drop it, it is an incomplete pass and not a fumble. Aaron caught 12 to 14 balls this year on the shovel pass.

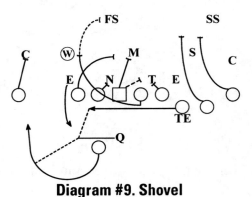

Diagram #9. Shovel

We can put the tight end in a multitude of places. We can run it from an attached or unattached formation. We can run it from the power set, or use motion from almost any set. The coaching point has to do with the pitch relationship to the quarterback. We tell him as he gets to the center, he has to stutter his feet so he keeps a four-yards-inside and two-yards-behind the quarterback relationship. We never want to be in a position where the end can force the quarterback to pitch and fall back on the tight end.

The quarterback runs parallel or slightly downhill. We want to draw the end upfield. We want to shovel the ball inside. If the defensive end sees the tight end coming underneath and closes on him, the quarterback keeps the ball. He turns upfield and finds the pitch key, which is generally the force defender.

The frontside down blocks, and the backside guard pulls for the Will linebacker in the B gap. If the Will linebacker pursues outside the B gap, the guard does not chase him. He turns up and blocks the next level of the defense. It could be the Mike linebacker or the safety. The Will linebacker running outside will be the pitch key for the quarterback if he is forced to keep the ball.

This is not a complicated play and the efficiency of the play is ridiculous. The pulling guard oftentimes ends up in space trying to block a defensive back. It is hard for a 300-pound lineman to block people in space. The buzzword we use is *come to balance*. When you work on this in the indoor program or in spring ball, you will see the lineman's

body position change when he gets the technique. He will be able to change direction.

We ran this play against Louisiana State University from an empty set while we were backed up to our end zone (Diagram #10). We consider the shovel pass a very safe play. The play we ran was a "check with me" shovel pass to what we call the "white" side of the defense. The white side is the uncovered guard, or wherever there is space at the line of scrimmage. The "black" side is the covered side. On this play, the tight end or slotback to the two-man side will be the shovel pass runner. In the diagram, the tight end became the pitchman. The tight end steps back and bellies back to become the pitchman.

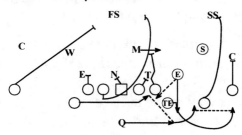

Diagram #10. Shovel Empty

We ran this screen pass 15 times this year (Diagram #11). We were successful 14 out of 15 times. This is a middle screen to the tight end. We tell the tight end to count two counts and go slow. It cannot be a quick two count. It is one-thousand-one, one-thousand-two. He comes behind the line of scrimmage slowly. He should catch the ball in the B-gap area. Both the tackles are dropping into a pass set and chopping their defenders. The center and two guards are blocking the Sam, Mike, and Will linebackers.

If one of the linebackers blitzes, we do not block him. We let him go. The quarterback is in the shotgun and has time to get the ball off. We had a lot of success with this play this year. The offensive tackle needs to set deep and get the defensive ends upfield. If there is a 3 technique aligned on the guard, the tackle cannot get involved with him. We want the guards and center to punch their blocks and throw them away from the B-gap area.

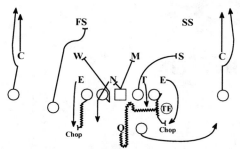

Diagram #11. Middle Screen

The tight end turns and shows both his numbers to the quarterback. When the quarterback can see both numbers, he knows there is no one between him and the tight end. The second reason is not to expose the ball. For the defender to get to the ball, he has to run through the tight end. If one of the down linemen reads the screen, the offensive lineman latches onto him and blocks the crap out of him.

We can align the tight end in the slot and motion him inside. We have protection schemes where he does the same thing. We can create a six-man protection by motioning the tight end into the backfield. If the tight end goes too fast, the backside linebacker will see the screen. This play is not too good against a man team, but it is great against any blitz team.

You cannot expect to put the tight end in a hip protection scheme and run the screen on third-and-long. You must have a protection scheme from the positions you want to throw the screen. If the only time you are in those positions you run the screen, it will not be a successful play. The guards and center have to punch before they turn the defenders loose. They cannot let them go from the line of scrimmage. They have to punch them to slow them down.

In our passing game, Aaron could run the entire scheme. We could split him and run deep patterns with him. We shifted him from attached positions to slot positions. That was a good indicator of how people were playing. It pointed out man cover in most cases. The tight end is a great indicator for coverage identification. It can also uncover a blitz

scheme. Shifts are better than motion. You can shift him from one side to the other or shift him from inside to outside.

The tight end is a great way to find 1-on-1 match-ups. When the tight end runs his patterns, he has to drive on the defender and create some space. We do not want to run into coverage, we want to widen defenders and create space in our route running. Against one high safety, we want to run the speed post into his area.

When you have an excellent receiving tight end, as we had, the defense cannot put a safety or linebacker on him. Most of the time, he gets the cover corner when he splits. We teach the tight end to step on the toe of the defender. We want him to close out the defender and maintain his space. He wants to put himself between the quarterback and the defensive back. We want to run away from the defender or put ourselves in a position to get the interference call.

Another pattern we throw to the tight end is the *delay pattern*. It is not a screen but run on the same timing. He sets in his blocking scheme and releases up the middle of the field. It is almost a checkdown pattern for the tight end. The pattern is designed for the Tampa-2 coverage. He shows pass and blocks for two counts. The Mike linebacker goes to the middle at 18 yards. The tight end has that area in front of the Mike linebacker to work.

We talk about a receiver's stick as a timing issue for the quarterback in the pass pattern. The quarterback has to feel the stick of the receivers. The receiver defines his stick and is ready to catch the football. The quarterback knows when the stick is coming and releases the ball. The receiver's body profile changes when he sticks the pattern. That way he can trigger his big muscles and power as he runs the route.

I appreciate your time gentlemen, and I hope you got something from this. I enjoyed being up here.

THE REDUCED 3-4 DEFENSE

Yale University

I appreciate you coaches coming to listen to me. I hope I do not bore you. A clinic is an opportunity to share ideas. One thing I want to say to you coaches, and I believe it with all my heart: you guys are on the front line of what I think is the most important job in America. I believe there are only two institutions in our country that allow young men to develop the way they used to develop. One of those institutions is the military. In the military, you still get discipline. You learn how to work hard and persevere. You learn all the things that football teaches. Football is the other institution.

We develop the athlete also, but it all starts with you. What you are doing is important. There is no other sport or profession that teaches the things football teaches. It teaches hard work, discipline, perseverance, team-building, and overcoming adversity. All the things you learn in life, you learn in football. That is why Fortune 500 companies are looking for former athletes to hire.

There are some misconceptions about the Ivy League. There are extremely high academic standards, and there is no question about that. Our incoming class will average 3.5 or higher on their GPA. The SAT is around 1800 on the base line. We are talking about sixes on all parts of the SAT. On the ACT, we are looking for a 27 score.

Those standards force us to recruit nationally. We have a player coming from Hawaii this year. We recruit from California the entire way back East. We have a couple of players from Pittsburgh on our team.

The last time I was in Pittsburgh, I was with the Jacksonville Jaguars. We played the Steelers in the second-to-the-last game of the season and beat them. We came back in the playoffs and beat them

again. I know that makes you coaches feel good about me. The thing I remember about that game was how physical and violent it was. It was what football was all about.

I am from Texas, and I had the opportunity to go several places to play. I chose Stanford because it gave me an opportunity to combine academics and athletics. That is why I chose to come to Yale. I believe in the study athlete. I believe that really exists. I believe you can do both and feel strongly about that.

I had a great coach and mentor to play for. I was recruited by Jack Elway. I played for Dennis Green, who was the coach for three years. We went form 3-8 to 8-4 in those three years. My senior year, Coach Waltz came back from the NFL, and we went 10-3. John Lynch was one of the players on that team. We developed as a team and finished on a good note.

I played in the NFL with San Francisco and made a Super Bowl appearance against the Dallas Cowboys. I have had a good coaching career in both college and pros, and I have been around some good defensive coaches and mentors. I want to tell you one thing: it is not the scheme that makes plays; it is the players.

Players make plays. I think our biggest job as coaches is evaluation. We have to find out what they can do and what they can do well. We have to put them into positions where they can succeed. You cannot force a square peg into a round hole. Coach Waltz used to say to us, "Don't tell me what he can't do; tell me what he can do." If we put the players in a position to fail, that is bad coaching. That is our fault because we need to put him in a position to be successful.

We are going to talk about the things we do defensively. However, I am not married to it. It changes with the different groups you get. That happens more in high school than it does in college. You do not have the opportunity to recruit what you need. We at least have the opportunity to find players who can do the things we need to do.

The most important thing we do is evaluation. Getting them to do it repeatedly is the second-most-important thing. If the player demonstrates that he can do it once, he can do it repeatedly. You have to tap into whatever is motivating him, and get him to do it repeatedly.

Six colleges have over 800 wins, and Yale is one of them. The other five are Michigan, Notre Dame, Nebraska, Texas, and Ohio State. Yale ranks number-two on that list. We have played football for 136 years. The game of football as we know it was invented on the campus of Yale. A coach by the name of Walter Camp invented the game and rules for it. When we talk about history and tradition, we made it. In the 1970s, the university presidents decided that the league was not going to pursue athletics at the expense of academics. They made a conscious decision not to "keep up with the Jones." However, the tradition of Yale football is alive and well.

There are some philosophical ideas I want to present about our defense:

- Be right.
- Be fast.
- Be violent.
- Be many.
- Be ball-conscious.

You need to know exactly what you are doing, and be right. You have to understand the scheme, what it requires you to do, and repeat it. You need to demonstrate that you can do that play after play.

Playing fast does not mean how fast the player is in his 40-yard dash time. How fast he thinks and how fast he runs are two things that do not necessarily correlate. Being fast for us means if the player runs 4.8 in the 40, that is the speed we expect him to play at. It does the player no good to be a 4.4 player who plays at 4.8 speed. As coaches, we have a lot to say about how that happens. In our staff meetings, we talk about "eliminating the gray areas." If the coach wants the player to play fast, give him two options. Give him one thing to do. If it does not happen, he does this, and that is all.

The thing that separates football from every other sport is the violence of the game. You have to be ready to punch somebody in the mouth on every single snap. They have to embrace the violence. One of my former coaches told me he would rather pull a player off the pile than throw one on it. We talk to our team all the time about playing with violence. We won four games this year, but we had an opportunity to win all 10 of them. We did not make the plays when we needed to. The thing we did do every game was play with great physical intensity. We were more physical than any team we played. Our problem was we did not execute. You have to play with great effort and violence. That gives you a chance. If you do not play with those things, you have no chance.

What does "be many" mean? That means get a bunch of players to the ball. The good thing about playing defense is you do not have to be exactly right every time. If you are not exactly right, you can overcome that with great effort. If you will swarm the ball, play fast, and get as many players to the ball as you can, you can overcome mistakes.

You must be ball-conscious. That is something coaches do not talk about enough. They talk about turnovers. We talk about takeaways. We want to take the ball away from the offense. A turnover is when the quarterback throws you the ball for an interception. We want to take the ball away from them. You cannot take the ball away from the offense unless you think about it. The defense has to be conscious about creating turnover. Turnovers do not happen because you want them to. You have to teach it and practice it.

We are essentially a 3-4-defense. We play with two standup outside linebackers (Diagram #1). We reduce the front. To the openside of the formation the Will linebacker plays a 5 technique on the offensive tackle. The defensive end to that side aligns in a 3 technique. The nose plays to the tight-end side in a 2i technique, and the tackle aligns in a 5 technique. The Sam linebacker stands up over the tight end. The inside linebackers are Mike to the tight-end side and Buck away from the tight end. The secondary bases out of a four shell.

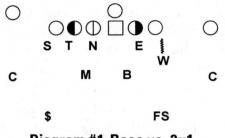

Diagram #1. Base vs. 2x1

I did a study when I was at San Diego State. They were the WAC conference at that time. I compared the teams that were playing two-high safeties as opposed to one-high safety. I found that teams who played the one-high safety gave up more big plays than teams that played two-high safeties. The percentages were 60 percent to 40 percent. If you have one safety and he makes a mistake, it is a touchdown. If you have two, you have a chance if one makes a mistake.

We will roll to three-deep, but we want to show a four-high shell every snap. I do not want the quarterback to look at the secondary and have an idea of what we are doing. The same thing holds true with the Will and Sam linebackers. I have them on the line of scrimmage, but they do not align there in the pre-snap. They walk up, back, in, and out. The 3-4 can give you an element of disguise.

We have three players with their hands in the dirt, and everyone else is moving around. I think that can cause some confusion. From the front, we can get into an Okie look or a true 30 look. We can set the front to the field, boundary, pass strength, or running strength. We can set the front for any situation.

We like to fit the personnel to the position they play. We want the Sam linebacker to be a space player. He can make a tackle on a back in space. The Will linebacker is a pass rush–type of player. We use him as the fourth rusher off the edge. When I was at San Francisco, that player was Charles Haley. We called him the rush end. For us, he is a stand-up linebacker. The inside players are defensive line–types. The tackle is more athletic and plays on the perimeter of our defense to the field. We want to protect the integrity of the field because big plays happen when the quarterback gets outside the containment.

I had an old coach say the entire structure of the defense breaks down when the quarterback gets outside of the containment. You need a contain player and force player to keep the ball bracketed. The end and nose are traditional shade players. We play a 2i as opposed to a shade. The reason I do that is because it makes you less susceptible to zone-scheme plays. If your nose is chasing the center on a down block every time, he will be caved down, and the line of scrimmage will be compromised.

We feel like our linebacker will be better than your center. They are more athletic. In the 2i technique, our nose will be able to control your guard, and the linebacker will be able to run away from your center on the combo block.

With the two-high look, we have the ability to play cover 2, cover 6, cover 3, or drop either of the safeties down to help with passing or run strength. We can move the safeties according to game plan to suit our needs for the extra man in the scheme. We have the ability to play "buzz." That drops the safety down into the box where he becomes the flat/curl defender. It is just another way to get to cover 3. From this alignment, it gives you a lot of flexibility.

If the offense goes to a 2x2 formation, we adjust with our Sam and Will linebackers and widen the tackle's technique (Diagram #2). With the popularity of the spread offense, the 3-4 gives you the chance to get more space defenders on the field. The obvious weakness is you lose an anchor point. That means you lose a defensive lineman. You have three players with their hands in the dirt instead of four. The trade-off is you have another athletic space-runner on the field. Our Will linebacker can stay in the game because he is a good space player and a good pass rusher.

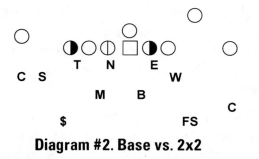

Diagram #2. Base vs. 2x2

The Will linebacker plays two yards inside the apex position of the slot receiver. We do not feel the slot can block our Will linebacker and keep him from boxing the play. Therefore, the integrity of the front is still intact, even though the 3 technique is inside the outside blocker.

Any defense defending the option has to be strong down the middle of the defense. To defend the option, you must stop the fullback. That is what the read zone is essentially. They want to hand the ball to the running back on the inside zone play. You have to make sure you can hold up with your interior line positions.

I used to read the end man on the line of scrimmage. I have gotten to the point where I think you have to be very specific as to what you read. We spend a lot of time coaching the eyes. You have to be specific as to what you tell your players to look at. Do not simply say, "Key the tight end." We tell them to look at his hip. If you are looking at what you are supposed to look at, you will go in the direction you are supposed to go. In relationship to a defensive player's reaction, the tighter you can make his focus, the better the chance of him doing exactly what you want him to do.

Our linebackers are in space, and we do not apex them. We align a yard or two inside what the normal apex position is. We have a coverage called "mix it" that allows us to play a three-over-two concept. The coverage is either cover 2 or cover 4 based on the release of the #2 receiver. That allows our Will and Sam linebackers to be box players. They are not coverage players.

When the offense splits the #2 receiver into the slot, most teams take the outside linebacker out of the box and leave the safety in the box as a kick player. I would rather have my linebacker play linebacker and my safety play safety. That is why we ask the outside linebacker to see the guard. He has enough depth off the ball where he can do that.

I listened to Bill Kenney last night talk about his counter runs and draw play. His tackles showed a pass set, while the guards were blocking down. Any time there is separation between the guards and the tackles, that is a draw play. If you are looking at the end man on the line of scrimmage, when you see the tackle come off the line, you think pass. If the linebacker sees the guard, he knows it is run all the way. If the guard uses a pass-set technique, we play the pass. That is why we think the guard is the truest read from that standpoint.

If the offense uses a 3x1 set, we adjust by sliding the 5-technique tackle (Diagram #3). With a tight end to the twin-receiver side, we move the 5-technique tackle to a 6i technique on the tight end, and his leverage point goes to the tight end. This alignment creates a firmer line of scrimmage. If you play with a 5 technique and a space player in the walked-off position, that to me is a soft edge. We give a Y call so the tackle gives a stronger anchor point on the edge. The space player can feel comfortable about the tight end not having a free release on him. The Will linebacker walks down to the 5-technique position on the backside. Coverage-wise, we can play all the same coverages as we did before.

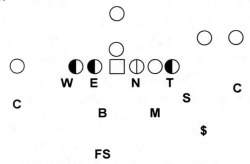

Diagram #3. Base vs. 3x1

We are seeing a proliferation of empty sets by the offense (Diagram #4). The thing about the 3-4 is it is easy to adjust because you have the two stand-up outside linebackers who can move in space. If you play a team that is trying to spread your defense, you do not have to substitute unless you feel the players on the field are in a mismatch. In this defense, we do not have to change our line assignments or coverages. We have to move out with the spread, which is no problem.

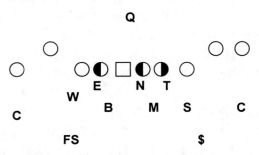

Diagram #4. Base vs. Empty

In the diagram, I put the tight end in a bastard split. It does not matter, but the Mike linebacker has to get into a relationship to the #3 receiver to that side. He is still in the box, but he is aware of the #3 receiver. The Sam linebacker is in relationship to the #2 receiver. To the weakside, if we were concerned about the 3 technique, we could move him to a 4i technique on the tackle but still read the guard's block.

We have very simple rules to align with the formation adjustments. If you can count to three, you can play in our defense. The defender always relates himself to the receiver he reads. We label the receivers with numbers starting from the outside going to the inside. The widest receiver to both side is #1, the next receiver inside is #2 and the next receiver to that side is #3. The numbering is the same on both sides. In our quarter coverages, the #2 receiver is the key receiver for the corners and safeties. The outside linebacker reads from #2 to #3. The coverages are related to receivers.

People who play quarters coverage against the triple set generally assign the release by the #3 receiver to the trips side to the free safety. With the empty set, the free safety has to stay with the #2 receiver to his side. The defender who has to make the adjustment to the #3 vertical is the Mike

linebacker. The strong safety tries to stay between the #2 and #3 receivers. However, if we want to play true zone, the Mike linebacker has to deepen up and get into a position to carry the #3 receiver. If the #3 receiver is a tight end, we can get away with doing that. However, if the #3 receiver is a wide receiver, we may have to use a nickel back or check coverages.

These are base rules for all these adjustments. When we game plan to play against the empty set, the first thing I am going to do is try to decapitate your quarterback. We have checks built into our defense to go to something different when the offense dictates it. If we were in zone, we would go to some kind of Tampa-2 and play maximum zone. If we were in man coverage, we would match up accordingly. When we match up, we match like personnel. We do not want a linebacker playing a wide receiver. The last thing we do is max blitz. We will bring one more than you can block. Even if the quarterback can get rid of the ball, we still are going to hit him.

This is another trips set, which we call a speed trips (Diagram #5). There are three wide receivers to the trips side, and the tight end is the single receiver. With this formation, the Sam linebacker comes to the three-receiver side. The tackle plays a 5 technique to that side. The nose is a 2i technique to the trips side, and the end is the 3 technique to the tight-end side. The Will linebacker aligns in the 9 technique on the outside shoulder of the tight end.

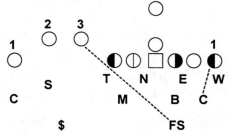

Diagram #5. Base vs. Speed Trips

In the secondary, the backside corner moves to what we call a C7 technique, which aligns him on the inside shoulder of the tight end at corner depth. To the three-receiver side, the Sam linebacker plays his relative position on the #2 receiver, and the Mike linebacker has a relative position on the #3 receiver. However, in this defense, the free safety has the #3 receiver on any vertical routes. The free safety moves to a position over the backside guard to be closer to his coverage but can still support back to the tight-end side on a running play.

We do not have a cover corner in our defense. We have corners who must be involved in the running game. Corners have to tackle, too. They have to get on their big-boy pads, get down, and explode on someone.

I want to show you one more adjustment to a 2x2 set with two tight ends (Diagram #6). The alignment is the same to the Sam linebacker's side of the defense. The adjustment is to the second tight end. The end still plays the 3 technique, and the Will linebacker plays a 9 technique on the outside shoulder of the second tight end. That is an age-old argument. For us, it is better for him to play in a 9 technique than to put the support player inside the tight end.

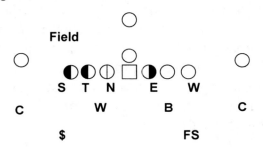

Diagram #6. Base vs. Two Tight Ends

The Will linebacker still boxes the outside and forces the ball into the C gap. We can fit the play with our backer linebacker from the inside and the free safety fitting to the outside of the C gap. The Buck linebacker spills the ball to the free safety. We want to keep the ball in the box.

We call our front a nine-man box. We want our safeties heavily involved in the running game. If we play cover 2, the corners are involved in the run game. If the offense runs the ball in a two-tight-end look, we expect the safeties to be heavily involved.

We align our outside linebackers in the walk-off positions at five-and-a-half yards deep. They have to be in position to see their keys and the ball. If they cannot see them from where they are, they have to adjust their alignment slightly so they can see. We believe in "ability alignment." The linebacker aligns as to what he needs to see or his ability to execute his assignment. That eliminates the gray area, and they can play fast.

When I was in Jacksonville, Greg Williams was there. He is the defensive coordinator at New Orleans this year, and they just won the Super Bowl. When he was at Jacksonville, he was a dog-crap coordinator. We had a young defense, got banged up during the season, and could not stop anyone. This year, he is the best thing since sliced bread. He had some veterans, and they played with great intensity. The scheme he runs is not very complicated, and we run the same thing.

He coaches to play fast and violent, and to create takeaways. That is the name of the game. Of the six games we lost this year, we lost the turnover battle in every one of them. That is what it all boils down to. If you play good defense, play fast, violent, and do not turn the ball over, you have a chance to win every game. It does not guarantee you will win the game, but it gives you a chance. There are no guarantees in life, but all you want is a chance.

The inside linebackers are reading the footwork of the backs in addition to the guards. They read zone step, counter step, and stretch steps of the back. We actually coach them to mimic the footwork of the backs. This gives you a chance to get a bonus linebacker on the play.

On defense, you generally have your linebacker attack the gap they are responsible for. They are working their fits into gaps. You have to understand what the offense is trying to do with the zone play. They are trying to make it a cutback play. If the linebackers key the footwork of the back, you have a chance to get two linebackers in the right place as opposed to one. The safety becomes the extra cutback player.

If you come to our practices and watch our linebacker coach, they work on the two-step read. They work their footwork off the read on the back.

They work two steps on the inside zone, stretch, and counter plays. They should know the play by the second step of the back.

Bootleg pass is a "play-the-play situation" for the linebackers. The bootleg will come off the stretch play-action. The linebacker should think bootleg off the stretch play and not the inside zone play. When the offense runs the bootleg, there will be two things that will happen. The back will give you stretch-play steps, and you will see what we call the "bootleg parade." That is all the fat-butted linemen running down the line of scrimmage. That should say "bootleg" to the linebacker.

Once the linebacker reads the bootleg, he turns over his outside shoulder and runs for a spot. We tell him to run toward the flag. He is not going to drop back to his normal zone drop. He plays the play, and gets to an area where the receivers are coming. He wants to pick up the crosser coming on the drag pattern. The linebacker who sees the bootleg first will be the backside linebacker. The frontside linebacker has to respect the stretch and is moving fast outside.

The backside linebacker plays the play and wants to make contact with the cross as he comes across the field. His pre-snap drops are gone, and he is playing a specific play. There are some specific plays where the linebacker plays the play. Those plays are draw, screen, and bootleg.

We have sprint-out rules for our linebackers. If the quarterback sprints with the ball to the right, the Sam linebacker runs through the flat all the way to the sidelines if necessary. The backside linebacker is the secondary contain rusher. The frontside linebacker runs right to the curl area. The sprint-out pass will be designated routes. They run a receiver to the sidelines, a receiver in the curl, and a backside post. We do not drop to our normal drop zones; we run straight to those spots and play football. We play the play. Whatever we were supposed to do before the play, we forget about and played the play.

The last formation I want to show is the 2x2 double-slot look (Diagram #7). In this alignment,

based the splits of the receivers, we have the ability to play a three-over-two concept. We pattern-read off the #2 receiver. The farther distance the Sam linebacker has to go in the curl zone, the wider he has to align. If the #2 receiver runs any out-breaking route, we roll the coverage into cover 2, and the corner has those routes. If the #2 receiver ran vertical, the safety takes him, and we play quarter coverage.

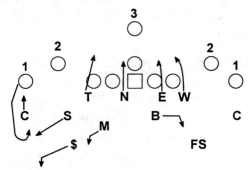

Diagram #7. Base vs. Doubles

The Sam linebacker reads the guard for pass or run read. When he sees the pass read, his eyes go to the #2 receiver. He keeps inside leverage on him until he reads the vertical route. He releases him to the safety and looks to get under the patterns of the #1 receiver if he is working to the curl area. The Sam linebacker is not pressured to carry the #2 receiver to the flat. If the #2 runs to the flat, the corner has him on his rolled up coverage.

If we want to get a four-man rush, the Will linebacker cheats down to the line of scrimmage and comes off the edge. The Buck linebacker takes the curl-drop responsibility to the weakside. Both sides are reading exactly the same. We play quarters or cover 2 off the read we get from the #2 receivers. We have a four-man rush scheme on most passing situations. The Will linebacker is generally the rush defender for his linebacker position.

All our fire-zone blitzes come off these looks. We play with the Sam linebacker into the field or passing strength. The tackle, nose, and Mike linebacker travel with the Sam linebacker. The 3-technique end, Buck linebacker, and Will linebacker go to the boundary side of the defense. We do have calls that will put the 3 technique into the strongside of the formation. The Will linebacker can rush or drop into coverage. However, he is generally the fourth rusher in our scheme.

I am a believer in exotic blitzes. I believe you have to be able to attack with a four strong, four weak, and four up the middle in your blitz package. When you want to hit the quarterback, you bring a maximum blitz package. If you bring five-man pressure with a free safety in the middle, you are rolling the dice. That does not guarantee you will get pressure on the quarterback. If you want to get pressure, you have to bring more than they can block or overload a side. If you overload a side, you have to do so against their protection scheme by a scouting report. You have to know where they are turning their scheme and where the backs are blocking.

If there is a "goat" on the offensive line that you want to attack, you can set the blitz for that. A goat is a weak offensive blocker the offense is trying to hide. We believe our blitzes are good against the run or pass. We have a way to make a distinction between our blitzes. If we are thinking run, we call "Cobra." If we are thinking pass, we call "reckless Cobra." That means we are going after the quarterback on the reckless blitz. We play the pass first, and react to the run. It is just the opposite for the "Cobra" call. We are playing run first, and reacting to the pass.

When the corner comes on the "reckless Cobra," he is looking to sack the quarterback, not to close the C gap. Do not let the strength of the defense be defeated. If you are playing a quarters coverage, and the offense completes the ball in the flat, that is all right because that is the weakness of the defense. You cannot be mad at your players for that. The strength of quarters coverage is stopping the vertical routes down the field. You cannot allow them to complete the ball in the strength of the defense.

On the Cobra, we are bringing the corner from the boundary side of the defense (Diagram #8). The defensive line angles to the wideside of the field. They slant at the adjacent linemen. They want to

get into the gap and up the field for penetration. The Will linebacker rushes up the field and is the contain rusher. We are trying to get a two-on-one against the blocking back in the backfield. The end, nose, and tackle are spiking to the field. The corner blitzes the C gap and up the field.

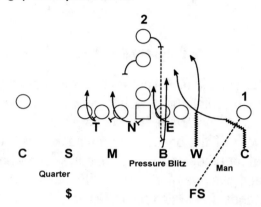

Diagram #8. Cobra

The Buck linebacker is responsible for the #2 receiver on this play. If the #2 receiver is aligned in the backfield and has a checkdown assignment, the Buck should pressure-rush him through the B gap. That gives you the overload you are looking for. I hope that the protection is turned to the tight end with the back blocking opposite. We have a four-man blitz coming from the backside. If the #2 receiver releases, the Buck linebacker picks him up in coverage.

We have a ricochet technique the slanting defender uses. The defensive linemen aim at the hip of the adjacent offensive lineman. They stunt into the gap and hit the offensive lineman. When they hit the lineman, they ricochet up through the gap and climb for penetration through the gap. The free safety plays man coverage on the #1 receiver. If the receiver cracks on the corner, the safety has to replace him.

In the "Ohio" stunt, we are bringing the Sam and Will linebackers off the edge (Diagram #9). We pinch the tackle and end into their inside gaps. The nose slants to the center and plays down the middle. If a pass were to show, he is the screen player. He is spying the back. He wraps around the center based on the release of the back. We are playing cover 2 in the secondary with two rolled-up corners. The Mike and Buck linebackers are the hook/curl players inside.

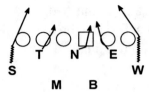

Diagram #9. Ohio

This is a simple five-man pressure scheme. We play zone behind the blitz. It is good versus the pass or the run. We want the linebackers to read the footwork of the backs. When a back runs a draw, they oftentimes use a step we call a "crow hop." It is a dead giveaway for the draw. He hops to the side and stands up waiting for the quarterback to bring him the ball. The linebacker should be mirroring the footwork of the back. When he hops over and stays square to the line of scrimmage, the linebackers should be doing the same thing.

When we run a backside blitz, the blitz runners have to continue to chase if the ball goes away from them. The outside linebacker has to get up the field and build a wall to stop the ball, and make it cut up. He has to force the ball back into the blitz and backside pursuer. Also, if the offense runs into the blitz, the blitz runner has to squeeze the run when he sees run. He reacts back to the run and does not open a seam to his inside. He has to help the inside linebacker fitting into the run.

When we run a blitz, we want to make sure the fits of the defender carry over in the blitz as well as the normal defense. We want to keep the ball bracketed on the proper shoulder every time we run a blitz. We want to bracket the ball from the outside moving to the inside and from the inside moving outside. The Will linebacker, even though he is blitzing, has to contain if he has a run coming to him. It does not matter whether we are playing cover 2 or cover 4; the fits for the defense are the same.

If the safety is supposed to fit inside the Sam linebacker on cover 2, he is supposed to fit inside the Sam linebacker on cover 4. The only difference is the distance he has to come. The Mike and Buck linebackers are spill players, and that is what they should be doing. If you have to think about that, you cannot play with the speed we want.

It is an honor for me to stand in front of a group like you. I think you are on the front lines of the last bastions of discipline and hard work in our country. Keep doing what you are doing, and if I can ever help you, do not hesitate to call.

NEW!

2010
COACH OF THE YEAR CLINICS Football Manual

Featuring lectures from several of America's most renowned coaches. Edited by Earl Browning.

$29.95 • 313 pages • 978-1-60679-104-2

Also available:

2004	2005	2006	2007	2008	2009

1-58518-896-4	1-58518-932-4	1-58518-969-3	978-1-58518-073-8	978-1-58518-719-5	978-1-60679-062-5
280 pp. • $24.95	288 pp. • $24.95	304 pp. • $24.95	288 pp. • $24.95	272 pp. • $24.95	288 pp. • $29.95

Title	Item #	Price	Qty	Total

Tax on materials for California residents only. Shipping & Handling: $7.50 for first item $1.50 for each additional item	PLUS	CA Tax 8.25%		
	PLUS	Shipping		
		TOTAL		

Name _____ Organization/School _____

Address _____

City _____ State _____ ZIP _____ Phone ( ) _____

Method of Payment: ☐ **VISA** ☐ **MasterCard** ☐ **Cards** ☐ **DISCOVER** ☐ Check # _____ ☐ P.O. # _____

Account # ☐☐☐☐ ☐☐☐☐ ☐☐☐☐ ☐☐☐☐ Expiration: ____/____ CVC #: __ __ __

Signature: _____ Email Address: _____

★★★★
COACHES CHOICE™
www.coacheschoice.com

Send check or money order to: **Coaches Choice**
P.O. Box 1828 Monterey, CA 93942
or call toll-free: (888) 229-5745 or fax: (831) 372-6075